MW00445861

50
STATES
1000
EATS

50 STATES 1000 EATS

WHERE TO GO · WHEN TO GO · WHAT TO EAT · WHAT TO DRINK

JOE YOGERST

NATIONAL GEOGRAPHIC
WASHINGTON, D.C.

Contents

Pages 2-3: Fishermen pull up king crab at a commercial fishery in southeast Alaska.

Opposite: Ice cream, cake, and meringue are flambéed tableside for a classic baked Alaska.

INTRODUCTION

We all have our own personal foodways, culinary habits, customs, and preferences gleaned from what our parents served us as children and what was passed down from generations before them.

Added to that are the gastronomic differences in the geographical places where we were born and raised, went to school, and later lived and worked. Travel introduces new flavors and textures. "Travel changes you," said Anthony Bourdain—both your palate and your soul. And it doesn't have to be through globe-trotting: As this book demonstrates, we have plenty to sample across Canada and the United States, foods very different from what we nosh on back home.

The roots of my personal foodways were the southern United States and the Great Lakes region. Although my mother was born and raised in Arizona, her siblings hailed from Arkansas and her mother from Tennessee. From fried chicken and biscuits with gravy to deviled eggs and black-eyed peas, southern comfort foods always filled our kitchen.

My father was from Buffalo, New York. As Catholics, we always had fish on Fridays, often in the form of creamed tuna so I wouldn't realize I was actually eating a sea creature. Hot dogs for lunch on a Saturday afternoon were another of his culinary rituals. Meatloaf smothered with tomato sauce, pork chops with applesauce, and corn on the cob were among his other favorites.

These two polar opposite food cultures came together as my parents raised a family in San Diego in the early days of California cuisine. The Tamale Factory (sadly no longer open) was my parents' idea of a big night out—and ended up stoking my lifelong affair with Mexican food, both the Californian and south-of-the-border varieties.

College introduced me to other global flavors. My first venture into Japanese cuisine was a restaurant on Westwood Boulevard near the UCLA campus; my initial adventure with Indian food was at an eatery near UC Berkeley. And I suppose that's part of the reason my first foreign trip was tramping the overland trail from Kathmandu to Istanbul, my entrée into Nepalese, Punjabi, Afghan, Iranian, and Turkish food.

Later I lived and worked in three of the globe's greatest food destinations: London, Hong Kong, and Singapore. By the time I moved back to the United States, many of the national and regional foods I had grown to love overseas had also made their way to North America.

When you think about it, the culinary histories of the United States and Canada have always been about fusion. Immigrants brought their techniques and recipes from Europe, Asia, Africa, and Latin America, blending their own cookery with Native American and First Nations staples like corn, beans, and squash, or the incredible bounty of the land and water.

Southern classics like dirty rice and jambalaya owe their origins to rice imported and cultivated by enslaved peoples from West Africa. Dishes that we consider quintessentially Italian—spaghetti and meatballs, marinara sauce, garlic bread, and cioppino—were invented by Italian immigrants rather than imported from across the ocean. The California roll (a delicious union of sushi and avocado) and Hawaii's *loco moco* (an Asian American mash-up of steamed rice, fried eggs, and a hamburger patty or teriyaki chicken) were the creations of Japanese, Polynesian, and Chinese immigrants adapting to new ingredients and homes.

In *50 States, 1,000 Eats,* I dive into all of those dishes and more. This book roves through the United States and Canada in search of classic dishes, culinary experiences, and incredible places to eat and drink. It includes gastronomic history, too, tributes to famous chefs, food innovators, and iconic brands. And though plenty of Michelin-starred restaurants are sprinkled through the chapters, roadside diners, mom-and-pop eateries, food trucks, farmers markets, and food halls are also touched on as integral parts of our world stew.

I hope this collection inspires you to sample new foods in your own kitchen, down the block, or maybe even on a road trip. Bon appétit!

—Joe Yogerst

RdV Vineyards' resident dog, Winter, oversees the harvest in Delaplane, Virginia.

United States

The oyster service at Woodberry Tavern in Baltimore, Maryland, includes the shellfish served three ways.

Alabama

Alabama cooks have long put their own spin on traditional southern favorites in a state that relishes rich flavors nurtured in the soil, sea, and the family kitchen.

There's nothing more sweet home(made) Alabama than **Lane cake**. The confection is named after Emma Rylander Lane of Clayton in southeast Alabama. Lane won several awards in the 1890s with her homemade "prize cake," first published in her popular *Some Good Things to Eat* cookbook (1898). The four-layer white sponge cake with a raisin bourbon filling later featured multiple times in *To Kill a Mockingbird*, Harper Lee's classic southern tale.

Boiled peanuts are another Alabama obsession. They come in numerous flavors. In fact, the Alabama Peanut Co. in Birmingham (founded in 1907) makes more than 100 different kinds, including southern-inspired flavors like Cajun, Sweet Tea, Collard Greens, and Dill Pickle.

You've also gotta crank back the clock for the origins of spicy **Alabama white barbecue sauce**. First created in 1925 by Robert "Big Bob" Gibson at his self-titled restaurant in Decatur, the white sauce, which goes onto smoked chicken, typically includes horseradish, vinegar, cayenne pepper, and mustard powder.

Wedged between the Tennessee River and the Gulf of Mexico, Alabama boasts prized seafood and freshwater fish. Between individual anglers and more than 80 farms, Alabama lands (and eats) more **catfish** than any other state besides neighboring Mississippi. And the popular **West Indies crab salad** may have been inspired by the Caribbean, but its origin is the Gulf Coast near Mobile.

CULINARY EXPERIENCES

Luverne hosts the **World's Largest Peanut Boil** every year over the long Labor Day weekend, when more than 30 tons (27 t) of peanuts are boiled and sold. Goobers (a southern term for peanuts) are again the focus at the **National Peanut Festival**, which also includes a rodeo, livestock shows, and country music concerts, in Dothan (November).

Among the state's seminal food events are the **Peach Jam Jubilee** in Clanton (June), the **Alabama Butterbean Festival** in Pinson (late September/early October), and the **Alabama Pecan Festival** in Mobile (November). Alabama is also home to numerous crawfish boils throughout the year, from Notasulga and Montgomery (both in April) to Cullman (March). **Alabama Restaurant Week** (August) spotlights excellent eateries across the state and often includes bakeries, craft breweries, and

THE BIG PICTURE

Founded: 1819

Population: 5.07 million

Official State Dessert: Lane cake

Also Known As: Yellowhammer State, the Heart of Dixie

Culinary Influences: Spanish, French

Don't Miss: Birmingham, Gulf Shores, Mobile

Claim to Fame: White barbecue sauce, fried green tomatoes, pecan pie

Grab a bucket of boiled or roasted peanuts at Birmingham's Alabama Peanut Co.

Big Bob Gibson Bar-B-Q has been drizzling its signature white barbecue sauce on smoked chicken and pulled pork since 1925.

wineries. Imbibers can sample vintages from different regions in a tour of the world's wines at Birmingham's **Magic City Wine Fest** (May).

RESTAURANTS TO DIE FOR

The James Beard Award–winning **Hot & Hot Fish Club** in Birmingham blends Alabama-sourced ingredients into cross-cultural dishes like Alabama gazpacho, creek shrimp tagliatelle, and chicken roulade with pork sausage and blistered okra. Around the corner on 3rd Avenue, **Ovenbird** is built around a different fusion: meat and seafood creations inspired by the live-fire cooking traditions of Iberia and South America. Save room for dessert at **Jeni's Splendid Ice Creams**, located mid-

way between the two restaurants.

Out in the Birmingham burbs, **Johnny's Restaurant** in Homewood continues the fusion trend with a mixture of southern comfort food and traditional Greek dishes like *keftedes* (meatballs) and *fasolakia* (stewed green beans and tomatoes). The area's Aegean immigrant roots also shine through in the Greek-style steak and seafood at **The Bright Star** in Bessemer.

Down in Mobile, seafood and fresh fish are the name of the game at top-shelf eateries like the **Noble South** with its classic shrimp and grits and fried catfish, as well as the crawfish cakes, blue crab claws, and Gulf shrimp chowder at **Dauphin's**, on the 34th floor of the Trustmark

Building. Downtown Mobile's sweet spot is **Three Georges** candy and soda fountain, where it's awfully hard to decide between the floats, shakes, or hand-dipped chocolates.

Among the culinary cornerstones of northern Alabama is the Cajun-inspired menu at **Simp McGhee's** in Decatur, named for an early 20th-century riverboat captain who patronized local bars with a beer-drinking pet pig. Riverside Decatur is also home to **Big Bob Gibson Bar-B-Q**, where Alabama white sauce was born and still thrives. And the city of Huntsville's German roots shine at **Hildegard's German Cuisine**.

Montgomery lies within easy striking distance of three intriguing

eaties in south Alabama. Tucked into a one-room school beneath a huge moss-hung tree that dates back to 1856, **Mossy Grove School House Restaurant** in Troy offers a full range of southern comfort foods, from West Indies salad and fried pickles to catfish fillet and broiled shrimp. **Gaines Ridge Dinner Club** in Camden is even older, located in an 1840s Greek Revival mansion that's allegedly haunted. Among its specialties are a shrimp and crabmeat casserole, fried catfish with hush puppies, and seafood gumbo. Southern standards like sweet potato casserole, turnip greens, and fried okra are also the forte of **Dorothy's Restaurant** on the Tuskegee University campus.

BOTTOMS UP!

Though both baseball greats Hank Aaron and Willie Mays could rightly be called the **Alabama Slammer**, the name actually refers to a bright red cocktail—ever present at University of Alabama Crimson Tide football tailgates—comprising Southern Comfort, amaretto, and sloe gin. Another Alabama-born libation is **Lynchburg Lemonade**, a bright yellow blend of lemon juice, lemon-lime soda, triple sec, and Jack Daniel's, first concocted by an Alabama bartender in the 1980s and named after the whiskey's Lynchburg, Tennessee, hometown.

Down on the coast, Mobile also boasts a lively bar scene. **The Haberdasher** excels in Old-Fashioneds and custom house cocktails made with Alabama bourbons and whiskeys. One of the city's top live music

Acclaimed pastry chef Dolester "Dol" Miles (now retired) welcomes guests to Birmingham's Bottega restaurant with her signature coconut pecan cake.

Take in the view as you sample dishes from Dauphin's French Creole menu on the 34th floor of the Trustmark Building in Mobile.

venues, **Callaghan's Irish Social Club** in the Oakleigh Garden District offers the possibility of chasing Irish whiskey sauce–topped bread pudding with a frothy Guinness.

Opened in 1899 and on the National Register of Historic Places, the **Peerless Saloon and Grille** in Anniston is Alabama's oldest bar. The arching mahogany bar made an appearance at the 1904 St. Louis World's Fair, while the Atlanta Room upstairs was once a popular brothel.

Alabama's oddest drinking establishment is probably the **Rattlesnake Saloon**. Tucked into an ancient limestone cave in Tuscumbia, the bar is named after the serpents who once occupied the cavern. Don't gasp when you see snake tails on the menu—they are actually fried green beans.

Though the city of Auburn boasts its fair share of rowdy student bars, those who seek solitude and a great cup of coffee might want to duck into the **Auburn Oil Company**, a former gas station that now doubles as a bookstore and gourmet coffee shop. ∎

GEORGE WASHINGTON CARVER & THE TUSKEGEE INSTITUTE

Hoping to improve the life of the "man farthest down"—especially poor Black farmers—George Washington Carver dedicated his career to discovering practical, self-sufficient agriculture techniques.

During his 47 years of research and teaching at Alabama's Tuskegee Institute (1896–1943), Carver promoted sustainable practices like crop rotation and alternative crops like peanuts, sweet potatoes, and soybeans. He developed more than 300 peanut recipes and products,

and created the Jessup wagon, a horse-drawn classroom that toured Alabama's farmlands.

Carver, whose many claims to fame include being the first African American to earn a bachelor of science degree, was declared the "Black Leonardo" by *Time* magazine in 1941 for his contributions to the arts and sciences. His image has graced U.S. coins and postage stamps, and a U.S. Navy ship and nuclear submarine were named in his honor.

Alaska

With an almost endless bounty on land and sea, the Last Frontier has evolved into a *new* frontier of cooking, prepared with the freshest possible ingredients from forest, farm, sea, and tundra.

Alaska stands far apart from the rest of the United States. Not just in geography, but also in food. No other state comes close in the quantity, variety, and accessibility of **fresh seafood** and **wild game**. Plus, Alaska farmers are able to cultivate abundant **wild berries** and **supersize vegetables** during a short summer growing season that averages around 19 hours of light each day.

Pick your *poisson*—**halibut, salmon, rockfish, pollack, black cod, scallops, Pacific oysters**, and **king, snow**, or **Dungeness crab**—and Alaska likely catches more of it than anywhere in the lower 48. The state boasts the top three ports for

annual seafood catches: in Dutch Harbor, Kodiak, and the Aleutian Islands.

Deer, elk, and **caribou** are the most popular game meats. You're more likely to find them as jerky, sausages, or trail sticks than on restaurant menus. Although much more common in the Alaska culinary world than elsewhere in the United States, **reindeer** are farmed animals, the descendants of herds imported long ago from Siberia.

Even though Russia sold Alaska to the United States in 1867 (the acquisition was dubbed "Seward's Folly"), there's still a lingering Russian influence in Alaska cuisine today. The most obvious is in the

Russian dish *pirok* (salmon pot pie), which commonly contains carrots, onions, bacon, and canned salmon. Diners are more likely to find pirok, **piroshki pies**, and other Russian delicacies in places like Kodiak Island that were colonized prior to Seward's Folly.

As a foodie footnote, it should be mentioned that **ranch dressing** was invented in Alaska. While managing a remote worksite in the early 1950s, plumber Steve Henson invented the creamy concoction to liven up otherwise lackluster provisions.

CULINARY EXPERIENCES

The best place to spot and photograph the state's Godzilla-size veggies is the **Alaska State Fair** in Palmer (August to early September). Among the fair record holders are a 64-pound (29 kg) cantaloupe, 82-pound (37 kg) rutabaga, 168-pound (76 kg) watermelon, 616-pound (280 kg) squash, and 2,051-pound (930 kg) pumpkin. The **Anchorage Market** (May to September) also boasts some pretty impressive veggies.

THE BIG PICTURE

Founded: 1959

Population: 734,000

Official State Fish: Giant king salmon (also known as chinook salmon)

Also Known As: The Last Frontier

Culinary Influences: Alaska Native, Russian, Scandinavian, Pacific Islander

Don't Miss: Juneau, Ketchikan, Homer

Claim to Fame: King crab, reindeer sausage, yak burgers

Travel by train to take in the unique beauty of Denali National Park.

Check out the long-legged specialties at Tracy's King Crab Shack in Juneau.

Alaska Railroad presents a "movable feast" in dining cars on passenger trains between Anchorage, Fairbanks, Denali, and Seward. Previous menus have included reindeer pasta, smoked salmon chowder, and buffalo chili. Meanwhile, the train's GoldStar bar mixes wild cocktails like the Brown Bear (hot chocolate and Irish cream) and the Polar Bear (blue curaçao and Sprite).

The **Copper River Salmon Jam** in Cordova (July) and the **Nome Salmonberry Jam Folk Fest** (July/August) count among the state's best food festivals. Meanwhile, professional mycologists and amateur shroom enthusiasts come together at the **Girdwood Fungus Fair** in September.

RESTAURANTS TO DIE FOR

Downtown Anchorage is rife with food choices, but restaurants tend to fall into those visitors favor and those with more of a local patronage. Among the latter is the **Haute Quarter Grill**, a popular steak and seafood restaurant that also sports a great cocktail menu. Another local favorite is **Bridge Seafood Restaurant**, which perches on a pier spanning Ship Creek. While relishing their halibut, rockfish, or king crab, diners can watch anglers casting for salmon in the creek.

Snow City Café tends to be more popular with visitors, especially during the summer season when cruise ships call on Anchorage. If there's an hour wait, walk a block down 4th Street to the **Sandwich Deck**, which serves equally tasty breakfast and lunch dishes.

Alaska's leading winter sports center, Alyeska Resort in Girdwood village, offers half a dozen eating options. Ride the aerial tram to the top of the mountain for the fine dining experience at **Seven Glaciers Restaurant** or the laid-back atmosphere and tasty pub grub at the **Bore Tide Deli & Bar**. Either way you get killer views.

With live music and a Latin-flavored menu, **Jazz Bistro on 4th** is a Fairbanks favorite. Alaska's largest inland city also has its quirky food and beverage spots, like **Skinny Dick's Halfway Inn** and **Ivory Jacks**. Between Talkeetna and Denali, there are plenty of places to dine along the Parks Highway.

Alpenglow Restaurant in Denali National Park offers awesome mountain views and a menu that runs a broad gamut from seared scallops and bourbon-cured beef fillets to an Alaska berry crisp with oatmeal streusel.

The outside deck of the **Long Rifle Lodge** restaurant along the Glenn Highway offers another stunning view: of Matanuska Glacier and the Chugach Range. Down the road in Palmer, **Turkey Red café** employs the agricultural abundance of the Matanuska Valley in Mediterranean-inspired dishes such as chicken pizzaiola, cioppino, and spanakopita as well as artisanal pastas and pizzas.

Tracy's King Crab Shack is the place to chow down on crab legs, cakes, bisque, and ceviche in Juneau. And they've got all three of the state's iconic crustaceans: king, snow, and Dungeness. Farther down the waterfront, **Pel'meni** specializes in Russian-style potato and beef dumplings.

BOTTOMS UP!

The state's Russian settlers often brewed **kvass** (aka liquid bread), an acquired-taste blend of water, sugar, and flour or stale bread fermented in barrels, sometimes flavored with berries, apples, or even beets. Every so often, a local brewery will produce a limited-edition kvass.

Inspectors prep a 1,603-pound (727 kg) pumpkin to be weighed at the Alaska State Fair in Palmer.

Toast the iconic Alaskan scenery with a local brew at Alyeska Resort in Girdwood.

Otherwise, it's mostly brewed (and consumed) in private.

The closest modern equivalent to kvass is probably the Alaskan Barley Wine at **Alaskan Brewing Company** in Juneau. Also try their other craft beers and those produced by **Denali Brewing** in Talkeetna. **Silver Gulch Brewing** in Fox claims to be the nation's northernmost brewery (64° north latitude). But the best brew view is on the rooftop terrace at **49th State Brewing** in Anchorage.

From the **Elf's Den Restaurant & Lounge** in North Pole to the **Salty Dawg Saloon** in Homer, Alaska boasts more than its fair share of funky bars. One of the most atmospheric is the **Golden Saloon**

in McCarthy, a popular watering hole for mountaineers, bush pilots, hunters, and hikers traversing through Wrangell–St. Elias National Park. Aptly named **Hangar on the**

Wharf in Juneau is tucked into an old seaplane hangar, while the **Inlet PubHouse** in Anchorage features outdoor winter seating in modern transparent igloos. ■

ALASKA'S TRADITIONAL INDIGENOUS FOODS

Alaska's Inuit and Native American peoples have been living off the land for at least 10,000 years, consuming an array of dishes sourced from what they could catch or forage.

Muktuk (whale skin and blubber) is eaten raw, boiled, or pickled. *Mikigaq* is fermented whale. Similar to jerky, *paniktak* is dried fish or meat. *Nigliq* is a rich goose soup, and bannock is an Alaska version of fry

bread. A dessert similar to ice cream called *akutaq* combines walrus, caribou, or moose fat with dried fish or meat and a variety of fresh berries.

Other than someone's home, the best place to sample these traditional foods is at the **Nalukataq whaling festival** in Utqiaġvik (Barrow), held in late June to mark the end of the traditional spring whaling season.

Arizona

Flavored with Mexican and Native American influences, Arizona's unique take on southwestern cuisine is paired with burgeoning winemaking and spirit distilling, sometimes in the most unlikely places.

THE BIG PICTURE

Founded: 1912

Population: 7.36 million

Official State Fish: Apache trout

Also Known As: Grand Canyon State

Culinary Influences: Mexican, Spanish, Navajo

Don't Miss: Phoenix, Sedona, Tucson

Claim to Fame: Chimichangas, Sonoran hot dog, cheese crisps

You probably wouldn't think of the frankfurter as one of Arizona's quintessential foods. That's because you've never come across the **Sonoran hot dog**, a bun-swaddled smorgasbord that includes pinto beans, tomatoes, and onions cloaked in mayo, mustard, and a jalapeño sauce. Although this amped-up wiener originated south of the border in Mexico's Sonora state, it's uber popular in Tucson, Phoenix, and elsewhere in southern Arizona.

The state's Hispanic heritage has influenced many other dishes that make up Arizona's unique brand of southwestern cuisine. **Tamales, burritos, huevos rancheros** (ranch-style eggs), and *raspados* (snow cones) all trace their roots to Mexico.

However, the **chimichanga** (deep-fried burrito) is considered an Arizona creation, with multiple Mexican restaurants in Tucson and Phoenix claiming its mid-20th-century invention. **Cheese crisps**—flat tortillas baked on a pizza stone and topped with poblano peppers and various cheeses—are another Arizona delicacy.

Arizona's local produce—harvested by Native Americans for thousands of years—has contributed the tiny but tangy **chiltepin chilies** and **nopal** (prickly pear cactus) to the state's culinary repertoire. Nopal appears in numerous forms, from

Fry bread crisps in a hot skillet inside a family hogan in Monument Valley, Arizona.

Chimichangas are deep-fried Tex-Mex favorites.

lemonade and cocktails to tacos and salads.

Although not a traditional Indigenous food, **fry bread** originated during the 1800s to supplement rations the U.S. Army handed out during its forced relocation of the Navajo people. From northern Arizona, fry bread has spread to many other Native American nations. Although it's often consumed with nothing more than honey, jam, or powdered sugar, the deep-fried bread is also the cornerstone of **Navajo tacos**.

An arid desert climate, sunny skies, and irrigation have boosted Arizona into one of the nation's top growers of **lettuce, lemons, cantaloupes, spinach, cauliflower**, and **dates**. The **chopped salad** (aka Arizona chopped salad or Stetson chopped salad) originated in Scottsdale during the 1980s. It features neat rows of smoked salmon, arugula, corn, tomato, couscous, pepitas, and dried currants or cranberries.

CULINARY EXPERIENCES

It may not have its origins in the Grand Canyon State, but Arizonans go gaga for salsa. Stretching 76 miles (122 km) between Pima and Clifton, the **Arizona Salsa Trail** includes more than a dozen top-notch Mexican restaurants.

One of those trail towns hosts the annual **Safford Salsa Fest** (September), which features a salsa-making competition, jalapeño-eating contest, and Taste of the Trail restaurant stalls. Among the state's other piquant events are the **Southern Arizona Salsa, Tequila & Taco Challenge** in Tucson (September) and **My Nana's Best Tasting Salsa Challenge & Jose Cuervo Margarita Mix-Off** in Phoenix (April).

The Valley of the Sun hosts several other culinary events throughout the year, including **Vegan Social**, a monthly outdoor vegan market on the second and third Saturday of every month, and the **Devour Culinary Classic** at the city's Desert Botanical Garden (February).

The **Navajo Nation Fair** in Window Rock (July) provides plenty of opportunity to sample Navajo/Diné cuisine. But the cooking portion of the fair's Miss Navajo contest has transitioned from fry bread (and its controversial origins) to traditional Navajo foods.

Nowadays, one of the state's top fry bread contests transpires in

Dancers don ceremonial regalia during a traditional performance at the Navajo Nation Fair in Window Rock.

Parker during the Colorado River Indian Tribes' **Native American Days Fair & Expo** (October). Farther downstream, half a dozen date palm plantations around Yuma welcome the public, including **Martha's Gardens Medjool Date Farm**. East on Interstate 8, **Dateland Date Gardens** sells a wide variety of date edibles, such as date butter, date barbecue sauce, dried dates, and tasty date shakes.

Among Arizona's best fresh produce emporiums are the **Heirloom Farmers Market** at five locations around Tucson throughout the week and the **Uptown Farmers Market** in Phoenix (Wednesday and Saturday).

RESTAURANTS TO DIE FOR

Phoenix may be larger, but Tucson holds its own against the state capital when it comes to food. Places like **CORE Kitchen & Wine**

Bar at the Ritz-Carlton Dove Mountain resort and the **Grill at Hacienda del Sol Guest Ranch** offer posh venues and superbly crafted cuisine. But the southern Arizona metropolis is more legendary for its modest but delicious Mexican eateries.

Opened in 1922, the original downtown branch of **El Charro Café** is considered the nation's oldest Mexican restaurant, as well as one of the places where the chimichanga was born. **El Güero Canelo** on the south side is nearly as famous, a bastion of south-of-the-border specialties like burros, tortas, street tacos, and Sonoran hot dogs, as well as the recipient of an "American Classics" honor from the James Beard Foundation.

Tucson is flush with "dogueros" (hot dog vendors) selling their own versions of the local delicacy. The **Ruiz Hot Dogs** food truck is a top spot, as is the adjoining **Los Chipilones** restaurant at 6th Avenue and 22nd Street in South Tucson.

It was inevitable that, given its popularity, Tucson's southwestern cuisine would drift up the food chain to stylish eateries like **BOCA** by former *Top Chef* contestant Maria Mazon, **Charro Steak & Del Rey** (created by the same family that runs El Charro Café), and **Tito & Pep** with its mesquite-fire fusion dishes. There's even a super-healthy version: the organic vegan and vegetarian cuisine at **Tumerico**.

Tucson satisfies its global cravings with sushi and ramen at **Kukai Japanese Kitchen**, Ethiopian fare at **Zemam's** and **Zemam's, Too!**, and a range of international dishes at **Feast**, which also hosts wine events like Portugal by Way of Tucson and Piedmont, Beyond Nebbiolo.

Perched on the northeast edge

SOWING SEEDS FOR THE FUTURE

The nonprofit Native Seeds/SEARCH program strives to identify, preserve, and foster the cultivation of seeds from traditional food plants in Arizona and the greater Southwest to boost sustainability and food security.

The program has dug into the heritage of 50 Indigenous communities as well as Mormon pioneers and Spanish padres to accumulate a seed bank that numbers more than

2,000 plant species, many of them rare and endangered.

The **Native Seeds/SEARCH Conservation Center** in Tucson features a drought-resistant food crop garden and a gift shop where visitors can purchase Native American artwork and handicrafts, as well as gardening and culinary books, desert skin care products, and, of course, seeds.

of Phoenix, Scottsdale is world-renowned for a dining scene that embraces the nouvelle four-course menus and wine dinners of the chic **Café Monarch**, the inventive modern Italian of **Virtù Honest Craft**, and laid-back **Citizen Public House** (with its famous original chopped salad and heirloom popcorn cooked in bacon fat).

Phoenix offers the state's easiest access to Indigenous cuisine. Fry bread (Navajo) tacos, hominy stew, and folded cheese crisps highlight the menu at **Fry Bread House** in Midtown, while the upscale restaurant **Kai** at Sheraton Grand at Wild Horse Pass resort offers grilled tenderloin of tribal buffalo, mesquite-cured duck with blue corn tamales,

prickly pear parfaits with saguaro and wolfberry leather, and other Native American–inspired dishes. In addition to its namesake dish, the city's **Emerson Frybread** food truck also serves mutton sandwiches, steamed corn stew, and Navajo tacos.

Although not quite as legendary as Tucson, the state capital offers a range of Hispanic restaurants from the traditional Mexican plates at **Rosita's Place** and the **Original Carolina's Mexican Food** to the sophisticated Sonoran dishes of **Bacanora PHX**. There's also Latin-flavored fusion at Chinese Mexican **Chino Bandido** (carnitas and machaca rice bowls) and French Mexican **Vincent on Camelback**

(duck tamales, smoked salmon quesadillas).

For the best views over the Valley of the Sun during your meal, you can pack a picnic and munch at the summit of South Mountain, or book a reservation at **Different Pointe of View** on the Tapatio Cliffs, **Compass Arizona Grill** at the top of the Hyatt Regency, or the elegant **Christopher's at Wrigley Mansion**.

Crank back the clock at **the Stockyards** steak house (opened in 1947) or **Durant's** with its red leather booths and wallpaper. But the chicest meal in town is **Binkley's**, where the set-menu feast starts with drinks, hors d'oeuvres, and a touch of caviar on the patio before

The glittering lights of Phoenix unfold from the dining room of Different Pointe of View at the Hilton Phoenix Tapatio Cliffs Resort.

moving inside the mansion for a multicourse dinner.

Rather than New Age eateries like one might expect, Sedona's culinary vortex includes the classic Italian of **Cucina Rustica**, Mediterranean fare of **René at Tlaquepaque**, and elevated Mexican at **Elote Café**. With tables an arm's length from the valley's legendary stream, **Cress on Oak Creek** offers the most romantic dining. But the award for most eccentric menu goes to the **Sedona Cowboy Club**, where you'll find rattlesnake sausage, prickly pear cactus fries, and bison pot roast.

BOTTOMS UP!

The Arizona desert may not seem like the most obvious place to cultivate grapes and make wine, yet the state's arid landscape nurtures three American Viticultural Areas: **Willcox** and **Sonoita AVAs** near Tucson and the **Verde Valley AVA** near Sedona.

Cultivating grapes that traditionally thrive in other hot, arid places like Spain and Argentina, outfits like **Rune Wines** in Sonoita, **Flying Leap Vineyards & Distillery** in Elgin, **Coronado Vineyards** in Willcox, and the educational **Southwest Wine Center** in Clarkdale continue to improve both their wines and visitor experiences.

Many a Verde Valley vintage is available for tasting and purchase at the **Spring Heritage Pecan & Wine Festival** in Camp Verde (March). At nearby **Vino di Sedona**, Arizona wines like Chateau Tumbleweed Miss Sandy Jones and Merkin Vineyards Chupacabra White are best sipped on the back patio while enjoying live music.

Eat the rainbow with an Arizona chopped salad.

A smoky sampling at Arizona Cocktail Weekend

Arizona Cocktail Weekend in Phoenix (March) features happy hours, educational seminars, and special events like the Cocktail Carnival, as well as a chance to sample drinks from the state's best mixologists. Much like with wine, the craft booze business is thriving thanks to outfits like **Whiskey Del Bac** in Tucson, the **Cider Corps** in Mesa, and **Superstition Meadery** in Prescott.

Come fall, Route 66 in northern Arizona renders a historic pathway between **Brews & Brats Oktoberfest** in Kingman, the funky **Museum Club** country-and-western bar in Flagstaff (opened in 1931), award-winning **Arizona Sake** in Holbrook, and **RelicRoad Brewing Company** near that famous corner in Winslow. ∎

GRAND CANYON WINE & DINE

Compared with most national parks, Grand Canyon offers a wide range of culinary options, including some that could hold their own in the outside world.

Lauded by *Wine Spectator* magazine, **El Tovar Dining Room** has a wine list that includes excellent Arizona vintages to complement its classic American surf and turf menu. Due west along the rim, **Arizona Steakhouse** at Bright Angel Lodge serves the park's best southwestern cuisine: dishes like citrus agave chicken tacos with jalapeño-lime slaw and avocado crema, and grilled salmon with prickly pear butter. However, the best food with a view is a roast turkey, tuna salad, or club sandwich at **Hermits Rest Snack Bar**.

Craft cocktails are all the rage at the rustically clubby **El Tovar Lounge**, where guests can quaff a prickly pear martini, Grand Canyon Mule, or draft beer from Williams, Arizona's Grand Canyon Brewing. The park's equivalent of a sports bar, **Yavapai Tavern** and its pine-shaded patio offer a dozen drafts, including Grand Canyon Prickly Pear Wheat.

Arkansas

Although Arkansas shares many culinary traditions with its southern neighbors, the state's natural bounty and human ingenuity have generated many unique foods and drinks.

A succulent **roasted or smoked turkey** is still the centerpiece of Thanksgiving in Arkansas, but the big bird is popular here any time of year—with stuffing and gravy, in subs and sandwiches, and even on pizza.

The state's **Atkins Pickle Company** produced briny cucumbers, okra, onions, and other edibles long before **Bernell Austin** opened a drive-in restaurant across the street in 1960. But it was Austin's audacious creation of the **fried dill pickle** that made the offbeat treat a statewide favorite.

Referred to variously as the Arkansas Traveler, Bradley Heirloom, and Pink Girl, the **pink tomato** is the official state vegetable *and* fruit. Expanding their color palette, Arkansas farmers also grow **purple hull peas** and **black apples** (actually a really dark red or deep purple).

THE BIG PICTURE

Founded: 1836

Population: 3.05 million

Official State Grape: Cynthiana grape

Also Known As: Natural State

Culinary Influences: French, Spanish

Don't Miss: Little Rock, Hot Springs, Eureka Springs

Claim to Fame: Possum pie, hubcap burgers, chocolate gravy

Arkansas accounts for around 40 percent of the nation's annual **rice** harvest as well as local dishes as varied as **barbecued rice** and **chocolate rice pie**. Although the state is no longer among the major spinach producers of the United States, Arkansas is the longtime home of **Allens' Popeye Spinach**, named for the famed cartoon character.

Fruit and berry cobblers are the state's favorite desserts. But its most unique sweet is **biscuits with chocolate gravy**, an Elvis Presley favorite, second only to fried peanut butter and banana sandwiches.

CULINARY EXPERIENCES

Iconic Arkansas edibles are the focus of three popular food events. Founded in 1956, the **Bradley County Pink Tomato Festival** in Warren (June) is the state's oldest continuously running festival of any kind. A brine drinking contest is one of the highlights of **Atkins Pickle Fest** (May). The **Alma Spinach Festival** (April)—in the self-proclaimed "spinach capital of the world"—includes a wacky lottery in which the winner is determined by dropping spinach leaves from the top

Dive into a heaping plate of fried pickles and dip.

The three-legged race gets competitive during the Watermelon Growers Games at the Cave City Watermelon Festival.

of a fire engine ladder onto a numbered grid below.

Among the state's other gastronomic jamborees are the **Cave City Watermelon Festival** (July), which features a free watermelon feast and a pancake breakfast in the First Baptist Church. **Art & Culinary Week** in Bentonville (September) offers an enticing blend of restaurants and food trucks, live music, and fine art and handicraft creations. Bentonville is also the focus of guided walking **Ozark Culinary Tours** hosted by Erin Rowe, author of *An Ozark Culinary History: Northwest Arkansas Traditions from Corn Dodgers to Squirrel Meatloaf.*

As the centerpiece of Little Rock's resurrected waterfront, the **River Market District** is home to a weekly farmers market (Saturdays from May to September) and **Ottenheimer Market Hall** with its range of international food options.

RESTAURANTS TO DIE FOR

Down the block from the Old State House, the Capital Hotel has wined and dined Little Rock's movers and shakers since opening in 1876. Its current dining iteration, **One Eleven at the Capital**, continues that tradition with classic American and southern cuisine served in an elegant dining room.

The more casual side of Little Rock dining is epitomized by

Cotham's in the City and a menu suffused with regional favorites like fried green tomatoes, fried okra, chicken and dumplings, turnip greens, and catfish. On the outskirts of town, **Cypress Social** complements delta dishes like blackened redfish, chicken and andouille gumbo, and New Orleans–style shrimp and grits with alfresco lakeside tables beneath huge shade trees. Après meal, feast on ice cream, milkshakes, or macarons at **Loblolly Creamery** in the SoMa district.

Ranging out from Little Rock, the **Grumpy Rabbit** in historic downtown Lonoke puts a global spin on traditional southern cooking with dishes like black-eyed pea hummus, crawfish poutine, and spicy spinach with chili queso. Established in 1928, **McClard's Bar-B-Q** in Hot Springs offers a mouthwatering array of beef and pork ribs, sausages, sandwiches, and tamale plates.

Burge's Hickory Smoked Turkeys & Hams in Lewisville started in 1953 as a backyard smokehouse before growing into a popular roadside diner with smoked meat sandwiches, po'boys, and barbecue plates.

Bentonville's innovative dining scene includes **Eleven Restaurant & Coffee Bar** at the Crystal Bridges Museum of American Art, the cool **Yeyo's Mexican Street Food**, and **the Hive**, a stylish establishment that raises southern cuisine to new heights with dishes like pan-roasted striped bass with creamy polenta, and pork belly with smoked cauliflower puree and fennel jam.

BOTTOMS UP!

Determined to create a better grape drink, traveling beverage salesman Benjamin Tyndle Fooks invented **Grapette** in the late 1930s and first sold his product in Camden, Arkansas. **Orangette** and **Lemonette** followed, and all three sodas became global hits. Still based in Arkansas, the company now produces more than 90 flavors of drink concentrates.

Another heritage beverage, **Mountain Valley Spring Water** has been bottled in the Ouachita Mountains near Hot Springs since 1871. Renowned for its health benefits, the water was part of the training regime of many professional boxers and Thoroughbred racehorses, as well as appearing on the dinner tables of 13 American presidents.

A far different libation is the focus of the **Arkansas Times Margarita Festival** in Little Rock, a September event that features bartender-blended concoctions from **La Terraza Rum & Lounge** and other top cocktail bars in the state capital.

Charlee's is one of numerous watering holes and restaurants in Little Rock's rollicking River Market area. Among its other after-dark denizens are **Cannibal & Craft** cocktail lounge and nightclub, the **Flying Saucer Draught Emporium**

Smothered goodness: biscuits with chocolate gravy

Margaritas of all flavors get prime billing at bars across Little Rock during the Arkansas Times Margarita Festival.

for craft beer, and **Willy D's Rock & Roll Piano Bar**.

Subiaco Abbey near Fort Smith makes Country Monks beer, brewed by the resident Benedictine friars. The taproom is open to the public on Saturday; profits support the welfare of the abbey's older monks.

As a college town, Fayetteville boasts a pretty rowdy bar scene, especially the stretch of **Dickson Street** just east of the University of Arkansas campus. For a mellower time, duck into **Pink House Alchemy** for a gourmet coffee or mocktail flavored with their farm-to-bottle bitters, shrubs, and syrups. ∎

OLD-TIME OZARK EATS

Much like the Native Americans they displaced, the Euro-American settlers and African Americans who populated the frontier-era Ozarks region were largely self-sufficient. In such a rugged, remote landscape, they had to be to survive.

Many of their edibles came straight from the land: They hunted for deer, possums, rabbits, raccoons, turkeys, and wild "razorback" pigs, and angled for trout and catfish. And they foraged for black walnuts, persimmons, pokeweed, muscadines, chicory, and Queen Anne's lace.

Nature's bounty translated into varied dishes, from ham hocks and squirrel meatloaf to wild berry cobbler and black walnut ice cream, as well as drinks like sumac lemonade and muscadine wine. The cultivation of corn, beans, okra, and other crops eventually expanded the Ozark diet.

You won't find squirrel meatloaf on the menu, but the **Skillet Restaurant** at Ozark Folk Center State Park in Mountain View serves other Ozark heirloom dishes like chicken and dumplings, fried okra, ham and beans, and blackberry cobbler.

California

With a bounty of fresh ingredients and a penchant for innovation, California has evolved into the global leader of farm-to-table dining, cross-cultural fusion foods, and restaurants with innovative themes and ambience to match the incredible cuisine.

THE BIG PICTURE

Founded: 1850

Population: 39.03 million

Official State Nuts: Almond, walnut, pistachio, pecan

Also Known As: Golden State

Culinary Influences: Spanish, Mexican, Japanese, Chinese

Don't Miss: Santa Barbara, San Francisco, Napa Valley

Claim to Fame: In-N-Out Burger, avocado toast, fish tacos

Long before "California cuisine" became a culinary catchphrase, residents of the Golden State were already cooking up unique foods. Some trace the state's gastronomic innovation to the gold rush era, when people from Europe, Asia, Latin America, and across the United States flocked to California hoping to strike it rich. Along with their dreams, they packed recipes from back home. But lacking traditional ingredients, cooks in the Sierra foothills mining camps and fancy restaurants of San Francisco had to find alternative ingredients and translate Old Country dishes into newfangled California foods.

That innovation continued long after the gold had petered out, aided and abetted in the early 20th century by the state's agriculture boom. California now grows more than 400 different crops, surpassing any other state and most foreign countries. Among the state's top 10 crops are **grapes, almonds, strawberries, pistachios, lettuce, tomatoes, walnuts**, and **rice**. The state also leads the nation in growing **artichokes, avocados, kiwifruit, dates, plums, raisins, celery, garlic, cauliflower, spinach**, and **carrots**. As the nation's top **milk** producer, California is also a leader in **artisanal cheese**.

It's no wonder that farm-to-table and California cuisine are almost synonymous. In fact, one of the genre's five major characteristics is fresh local ingredients—not just fruits, nuts, and vegetables, but also seafood and meats. California-style cooking is also notoriously unfussy, simple, and easy to make at home. If the cuisine had a motto, it would probably be "Let the food tell its own story." It's also often chef driven—what other state has created or attracted so many celebrity chefs?

In keeping with the state's gold rush roots, international influences are very much welcome. Californians are genius at transforming dishes from other culinary cultures into quintessential California fare. Like **fish tacos**: originally from Mexico but now an integral part of the Southern California beach dining scene. And the **California roll** with avocado and crab, invented in Canada but now a signature item at nearly every sushi restaurant in the Golden State. Among the latest cross-cultural food fads are **ramen** and dishes made with **matcha** (green tea) from Japan, **poke** from Hawaii, and **Cali-Baja** blends.

First introduced in L.A. in the 1960s, the popular California roll features real or artificial crab and avocado.

The flavors—and flames—heat up at the Gilroy Garlic Festival.

That's not to say that California doesn't have indigenous dishes. With its flavorful blend of chicken, bacon, hard-boiled eggs, and super-fresh vegetables, the **Cobb salad** was first created at the Brown Derby in Hollywood after World War I and named after the restaurant's owner. Even though it's been around since Wild West days, **avocado toast** is enjoying a renaissance as a hip lunch or breakfast dish.

San Francisco was the genesis of several iconic California dishes, including **sourdough bread, Ghirardelli chocolate, cioppino,** and the thin-crust **California pizza**

topped with various cheeses and fresh veggies. In the Los Angeles area, the **cheeseburger** was pioneered at a Pasadena sandwich shop in the 1920s, and **Chinese chicken salad** at Madame Wu's restaurant in Santa Monica in the 1960s. And Southern California eateries morphed traditional Mexican dishes into local standards like **Korean tacos** and the avocado-infused **California burrito**.

CULINARY EXPERIENCES

Name a California food product and chances are that it's the focus of a festival somewhere in the

Golden State. Visitors can munch deep-fried dates wrapped in bacon or slurp delicious date shakes at the **National Date Festival** in Indio (February). **California Artisan Cheese Festival** in Sonoma County (March) includes an evening cheese crawl through the Barlow outdoor market in Sebastopol.

First staged in 1959, the **Artichoke Festival** in Castroville (June) features chef demonstrations, an artichoke-themed quilt competition, and a stand-up comedy show called Thistle Be Funny (get the joke?). There's **San Joaquin Asparagus Festival** in Stockton (April), **Eggplant**

The same mother cultivated from a gold miner's starter serves as the base for breads at San Francisco's Boudin Bakery.

Festival in Loomis (October), **Pistachio Festival** in Newberry Springs (November), and **Mountain Mandarin Festival** in Auburn (November). Knott's Berry Farm theme park in Orange County revels in its agricultural roots during the **Knott's Boysenberry Festival** (late April through early May).

Many culinary events combine libations and local foods. The **Mendocino Crab, Beer & Wine Festival** (January) features a crab cake cook-off with wine tastings, crab and beer tastings, a family-style cioppino

dinner, and an all-you-can-eat crab feast. The **BottleRock** festival in the Napa Valley complements its wining and dining with top-shelf music acts. **Sample the Sierra** at Lake Tahoe (June) features the creations of local chefs, vintners, and craft beer brewers.

Public markets that mix small food and beverage outlets with stalls that sell ingredients and kitchenware have become a huge deal in California over the past decade. Leading the way are high-profile bazaars that offer great

eats and drinks in historic venues like **Grand Central Market** in downtown Los Angeles and the **Ferry Plaza Farmers Market** along the Embarcadero waterfront in San Francisco. San Diego has transformed old naval training buildings into the bustling **Liberty Public Market** in Point Loma. **The Public Market** in Emeryville on the east side of San Francisco Bay occupies the remains of an old paint factory. **Santa Barbara Public Market** may look like something left over from the Spanish colonial era, but it's actually one of the state's newer food hall, unveiled in 2014.

Californians have been buying fresh produce at farmers markets since the 19th century. Among the oldest is the **Original Los Angeles Farmers Market** next to CBS Television City in the Fairfax district. Opened in 1934, it's a longtime hangout of Hollywood actors, directors, and scriptwriters. Some of the outlets are legendary: **Du-par's** diner has been around since 1938, **Marconda's** butcher shop since 1941, Bennett's Ice Cream stall since 1963.

Some of the state's other farm-to-fork forums are the **Sacramento Sunday Farmers' Market** in the state capital, the **Groovy Zen Kaleidoscopic Farmers' Market** in Sebastopol, the **Downtown SLO**

Farmers' Market in San Luis Obispo on the Central Coast, and the **Chino Family Farmstand** in the San Dieguito River Valley near San Diego.

Night markets are a more recent trend fueled by California's large and varied Asian population. The largest is **626 Night Market** at the Santa Anita Park Thoroughbred racetrack in the eastern suburbs of Los Angeles. Named for the San Gabriel Valley's telephone area code, the sprawling summertime market features more than 300 vendors and a wide variety of Asian foods. Among the other after-dark feasts in the L.A. metro area are the **Asian Garden Night Market** in Westminster and the **Ave 26 Family Night Market** in Pico Rivera.

RESTAURANTS TO DIE FOR

Los Angeles/Orange County

Although you can eat just about any type of food from nearly every corner of the globe in the vast Los Angeles environs, the City of Angels excels at three types of dining: Asian cuisine, Latin American dining, and legendary Hollywood hangouts.

The city boasts 11 Japanese restaurants with at least one Michelin star and even a trio with two of the coveted kudos: **Sushi Ginza Onodera** in West Hollywood, **Hayato** in the wholesale produce market near downtown, and the **n/naka** kaiseki (small plate) restaurant on the west side.

Don't miss the Ghirardelli Chocolate Experience at the historic Ghirardelli Square in San Francisco.

Ethnic neighborhoods and their respective eats are scattered across the metro area. Downtown L.A. is flanked by **Chinatown, Little Tokyo**, and **Koreatown**. Hunkered beneath the Hollywood sign are **Thai Town** and **Little Armenia**. Farther out are **Little Saigon** in Westminster, **Little India** in Artesia, and a long stretch of Las Tunas Drive in the **San Gabriel Valley** with just about every Asian cuisine you could ever imagine.

Boyle Heights has morphed into the go-to place for street tacos, with **Los Cinco Puntos, Carnitas El Momo**, and **Mariscos Jalisco** food truck among the best. Authentic south-of-the-border dishes lure locals to **Rocio's Mexican Kitchen** in Bell Gardens and **Birrieria Apatzingan** in Pacoima, while the Michelin-starred **Taco Maria** in Costa Mesa offers modern, artistically presented Mexican cuisine.

Celebrities dine in the garden at the **Chateau Marmont** on Sunset Boulevard or beachside at **Nobu Malibu** while their agents make

Peruse the extensive selection at Molinari Delicatessen in North Beach, San Francisco.

Californian contemporary cuisine meets Italian at San Francisco's three-Michelin-starred Quince.

deals at the **Polo Lounge** at the Beverly Hills Hotel. Scripters are more likely to gather at **Musso & Frank Grill** on Hollywood Boulevard to commiserate on how showbiz doesn't respect writers.

San Francisco Bay Area

If one place pips L.A. for top dining in California, it's the San Francisco Bay Area. San Francisco alone has more than 4,400 restaurants, with more than 50 boasting

THE THREE QUEENS OF CALIFORNIA CUISINE

No one person is credited with inventing California cuisine. But three women were responsible for launching the state's food culture into a stratosphere that Paris and New York City previously dominated.

After moving to Pasadena in 1937, food writer and critic **Helen Evans Brown** began advocating the use of fresh local ingredients and international influences. She never called them farm-to-table or fusion foods,

but her recipes in *Helen Brown's West Coast Cook Book* (published in 1952) are exactly that. Brown's culinary mind-set influenced other foodies like James Beard, Craig Claiborne, and fellow Pasadena denizen Julia Child.

While studying abroad, college student **Alice Waters** learned how the French used super-fresh meats, fish, and produce in their homes and restaurants. Armed with that knowledge, she opened Berkeley's Chez

Panisse—one of the first restaurants to emphasize a farm-to-table style that would later be called California cuisine.

Though her forte was French cooking, **Julia Child** proved that a virtually unknown chef and cookbook author from California could become a global icon and ambassador of good food. Later in life, she launched a Santa Barbara–based foundation to promote gastronomy and the culinary arts.

Breakfast of champions: huevos rancheros and homemade tortillas at MishMash Burgers, BBQ & Stuff in San Diego

Michelin stars. The culinary hot spots of 50 years ago—like **Chinatown, North Beach**, and **Fisherman's Wharf**—have been surpassed by new dining mavens like **SoMa (South of Market), Cow Hollow,** the **Richmond**, and the **Mission**.

California cuisine reaches a delectable peak at **Quince** in Jackson Square, which sources many of its ingredients in partnership with Fresh Run Farm in Bolinas. On the waterfront side of the Financial District, **Angler SF** offers locally sourced seafood like Tomales Bay oysters and Monterey Bay abalone. Tucked

between the steel-and-glass towers of SoMa are acclaimed eateries like **Benu** with its decadent fixed menus and the Morocco/California fusion food at **Mourad**.

The eclectic Mission District offers an enticing choice between vintage Mexican restaurants like **El Faro** and **La Taqueria** and neighborhood newbies like **Californios** with its innovative Mexican food, the fabulous New American cooking at **Lazy Bear**, or the exotic Nepalese cuisine of **Dancing Yak**. Flipping the script even further, the city's best dim sum is no longer in Chinatown but at **Dragon Beaux** in the

Richmond District. Ironically, the Chinatown area now boasts some of the city's best South Asian dining with the Cal-Indian cuisine at the ritzy **Campton Place**.

North Beach institutions like the **Victoria Pastry Company** (opened in 1914) and **Molinari Delicatessen** (founded in 1896) reflect the area's Italian roots. But the overflow from nearby Chinatown has gifted the neighborhood with edgy Asian eats like **Red Window** (which really does have a red takeout window in the back). Elegant Italian awaits on the other side of Nob Hill at **Acquerello** in Polk Gulch.

Even after half a century, **Chez Panisse** in Berkeley remains the gastronomic gold standard for the East Bay. But Oakland is on the rise, thanks to transpacific fusion food at **Commis** and the Colombia-meets-California cuisine at **Mägo**. Down the peninsula, the Silicon Valley tech boom has spawned culinary experiences like the French haute cuisine at **Bistronomie by Baumé** in Palo Alto, the tony **Village Pub** (which is anything but a pub) in Woodside, and **Saffron** for elevated Indian cuisine in Burlingame and San Carlos.

The legendary **French Laundry** is still the epitome of extraordinary dining in the Napa-Sonoma wine country. But in a region renowned equally for food and wine, there are heaps of other great eats: **Barndiva** in Healdsburg and **Farmstead at Long Meadow Ranch** in St. Helena for the freshest farm to fork, **Bottega** in Yountville for refined Italian, and **Gott's Roadside** diner in St. Helena for Napa's best burgers.

South of the Bay Area, **Nepenthe** offers jaw-dropping views of the Big Sur coast as you munch Ambrosia Burgers, and the acclaimed **Aubergine** in Carmel-by-the-Sea features an eight-course tasting menu that could easily define California cuisine. The **Steinbeck House Restaurant** in Salinas serves Cobb salad, cream of asparagus soup, and other Golden State favorites in the Victorian home where the author grew up.

San Diego

Like eaters in other California urban areas, San Diegans have benefited from the rise of restaurant-rich ethnic neighborhoods since the 1980s.

Convoy Street in Kearny Mesa is flanked by scores of Asian eateries, from super-hip spots like **RakiRaki Ramen** and **SomiSomi** dessert shop to more traditional restaurants like **Tofu House** for Korean hot pot and **Jasmine** for Chinese seafood. Little Italy near downtown San Diego has evolved into an eating oasis where diners can choose from **Bencotto** and its exceptional Italian cuisine, the Asian fusion at **Harumama Noodles + Buns**, or dishes from that other down under at **Queenstown Public House**.

Upscale restaurants like **the Marine Room** and **George's at the Cove** continue to attract well-heeled eaters to La Jolla. But you can dine just as enjoyably—for a fraction of the price—at farm-to-table **Girard**

The sweet pea custard adorned with edible flowers at Lazy Bear in San Francisco's Mission District

Gourmet or **Bubba's Smokehouse BBQ**. Just north of La Jolla, **Addison Restaurant** in Carmel Valley recently became the first Southern California restaurant to earn three Michelin stars.

Surfers were the original denizens of many of the most popular eateries in San Diego's beach burbs. They range from **Hodad's** for burgers in Ocean Beach and **Kono's Café** for breakfast burritos beside Crystal Pier in Pacific Beach to the rad sandwiches at **Board & Brew** in Del Mar and primo fish and shrimp tacos at **Fish 101** in Encinitas. Props for the best waterfront views go to the outdoor terraces at **Jake's Del Mar** and **Island Prime** on Harbor Island.

BOTTOMS UP!

Franciscan padres were the first to discover that California's climate and soils were ideal for cultivating grapes that could be crushed into wine. Even during Prohibition, the pious **Christian Brothers** in the Napa Valley continued the tradition, ostensibly for altar wine.

The state's production grew substantially after World War II, as Americans slowly but surely learned to love wine. However, it wasn't until the 1976 Judgment of Paris—when a Cabernet Sauvignon produced by Napa's **Stag's Leap Wine Cellars** beat the best French reds—that California wine exploded onto the global scene.

Nowadays the state boasts 139 American Viticultural Areas (AVAs) spread across 49 counties. Responsible for more than 80 percent of U.S. wine production, California has grown into the globe's fourth largest winemaker behind Italy, France, and Spain.

With more than 400 wineries—including prestigious names like **Inglenook, Beaulieu, Opus One, Sterling, Chateau Montelena, Rutherford Hill, Domaine Carneros, Far Niente**, and **V. Sattui**—the Napa Valley remains the pinnacle of California wine. But Sonoma, Santa Barbara, Central Coast, Mendocino, and upstarts like the Sierra Foothills and Temecula offer vintages and visitor experiences that are just as rich (and often a lot less crowded).

While the rest of the state was sipping wine, San Diego was busy brewing craft beer. Opening in 1989, **Karl Strauss** (downtown and Sorrento Valley) was the first of more than 150 craft breweries spread across the county. As *Time Out* exclaimed, "San Diego is to craft beer what Napa is to wine."

Dine with a speedy view on the Gourmet Express lunch train with Napa Valley Wine Train tours.

Outfits like hilltop **Stone Brewing** (Escondido and Liberty Station) and **Ballast Point** (in Miramar and Little Italy) have earned national reputations. Yet some of the best beer is found at off-the-beaten-path suds makers like **New English** in Sorrento Valley, **Border X** in Barrio Logan, and **White Labs** in Miramar.

Among the Golden State's other purveyors of award-winning amber nectar are **Lagunitas Brewing Company** in Petaluma, **Firestone Walker** in Paso Robles, **Temescal** in Oakland, **Russian River Brewing** in Santa Rosa, and **Highland Park Brewery** in L.A.'s Chinatown.

From the **Appletini** and **White Russian** to the nonalcoholic **Shirley Temple**, California has spawned numerous cocktails. The **mai tai** may sound tropical, but it was first concocted during World War II at **Trader Vic's** bar in Oakland (having since relocated to nearby Emeryville). The classic **Tequila Sunrise** was born in the early 1970s across the bay at

The Buena Vista café in San Francisco serves up 2,000 Irish coffees a day.

the **Trident** in Sausalito. And though not strictly a cocktail, **Irish coffee** traces its American roots to the **Buena Vista Café** near Fisherman's Wharf in San Francisco.

Angeleno lounge lizards gravitate toward killer sunset views—like

Moonshadows and the **Barefoot Bar**, both along Pacific Coast Highway in Malibu—or totally off-the-wall drinking places. Scores of joints fit into the latter category, including the **Spare Room** bowling alley and cocktail lounge in Hollywood, the **Tonga Hut** tiki bar in North Hollywood, and the new **Let's Go! Disco & Cocktail Club** in the Arts District, which styles itself after a garish 1970s Italian discotheque. Among the city's most photogenic bars is **the Wolves**, with its stained glass ceiling and ornate Old World decor in downtown L.A.

The City by the Bay also boasts its fair share of lovable dives. Opened in 1937, **Li Po Cocktail Lounge** in Chinatown offers a Buddhist shrine, a large neon lantern that appeared in the 1947 movie *The Lady From Shanghai,* and drinks like the Chinese Mai Tai and Tokyo Tea with vodka, gin, rum, tequila, and triple sec. Famous for its dry martinis, the Middle Eastern–themed **Zam Zam** bar in the Haight attracted GIs during World War II and hippies during the flower power era. ■

THE KINGS OF CALIFORNIA FAST FOOD

As one of the first places to fully embrace car culture, California pioneered things like the drive-in church, drive-through bank, and, most significantly, fast-food restaurants. Like Levi's jeans, skateboarding, and other Golden State creations, the fast-food phenomenon spread around the world.

In 1940, brothers Richard and Maurice **McDonald** started a burger stand in San Bernardino and expanded that initial restaurant into a chain with golden arches as its symbol. A year later, Robert Peterson launched his **Jack in the Box** chain with a single outlet in San Diego.

Harry and Esther Snyder took the concept a step further in 1948 by

opening the state's first drive-through eatery in the L.A. suburb of Baldwin Park. Perfectly describing what patrons would do, they christened their restaurant **In-N-Out Burger**.

By the early 1960s, California's appetite for quick, casual eats had expanded beyond burgers and fries. Glen Bell cleverly incorporated his own last name into the **Taco Bell** chain he founded in the L.A. suburb of Downey. John Galardi, one of Bell's young protégés in the taco business, decided that an A-frame edifice and oddball name would make his first **Wienerschnitzel** restaurant in Wilmington stand out from the increasingly crowded fast-food field.

Colorado

A crossroads of Rocky Mountain and southwestern cuisine, the Centennial State offers some of the best eats in the American West in a culinary scene that includes big cities, chic ski resorts, and small-town diners.

THE BIG PICTURE

Founded: 1876

Population: 5.84 million

Official State Fish: Greenback cutthroat trout

Also Known As: Centennial State

Culinary Influences: Mexican, Chinese, Italian

Don't Miss: Telluride, Denver, Aspen

Claim to Fame: Rocky Mountain oysters, Denver omelet, the Snowball

Some of Colorado's iconic foods trace their roots to the frontier era while others are far more modern inventions.

The ubiquitous **Denver omelet** may have been pioneered by 19th-century cattle drive chuck wagon cooks or by Chinese railroad workers as a modified egg foo young. Also called the western omelet, it features diced ham, onions, and green peppers, cheddar cheese, and a touch of spice or salsa to give it a little kick. Pair it with bread and it becomes a **Denver sandwich**.

Other frontier favorites were **mountain trout** and **Rocky**

Mountain oysters, a deliberately misleading pseudonym for flour-dusted, deep-fried bull testicles. The sheep version is called **lamb fries**.

Steak Oscar was another favorite in the Colorado goldfields, at least for those who had already struck it rich. Allegedly invented by King Oscar II of Sweden and Norway (and originally made with veal), the luscious dish is created by complementing filet mignon or another prime cut of beef with hollandaise sauce and grilled asparagus.

Despite its frontier-sounding name, the **Fool's Gold Loaf sandwich** is a mid-20th-century creation invented in the 1970s at Denver's

now defunct Colorado Mine Company restaurant. The humongous sandwich comprises a massive amount of peanut butter, grape jelly, and bacon stuffed inside a hollowed-out bread loaf. It's said that Elvis Presley got his recipe for the offbeat hoagie directly from the restaurant, and it's often called the Elvis sandwich outside of Colorado.

Two other supersize dishes are **Colorado-style pizza**, with its extra-thick crust and plentiful toppings, and **spaghetti pie**, a casserole-like dish featuring pasta, ground beef, cheese, eggs, and assorted diced vegetables.

Colorado's rich soil and favorable climate generates sought-after farmers market items like **Olathe sweet corn** from the prairie counties, **Palisade peaches** from the Grand Junction area, and sweet **Rocky Ford cantaloupe** from the Arkansas River Valley. Southern Colorado is renowned for **Pueblo chilies**, a variety of mirasol pepper that adds a kick to many regional dishes.

CULINARY EXPERIENCES

Denver's premier food fest, **A Taste of Colorado** normally takes place over a long September

An assortment of cheeses at Haystack Mountain creamery in Longmont

Dine in the sky at Telluride's Alpino Vino, the highest-elevation restaurant in North America at 11,966 feet (3,647 m).

weekend in the state capital's Civic Center Park. However, the organizers have (on occasion) spread the feast—which features just about every type of food and drink you can find in Colorado—over four Sundays between May and August in conjunction with ¡Viva! Streets Denver, when motor vehicles are verboten on many downtown streets.

Way down south, the **Pueblo Chile & Frijoles Festival** (September) highlights two of that region's most celebrated foods. Culinary events like a jalapeño-eating contest, farmers market, and chili and salsa showdown are complemented by a hot-air balloon fest and Chihuahua parade.

Rocky Mountain towns host several of the state's top-shelf food and drink events, like the **Food & Wine**

Classic in Aspen (June) with its all-star lineup of celebrity chefs and winemakers. One of the nation's oldest food festivals, **Strawberry Days** in Glenwood Springs (June) has been a tradition since 1898. An old-fashioned hometown parade is the main event, but for lots of folks, the highlight is free ice cream with strawberries.

Farther down the Colorado River (and Interstate 70), the **Palisade Fruit & Wine Byway** features wineries and tasting rooms, farm stands, U-pick orchards, and farm tours along three loops outside the western Colorado city. If you don't want to drive or bike the routes yourself, local outfitters offer transport in horse-drawn carriages, pedal bikes, and other conveyances.

Like many American urban areas,

Denver has gone gaga for food halls, with half a dozen in the city center alone. Opened in 1881 and still the city's rail passenger hub, **Denver Union Station** boasts 10 gastronomic choices ranging from casual spots like **Milkbox Ice Creamery** and **Acme Delicatessen** to craft cocktails at the art deco **Cooper Lounge** or fine dining at **Stoic & Genuine Seafood & Oyster Bar**.

Over on the other side of Coors Field baseball stadium, the **Denver Central Market** (opened in 1928) has helped spark a revitalization of the River North (RiNo) Art District with its combination of gourmet ingredient vendors like the **Local Butcher** and **Tammen's Fish Market**, and low-key hangouts like **Vero Italian** and **Curio** bar.

Elsewhere along the Front Range,

Boulder's **Rosetta Hall** harbors eight restaurants and two bars, while the innovative **Exchange** in Fort Collins tucks its dine and drink outlets into reused shipping containers.

RESTAURANTS TO DIE FOR

Colorado may not seem like the most obvious place for awesome Italian food, yet many of the state's finer dining establishments are either traditional Italian or inspired by Italy's rich culinary culture.

The latest creation from James Beard Award–winning chef Alex

Seidel, **Mercantile Dining & Provision** inside Denver's restored Union Station offers a compelling pasta menu with less known dishes like *mafalde* (named for Princess Mafalda of Savoy), *cappelletti* (little hats), and caramel candy–shaped *caramelle*. Around the block is **Tavernetta**, where patrons can sip a Venetian spritz with their *bistecca alla Fiorentina* (Florentine steak) or *fagiano alla cacciatora* (hunter's stew).

Denver's international food scene stretches all the way from the **African Grill & Bar** in suburban

Lakewood with its wide variety of African dishes, to the Chinese tapas of **Hop Alley**, a cool little RiNo restaurant that adopted a derogatory term for Denver's onetime Chinatown as its name. Latin American cuisine is the focus of the cutting-edge **Comal Heritage Food Incubator**, which spotlights aspiring immigrant and refugee chefs.

A few blocks from Coors Field, **Biker Jim's Gourmet Dogs** grills some of the world's most unusual wieners, including rabbit, ostrich, and rattlesnake dogs. Top off a meal with a cone from **Sweet Cow Ice Cream**, with seven outlets in the Denver metro area.

Down in Colorado Springs, **Ristorante del Lago** at the legendary Broadmoor resort offers Bellinis and Venetian poached eggs for breakfast, and gourmet, wood-fired pizzas for dinner. The swish resort is also home to **La Taverne**, a classic steak house that specializes in Colorado black Angus beef and premium pork chops, lamb chops, and Colorado mountain trout.

At the foot of the Rockies south of town, **Juniper Valley Ranch** serves frontier-era grub like skillet-fried chicken, okra casserole, and handmade biscuits with apple butter inside a century-old adobe ranch house. Creative southwestern cuisine is the focus of the four-course tasting menus at **Four by Brother Luck** in downtown Colorado Springs.

An hour down the interstate, Pueblo is the epicenter of Colorado's southwestern and Mexican cooking. An extensive margarita menu and plenty of mirasol chilies on just about everything has made the **Cactus Flower Mexican Restaurant & Cantina** a go-to spot for locals. Although its Mexican food originally catered to the city's

Tending the garden with the grassroots nonprofit Slow Food Nations, Denver

Nick Andurlakis (pictured) served Elvis Presley his first Fool's Gold Loaf sandwich in 1976.

steelworkers, the **Mill Stop Cafe** has become a popular foodie destination. Injecting Pueblo with a splash of global cred, **Mr. Tandoori Urban Bar & Grill** serves northern Indian-style roasted meats and curries with all the condiments.

The forte at Boulder's **Frasca Food & Wine** is northern Italian Alpine cuisine, including a six-course Friulano tasting menu that can be paired with Italian wines. North America's highest-elevation restaurant is **Alpino Vino** in Telluride, where winter skiers or summer hikers can recharge on paninis or pasta.

Elsewhere in the high country, **Hearthstone** in Breckenridge excels at Colorado ranch-raised and game dishes like lamb, beef, elk, and bison. Celebrity chef Nobu Matsuhisa's refined Japanese cuisine is the star at **Matsuhisa Aspen**, while Colorado-Asian fusion reaches fever pitch at Vail's **Sweet Basil** with dishes like pork belly miso ramen and tempura mahi-mahi tacos.

The **Drunken Goat** in Edwards has a thing for fine wine, artisanal cheese, and offbeat dishes like warm brie brûlée, deviled-egg bruschetta, and prosciutto-wrapped Medjool dates. Or get your cheese fix—like Rocky Mountain Raclette and Buena Vista Blue—directly from the source at **Jumpin' Good Goat Dairy** in Buena Vista.

Many of Colorado's endemic dishes have become rare and endangered species. Opened in 1893, the Buckhorn Exchange is Denver's oldest restaurant and one of the few places with Rocky Mountain oysters (as well as elk, buffalo, and rattlesnake) on the menu. Steak Oscar remains a popular choice at **Del Frisco's Double Eagle Steakhouse** in the Denver Tech Center. Since Nick's Café in Golden closed in 2022, it's basically impossible to find a restaurant-made Fool's Gold Loaf sandwich. Thirty miles (48 km) west of Denver, **Beau Jo's** in Idaho Springs bakes what is arguably the state's best Colorado-style pizza.

BOTTOMS UP!

With nearly 300 craft breweries, Colorado is one of the nation's top three artisanal suds

Tacos and Tocatlán-style chicken at Comal Heritage Food Incubator, which supports immigrant entrepreneurs in Denver

producers. Denver certainly boasts its fair share of microbrewing outlets—and hosts the **Great American Beer Fest** in September—but Boulder and Fort Collins are the twin kings of Colorado's hipster beer scene.

Fort Collins offers more than two dozen spots to wet your whistle, including longtime favorites like **New Belgium Brewing** with its enormous lawn and **Odell Brewing Co.**, which hosts music fests on its expansive patio. The

award-winning **Avery Brewing** is top dog in Boulder.

Out in the hinterland, **Casey Brewing & Blending** in Glenwood Springs makes some of the best beer in western Colorado. With more libations than any other brewery on

OSO ADVENTURE MEALS

While backpacking together and dining on lackluster freeze-dried meals, Colorado's Dom Barrera and Mexico's Felipe Vieyra shared stories about their grandmothers' home cooking and dreamed about creating better trail food. Rather than just talk, the duo sprang into action and founded Oso Adventure Meals with

a couple of other friends and family members.

Combining their own funds with Kickstarter donations, they built a Denver-based company that transformed many of their *abuelitas'* recipes into Mexican-inspired gourmet dehydrated meals for hiking, mountain biking, ski touring, and

camping. The range includes huevos rancheros, Mexico City enchiladas, posole soup, and a veggie enchilada bowl.

Oso is also active in encouraging more Black, Indigenous, and people of color (BIPOC) in Colorado and elsewhere to undertake outdoor adventures in the Centennial State.

the BeerAdvocate list of the top-rated beers in Colorado, **WeldWerks Brewing Co.** draws dedicated beer drinkers to Greeley.

Although Colorado and wine are rarely mentioned in the same sentence, the Western Slope of the Rockies is home to the state's foremost wine regions: the **Grand Valley AVA** along the Colorado River around Palisade and Grand Junction, and the **West Elks AVA** near Black Canyon of the Gunnison National Park.

Founded in 1978, **Colorado Cellars** in Palisade is the state's oldest and largest winemaker. **Red Fox Cellars** is renowned for offbeat libations like Roasted Chile Dry Cider and Loco-Motive Tequila Barrel Aged Chardonnay. But **Carlson Vineyards** offers the most intriguing name (and wine label): Tyrannosaurus Red. ■

A medley of five IPAs from Horse & Dragon Brewing Company in Fort Collins

Connecticut

Between its abundant farms, lengthy coastline, and energetic urban areas, Connecticut has developed a diverse and intriguing food culture with distinctive dishes and offbeat drinks.

Connecticut is one of those states that overlaps on two distinct culinary traditions: New England and New York City. Though largely rural, and with a long shore on the Long Island Sound, it also boasts gritty cities with old-time urban attitudes when it comes to food.

So, it should come as no surprise that one of the state's iconic foods melds both traditions: **white clam pizza**. Prepared with littleneck clams and Pecorino Romano cheese, with a sprinkling of herbs and garlic, the pizza is "white" because it doesn't feature red tomato sauce. Both the white clam and the red-sauced **apizza** (aka New Haven–style pizza)—with its especially tasty, superthin crust—have spread from New Haven to the rest of the state.

New Haven is also the birthplace of the **steamed cheeseburger** and possibly the **hamburger** itself. According to the Library of Congress, Danish immigrant Louis Lassen sold the first ever hamburger sandwich from his lunch wagon in 1895.

When it comes to maritime eats, **Blue Point oysters** are a local delicacy. The state's favorite fish since precolonial days is the humble **shad**, which migrates up the Connecticut River and other waterways each spring. In 2003, the shad was named the official state fish.

Native to the Middle East, the **quince** tree has found a welcome home in Connecticut as both a flowering ornamental tree and fruit producer. The sweet, golden, pear-shaped fruit features in pies and preserves.

Even though Connecticut is often called the Nutmeg State, the tropical spice tree doesn't grow in colder climes. The name actually derives from unscrupulous entrepreneurs (called "nutmeggers") who tried to pass off fake wooden nutmegs as the real deal during colonial times. However, the state does produce plenty of **apples** that find their way into cider, pies, and popular apple doughnuts.

Pepperidge Farm was founded by Fairfield housewife Margaret Rudkin in 1937. From homemade bread, she expanded into cookies and Goldfish crackers, and along the way penned the first cookbook to make the *New York Times* best-seller list.

CULINARY EXPERIENCES

Shuck and suck the bounty of Long Island Sound at the **Milford Oyster Festival** in August or learn how to

THE BIG PICTURE

Founded: 1788

Population: 3.63 million

Official State Cookie: Snickerdoodle

Also Known As: Constitution State, Nutmeg State

Culinary Influences: Italian, English

Don't Miss: New Haven, Hartford, Mystic

Claim to Fame: Pepperidge Farm foods, white clam pizza, steamed cheeseburgers

Garlic, olive oil, cracked red pepper, and oregano provide the base for the littleneck clam pizza at Zuppardi's Apizza in West Haven.

Shuckers battle for the top spot in the oyster-shucking competition at the Milford Oyster Festival.

grow and cook with the "stinking rose" at Bethlehem's **Garlic & Harvest Festival** in October.

Taste of New Haven offers a variety of guided food walks including pizza, tapas, taco, and french fry tours. Their six-hour Pizza Lovers Tour features a dozen different pies, including the iconic white clam and apizza. Another guilty pleasure is the focus of the **Connecticut Chocolate Trail**, with stops at gourmet chocolatiers in Hartford, Litchfield Hills, Fairfield County, and Mystic.

A number of Connecticut working farms offer summertime dinners and other culinary events. **Stone Acres Farm** in Stonington stages a Summer Nights pop-up dinner series with vegan, vegetarian, and pescatarian options. **Rosedale Farms & Vineyards** in Simsbury hosts a variety of summer foodie

feasts, from a Father's Day lobster meal to events that revolve around Asian and Indian cuisine and Connecticut craft beer. **White Gate Farm** in East Lyme offers farm-to-table celebrations and dinners, critter tours for kids, and a variety of classes ranging from chicken processing to flower arranging.

RESTAURANTS TO DIE FOR

Connecticut's most celebrated eateries aren't fancy Michelin-starred affairs but rather a couple of vintage New Haven joints serving two of the state's favorite foods. Opened in 1925, **Frank Pepe Pizzeria Napoletana** in the Little Italy area is renowned for white clam pizza and as the originator of apizza, while little brick **Louis' Lunch** near New Haven Green has been serving classic burgers for more than a century. It

may look vintage—given its location in an old auto shop—but **Camacho Garage** in the city's Westville neighborhood is a hip, new restaurant that specializes in ceviche, tacos, and other Mexican street foods.

Soak up the maritime ambience and New England–style seafood at the **Oyster Club** in Mystic, where summertime diners can opt for a table in the "tree house" with its open-air bar and views of the Mystic River. In nearby Noank village, **Abbott's Lobster in the Rough** has been serving the spiny sea creatures and other shellfish on a deck and grassy area overlooking Long Island Sound since 1947. Farther west along the shore, **Lobster Landing** in Clinton fixes what many aficionados consider the state's best lobster rolls.

The Hartford area boasts many of Connecticut's best restaurants, including **the Charles** in Wethersfield Village. The structure might be ancient (constructed in 1790), but the restaurant is new (opened in 2020) and the recipient of numerous awards and accolades. Perched along the Farmington River in Tariffville, **Present Company** serves cutting-edge French American cuisine on ever changing tasting and prix fixe menus.

Millwright's Restaurant in Simsbury offers upscale American fare in a woodsy dining room, an open-air covered bridge with waterfall views, or a stone-walled tavern. The industrial chic decor at **Viron Rondo Osteria** in Cheshire is nearly as delicious as the contemporary Italian food. An hour's drive west of Hartford, **Community Table** in Litchfield County relies heavily on ingredients from local farms to create innovative fish, fowl, and meat dishes.

A rustic waterside welcome greets guests at Lobster Landing in Clinton.

BOTTOMS UP!

If Connecticut were to have an official state cocktail, it would probably be the **Brass Monkey**. The blend of orange juice, vodka, and dark rum has been around for years, but it didn't become widely popular until the 1970s, when Hartford-based **Heublein Spirits** launched a premixed bottled version that later featured in a Beastie Boys song.

Birch beer is another favorite libation. Although normally a non-alcoholic soda, it can be fermented into an alcoholic version. **Foxon Park Beverages** in East Haven has been making white birch beer soda since the 1920s.

Connecticut certainly owns its fair share of dive bars, craft breweries, and swish cocktail lounges. But the more offbeat places stand out from the crowd. **Little River**

MARTHA STEWART

Martha Stewart may have been born and raised in New Jersey, but she rose to fame as a cookbook author, home decorator, and television personality during her long residence at Turkey Hill farm in Connecticut (from 1971 to 2007).

While tending to the greenhouse and vegetable garden at Turkey Hill, Stewart developed many of her best-selling cookbooks, including *Martha Stewart's Quick Cook*, *Martha Stewart's Hors d'Oeuvres*, and *Martha Stewart's Pies & Tarts*. She also launched a self-titled homemaking magazine, a home merchandise line, and a popular TV show.

One of her latest ventures was *Martha & Snoop's Potluck Dinner Party*, an offbeat food and variety show she co-hosted with rapper Snoop Dogg.

Grab a refreshing margarita and a sampling of tacos at Milford's Dockside Brewery.

Restoratives in Hartford offers an intriguing choice of cocktails, grogs, possets, and punches like the Bad Hombre (tequila, mezcal, lemon, and truffle honey) and Kingston Buck (Jamaican rum, ginger beer, lime, and amaro).

More than a dozen billiard tables and an entire wall of dartboards complement the draft beers at **Branford Cue & Brew** near New Haven. For those who prefer alfresco drinking, the **Hops Company** in Derby renders craft brews and designer pizzas in a shady outdoor beer garden, while **Dockside Brewery** in Milford offers a large outdoor area beside the Housatonic River. ∎

Delaware

With a long coast and pastoral hinterland, Delaware makes it easy for home cooks and restaurant chefs to prepare farm-to-fork and sea-to-table dishes.

Delaware may have an ox on its coat of arms and the blue hen as the official state bird, but its culinary claim to fame is seafood.

Served fresh or fried, **Delaware Bay oysters** are renowned for their subtle flavor, while creamy, white **Delaware clam chowder** distinguishes itself from the New England variety with the addition of pork and, on occasion, corn. **Dilly crab dip**—flavored with dried dill weed, lemon juice, and a dab of hot sauce—is another favorite.

Landed along Brandywine Creek and the lower Delaware River, **walleye** is most often grilled or served as fish-and-chips with Delaware-style **vinegar french fries** (marinated in cold vinegar before cooking).

Like those in other mid-Atlantic states, Delaware diners love their

scrapple, a blend of pork scraps, cornmeal, and flour molded into a loaf and often served for breakfast either on its own or as a sandwich.

You will find a host of chicken dishes across the state, including local favorites such as **cream chicken, rotisserie chicken, chicken divan, chicken pasta,** and **barbecued chicken salad**.

Despite its name, Delaware's **pretzel salad** is actually a three-level cake featuring layers of crushed pretzels, cream cheese, and strawberry or pineapple slices in Jell-O.

CULINARY EXPERIENCES

Delaware's signature food event is the **Bridgeville Apple-Scrapple Festival**, where eaters can sample the "prime rib of scrapple," scrapple waffles, scrapple bagels, and other

THE BIG PICTURE

Founded: 1787

Population: 1.02 million

Official State Dessert: Peach pie

Also Known As: First State, Diamond State

Culinary Influences: English, Dutch, German

Don't Miss: Rehoboth Beach, Wilmington, Dover

Claim to Fame: Fries with vinegar, dilly crab dip, Delaware Bay oysters

versions concocted by the town's century-old RAPA Scrapple Factory.

New Castle, the state's northernmost county, hosts the uber-popular **Old-Fashioned Ice Cream Festival** in June with fireworks and live music, as well as the year-round **New Castle Farmers Market** (Thursday–Sunday), which features a Pennsylvania Dutch food section. **Spence's Bazaar & Amish Market** in Dover offers traditional dishes.

Eating Rehoboth offers walking food tours that cover five different eateries in the popular seaside town between May and November. The coastal zone is also the place for culinary classes at **Paul's Kitchen** in Lewes and **Big Fish Grill** in Rehoboth Beach, as well as **SoDel Concepts** educational wine dinners at various locations.

Delmarva Discovery Tours in Dewey Beach explores food and drink along the coast on wine, garden, and brewery tours, as well as a farm tour that includes cuddling baby goats.

Meanwhile, you can catch your own dinner on Delaware Bay and open Atlantic fishing trips with outfits like **Fisherman's Wharf charters** in Lewes.

The local favorite strawberry pretzel salad

Try the beer-battered fish-and-chips at Jessop's Tavern, housed in a historic building from 1674, in New Castle.

RESTAURANTS TO DIE FOR

As Delaware's largest city, Wilmington flaunts much of the state's finest dining with a host of restaurants with contrasting locations, ambience, and gastronomic choices.

Opened as a bakery in 1798 and converted into a tavern during the War of 1812, the elegant **Columbus Inn** recently debuted a revamped menu with surf and turf classics and craft cocktails. The moody red-and-black decor imbues **Harry's Savoy Grill** with the feel of a classic mid-century steak house.

True to its name, **Big Fish Grill on the Riverfront** renders seafood on the banks of the Christina River with fried oysters, crab cake sandwiches, and Pot 'O Mussels among the choices. **Feby's Fishery** on Wilmington's suburban west side offers both sit-down seafood and a fish market for those who want to prepare scallops, oysters, crab, and fresh-off-the-boat fish at home.

Wilmington's Little Italy district harbors half a dozen Italian eateries, including **Mrs. Robino's Restaurant**, opened in 1940. The spread includes homemade pastas, gourmet pizzas, parmigiana dishes, and less common Italian specialties like broccoli rabe. St. Anthony of Padua Church in the same neighborhood hosts the weeklong, food-filled **St. Anthony's Italian Festival** in June.

On the southern outskirts of Wilmington, the cute little roadside **Dairy Palace** in New Castle has been churning out soft-serve ice cream, sundaes, and shakes since 1956.

In southeastern Delaware, Rehoboth Beach is the state's other culinary hub. **Henlopen City Oyster House** serves some of the shore's best seafood, with a menu that runs a broad gamut from vodka or champagne oyster shooters to caviar, crab cakes, and a fabulous smoked fish board. A block off the boardwalk, **Blue Moon** complements its seafood with live cabaret, jazz, drag shows, musical tributes, and old-fashioned bingo with Sister Dot.

Dive into a delicious filet mignon or New York strip at **1776 Steakhouse**, and then tee off at the neighboring miniature golf course. Or hustle down to the Rehoboth Boardwalk for legendary seaside treats like **Kohr Brothers** frozen custard or **Thrasher's** french fries.

Away from the beach, **Rosenfeld's Delicatessen** offers more than 100 breakfast, lunch, and dinner choices, including lox and bagels, Reubens, borscht, blintzes, and chopped liver.

Grey Fox Grille & Public House is one of the posher places for Dover dining, with a menu that features tantalizing chicken and salmon dishes served with live music on weekends. **Cool Springs Fish Bar and Restaurant** is the best choice for seafood in the state capital, while **Hall's Family Restaurant** excels at inexpensive comfort foods.

BOTTOMS UP!

Beer drinkers who may not be able to name the state capital (Dover!) can almost always declare that it's the home of beloved **Dogfish Head** craft beer. Dogfish HQ in Milton offers a factory tour and tasting room, and is home to a 40-foot-tall (12 m) steampunk tree house sculpture made from various reclaimed and recycled materials. There's a Dogfish outpost in Rehoboth—**Dogfish Head Brewings & Eats**—just steps from the boardwalk where you can try seasonal brews alongside wood-fired pizza, crab and corn chowder, and a bevy of sandwich options.

Nearby in Dewey Beach, you'll find **the Starboard**, a legendary Sunday brunch spot known for its make-your-own Bloody Mary bar. Check out **Dewey Beer Co.** across the street for a rotating selection of craft beer and an eclectic menu that includes everything from burgers to Chorizo Lo Mein.

By the way, Dover hosts the annual **Delaware Beer, Wine & Spirits Festival** in August at the

Gruyère, Comté, and raclette top the classic French onion soup at Le Cavalier in Wilmington.

The Old-Fashioned Ice Cream Festival at Rockwood Park in Wilmington

Delaware Agricultural Museum and Village.

Founded in 1724, more than 270 years before Dogfish, **Jessop's Tavern** in New Castle is the state's oldest drinking establishment. It opened during an era when William Penn and Baron Baltimore were still arguing over who rightfully controlled the Delaware colony.

Inland from Rehoboth Beach, **Nassau Valley Vineyards** is the state's most prominent vintner, but the coastal region is also home to Viking-themed **Brimming Horn Meadery** and **Grain on the Rocks** on the Cape May ferry pier in Lewes, which serves craft beer and gourmet coffee with waterfront views of Delaware Bay and Cape Henlopen. ∎

DELAWARE COOKBOOKS

Delaware's history is incredibly rich in cookbooks. Among the more modern tomes are *In Season: A Coastal Delaware Cookbook* (2022) by Schell Brothers, the company that owns and operates the Coffee House café in Rehoboth Beach; *The Delaware Heritage Cookbook* (1988), which includes recipes from locals; and *First State Plates: Iconic Delaware Restaurants and Recipes* (2005) by Pam George.

Others are collector's items, like the Delaware State Society Daughters of the American

Revolution's spiral-bound *Delaware DAR Historical Cookbook* (1990) and *The First State, First Lady's Recipe Book* (1976) by Frances Allmond.

The biggest prize is the *Trinity Parish Cook Book*, compiled and illustrated in 1892 by the ladies of Trinity Church in Wilmington. Republished by Leopold Classic Library in 2015, the book contains recipes for heirloom dishes like Lewes Overnight Pone Cornbread, World War I Cake, Wild Dove in Cherry Sauce, and Baked Muskrat.

District of Columbia

The nation's capital compensates for its lack of heirloom dishes with a robust dining and drinks scene worthy of its standing as a global power center.

THE BIG PICTURE

Founded: 1790

Population: 671,800

Official Fruit: Cherry

Also Known As: Our nation's capital

Culinary Influences: French, African American, Italian, Spanish

Don't Miss: Capitol Hill, National Mall, Dupont Circle

Claim to Fame: Half smokes, mumbo sauce, pupusas, jumbo pizza slices

Carved from the state of Maryland in 1790, the nation's capital shares a taste for blue crabs, oysters, and other delectable denizens of the Chesapeake Bay. But with more than 200 years of home cooking, D.C. was bound to develop several endemic dishes.

The meaty **"G" Man sub sandwich**—stuffed with double ham, pepperoni, salami, mortadella, and provolone and fontina cheeses—was invented at Mangialardo's Italian deli in the 1970s allegedly after two FBI agents asked for those exact ingredients on their sandwiches.

A blend of beef and pork, the **half-smoked sausage** (aka half smokes) has been a D.C. mainstay since the 1950s. Although no one knows for sure, the name apparently derives from the fact that the sausage is lightly smoked before grilling. Eaten in a hot dog bun and smothered in chili, chopped onions, and yellow mustard, the half smoke was said to be a favorite of both Anthony Bourdain and Barack Obama.

Another local food with roots in the 1950s is **mumbo sauce**, a tomato-based sweet-and-sour condiment that goes great with chicken, french fries, Chinese takeout, and many other dishes. Many D.C. restaurants make their own and there are several commercial varieties including Capital City.

CULINARY EXPERIENCES

Not to be confused with Washington's **Union Station**, which boasts its own bevy of bars and restaurants, **Union Market** has morphed from a wholesale food emporium founded in the 1930s into a popular dining and drinking area one local magazine calls "D.C.'s hippest feasting ground." Its dozens of offerings range from Argentine, Korean, Egyptian, and South Indian cuisine to **Ice Cream Jubilee, Bread Alley** bakery, and gourmet Italian at Michelin-starred **Masseria**.

Much older and earthier, the city's **Eastern Market** began serving patrons just a few years after the Civil War (1873). It's primarily a farmers/flea market with the food stalls indoors—including Mexican

D.C.'s signature sandwich: the "G" Man, loaded with ham, salami, mortadella, pepperoni, fontina, and provolone, at Mangialardo's

The iconic exterior of Ben's Chili Bowl

street food, crepes, and southern comfort dishes—and arts and craft vendors outside.

The capital stages several huge chow-downs each year, including the **Giant National Capital Barbecue Battle** (June)—which takes over four blocks of Pennsylvania Avenue between the White House and Capitol Building—**A Taste of the DMV** (D.C., Maryland, and Virginia) food and cultural festival (July), and the festive, food-filled **Downtown Holiday Market** (November–December).

DC Metro Food Tours offers guided forays through Georgetown, Dupont Circle, Capitol Hill, Adams Morgan, Little Ethiopia, and Old Town Alexandria on the other side of the Potomac. **Capital Harvest on the Plaza** farmers market sets up every Wednesday between May and October in Wilson Plaza outside the Ronald Reagan Building & International Trade Center near the White House.

RESTAURANTS TO DIE FOR

The District is one of only six American urban areas with Michelin-starred restaurants, and three of the capital's eateries have earned a coveted two stars.

Located in the hip U Street Corridor, **Jônt** offers a 14-seat tasting counter and Japanese-influenced tasting menus you're not likely to find anywhere else—like Murasaki sweet potatoes, Dulcey ganache, mascarpone, and white miso caramel or nori pancakes with carrots and braised lamb.

Down in the Capitol Hill neighborhood, **Pineapple & Pearls** bucks the fine dining fashion trend by telling patrons they can dress any old way they want (but suggests flamboyantly) to devour its exquisite four-course tasting menu. A block from Ford's Theatre, the uber-intimate **minibar** by José Andrés seats just 12 for the Spanish maestro's latest creations.

Cranes specializes in small, artfully presented Iberian Japanese dishes they call Spanish kaiseki. Innovative modern Indian cuisine and cocktails are the twin attractions of **Daru** in northeast D.C., recently named one of the nation's top 50 restaurants. And **the Dabney** in artsy, brick-paved Blagden Alley offers updated takes on mid-Atlantic favorites like oysters, rockfish, and scrapple.

Among the District's more traditional seafood choices are **Pearl Dive Oyster Palace** with its sidewalk counter seating and funky upstairs bar; the **Rappahannock Oyster Bar** opposite the city's Municipal Fish Market; and **BlackSalt** near the Palisades, which doubles as a restaurant and neighborhood fishmonger.

Located below the Mason-Dixon Line, D.C. also excels at southern cooking and soul food. Since it first opened in 1958, **Ben's Chili Bowl** (five locations in the metro area) has been the go-to place for half smokes with chili and Virginia-style banana pudding. **Po Boy Jim Bar & Grill** does its signature sandwiches just like they're done in New Orleans.

Tucked inside the National Museum of African American History & Culture, **Sweet Home Café** offers an Afrofuturist menu with dishes like crispy pork sweet potato mofongo and ham hock collard greens dip served with flatbread.

BOTTOMS UP!

It's telling that among the first commercial establishments to open in the District when it was declared the national capital were bars. The **Old Ebbitt Grill** is the modern reincarnation of a bar that originally opened in 1856. Dubbed the "Saloon of Presidents," it

Don't miss the fried rock shrimp at local favorite Shōtō in the heart of downtown.

The Highlander cocktail at barmini

famously served a number of chief executives including Ulysses S. Grant and Teddy Roosevelt.

With walls covered in caricatures and cartoons of many of the leading political figures of the past half century, **Off the Record** bar in the fabled Hay-Adams hotel really does feel like the sort of place where Deep Throat passed his secrets to Woodward and Bernstein.

Not all the city's watering holes are as old as dirt. The king of D.C. craft beer, **ChurchKey** offers more than 500 handpicked varieties from around the world, including 50-plus draft and cask beers. José Andrés's **barmini** affords the famed Spanish chef and food philanthropist a chance to experiment with cocktails like the gin-based Matcha Tot-Tea,

LN2 New York Sour, and frosty Daphna with liquid nitrogen. Down on the river, **Tiki TNT Rum Bar** goes full tropical with modern takes on classic island cocktails.

D.C.'s best pub crawl route is 18th Street NW in Adams Morgan,

with joints including the over-the-top **Le Mont Royal** disco bar, the **Green Zone** for creative cocktails and Middle Eastern bites, and **Jack Rose Dining Saloon** with its phenomenal whiskey wall (2,700 bottles and counting). ■

U.S. SENATE BEAN SOUP

Of all the laws the U.S. Senate has passed over the centuries, one of the oddest is a mandate that navy bean soup must be served daily in the Senate Restaurant. Two bygone senators claim to have introduced the resolution. But the original recipe was created by Idaho's Fred Dubois, who served two terms in the 1890s and early 20th century.

The current recipe calls for two pounds (0.9 kg) dried navy beans, four quarts (3.8 L) hot water, 1.5 pounds (0.7 kg) smoked ham hocks, one chopped onion, two tablespoons (28 g) butter, and a pinch of salt and pepper. A heartier version, which corresponds more closely to Dubois's original concoction, includes mashed potatoes, celery, garlic, and parsley.

Florida

Fresh ingredients and diverse cultures, alongside stunning waterfront locations and vibrant urban scenes, are the main ingredients of Florida's incredibly rich culinary stew.

Florida's unique geography—a giant thumb extending into the Caribbean and Gulf of Mexico—and its settlement patterns have stoked not one but four distinct culinary landscapes.

Founded by the Spanish in 1565 and the nation's oldest continuously inhabited European settlement, St. Augustine carries on Iberian cooking traditions with dishes like **Minorcan clam chowder**, made with potato, tomato, onion, bell pepper, a boatload of herbs and spices, and locally grown **datil peppers** to give it some kick.

After Florida became part of the United States in 1819, American settlers in the panhandle region introduced southern comfort foods

THE BIG PICTURE

Founded: 1845

Population: 22.2 million

Official State Fruit: Orange

Also Known As: Sunshine State

Culinary Influences: Italian, French, Creole, Spanish, Caribbean, Cuban

Don't Miss: Miami, Orlando, Key West

Claim to Fame: Key lime pie, gator tail, stone crabs

like **fried green tomatoes, boiled peanuts, shrimp and grits**, and **sweet tea**. Early settlers also discovered locally available foods like **alligators, stone crabs**, and **Apalachicola oysters**. And they presumably tossed a variety of endemic ingredients into a gumbo that came to be called **Sunshine State Cioppino**.

By the end of the 1800s, settlement had moved farther down the peninsula in search of beach resort towns and inland areas where subtropical fruits could thrive. Almost overnight, Florida became one of the world's leading **orange, grapefruit**, and **kumquat** growers. The state even invented its own citrus—the **Orlando tangelo**—a hybrid of the Dancy tangerine and Duncan grapefruit developed in Lake County in 1897. The state's booming citrus industry birthed popular desserts like **Key lime pie** and **sour orange pie**.

During the 20th century, immigrants from Cuba, Haiti, and other islands revolutionized the Florida eating scene. The **Cubano** with roast pork, smoked ham, and Swiss cheese became Florida's trademark sandwich. Cooks from the Caribbean

The famous Cubano sandwich

February means harvest time for oranges at a grove in Fort Meade.

also introduced dishes like ***arroz con pollo*** (rice with chicken), ***pastelitos de guayaba*** (cheese and guava pastries), **plantains, empanadas**, and **conch fritters**.

CULINARY EXPERIENCES

The Florida Panhandle celebrates its maritime bounty with a slew of autumn events, including the **Destin Seafood Festival** along the city's Harbor Boardwalk and the month-long Destin Fishing Rodeo (October), the **Pensacola Seafood Festival** with its signature tapas-size samples (September–October), and the long-running **Florida Seafood Festival** in Apalachicola (November)

with an oyster-shucking contest and other events in the historic downtown district.

Farther down the state's Gulf Coast, the **Ford International Cuban Sandwich Festival** invades Centennial Park in Tampa's Ybor City neighborhood over Memorial Day weekend (May), while Florida's favorite shellfish is the focus of **Frenchy's Stone Crab Weekend** in Clearwater Beach (October).

Participants compete to see who can drop an entire Key lime pie from the top of a lighthouse—and not have it splatter—during the **Key Lime Festival** in Key West during Fourth of July week. The event also

features Key lime baking classes, rum tastings, and a master class in caring for Key lime trees. The limelight falls on a different citrus during the **Kumquat Festival** in Dade City (January) in the heart of central Florida's kumquat country.

Miami Culinary Tours offers private and group outings of the vibrant food and beverage terrain in Little Havana, South Beach, the Design District, and the Wynwood (Little San Juan) neighborhood north of downtown with its colorful murals and Latin-flavored eateries.

Like other metro areas, Miami-Dade is not immune to the food-hall fad. Among the unique concepts

Eat your heart out—and win a pie-eating competition—at the Key Lime Festival in Key West.

are **Lincoln Eatery** in Miami Beach with its rooftop Sky Yard music events and dance parties; the industrial chic **Citadel** in the up-and-coming Little River district; **1-800-Lucky** in Wynwood, which styles itself after an Asian night market; and **Okeydokey** food hall in Brickell with three floors of eats, drinks, and live entertainment.

Founded in 1938, the daily **Jacksonville Farmers Market** is the oldest of its kind in Florida, with more than 100 stalls hawking locally grown organic edibles and ethnic foods. The weekend-only **Yellow Green Farmers Market** in Hollywood recently launched a new air-conditioned pavilion called **the Station** with specialty eateries.

Not every Florida food encounter fits a well-defined culinary category. On the edge of the Everglades, the **Robert Is Here Fruit Stand & Farm** is renowned for both its fresh tropical produce and incredible fruit smoothies and milkshakes. The monks at **Wat Mongkolratanaram Thai Temple** (often called Wat Tampa) in West Tampa organize a Sunday market with goodies like crab Rangoon, pad Thai noodles, spring rolls, and Thai iced tea.

RESTAURANTS TO DIE FOR

Miami/Palm Beach

It doesn't get any more old-school than breakfast or brunch at **The Circle** restaurant in The Breakers.

Reminiscent of the 1920s, when the legendary beachfront hotel first opened, the dining room is crowned by a massive chandelier from a domed, frescoed ceiling with Italian Renaissance scenes.

Although now skippered by the esteemed Thomas Keller, the **Surf Club** at the Four Seasons in Surfside is another throwback, in this case to the mid-20th century, when Elizabeth Taylor, Winston Churchill, and other celebrities were guests. Two other oldies but still goodies are **Versailles**, purveyor of the city's best Cuban cuisine for more than 50 years, and Miami Beach's **Joe's Stone Crab**, which opened in 1913 as a modest seafood lunch counter.

With an outdoor terrace and

picture windows looking out on downtown Miami and down on the Miami River, the rooftop **Area 31** at the Kimpton Epic Hotel renders elevated surf and turf and one of the city's best dinner table views. Another sleek, upscale eatery, **Cote Miami** in the Design District marries the classic American steak house to Korean barbecue, while **Fiola Miami** in Coral Gables delivers an Amalfi Coast raw bar, laid-back aperitivo hour, and modern Italian cuisine.

You won't need to take out a second mortgage to dine on fine Cuban at **Enriqueta's Sandwich Shop** in the Edgewater district or to dig into sumptuous cakes, cookies, and croissants at **Zak the Baker** in nearby Wynwood. Located beside the Little Haiti Cultural Center in North Miami, **Piman Bouk Restaurant** serves *bouillon cabrit* (goat stew), *poisson gros sel* (salt fish soup), *griot de porc* (fried pork), and other Haitian specialties.

The awesome eats continue north of Miami, all the way up the shore to Jacksonville. Any foodie trip up the Scenic & Historic A1A Coastal Byway should include stone crab claws from the raw bar at **Swifty's** restaurant at the chic Colony Hotel in Palm Beach, steamed rock shrimp at **JB's Fish Camp** in New Smyrna Beach, Minorcan conch chowder at the **Conch House Marina Resort restaurant** in St. Augustine, and mesquite-grilled steak with diver scallops at **Eleven South** in Jacksonville Beach.

Orlando/Winter Park/ Disney

Beyond the fast-food joints and chain restaurants that dominate so much of the Orlando dining scene, the central Florida city offers some of the state's best Asian eats.

Don't skip dessert at Thomas Keller's Surf Club in Surfside.

With branches in the Milk District/Colonial area and Sand Lake, **Kabooki Sushi** offers James Beard Award–nominated Japanese cuisine, including omakase and kaiseki (small plates). Curry ramen with Thai flavors and *chuka* (cold ramen salad)

are among the innovative noodle dishes at **Domu**, inside the East End Market in the Audubon Park Garden District. M. C. Escher could have easily designed the astonishing black-and-white decor at **Twenty Pho Hour** on the south side, a Vietnamese

AN ORANGE A DAY …

It's said that Ponce de León planted Florida's first orange trees in the early 16th century. But given the short amount of time he spent there—and the fact that all the settlers he brought along fled after the Spanish conquistador was mortally wounded in a clash in 1521 with the local Calusa people—that origin story remains highly suspect. More likely, the Spanish who later founded St. Augustine planted the first orange seedlings on the North American mainland.

Jesse Fish—an English smuggler, slaver, and all-around scam artist—planted the first commercial crop in 1763 and was soon shipping oranges and their juice in wooden

barrels from Spanish Florida to the 13 American colonies.

Production remained relatively small until after the Civil War, when railroads reached central and southern Florida and orange growers could ship their fruit in bulk to northern markets. As "Orange Fever" spread, thousands more acres were planted, and some growers made tremendous fortunes.

Nowadays the state nurtures more than 74 million citrus trees that produce roughly half the nation's orange crop and nearly all its orange juice and frozen orange concentrate each year. Overall, the fruit contributes around $9 billion per annum to the Florida economy.

restaurant that bills itself as America's first 2D noodle bar.

Butcher's cuts are the specialty at the **Ravenous Pig**, a hip gastropub and beer garden in Winter Park that also offers seafood, pasta, and creative starters like chorizo-stuffed braised squid and a ciabatta truffle loaf. In nearby Maitland, **Luke's Kitchen & Bar** lives up to its "Orlando Restaurant of the Year" repute with dishes like swordfish schnitzel with snap peas, wahoo ceviche, and Key lime semifreddo.

Among the scores of eating options inside the Magic Kingdom, several soar above the rest. **Wine Bar George** at Disney Springs can pair its artisanal cheese and charcuterie boards with more than 140 different wines. A longtime advocate of traditional southern cuisine, celebrity chef Art Smith's **Homecomin'** restaurant serves old-time Florida favorites like fried chicken, shrimp and grits, fried green tomatoes, hush puppies, and moonshine cocktails.

For something completely different, **Tiffins Restaurant** at Disney's Animal Kingdom does exotic African-Asian dishes like Indian-style butter chicken, chermoula-marinated tofu, and South Africa braai-spiced veal.

A platter of stone crab claws

Fried perfection: conch fritters and a zippy dipping sauce

And just for fun, **Space 220** at EPCOT simulates dining in a space station orbiting Earth. (You'll need park reservations to visit these two spots, though.)

Tampa–St. Petersburg

Even though it's overshadowed by multicultural Miami when it comes to ethnic eats, the Tampa Bay area easily holds its own when it comes to global dining.

Long before there was a Little Havana, Tampa's Ybor City was the state's preeminent Hispanic neighborhood, populated by Cubans, Spaniards, and other immigrants who came to work in the area's cigar factories. Founded in 1905, **Columbia Restaurant** is both an architectural gem and a culinary landmark that serves dishes like *ropa vieja*, Cubano sandwiches, gazpacho, and tapas plates.

That same year, Greek immigrants began sponge diving in the Gulf waters off Tarpon Springs. In addition to their heavy rubber suits

CONCH REPUBLIC

As both a protest against federal government policies and a novel way to promote tourism, a group of Key West residents declared the island's independence from the United States in 1982. They christened their new territory the Conch Republic and eventually created their own flag, national anthem, and passports.

The birth of the little faux nation also elevated the profile of one of the island's favorite foods: the conch. Although fritters are the most common way of cooking the large, meaty, shell-dwelling sea snail, it can also be served in chowder, ceviche, or paella, or fried or cracked.

Among the city's foremost purveyors are **Conch Republic Seafood Company** in the Key West dockyards area, the **Conch Shack** on busy Duval Street, **Eaton Street Seafood Market**, and the legendary **Louie's Backyard**.

Dine while "orbiting" Earth at EPCOT's Space 220.

and metal helmets, they brought foods from the homeland now served at **Mykonos** restaurant and **Limani** takeout near the Tarpon Springs Sponge Docks. At **Jerk Hut** in North Tampa, dishes like curry goat, *escovitch* fish, mannish water, and jerk pork reflect a more recent wave of immigrants from Jamaica.

The bay area's waterfront choices include gumbo, grouper, and garlic crab fries at the funky little **Frenchy's Original Cafe** at Clearwater Beach, **Salt Shack on the Bay** in Tampa, and **Coconut Charlie's** at St. Pete Beach with its killer sunsets. Dedicated to the region's Native American foodways and Florida's native

ingredients, **Ulele** restaurant has transformed an old brick waterworks building on the Tampa Riverwalk into a bastion of grilled barbacoa meats and seafood.

It may not have a dreamy shoreline location, but the ever experimenting **Edison: Food + Drink Lab** in Hyde Park creates provocative dishes like molten crab cake with garlic cornbread, roasted bone marrow with scallop crudo, and buttermilk fried chicken with kimchi and shiitake mushrooms.

Across the water in St. Petersburg, **the Chattaway** is a lovable mishmash of British kitsch and tropical garden with a menu that

stretches all the way from English high tea to salads, soups, and burgers. Don't let the offbeat location fool you: **The Library** restaurant on the Johns Hopkins medical campus serves one of the city's best weekend brunch spreads.

BOTTOMS UP!

When sampling tropical cocktails in Florida, the challenge isn't finding drinks that nearly every bar south of Jacksonville seems to serve, but rather sipping these iconic concoctions in a setting that complements the drink.

There's nothing quite like quaffing a classic mojito at the **Ball &**

Chain, a historic Little Havana saloon that debuted in 1935, or a Papa Dobles daiquiri at **Sloppy Joe's**, the Key West bar where Ernest "Papa" Hemingway swigged them back in the day.

You can still gulp Rum Runners at the **Tiki Bar** on Islamorada, where the cocktail was invented in the late 1950s, or a creamy iced Kahlúa and rum Bushwacker at the divey **Sandshaker Lounge** in Pensacola Beach, where the chilly treat was conceived in the 1970s.

From relative newcomers like the rum-centric **Cafe La Trova** in Little Havana and **Broken Shaker** with its tropical outdoor patio in Miami Beach, to legendary dives like the neon-studded **Mac's Club Deuce** in South Beach (opened in 1926) and **the Bar** in Coral Gables (founded

in 1946), the Miami metro area boasts one of the world's best bar collections.

Even beyond Miami, the variety of bars in the Sunshine State is mind-blowing. True to its name, the **Flora-Bama Lounge** beach bar on Perdido Key strides the state line. Patrons at the **Wreck Bar** in Fort Lauderdale can view mermaid shows in the giant fish tank behind the bar. Sip artisanal ouzo at the **Tarpon Springs Distillery**, or catch a classic flick with your booze and bites at **Gigglewaters Social Club & Screening Room** in Safety Harbor.

Florida doesn't grow a lot of grapes, which means the **Florida Orange Groves Winery** in St. Petersburg makes its beverages with other fruits. The lineup includes Mango Mamma, Barrel-Aged

Guava, Key Limen, and Orange Sunshine wines.

Alternative ingredients are also the modus operandi at **Ice Plant** bar in St. Augustine, where signature cocktails feature unconventional items like chipotle- and rosemary-infused tequila, Ecuadorian agave spirit, hibiscus, lavender, and cantaloupe.

And don't assume Walt Disney World is just for kids. The Magic Kingdom sports two dozen drinking spots, many of them with movie themes like **Oga's Cantina** *(Star Wars)*, **Jock Lindsey's Hangar Bar** *(Indiana Jones),* and the **Enchanted Rose** *(Beauty and the Beast).* Outside the House of Mouse, **Reyes Mezcaleria** in downtown Orlando stocks more than 150 varieties of tequila, mezcal, and other agave-based drinks. ∎

Colorful mocktails at Safety Harbor's Gigglewaters Social Club & Screening Room

Georgia

Georgia complements its southern soul food roots and moonshine legacy with a sophisticated, urban food and beverage scene that embraces opulent upscale restaurants, a variety of multicultural eats, and newfangled food halls.

As one of the bastions of southern cooking, Georgia features restaurants and home kitchens that are rife with classics like **collard greens, fried green tomatoes**, and **hoppin' John** (rice and black-eyed peas). Although not as widespread as it once was, **meat and three**—your choice of pork, ham, fowl, etc., and three sides—is another old-time Georgia favorite.

But nothing rises to the level of **chicken**, served fried as the main event with dumplings, biscuits, or in a sandwich. In fact, chicken is so sacred among some Georgians that the city of Gainesville ("poultry capital of the world") passed a law in 1961 making it illegal to eat fried chicken with anything other than your hands.

More than half the state's **peanuts** (Georgia's official state crop) go into **peanut butter**. **Peaches** are used in all sorts of dishes, from cobbler and ice cream to peach martinis and the

THE BIG PICTURE

Founded: 1788

Population: 10.9 million

Official State Prepared Food: Grits

Also Known As: Peach State, Goober State

Culinary Influences: Spanish, African American, Creek and Cherokee

Don't Miss: Savannah, Atlanta, Golden Isles

Claim to Fame: Coca-Cola, Waffle House, peaches, chicken and dumplings

Peach State Lite beer brewed in Athens, Georgia. Among other iconic crops are **pecans**, flavorful **sweet corn**, and delicious **Vidalia onions**.

Pimento cheese (also seen as pimiento cheese) is so popular it's called the "pâté of the South." Made with Georgia-grown pimento peppers, the spread first became a huge hit during the early 20th century and is nowadays found in everything from **deviled eggs** to the **pimento cheese sandwiches** served at the annual Masters golf tournament in Augusta.

The town of Brunswick, Georgia, and Brunswick Counties in both North Carolina and Virginia, fight over the origin of **Brunswick stew**. Originally made with squirrel, the hearty meal is more likely to feature chicken or pork these days, along with tomatoes, onions, and other vegetables.

CULINARY EXPERIENCES

The state's quintessential crops are the focus of the **Georgia Peach Festival** in Fort Valley and Byron (June), the **Plains Peanut Festival** in President Jimmy Carter's

Ring in the New Year with hoppin' John, kale, and cornbread.

Catch the sunset against the Atlanta skyline at fast-food hot spot the Varsity.

hometown (September), and the **Vidalia Onion Festival** (April), in the onion's place of origin, Vidalia. The latter city is also home to the **Vidalia Onion Fountain** and the **Vidalia Onion Museum** with its educational, interactive exhibits and the world's smallest registered Vidalia onion field.

What else do hungry Georgians have on their minds? How about succulent grilled meat at the **Pigs & Peaches BBQ Festival** in Kennesaw (August) and the **Big Pig Jig** barbecue cook-off in Vienna (November). Down on the coast, it's all about aquatic edibles at the **Woodbine Crawfish Festival** along the Satilla River (April), **St. Marys Seafood Festival** (October), and **Kingsland Catfish Festival** (November).

Featuring chefs from the city's top restaurants, **Taste of Atlanta** showcases four all-inclusive tasting experiences between July and November in four different parts of the metro area, including a Grand Tasting near downtown in October. Smaller in scale but just as tasty, **Atlanta Black Restaurant Week** (August) highlights the culinary genius of the city's Black chefs.

Unexpected Atlanta Tours offers a guided food walk of the city's historic Grant Park neighborhood that includes eight modern and southern fusion tastings at three eateries. Down on the coast, the **Savannah Taste Experience** renders four interesting tours of Georgia's ultimate foodie city, including Southern Fried Expectations and Walktails & Bar Bites Happy Hour.

Atlanta has jumped on the food hall bandwagon with culinary clusters like **Ponce City Market** in the Old Fourth Ward, **Politan Row** in Midtown, and **Krog Street Market** in Inman Park. Celebrity chef Andrew Zimmern is part of the brain trust that created **Chattahoochee Food Works** on the Upper Westside. Housed inside a vintage industrial warehouse, the complex harbors 31 food outlets ranging from **Sakura Ramen Bar** and **Belén de la Cruz** (known for its empanadas) to **Cosmic Candy** and **Morelli's Ice Cream**.

Marietta Square Market in northwest Georgia carries a similar vibe in a revitalized warehouse with 20 culinary options, including **B.A.D. Gyal Vegan** Caribbean fusion, **Cousins Maine Lobster**, and **Siete Tacos + Tequila**.

RESTAURANTS TO DIE FOR

Atlanta's culinary options range from the refined, romantic **Canoe** on the banks of the Chattahoochee River and the sublime surf and turf of **Nikolai's Roof** on the 30th floor of the downtown Hilton Hotel to burgers and fries at **the Varsity**, opened in 1928 and now the "world's largest drive-in" with space for 600 vehicles.

Other legendary eating spots include the **Busy Bee Café** (opened in 1947) for classic soul food and **Mary Mac's Tea Room** (established in 1945) for authentic southern comfort food. Even older, **the Colonnade** has served fried chicken, catfish, and pork chops since 1927.

BELTLINE BITES

A looping railroad right-of-way around central Atlanta is gradually being transformed into a hiking and biking greenway called the BeltLine that will eventually link dozens of neighborhoods along a 22-mile (35 km) corridor.

Large segments of the route (on the city's east and west sides) are finished, and as predicted by its planners, the project has sparked redevelopment along much of its length. What they may not have anticipated is the BeltLine becoming a major magnet for food and beverage aficionados.

The Eastside Trail between Piedmont Park and Reynoldstown has fostered the **Ponce City Market** and **Krog Street Market** food halls, and more than two dozen individual bars and restaurants. Choices range from Cajun and creole at **TWO Urban Licks** to **Barcelona Wine Bar**, **Bell Street Burritos**, and **Shake Shack**.

Although not as well fixed with restaurants, the Westside Trail boasts a craft beer hub opposite Rose Circle Park and the BeltLine zero mile marker. Housed in restored industrial buildings, the collection includes **Boxcar at Hop City, Best End Brewing, Wild Heaven Beer**, and **Monday Night Brewing's Garage** taproom.

It doesn't get more iconic than the fried green tomatoes at the Whistle Stop Café in Juliette, the shooting location for the *Fried Green Tomatoes* film.

Stop by the Vidalia Onion Museum to meet the town of Vidalia's mascot, Yumion, and learn about the city's onion-y nicknames.

Among the city's newer gastronomic stars are **Slutty Vegan ATL** on the west side, northside **Taco Mac** for chicken wings and more than 60 craft beers, and the **Flying Biscuit Café** chain for its biscuits, grits, and chicken and waffles. Taking both food and ambience up a few notches, **Lucian Books and Wine** in the upscale Buckhead neighborhood does triple duty as a stylish bookstore, wine bar, and restaurant with dishes like polenta with black truffles, ratatouille with squid ink and salsa verde, and a caviar omelet with crème fraîche.

With excellent Vietnamese, Thai, Malaysian, Indonesia, Persian, and regional Chinese restaurants, the Atlanta metro area might be the best place in the Southeast for Asian food. It's known for its Korean cuisine, especially **Gwinnett Place Mall** in Duluth, where eateries like **Stone Bowl House Woo Nam Jeong** and **Seo Ra Beol BBQ** count among the local favorites.

Even more so than the state capital, Savannah is renowned for elegant fine dining at establishments like the **Olde Pink House** and **Elizabeth on 37th**. But what makes the dining scene extra special are restaurants with quirky or offbeat locations, such as **the Grey**, which is situated in a restored 1938 art deco Greyhound bus station. A throwback to the boardinghouse of old, **Mrs. Wilkes' Dining Room** serves meals at communal tables in a four-story brick structure where you can also rent rooms. **Husk Savannah**, with its modern takes on southern cuisine, occupies one of the city's most haunted houses.

There are no better places to sample some of Georgia's quintessential foods than their origin towns. **Marshside Grill** in Brunswick serves its tasty Brunswick stew with views across the MacKay River wetlands and a chance to kayak the watery wilderness before or after lunch with the adjacent SouthEast Adventure Outfitters. In addition to sautéed onions, **Steeplechase Grille & Tavern** in downtown Vidalia flavors many of its dishes with the pungent bulb, including its Philly cheesesteak and signature chicken.

A longtime hangout of the Allman Brothers Band, **H&H Soul Food** in Macon is one of a dwindling

number of Georgia restaurants still serving meat and threes, with collard greens, fried okra, and deviled eggs among the possible sides. **Chicken Salad Chick** in poultry-smitten Gainesville features a chicken-focused version of meat and three, plus pimento cheese dishes and a dozen different kinds of chicken salad.

The folksy little **Whistle Stop Café** in Juliette gained worldwide fame in the movie *Fried Green Tomatoes* (1991) and continues to serve its signature dish straight up or in a salad, as well as other Georgia favorites like fried chicken and catfish fillets.

BOTTOMS UP!

Illegal hooch once thrived in the Georgia backwoods. But nowadays moonshine is legal, out of the woods, and very trendy. **Dalton Distillery** in northwest Georgia makes its Raymond's Reserve moonshine using a 100-year-old recipe, while **Grandaddy Mimm's Distilling Co.** in Blairsville crafts 10 different types of firewater, from 40-proof fruit-flavored moonshines to the 140-proof Mule Kickin'.

The **Mountain Moonshine Festival & Car Show** in Dawsonville City (October) highlights the town's legacy in both distilling and NASCAR history—the two often went hand in hand in olden days. Classic cars and locally crafted spirits are also the double feature at the **Georgia Mountain Moonshine Cruiz-In** in Dalton (July).

Some of that modern moonshine makes its way to Atlanta and into the craft cocktails that feature at hipster bars like the **Parlor** cocktail

A spread of ribs, brisket, barbecue tacos, and sides

Hit up Dead End Drinks in Atlanta for spooky good atmosphere alongside hauntingly good eats and drinks.

den in Castleberry Hill and **Dead End Drinks** at the historic Pullman Yards. Atlanta also boasts a strong craft beer scene via the likes of **New Realm Brewing Company** beside the BeltLine trail and **Scofflaw Brewing** on the Upper Westside.

Given its melodious reputation, Savannah excels at moody music joints. **The Wormhole** may not look like much from the outside, but it's top-shelf when it comes to live music and comedy. **Jazz'd Tapas Bar** serves tapas and craft cocktails with its nightly live acts, while **Rancho Alegre** lays on the Latin tunes. ∎

THE GREAT NATIONAL TEMPERANCE BEVERAGE

John Stith Pemberton is famously credited with concocting the formula for Coca-Cola in 1886. But what's not as widely known is that the Georgia pharmacist, a veteran of the Confederate Army, was searching for a way to ease his lingering pain from a saber wound inflicted during the Civil War.

Pemberton began marketing his blend of cocaine (extracted from coca leaves) and caffeine (extracted from kola nut), sugar, and carbonated water as a "brain tonic" and "great national temperance beverage" that could aid everything from sexual performance to hysteria and melancholy.

By the early 1890s, Asa Griggs Candler, another Georgia pharmacist, had purchased the formula and founded the **Coca-Cola Company** in Atlanta. Cocaine was removed in 1903 due to a wake of public pressure, and the caffeine was greatly reduced in 1911 by government mandate, but that didn't stop Candler from catapulting Coke into the national drink that Pemberton had always envisioned.

Hawaii

Hawaiian cookery blends the state's Polynesian heritage with ingredients introduced by Asian immigrants and also features tropical island takes on American favorites, culminating in one of the globe's most diverse food scenes.

THE BIG PICTURE

Founded: 1959

Population: 1.44 million

Official State Tree: Kukui (candlenut)

Also Known As: Aloha State

Culinary Influences: Polynesian, Japanese, Chinese, English

Don't Miss: Honolulu, Kona, Waikiki

Claim to Fame: Shave ice, saimin noodle soup, poi

Let's get this on the table immediately: The beloved Hawaiian pizza, with pineapple and ham, is not indigenous to the Aloha State. It was first created in Ontario, Canada, in 1962 by Sotirios "Sam" Panopoulos. Those who want to sample a true Hawaiian pie should seek out a **Spam pizza** instead.

But plenty of other famous dishes do have their origins in the mid-Pacific archipelago. Often called a superfood because it's packed with vitamins and minerals, **poi** traveled to Hawaii and the rest of Polynesia from the Marquesas Islands of French Polynesia on oceangoing outriggers. Normally made from mashed taro root, the pasty, purplish concoction can be eaten as a side dish or dessert.

Laulau, another popular Polynesian dish, is taro leaves stuffed with meat or fish, then steamed on a stove top or in an *imu* (underground oven). Imus are essential to other popular Hawaiian dishes like savory **kalua pig** and **kalua turkey**. Wrapped in banana leaves, the entire animal is cooked over basalt stones heated by a wood fire. An imu feast often includes **haupia**, a gelatinous dessert made with coconut milk and thickened with arrowroot, cassava, or cornstarch.

Similar to the ceviches of Latin America, Filipino *kinilaw*, or the *'ika mata* of the South Pacific, **poke** is raw seafood (usually ahi tuna) cut into small pieces, marinated with soy sauce and sesame oil, garnished with scallions and *limu* (edible ocean plants), and sometimes served with a side dish of steamed rice. However, there are *many* variations.

Asian immigration had a huge impact on the state's culinary scene. Hawaii's delicious **saimin noodle soup**, inspired by Japanese ramen and Chinese soups, features barbecued pork, *kamaboko* (fish cakes), dashi stock, and perhaps seaweed or scallions. In that same vein, **manapua** (steamed buns) stuffed

Book way in advance to nab a table and enjoy the Ahi Tahitian with lime, coconut milk, and crisps at Maui's family-owned Mama's Fish House.

Preparing for a traditional hula and feast at Old Lāhainā Lūʻau in Maui

with barbecued pork are island versions of Chinese *char siu bao*. Meanwhile, Hawaii's cool and colorful **shave ice** is a direct descendant of the *kakigōri* introduced by Japanese plantation workers more than 100 years ago.

Spam *musubi*—a small slice of Spam and steamed rice wrapped in dried seaweed—is a mash-up of American and Japanese influences. *Malasadas* (eggy doughnuts sans the holes) were introduced to the islands by 19th-century Portuguese farm laborers. Hawaii's craziest concoction, *loco moco*, is a mound of white rice topped by a hamburger patty, fried egg, and brown gravy.

Hawaiian cattle ranching was born in 1793, when British explorer George Vancouver gifted King Kamehameha I with six cows and a bull. Mexican vaqueros were hired to mentor local *paniolo* (cowboys) and eventually the Big Island was producing the beef used in loco moco, **pipi kaula jerky, teriyaki short ribs**, and **Hawaiian beef stew**.

CULINARY EXPERIENCES

The islands' largest and most significant food happening is the **Hawaii Food & Wine Festival** in October. Spanning three weekends and three islands (Oahu, Maui, and Hawaii), the event features more than 150 chefs from Hawaii and the mainland, gourmet meals, culinary demonstrations, recipe contests, and beverage tastings.

Smaller food fests tend to focus on particular aspects of Hawaiian gastronomy. The super-twisty Hana Highway leads to the **East Maui**

Taro Festival (April), actually held in Hana, which features various dishes made from taro leaves and roots, as well as other tropical crops grown on the island's lush east side. Over on the Big Island, the Kona Coffee Cultural Festival (November) showcases brews from more than 35 local coffee farms, as well as art shows, live entertainment, panel discussions, barista demonstrations, and farm tours. The Waikiki Spam Jam (April) offers an incredible range of Spam dishes from Oahu restaurants, including Spam musubi, pizza, street tacos, nachos, burritos, poke, and mai tais served in Spam cans.

Oahu also hosts several regular food gatherings. Eat the Street involves 40-plus food trucks and vendors who congregate on the last Friday of every month on Honolulu's Kaka'ako Waterfront Park. Every weekend, around a dozen food trucks huddled beneath coconut palms in Kahuku on the North Shore dispense a broad range of edibles, from Vietnamese and Thai to corn dogs, hamburgers, and tacos. The North Shore is also home to the Hawaii State Farm Fair (July) and its eclectic blend of food vendors, eating contests, livestock shows, and a country market on the historic Kualoa Ranch.

In addition to its popular downtown Honolulu walking tour, Hawaii Free Tours offers two paid culinary tours, one that focuses on local foods and the other on off-the-beaten-path food experiences. Hawaiian Food & Photo Tour renders an opportunity to sample and shoot dishes like Spam musubi, malasada, shave ice, and poke.

Luaus are a flashy mash-up of Hawaiian foods and traditional

Pineapples grow near the ground on *Ananas comosus* shrubs.

Pouring out flavors at Matsumoto Shave Ice in Haleiwa, Oahu

Hawaiian and Polynesian dance and music, with maybe a little fire twirling. Most of the big beach hotels and resorts stage their own luaus at least once a week, catered to tourists. The daily luaus at the Polynesian Cultural Center on Oahu's North Shore and the Old Lāhainā Lū'au in Maui are larger affairs, while smaller shindigs—like the Smith Family Garden Luau in Kauai—are more intimate.

RESTAURANTS TO DIE FOR

Some of the best native Hawaiian food is served at food trucks, night markets, and neighborhood cafés rather than in fancy restaurants. Haili's Hawaiian Foods in Honolulu's Kapahulu district has been serving incredible kalua pig, laulau, poke, and haupia since 1958 (only open for lunch). Over in Kaka'ako, the Highway Inn serves an even wider range of local

HAWAII'S JUICY GOLD RUSH

Though other places prospered on golden metal, the Hawaiian Islands had a different kind of gold rush: the pineapple boom of the early 20th century. Although native to South America, *Ananas comosus* flourished in Hawaii's tropical climate and rich volcanic soil.

"Pineapple King" James Dole built plantations on Oahu and a canning factory near Honolulu Harbor so his canned pineapple could be easily

shipped abroad. After Dole purchased Lanai in 1922, the island grew into the source of 75 percent of global pineapple exports.

By the 1990s, cheaper production in other tropical lands had busted Hawaii's pineapple boom. Visitors can learn about Hawaii's pineapple past—and its controversial legacy on the islands—at the Dole Plantation on Oahu or by joining a Maui Pineapple Tour in Makawao.

favorites, including loco moco, Hawaiian beef stew, and squid *lu'au*. On the North Shore, the reincarnated **Waiahole Poi Factory** offers hand-pounded poi with a variety of traditional island dishes.

Hawaiian food goes nouvelle at **Mud Hen Water** in the city's Kaimuki district. Akule with limu butter, beet poke with avocado and macadamia nuts, and pork *sisig* (sizzling pig's head) are some of the creative dishes on the brunch and dinner menus. Chef Kevin Lee has crafted delectable East-West tasting menus, with dishes like sisig lasagna and Samoan crab in chilled truffle corn soup, at the upscale **PAI restaurant** in downtown Honolulu.

The **Original Roy's in Hawaii Kai** near Oahu's east end adds island touches to Japanese and Chinese cuisine.

Mama's Fish House is a long-time favorite on Maui's North Shore, so popular that reservations should be made months in advance. The payback for all that effort is dishes like macadamia nut crab cakes and Mama's ahi and mahi-mahi curry. On the other side of Maui, the elegant **Lahaina Grill** spawns the island's best surf and turf menu.

Lower down Maui's food chain (but just as delicious) are the Asian-inspired shared plates and sake cocktails at **Star Noodle** in

Lahaina and **Paia Fish Market** at three locations around the island.

Merriman's Waimea is the undisputed champion of fine dining on the Big Island. Located in the heart of paniolo cowboy country, it's the brainchild of celebrated chef Peter Merriman, an early advocate of Hawaiian regional cuisine and farm-to-table dining.

Some of the Big Island's best grub is served by small joints that locals favor. Ask about the daily special at **Da Poke Shack** in Kona or order one of their signature dishes, like spicy garlic sesame poke or traditional poke with *limu kohu* (a seaweed) and Hawaiian salt. **Kilauea General Store** in Volcano village (just outside of Volcanoes National Park) makes awesome sandwiches, cookies, and smoothies. **Punalu'u Bake Shop** near the south coast is the go-to place for Hawaiian sweet bread, malasadas, and tropical fruitcake.

Kauai's edible offerings range from oceanfront Pacific Rim dining at the **Beach House** on the South Shore to **JoJo's Shave Ice** and the **Hanalei Bread Company** on the North Shore.

BOTTOMS UP!

Much like the pineapple and ham pizza, the **mai tai** wasn't invented on the islands, but rather in California, long before it became Hawaii's signature cocktail. For those who want to quaff something that truly originated in the 50th state, the **Blue Hawaiian** (rum, pineapple juice, and blue curaçao) is probably the best bet.

Hawaii has evolved its own variations of popular drinks, including the **Hawaiian Martini** (vodka, grenadine, orange juice, and pineapple juice), the **Pineapple Moscow Mule**

Grab a dozen *malasadas* (Portuguese fried doughnuts) from Hawaii's original malasadas hot spot, Leonard's Bakery in Honolulu.

Watch a demonstration and sample the poi (steamed and hand-pounded taro root) at Waiahole Poi Factory in Honolulu.

(vodka, ginger beer, lime juice, and pineapple juice), and the **Hawaiian Margarita** (tequila, triple sec, coconut water, lime juice, and pineapple juice).

Pineapple juice also features in the Mai Time Light beer made by **Kona Brewing Co.** on the Big Island, while hibiscus flowers flavor the Route 70 Saison at **Lanikai Brewing Co.** on Oahu. Coconut Hiwa Porter and Pineapple Mana Wheat are among the beers dispensed by **Maui Brewing** at four taprooms in Maui and Oahu or after a tour of their brewery in Kihei.

Located on the lush lower slope of Haleakalā volcano in Upcountry Maui, **MauiWine** at Ulupalakua Ranch is the best known of Hawaii's three commercial winemakers. Built for hosting visits by Hawaiian monarch David Kalakaua in the late 1800s, MauiWine's King's Cottage Tasting Room provides a historic venue for sampling six varieties of grape wines and the winery's signature pineapple and passion fruit wines.

Upcountry Maui is also home to **Hali'imaile Distilling Company** and its tasting room. Their libation-filled repertoire includes rum, vodka, whiskey, and gin crafted with locally grown tropical fruits and botanicals. And yes, they do have a pineapple-infused spirit—Paniolo Blended Whiskey—as well as the Kona coffee–tinged Mahina Premium Rum.

The Kona District on the west side of the Big Island produces what many connoisseurs consider some of the world's best **coffee**. Planted in 1828, Kona's first coffee was grown from Brazilian cuttings. However, the business didn't thrive (or start to become an international sensation) until Guatemalan coffee plants were imported in the 1890s. Learn more about Hawaiian joe at the **Kona Coffee Living History Farm** in Captain Cook village. ∎

Idaho

Sure, they've got a lot of potatoes in Idaho, but the Pacific Northwest state offers plenty of other tasty options, from wild game and mountain trout to offbeat desserts.

THE BIG PICTURE

Founded: 1890

Population: 1.94 million

Official State Vegetable: Potato

Also Known As: Gem State

Culinary Influences: Basque

Don't Miss: Boise, Sun Valley, Ketchum

Claim to Fame: Jim Spud baked potatoes, ice-cream potato, finger steaks

When Reverend Henry Spalding planted Idaho's first **potato** crop in the 1830s, he had no way to know that the humble tubers would someday symbolize the entire state and become one of the planet's most popular foods. Turns out, the rich volcanic soil of the Snake River watershed, combined with warm days, cool nights, and easy access to irrigation water, is ideal for growing spuds.

Idaho produces around a third of the U.S. crop and more than 30 potato varieties. At least 90 percent of that annual yield is french fry–perfect **russet potatoes**. Residents of the Gem State like their standard **fries, Tater Tots, potato salad, hash browns**, and **mashed potatoes** as much as anyone else. But they've also pioneered unique variations on classic recipes like **red flannel hash, monkey fries**, the mashed potato–stuffed **Idahoan sandwich**, and steak-filled **Jim Spuds**.

Speaking of meat and potatoes, Idaho offers plenty of farm-raised and wild game options from **bison burgers** and **finger steaks** to **Lava Lake rack of lamb**. With so many lakes and rivers, freshwater fish are also abundant. Grilled, broiled, or panfried **trout** makes it onto many restaurant menus.

The state's love affair with spuds extends into desserts. Well, sort of. The **ice-cream potato** is cocoa-covered vanilla ice cream shaped to resemble a baked potato. In that same vein, the **Owyhee Idaho Spuds**—made by the Idaho Candy Company in Boise since 1918—are chocolate and marshmallow candy bars rather than actual potato snacks.

Locals are liable to make their ice-cream potatoes with farm-fresh vanilla from Reed's Dairy, a family business founded in 1955 in Idaho Falls and now available at outlets in six cities. **Huckleberries**, the official state fruit, make a perfect companion to any ice-cream serving or as jam, syrup, tea, candy, barbecue sauce, and even lip balm.

CULINARY EXPERIENCES

September 1 is the traditional kickoff of the Idaho potato harvest. The town of Shelley near Idaho Falls celebrates the harvest three weeks later with its **Idaho Spud Day**. First staged in the 1920s, the festival features potato sack races, a potato-picking competition, Miss Sweet Potato and Miss Russet

Cocoa powder coats the outside of vanilla ice cream in the shape of the state's famous spud for the Idaho Ice Cream Potato at Boise's Westside Drive In.

A priest blesses a flock during the Big Sheep Parade at the Trailing of the Sheep Festival in Ketchum.

Pageants, and a free baked potato lunch.

One of the state's most intriguing food events is the **Trailing of the Sheep Festival** in October. Though not quite an Idaho version of the running of the bulls, it does involve helping sheepherders and border collie sheepdogs herd 1,500 sheep through downtown Ketchum. Whether in cooking classes or lamb tastings, visitors have plenty of ways to sample the end product.

Refugee Restaurant Week in October features immigrant chefs and restaurants in Boise and the surrounding Treasure Valley. The celebrated array of dishes from around the world raises awareness of Idaho's flourishing ethnic food scene. The same folks sponsor a **World Refugee Day** in June with food vendors at Boise's Grove Plaza. The Sun Valley region boasts two of the state's best fresh food spreads: **Wood River Farmers Markets** in Hailey and **Ketchum Farmers Market**.

RESTAURANTS TO DIE FOR

Barbacoa's over-the-top decor (check out the chandeliers), vaulted wine cellar, and lakeside setting set the table at Boise's most intriguing restaurant, an open-fire-grill affair that creates marvelous Latin American cuisine. The equally chic **Trillium** transforms Idaho favorites through modern dishes like huckleberry short ribs, bison meatloaf, and bronzed steelhead trout. The third in the triple crown of swank Boise dining spots, **Chandlers** pairs the city's best steaks and seafood with live jazz and a cool martini bar.

Yet Boise isn't all highbrow. **Westside Drive In** offers a trip back to the 1950s via its Daddy-O burger, spaghetti and meatballs, classic baked potatoes, cream soda, and other comfort foods. True to its name, **Bacon Boise!** adds crispy fried pork bits to just about anything: omelets, grits, cinnamon rolls, sandwiches, wraps, and Bloody Marys. French fry fanatics can sample six varieties cut five different ways (regular, homestyle, curly, shoestring, or po'ball—a deep-fried ball of mashed potatoes) at the three **Boise Fry Company** cafés in the state capital.

Perched on the seventh floor of the upscale Coeur d'Alene Resort,

Beverly's restaurant takes full advantage of the geography with views across the water to tree-studded mountaintops and a Pacific Northwest menu that revolves around steak and seafood. Alternatively, sink your teeth into Full Oinker, American Ooze, or Huckleberry Heaven sandwiches at **Meltz Extreme Grilled Cheese**. Farther north in the panhandle, **Baxters on Cedar** transforms the Sandpoint dining experience with dishes like Moroccan lamb sliders, Korean pork salad, and cioppino.

Given its status as a hip snow sports destination, Sun Valley offers a broad range of grub from dishes like sturgeon and Wagyu beef at **the Covey** in Ketchum to the locally sourced greens, meats, and fish at **CK's Real Food** in Hailey.

Down in the flatlands of southern Idaho, **Elevation 486** in Twin Falls renders views of the Snake River gorge and a menu spangled with local specialties like rack of lamb, ruby red trout, and crispy Idaho potato skins. **Smitty's Pancake & Steak House** is the reigning king of comfort food in Idaho Falls.

BOTTOMS UP!

It was inevitable that Idahoans would hit on the bright idea of making vodka with their home-grown spuds. The state flaunts several excellent spirit makers, including **44° North Distillery** in Shelley and **Grand Teton Distillery** in Driggs. Both make huckleberry- and cherry-flavored vodkas.

In addition to some pretty wicked drinks, Ketchum's **Pioneer Saloon** hosts a collection of Hemingway memorabilia, Native American

Halibut tops a bed of fresh vegetables at Chandlers in Boise.

artifacts, and vintage Western movie posters, and offers plenty of great wines to accompany their fabled Jim Spud baked potatoes.

Like neighboring Northwest states, Idaho has also ventured into grape cultivation and wine production. The **Lewis-Clark Valley AVA** in west-central Idaho, one of the nation's newest viticultural areas, produces 20 varietals at nine different wineries, including **Colter's Creek Winery** in Juliaetta and the dog-friendly **Two Bad Labs Vineyard** in Lewiston. ■

BOISE'S BASQUE BLOCK

Basque immigrants settled in Idaho during the late 19th and early 20th centuries. Many were expert sheepherders, but a good number also opened restaurants that initially served the local Basque population before a wider range of people embraced the new-to-them cuisine.

Boise boasts more residents of Basque ancestry than any city outside of Spain or France. The city's downtown Basque Block neighborhood offers several ways to sample Basque cuisine, including **Leku Ona** restaurant, **Bar Gernika**, and the **Basque Market** café with its popular *pintxos* (tapas) plates, paella cooking classes, and Iberian wines.

The Block is also the epicenter for events like the **Sheepherders Ball** (December) and the feast day of **St. Ignatius of Loyola** (July).

Chef Tony Eiguren (left) serves up fragrant paella at Boise's Basque Market.

Illinois

From deep-dish pizza to pumpkins and popcorn, Illinois offers a feast of classic American foods, as well as some of the nation's top restaurants.

THE BIG PICTURE

Founded: 1818

Population: 12.6 million

Official State Snack Food: Popcorn

Also Known As: Prairie State

Culinary Influences: Italian, Austrian, Polish, German, Swedish, Irish

Don't Miss: Chicago, Springfield, Galena

Claim to Fame: Cracker Jack, deep-dish pizza, Italian beef sandwich, Chicago hot dogs

Fueled by the industrial revolution and America's unrelenting westward expansion, Chicago exploded from a lakeside village of 4,000 in the 1840s to one of the world's largest cities by the end of the 19th century. Many of its new residents were immigrants, who blended dishes from their native homes with Midwest ingredients to create distinctive Chicago foods.

Nothing is more iconic to the Windy City than **Chicago-style deep-dish pizza**, defined by a crust that rises two, or maybe even three inches, above the base. Its origin story stretches back to World War II and the inventive chefs at Pizzeria Uno who tried to create a pizza that was truly a pie rather than a flatbread.

Another Chicago favorite, the **Italian beef sandwich** traces its origins to Italian American Anthony Ferreri, who made the sandwiches at home and sold them off the back of his truck. By the late 1930s, Al's #1 Italian Beef restaurant was serving the sandwich as the front of a bookmaking joint in the back of the shop. The sandwich comprises a French roll stuffed with superthin beef (simmered in its own juices) topped with giardiniera (pickled vegetables) and sliced bell peppers and flavored with olive oil, garlic, and Italian herbs.

Chicken Vesuvio also sprang from the imaginations of the city's Italian American cooks. Named after a long-ago Chicago restaurant,

which itself was named for the volcano that destroyed Pompeii, the dish features sautéed bone-in chicken and potatoes baked in a broth of garlic, oregano, olive oil, and white wine until the chicken skin is a deep golden brown.

Austrian immigrants brought the beef frankfurter to the Second City, where it evolved into a "loaded" version called the **Chicago hot dog**, which is topped with sliced onions, pickles, tomatoes, peppers, relish, and yellow mustard. Arriving from Belgium in the 1890s, the DeJonghe brothers opened a restaurant that specialized in **Shrimp DeJonghe**: peeled shrimp covered in breadcrumbs and cooked with sherry and various herbs and spices. A flambéed cheese dish called **flaming saganaki** originated among the city's Greek Americans.

Chicagoland satiates its sweet tooth with several goodies, including the **Rainbow Cones** first served in 1926 by "Grandpa Joe" Sapp and his wife, Katherine, at their Rainbow Cone ice-cream stand in Evergreen Park. The legendary ice-cream cone features five flavors: chocolate, strawberry, Palmer House (vanilla

Pumpkins line the walkway at Morton Arboretum in DuPage County.

Cheese-pull perfection: Chicago's deep-dish pizza hides serious fillings beneath a tomatoey topping.

with cherries and walnuts), pistachio, and orange sherbet. Although invented in Seattle, **Frango mints** became one of the most popular items at the Marshall Field department store candy kitchen.

Chicago isn't Illinois's only innovator. Springfield was the birthplace of the **horseshoe open-faced sandwich**, which in its original form featured a horseshoe-shaped slab of ham on toast covered in french fries and cheese sauce.

As the nation's second biggest corn producer after Iowa, the Land of Lincoln is a great place to sample **corn on the cob, corn chowder,** and other maize-based dishes. Meanwhile, **popcorn** is the official state snack food (sample **Chicago-style popcorn**—a blend of caramel and cheddar popcorn—at Garrett Popcorn, a favorite of the Obamas). **Pumpkins** are also a big deal. In fact, Illinois produces twice as many of the orange squashes as the next best state.

CULINARY EXPERIENCES

Two of the state's iconic crops step into the limelight during the **Mendota Sweet Corn Festival** in LaSalle County (August) and the **Morton Pumpkin Festival** near Peoria (September). The former features a free hot buttered sweet corn boil, corn dogs, kettle corn, and other fairground favorites, while the latter offers all sorts of pumpkin swag, a pumpkin-decorating contest, pumpkin weigh-ins, and a Pumpkin History & Mystery Geocaching Adventure.

Illinois hosts hundreds of fresh-off-the-farm emporiums, including the **Farmers' Market of Carbondale**, Urbana's **Market at the Square**, the **Old Capitol Farmers Market** in Springfield, and **Farmers Market + At the Dole** in Crystal Lake on the outer edge of Chicago.

The five-layered Rainbow Cone is a must-have summer treat.

The state's most unusual farm stall lies inside the Rotunda Building at **O'Hare International Airport**, where salads and sandwiches are made with produce grown in the adjacent indoor garden, the world's first aeroponic farm inside an airport.

Or you can travel straight to the source and visit farm families with deep roots in Illinois agriculture. Owned and operated by seven generations of the same family, **Marcoot Jersey Creamery** in Greenville makes artisanal cheese, homemade ice cream and popcorn, sweet clover honey, and top-quality beef. The **Great Pumpkin Patch** near Decatur invites visitors to experience fall harvest season on a working farm tilled by the same family since the 1850s, and pop into their bakery year-round.

During the summer, **Locavore Farm** on the prairie south of Chicago offers a Dine on the Land dinner series that includes a multicourse feast served on a 110-foot (35 m) wooden table of dishes prepared with local ingredients produced via regenerative agricultural practices.

The Windy City's premier culinary event is **Taste of Chicago** in Grant Park (September). Founded in 1980 and deemed the world's largest food festival, the three-day event attracts around four million people to vendors that make many of the city's iconic dishes. The event has spawned spin-offs like the Latin American–focused **Taste of Chicago Little Village** and the soul food–infused **Taste of Chicago Pullman** (both in June).

The **Chicago Food Truck Festival** offers two events: at the South Loop (June) and LaBagh Woods on the North Side (October). Among the dozen or more movable feasts are **Soul Kantina** for southern cooking, **Happy Lobster** for seafood, and **El Campeon** for piña coladas and south-of-the-border favorites.

Year-round, **Time Out Market Chicago** offers about two dozen gourmet food and beverage outlets inside a huge industrial space in the Fulton Market District. The global lineup includes Lebanese, Korean, Polish, Colombian, Hawaiian, Indian, Vietnamese, Mexican, and Greek cuisines.

Learn how to make tamales, dumplings, pasta, and other dishes during a class at **Cooking Fools**, a myriad of South Asian dishes at **Ranjana's Indian Cooking Classes**, and a wide variety of foods at **Marcel's Culinary Experience**, all of them in the Chicago metro area. Or learn everything there is to know about amber nectar at **Map Room Beer School**, at the geography-themed bar of the same name in the Bucktown neighborhood.

RESTAURANTS TO DIE FOR

The Second City can give anyone a run for their money—including the Big Apple and City of Angels—when it comes to the quality and quantity of food.

Perched atop Chicago's food pyramid are legendary establishments like the three-Michelin-starred **Alinea**, where American molecular gastronomy was pioneered by chef/owner Grant Achatz, and **Frontera Grill**, where Oklahoma-born chef Rick Bayless creates innovative Mexican cuisine with Midwest ingredients. Another cross-cultural star is **Bavette's Bar & Boeuf**, where Chicago's fabled top-quality beef gets a French twist.

Smyth + The Loyalist in the West Loop offers two distinctly different dining experiences at the same venue. Tucked upstairs, two-Michelin-starred Smyth offers upscale tasting menus with wine pairings; on the ground floor the Loyalist is more casual but no less tasty, with a brasserie-style menu spangled with French comfort foods. Belying its grandiose name, **Giant Restaurant** in the Logan Square area suffuses its tiny dining room with enormous flavors. *Top Chef* alum Stephanie Izard has also made a name for herself in the Chicago food scene with **Girl & the Goat**.

Despite launching during the height of the pandemic, several new eateries have risen to the top of

Sample from 18 different food concepts—including West Indian, Asian fusion, and barbecue—at Time Out Market Chicago.

Chicago's dining charts. **Dear Margaret** in Lake View specializes in French Canadian dishes like poached scallops, duck leg cassoulet, and maple-vanilla crème brûlée. With locations in Lincoln Park and Fulton Market, **Evette's** offers a tasty mash-up of Mexican and Lebanese classics.

Many of the Windy City's oldies but goodies are still alive and kicking: the original **Pizzeria Uno** near the Miracle Mile for Chicago-style deep-dish pizza; the original **Al's #1** on Taylor Street for Italian beef sandwiches; and the **Original Rainbow Cone** on Navy Pier and the Museum Campus for summertime frozen treats.

Superdawg Drive-In in Norwood Park has been serving overstuffed Chicago-style hot dogs since 1948. Established in 1942, **Manny's Cafeteria & Delicatessen** in the South Loop is the place to nosh on pastrami sandwiches, liver and onions, potato pancakes, and other deli standards. On the southwest outskirts of Chicago, **White Fence Farm** in Romeoville has been luring in fried chicken aficionados since 1954.

Located near the Old State Capitol and the Lincoln Presidential Library, **Maldaner's** is Springfield's oldest restaurant (established in 1884) and still one of the city's best spots for soups, salads, and steaks. In addition to its Irish pub fare, **D'arcy's Pint** offers 15 different "shoes" (horseshoe sandwiches) smothered in french fries and cheese sauce. Nearby **Charlie Parker's Diner** is also renowned for meat and vegetarian shoes as well as all-day breakfast. Located on historic Route 66 on Springfield's

Add a farm-fresh egg to your fried chicken sandwich during brunch at another Chicago must-visit: Honey Butter Fried Chicken.

CRACKER JACK

Candied popcorn with peanuts was a popular snack in some parts of the United States by the end of the 19th century. But the German-born Rueckheim Bros. transformed it into a national phenomenon when they founded Chicago's Cracker Jack company in 1896.

They became such a huge hit at Cubs and White Sox baseball games that Jack Norworth and Albert Von Tilzer included Cracker Jack in their immortal "Take Me Out to the Ball Game," composed in 1908.

The snack's popularity soared even higher after the introduction of official mascots Sailor Jack and Bingo the dog, as well as the addition of a small game or toy in each box.

Over the years, Cracker Jack has become part of American pop culture with appearances in everything from the movie *Breakfast at Tiffany's* to a hit Meatloaf song. Leaping into modern times, the brand introduced Cracker Jill in 2022 to honor women who break down sports barriers.

The famous Pizzeria Uno in Chicago

south side, **Cozy Dog Drive In** serves its corn dogs with a side of history: The joint is reputed to be where the hot dog on a stick was born in 1946.

Peoria wasn't much of a dining destination until 2013, when chef Dustin Allen opened **Edge** just north of the city in Peoria Heights. His elevated "peasant food" includes pork chops in a plum sage sauce, cured meats and cheeses, and steak with chimichurri and grilled leeks. Anyone driving between St. Louis

and Indianapolis on Interstate 70 should make a point of eating at the **Firefly Grill** in Effingham for their gourmet pizzas and pastas, premium steaks and chops, or a selection of tapas-style small plates.

BOTTOMS UP!

Skip the run-of-the-mill student bars in the state's college towns and head straight for more intriguing drinking establishments like **Blind Pig Brewery** in Champaign and **Hangar 9** brewery in Carbondale

with its live tunes and cabaret shows. There's more great beer throughout the state, sometimes in the most unlikely places, like the **Lone Buffalo by Tangled Roots Brewing Company** near Starved Rock State Park.

As one of the nation's fastest-growing winemaking states, Illinois offers scores of wineries and several American Viticultural Areas (AVAs). The **Shawnee Hills Wine Trail** in southern Illinois links 11 wineries as it meanders 40 miles (64 km)

Sheepadoodle Rufus leads the way through the vines at Galena Cellars Vineyard & Winery.

A collection of fall cocktails at the Gage

Loop neighborhood. The innovative spirits maker also offers organic grain vodka, gin, rum, bourbon, aquavit, and other bitters.

One of America's great drinking towns, Chicago offers a seemingly infinite number of watering holes. Among the city's more sophisticated digs is **the Gage**, an upscale bar opposite Grant Park renowned for its extensive wine cellar and single barrel whiskey selection. Shaken or stirred, the speakeasy-style **Violet Hour** in Wicker Park offers a James Beard Award–winning cocktail program.

Music and mixology go hand in hand at joints like the **Green Mill** cocktail lounge, offering live jazz and other tunes since 1907, as well as Uptown Poetry Slams on the third Sunday of every month. Blues and beer lure patrons to **Kingston Mines**, a historic music club near the DePaul University campus. Panoramic views of the Chicago skyline, Grant Park, and Lake Michigan are the lure at **Cindy's Rooftop** at the summit of the Chicago Athletic Association building. ∎

through the rugged terrain between Carbondale and the Ohio River. Tucked up in the state's northwest corner, the Illinois segment of the **Upper Mississippi River Valley AVA** harbors wineries like **Galena Cellars** and **Rocky Waters** that specialize in growing hearty grapes that can withstand cold weather.

Besides an awesome movie snack, Illinois corn contributes to a variety of spirits. **Whiskey Acres Distilling** in DeKalb makes bourbon, rye, and vodka, as well as a special-edition Blue Popcorn Bourbon. Galena resident Ulysses S. Grant knew a thing or two about bourbon, a heritage that endures at the riverside city's **Blaum Bros. Distilling Co.**, which offers great tours and a cocktail bar.

"Weeding Out the Weak Since 1933" is the motto of **Jeppson's**

Malört *bäskbrännvin,* a Swedish-style bitters digestive now produced by **CH Distillery** in Chicago's West

PROHIBITION IN CHICAGO

As the headquarters of the powerful, anti-alcohol Woman's Christian Temperance Union (WCTU) and a bootlegging hub, the Chicagoland area was a major player on both sides of Prohibition.

The "Black Sox" World Series game-fixing scandal in the fall of 1919 showed that Chicago was a town willing to bend—or break—the rules. So when the 18th Amendment was passed in December of that year, the Windy City was the perfect epicenter for flouting the law.

With around a quarter of municipal revenues derived from alcohol

licensing, many of Chicago's city officials were more than willing to turn a blind eye to the city's thriving speakeasies and booze production, much of it controlled by the mob.

Crime boss "Big Jim" Colosimo—who already ran gambling and prostitution rackets—quickly transitioned into liquor production and distribution. After he was assassinated in 1920, Johnny Torrio and eventually Al Capone took control of the Chicago mob. With local politicians in his pocket, Capone based his criminal empire in suburban Cicero.

Indiana

From vintage diners and fine dining establishments to sandwiches and sweet things, Indiana's food scene offers victuals to please just about any taste.

THE BIG PICTURE

Founded: 1816

Population: 6.83 million

Official State Pie: Sugar cream pie

Also Known As: Hoosier State

Culinary Influences: German, Irish, African American

Don't Miss: Indianapolis, Fort Wayne, South Bend

Claim to Fame: Triple XXX Root Beer, Coney dogs, German sausages

It's not Indiana's official state food just yet—although the state senate did pass a resolution recommending that honor—but admiration for the **sugar cream pie** is widespread between Lake Michigan and the Ohio River, so much so that it's often called the Hoosier pie. A simple blend of flour, cream, brown sugar, vanilla, milk, eggs, and nutmeg, the pie was most likely introduced to the state by 19th-century Quaker settlers. If sugar cream pie isn't available, Hoosiers will gladly settle for cake-like **persimmon pudding**.

They also crave the **pork tenderloin sandwich**, which is basically a wiener schnitzel with condiments inside a hamburger bun. According to the state government website, the sandwich was invented at Nick's Kitchen in Huntington, Indiana, around 1908.

Some of Indiana's other beloved (and somewhat offbeat) lunch picks are the **fried bologna sandwich, fried brain sandwich** (made with cow or pig brains), and a hearty **beef Manhattan**, which involves a slice of roast beef on white bread smothered in mashed potatoes and gravy. On the other hand, **fried biscuits with apple butter** is a bygone Indiana breakfast favorite.

CULINARY EXPERIENCES

The Indiana calendar is flush with food events in every corner of the state. Dig into persimmon pudding at the **Mitchell Persimmon Festival** or pig out on swine dishes at the **Tipton County Pork Festival** (both in September). Savor southern Indiana's freshwater fish at the **Shoals Catfish Festival** along the White River over the Fourth of July weekend, or snap photos of the colorful popcorn-decorated floats at the **Valparaiso Popcorn Festival** after Labor Day.

Among the state's many urban food festivals are **TASTE of Tippecanoe** in Lafayette (June), the **Festival of Gingerbread** in Fort Wayne between Thanksgiving and Christmas, and the **Eiteljorg**

Cinnamon and brown sugar heighten the flavors of persimmon pudding.

A festive float at the Valparaiso Popcorn Festival

Indian Market & Festival in Indianapolis (June) on the grounds of the state capital's Eiteljorg Museum, a showcase for Native American art and culture.

RESTAURANTS TO DIE FOR

An Indianapolis eating institution since 1902, **St. Elmo Steak House** is often named among the nation's best surf and turf restaurants. Steak with lobster tail—accompanied by shrimp cocktail and navy bean soup—remains its signature feast in memorabilia-filled dining spaces that seem little changed in 100 years.

Another heirloom eatery in downtown Indy, **Shapiro's**

Delicatessen opened in 1905 and remains one of the city's premier sandwich makers. **Small Batch Soups by Soupremacy** complements its salads and paninis with wonderful lobster bisque, chicken noodle, and other fluid feasts. East of downtown, **Historic Steer-In** diner has fed hungry eaters for more than 60 years with their signature Twin Steer burger and family meals.

Broad Ripple Village in north Indy delivers dozens of eating options, from modern French cuisine at **Petite Chou Bistro & Champagne Bar** and the elegant brunch or afternoon tea at the **Cake Bake Shop** to immense pork tenderloin sandwiches and Indiana

basketball memorabilia at **Plump's Last Shot**.

South Bend anchors the northern Indiana food scene with outstanding eats at the upscale **LaSalle Grille**, on the ground floor of downtown's oldest commercial building (built in 1868), and the stylish **Tippecanoe Place**, lodged inside an 1880s Studebaker family mansion. Among the city's other culinary stars are **Café Navarre** for elevated seafood and **Pejza's Lydick Patio** for pork tenderloin sandwiches and its popular first Thursday of the month Polish dinners.

In neighboring Elkhart, **Artisan** restaurant showcases the modern American cooking of chef/owner

Oasis Diner lights up the night in Plainfield.

Kurt Janowsky. Continuing the flavorful journey along Highway 20, **Blue Gate Restaurant & Bakery** in Shipshewana crowns an Amish marketplace that also offers concerts, handcrafted wooden furniture, and old-time buggy rides.

Nicknamed "Indiana's city of

ORVILLE REDENBACHER

There's a good reason that Orville Redenbacher's name is almost synonymous with popcorn. He didn't invent the popular movie and campfire snack, but the Indiana native was instrumental in shaping the evolution of popcorn from a regional novelty to worldwide culinary phenomenon.

Born in Brazil, Indiana, in 1907, he earned an agronomy degree at Purdue University and began experimenting with corn hybrids to find the perfect strain for popcorn. Redenbacher and his partner eventually settled on a "RedBow" hybrid—delicious, light and fluffy, and with a 44:1 ratio of popped to unpopped corn—that would become the keystone of his popcorn empire.

With his horn-rimmed glasses, bow tie, and wavy gray hair, Redenbacher became the star of the brand's humorous TV ads and a celebrity in his own right before he passed away in 1995.

---

restaurants," Fort Wayne's options range from Burmese at **NineHouse** to Asian fusion at **Nawa** to beer and brunch at the **Hoppy Gnome** and the **Famous Coney Island Wiener Stand** (opened in 1914).

Oasis Diner in Plainfield—an authentic Mountain View unit manufactured and moved to Indiana in 1954—makes it easy to combine a root beer float or chocolate shake with your pork tenderloin sandwich. The last of what was once a statewide chain, **Triple XXX Family Restaurant** in West Lafayette started life in 1929 as a root beer "thirst station" before evolving into a full-fledged restaurant with burgers, dogs, and the obligatory (for diners in Indiana) pork tenderloin sandwich.

Fully committed to Indiana food culture, **the Narrows** restaurant at Turkey Run State Park near Mitchell serves tenderloin pork and beef Manhattan sandwiches, fried biscuits with apple butter, and sugar cream pie. However, **Cammack Station** in Muncie is one of the few eateries that still serves fried bologna sandwiches.

Just west of the Indiana University campus, 4th Street is Bloomington's hotbed for Asian cuisine, a stretch that includes Korean, Chinese, Turkish, and Thai and Indian at favorites like **Anyetsang's Little Tibet Restaurant**.

Northwest Indiana continues to up its culinary game with offerings like the eclectic **Culinary Misfits** in Crown Point and the terrific Thai cuisine at **Asparagus** in Merrillville. If you just want to snack, the **Albanese Candy Factory** (gummies!) and **Chicagoland Popcorn** are just a few miles farther down the Lincoln Highway. The **Miller Pizza Co.** in Gary's lakeshore Miller Beach area makes the area's best Chicago-style pies.

BOTTOMS UP!

The **Hoosier Heritage**—a blend of Knob Creek rye whiskey, apple cider, maple syrup, and lemon juice—is Indiana's unofficial state cocktail. The state's other home-grown libation is the **Elmo Cola** (bourbon whiskey, vanilla, and dark cherry juice), conceived at St. Elmo Steak House.

Erected in 1918 as an auto parts factory, the historic Circle City Industrial Complex harbors spirituous tenants like the **Fowling Warehouse** bowling alley and sports bar, **Centerpoint Brewing**, and chocolate and wine pairing sessions at **SoChatti**.

Sip more homegrown suds at the

Indulge in classic fare at St. Elmo's Steak House in Indianapolis.

Indiana Microbrewers Festival (July) at Military Park in the state capital, as well as **Books & Brews** in north Indy, a combination brewpub and bookstore that also sells a wide selection of board games and collectibles (think Pokémon).

Pre- and post-game action for Fighting Irish football and basketball games takes place at the **Fiddler's Hearth** Irish pub in downtown South Bend or stylish **Rohr's** tavern on the Notre Dame campus, where bartender Patrick "The Murf" Murphy has been pouring drinks for half a century. ■

Iowa

Corn may be king in the Hawkeye State, but Iowa offers plenty of other tantalizing foods, both homegrown and from faraway shores.

THE BIG PICTURE

Founded: 1846

Population: 3.2 million

Official State Vegetable: Sweet potato

Also Known As: Hawkeye State

Culinary Influences: Czech and Slovak, Dutch

Don't Miss: Des Moines, Amana Colonies, Cedar Rapids

Claim to Fame: Pork tenderloin sandwich, kolaches, Dutch lettuce salad

Corn easily tops the Iowa crop charts in terms of both acreage and value. In fact, the Hawkeye State is the nation's single largest producer of maize. In addition to corn on the cob, the golden kernels end up in all sorts of dishes, from casseroles and cornbread to relishes, soups, and salads.

Iowa also leads the nation in **pork**, producing nearly three times as much as runners-up Minnesota and North Carolina. It's also the main ingredient in one of the state's signature dishes, the **pork tenderloin sandwich**. Another lunchtime favorite is the **loose meat sandwich**, which blends ground beef, chicken, or beef stick and sometimes diced onion or dill pickles (but without the thick sauce that would make it a sloppy joe), all served on a hamburger roll or kaiser bun.

Along with everything else in their covered wagons, European pioneers brought recipes from home, foods now considered Iowa dishes. One, the **Dutch letter**, is an ultraflaky S-shaped butter pastry filled with almond paste and sprinkled with granulated sugar. Iceberg or romaine, hard-boiled eggs, bacon, onions, and potatoes with a tangy dressing are the main ingredients in **Dutch lettuce salad**.

Introduced by Czech immigrants, the **kolache** is a popular pastry normally filled with fruit or berries but also offered as a savory meat snack or a breakfast dish with cheese, eggs, and bacon. It's also possible to sample other Middle European treats like **pierogi** (dumplings) and *klobasa* (smoked sausages), although not as widely available.

CULINARY EXPERIENCES

With more than 85,000 farms, Iowa produces plenty of fresh meat, dairy, fruit, and produce to sell at farmers markets around the state. The **Downtown Farmers' Market** in Des Moines offers eats from 50 counties. **Cedar Rapids Downtown Farmers Market** is one of the largest, boasting more than 150 vendors. Founded in 1845—a year before Iowa became a state—**Dubuque Farmers Market** is the oldest, while **Freight House Farmers Market** offers a location beside the Mississippi River in Davenport.

Iowa's agricultural bounty is also on display at the **Iowa State Fair** in Des Moines (August), which features the **Farm Bureau Cookout Contest** with local meats, buckets of **Barksdale's State Fair Cookies**, and a **Butter Cow** sculpture mascot, a tradition that started in 1911.

Iowa's ethnic eats take center

Race to the finish during a pie-eating contest at the annual Iowa State Fair.

Golden rows of corn blanket the Iowa countryside.

stage at **St. Ludmila's Kolach Festival** in Cedar Rapids (June) and the **Tivoli Fest** at the Museum of Danish America in Elk Horn (May) with its smorgasbord of Nordic foods.

The **Prairie States Mushroom Club** near Cedar Rapids invites amateur mycologists and anyone else with a keen interest in fungi to join them for Saturday morning forays in different parts of the state to forage for morels, porcini, hen of the woods, goat's beard, puffballs, coral and oyster mushrooms, and other edible varieties.

RESTAURANTS TO DIE FOR

Vintage cafés, diners, and bakeries—many in small towns—are often the best places to sample Iowa's signature dishes.

The **Lucky Pig Pub & Grill** in Ogden is renowned for a hogzilla-size pork tenderloin sandwich called Porky's Revenge, while the tiny **Canteen Lunch in the Alley** in Ottumwa is famed for a loose meat sandwich that rose to fame on the original *Roseanne* television show. **Coffee Cup Café** in Sully serves a much acclaimed Dutch lettuce salad, while **Cornbred Barbecue** in Ames offers cornbread pudding, street corn salad, homemade kettle corn, and sweet corn on the cob with many of its entrées.

In addition to the **National Czech & Slovak Museum & Library**, the **Czech Village & New Bohemia** in Cedar Rapids boasts abundant ethnic eateries. **Sykora Bakery** excels at freshly made kolache, *houska* (braided bread), *bábovka* (Bundt cake), *koprovka*

soup, and Bohemian rye bread. Despite its name, Des Moines's **Cajun Belle** drive-in is a favorite stop for sweet and savory kolaches.

Founded in 1847 by immigrants from the Netherlands, Pella is the state's hotbed of Dutch cuisine. Nearly as old as the town, **Jaarsma Bakery** makes classic Dutch letters, almond-flavored *gevulde speculaas* (bars), St. Nicholas cookies, and *bokkenpootjes* (almond pastries). Down the block, **Vander Ploeg Bakery** offers a similar selection of pastries and cookies, plus an amazing array of fruit-flavored, Dutch-style breads (apple cinnamon, lemon blueberry, orange cranberry walnut, etc.).

Rather than steak houses, as one might expect of a Midwest capital city, the Des Moines dining scene is surprisingly cosmopolitan. Local

grub ranges from the exotic Nepalese dishes of **Kathmandu Restaurant** and modern takes on Latin American favorites at **Bar Nico**, to the big red **Veggie Thumper** food bus and the **Cheese Bar** with its Swiss fondue and raclette, gourmet mac and cheese, and amazing charcuterie boards.

Jesse's Embers or the newly launched **Irina's Steak & Seafood** can satisfy cravings for a nice, juicy piece of meat. However, the pièce de résistance of Des Moines fine dining is **Aposto**, an elegant Mediterranean eatery tucked into a lovingly restored Victorian mansion.

Dubuque is giving the capital city stiff competition at the upper end of the eating market with restaurants like **Brazen Open Kitchen** in the historic Millwork District. Former Iowa chef of the year Kevin Scharpf uses locally sourced ingredients to create dishes like carrot-apple soup, braised lamb and kale pizza, and Amish fried chicken with Red Rock cheddar and cornbread. Date night in Davenport could mean a visit to **Duck City Bistro** and a menu spangled with classic dishes like filet mignon, Alaska king crab, and, of course, duck breast.

BOTTOMS UP!

It's not anywhere near Mexico or a tropical island, but Iowa's unofficial state cocktail is the **Frozen Blue Margarita**. It's allegedly inspired by an old wives' tale that West Okoboji Lake in the state's northwest corner is one of only three true blue-water lakes on the entire planet. If you don't see it on the cocktail menu at

Authentic Dutch pastries await at family-owned and -operated Jaarsma Bakery in Pella, which has been in business since 1898.

Iowa Girl Eats' Jennifer Aniston Salad is packed with quinoa, cucumbers, chickpeas, red onion, and fresh herbs.

waterfront hangouts like the **Barefoot Bar** or **the Gardens**, ask the bartender for a traditional margarita with blue curaçao.

Iowa isn't all about corn; it also boasts more than 100 small vineyards that turn their grapes into wine. Vintners like **Prairie Crossing Vineyard and Winery** and **Bodega Victoriana** in the state's southwest corner fall within the Loess Hills District AVA, while winemakers like **Stone Cliff** and **Wide River Winery** along the state's eastern edge are part of the Upper Mississippi River Valley AVA.

With tight state government restrictions on distilling until recently, Iowa is late to the craft spirits wave sweeping the nation. But it's catching up fast with flavorsome beverages from **Mississippi River Distilling Company** in LeClaire and Davenport and **Iowa Distilling Co.** near Des Moines. ■

THE QUEEN OF GLUTEN FREE

When Iowa lifestyle blogger Kristin Porter was diagnosed with celiac disease in 2013, she took a deep dive into ways that she and others who suffer from the autoimmune disorder could eat healthy without sacrificing flavor.

Since then, Porter has become the "queen of gluten free" and a godsend to thousands of eaters with special dietary needs. In addition to her *Gluten-Free for Beginners* cookbook, she pilots the popular **Iowa Girl Eats** website, which is filled with recipes for gluten-free, dairy-free, low-carb, low-fat, vegan, and vegetarian diets. Recipes range from her famous Jennifer Aniston Salad and Thai Sweet Potato Curry to Iowa-inspired dishes like Sweet Corn Soup and Grilled Pork Tenderloin.

Kansas

Carry on, wayward eaters. In Kansas, the menu varies from Kansas City's vaunted barbecue culture to myriad farm-based dishes and heirloom Volga German cuisine.

Several of the great cattle-driving routes of the Old West—the Chisholm Trail, Shawnee Trail, and Western Trail—ran to railheads in Kansas, where the cows were shipped east. Those epic migrations are long gone, but the state retains its reputation for top-notch beef served as straight-up **steak**, succulent **pot roast**, or barbecued **ribs** and **burnt ends**.

Ground beef features in the state's **crumbly burgers** as well as Kansas **chili** (often served with **cinnamon rolls**) and the beloved **bierock**, a savory pocket sandwich that 19th-century Volga German immigrants from Russia introduced along with soft **zwieback** bread rolls and sweet *grebble* (fried dough).

True to the nickname, the Sunflower State is one of the nation's largest **sunflower** growers, and the bright yellow blooms in late August to early September draw photo-snapping residents and visitors. Kansas also ranks among the top producers of **wheat**, one of the grains making its way to the state's artisanal bakeries and breadmakers.

CULINARY EXPERIENCES

The nation's foremost grilled meat event, the **American Royal World Series of Barbecue** at Kansas Speedway (September–October) serves up chicken, pork, beef brisket, sausage, sides, and dessert competitions waged by teams from around the globe.

THE BIG PICTURE

Founded: 1861

Population: 2.94 million

Official State Fruit: Sandhill plum

Also Known As: Sunflower State

Culinary Influences: Swedish, German, Hmong

Don't Miss: Wichita, Lawrence, Lindsborg

Claim to Fame: Barbecue ribs, chili with cinnamon rolls, barbecue

Two events celebrate Kansas-grown wheat: the **National Festival of Breads** (June) in Manhattan and good, old-fashioned **Country Threshing Days** (August) in Goessel. Borscht, pierogi, zweiback, and other Volga German delicacies are the culinary attraction at the annual **Kansas Mennonite Relief Sale** at the fairgrounds in Hutchinson.

With around 60,000 farms and ranches, Kansas offers myriad agritourism options. **Gieringer's Family Orchard & Berry Farm** near Edgerton offers U-pick peaches, apples, pumpkins, sweet corn, sunflowers, and berries as well as a four-course Feast in the Fields meal beneath the peach trees. Blackberry picking, a café with blackberry-infused baked goods, and a creamery that produces artisanal goat milk cheeses are the culinary temptations at **Elderslie Farm** near Wichita.

Opened in 1937, the **Nifty Nut House** in Wichita stocks a mind-blowing array of nuts, candies, chocolates, dried fruit, and other snacks. The city is also home to **Cocoa Dolce** and its artisan chocolates, chips, bites, macarons, and cookies.

Kansas chili is often served with a cinnamon roll on the side.

Watch the flame-packed action over a plate of barbecue via the open kitchen at Q39 South in Overland Park.

RESTAURANTS TO DIE FOR

Nobody does it better than **Joe's Kansas City Bar-B-Que**. Set inside an old gas station on the Kansas side of the metro area, this longtime local favorite is renowned for specials like the Hogmaniac dinner, Rocket Pig pulled pork sandwich, and burnt ends by the pound. **Q39 South** in Overland Park blends classic barbecue plates and sandwiches with offbeat dishes like smoked beef brisket poutine and pork belly tacos.

It may be hundreds of miles from the Rio Grande, but KCK does great Mexican, too. **Jarocho** in the Armourdale neighborhood specializes in south-of-the-border seafood delights like ceviche tostadas, blue crab queso, and chipotle jumbo shrimp. The specialty at **Chentes on the Hill** on Strawberry Hill is Mexican-flavored pizzas topped with chorizo, carne asada, and salsa verde.

Out in the burbs, the **Restaurant at 1900** in Mission Woods is tucked inside an elegant mid-century modern building with tulip columns. The restaurant, helmed by James Beard Award semifinalist chef Linda Duerr, is known for innovative Euro-American cuisine. At the nearby Shops of Prairie Village, **Story Restaurant** offers novel takes on New American cuisine in a chic minimalist space. Upscale surf and turf—and amazing soufflés, brûlées, and cheesecakes—are the spoils at **801 Chophouse** in Leawood.

The state's most stylish steak house, **Scotch & Sirloin** in Wichita complements its prime rib, filet mignon, and seafood with an extensive wine wall it calls the "Napa Valley of the Midwest." Some would say the crumbly burgers at the city's **Nu-Way Drive-In** are just as tasty.

Road trippers can break up the long, boring drive across Kansas on Interstate 70 by savoring the prairie-flavored French and Italian cuisine at the **White Linen** in Topeka or sampling one of the 48 ice-cream flavors available at the student-staffed **Call Hall Dairy Bar** at Kansas State University in Manhattan.

Crank back the clock to frontier days by digging in to the popular Friday night buffet at **Sommerset**

Sip and stay a while at brewpub Tallgrass Tap House in Manhattan.

Café inside the clapboard Sage General Store in Dover. Out on the tallgrass prairie, the **Grand Central Grill** in Cottonwood Falls has been cooking up good stuff since 1884. You can decide who fixes the best fried chicken: **Chicken Annie's** or **Chicken Mary's**, which are just 400 feet (122 m) apart in Pittsburg.

BOTTOMS UP!

Reputedly the oldest bar and restaurant west of the Mississippi, **Hays House Restaurant and Tavern** in Council Grove first opened its doors in 1857 as a stopover on the Santa Fe Trail. Some of the craft cocktails—like the whiskey-based Red Eye—are made with spirits from the boutique **Boot Hill Distillery** in Dodge City.

With a resident population of

Sunflowers brighten the landscape at a Kansas farm.

avid beer drinkers, Kansas college towns have sprouted numerous craft breweries. Among the best are **Free State Brewing Company** in Lawrence and **Tallgrass Tap House** in Manhattan.

Out on the plains south of Kansas City, **Louisburg Cider Mill** has grown from a humble roadside cider stand in the 1970s into a prairie village setting that produces apple cider, lemonade, and three flavors of Lost Trail Soda (including sarsaparilla) and hosts a two-day **Ciderfest** in late September.

You probably won't run into Dorothy or the Tin Man, but **Oz Winery** in Wamego (between Topeka and Manhattan) offers *Wizard of Oz* swag and memorabilia, as well as locally produced wines that follow the movie theme, like Yellow Brick Road Chardonnay and Emerald City Lights Sauvignon Blanc. **Liquid Art Winery & Estate** west of Manhattan offers another take on Flint Hills wine. ■

HARVEY HOUSE

Founded in Topeka in 1876, Harvey House was a collaboration between British restaurateur Fred Harvey and the Atchison, Topeka & Santa Fe Railway to develop restaurants at popular train destinations in the American West. Harvey's empire grew from the depot lunchroom in Topeka into a chain of 45 restaurants in a dozen states known for both their fine dining and iconic Western architecture.

As business soared and its reputation spread, Harvey House also ventured into railroad dining cars and tourist hotels. Among those that still exist are **El Tovar Hotel** at the Grand Canyon, the **Inn & Ranch at Death Valley**, and **La Fonda** on the Plaza in Santa Fe.

Kentucky

Bourbon, burgoo, and barbecue flavor a Kentucky dining scene that traces its gastronomic roots to drinks and dishes pioneered during frontier days.

THE BIG PICTURE

Founded: 1792

Population: 4.51 million

Official State Fruit: Blackberry

Also Known As: Bluegrass State

Culinary Influences: African, Scottish, English, German

Don't Miss: Louisville, Lexington, Paducah

Claim to Fame: Hot brown sandwiches, bourbon, Benedictine dip or sandwiches

One thing that Stephen Foster forgot to mention in "My Old Kentucky Home" is what the inhabitants were eating while the young folks were rolling on the floor and the birds were making all that music.

The Bluegrass State craves plenty of foods that it shares with its southern neighbors, from **country ham** and **corn pudding** to **spoon bread** and **fried chicken**. But some dishes are uniquely Kentuckian.

Legend holds that the Kentucky version of **burgoo stew**, which includes whatever vegetables and meat might be available at any given time, came out of Lexington. On the other hand, **rolled oysters** (deep-fried oysters encased in cornmeal and cracker crumbs) are a Louisville favorite. So is the **hot brown sandwich**, an open-faced blend of turkey and bacon smothered in a cheese sauce originally contrived in the 1920s by cooks at the city's Brown Hotel.

Bacon is also a key ingredient of the traditional **wilted lettuce salad**, which actually uses super-fresh lettuce (and either onion or radish) that is dressed with hot bacon drippings to gently wilt the lettuce. Another oldie but goodie is **pocket**

Smothered with cheese and a creamy sauce, the Kentucky hot brown sandwich is a knife-and-fork favorite.

Watch the world's largest stainless-steel skillet fry up chicken during the World Chicken Festival in London.

dressing, a combination of corn-bread, biscuits, eggs, chopped vegetables, herbs, and turkey broth that is baked into balls that fit easily into the pockets of hunters and farmers or, these days, hikers and bikers.

Like many other southern states, Kentucky does its own thing with **barbecued meats**. Actually, two things. Pork is the meat of choice in the western part of the state, while mutton is the king of barbecue out east.

From potent **bourbon balls** and **apple stack cake** (which looks far more like breakfast pancakes than dessert) to soufflé-like **cheese pudding** and a marshmallow-

and-caramel concoction called *modjeska*, Kentucky kitchens also produce an amazing array of sweet things for dessert or between-meal snacks.

CULINARY EXPERIENCES

Forget the horses! The **Kentucky Derby** offers a feast of dishes rarely found beyond Churchill Downs. Racegoers can supplement their mint juleps with Benedictine mini sandwiches filled with a cream cheese spread, pork cracklin' with pimento cheese, bourbon-dosed pecans, or a Derby sundae smothered with bourbon chocolate sauce.

One of Kentucky's oldest annual

food events, **Marion County Country Ham Days** in Lebanon (September) features numerous special events from a hay toss and pig pen relay to an evening hot-air balloon "glow" and a Saturday morning breakfast during which 4,000 pounds (1,814 kg) of ham are served.

Laurel County, the location of the first Kentucky Fried Chicken restaurant, also hosts the **World Chicken Festival** (September). The four-day event includes Colonel Sanders look-alikes, chicken imitation and rooster-tail mullet contests, a survival egg drop, and a chicken trivia game.

Sugaray Rayford performs during the 2022 W.C. Handy Blues & Barbecue Festival in Henderson.

One of the nation's largest free music events, **W.C. Handy Blues & Barbecue Festival** in Henderson features both styles of Kentucky grilled meats in venues along the Ohio River. In the western foothills of the Appalachians, the **Mountain Mushroom Festival** in Irvine features a mushroom cook-off, mushroom hunting, a mushroom market, and a mascot called Morey Morel.

RESTAURANTS TO DIE FOR

Set inside an 1845 antebellum manse on the National Register of Historic Places, **Holly Hill Inn** near Lexington is renowned for elevated southern cuisine and its vast selection of wines and bourbons, as well as dining experiences like a five-course Aphrodisiacs menu on Valentine's Day.

Windy Corner Market on the north side of Lexington offers many of the state's iconic foods—hot brown sandwiches, deep-fried oysters, country ham, and fried chicken—as well as snacks like bourbon-spiked chili and bourbon-chili nachos flavored with the state's favorite libation.

Some of the state's best meals are found in the rural Bluegrass region around Lexington. Savor mushroom galette, steak frites, onion grilled cheese sandwiches, and other French-inspired dishes at **Heirloom** in Midway. Or sample southern culinary classics like fried catfish, "yellow-legged" fried chicken, and corn pudding at the elegant **Beaumont Inn** in Harrodsburg. Burgoo stew with sour cream cornbread and black-eyed peas is the signature dish at the **Trustees' Table** restaurant in historic Shaker Village of Pleasant Hill.

In addition to being home to the original hot brown sandwich, the upscale **English Grill** at the Brown Hotel in Louisville offers all-time favorites like filet mignon, rack of lamb, and duck breast, as well as a five-course feast at a chef's table in the kitchen.

Opened in 1909 in the eastern Kentucky coal country, Berea's

THE COLONEL

Born in Indiana, Harland Sanders worked his way through the South as a steamboat pilot and railroad worker before gathering enough cash in 1930 to open a roadside restaurant in Corbin, Kentucky, that served fried chicken made with his "secret" blend of 11 herbs and spices.

By 1950, he had assumed the "Colonel Sanders" persona, characterized by a white suit and his snow-white mustache and goatee. He briefly served in the military but didn't become a colonel until decades later when the governor of Kentucky awarded him that honorary title.

Two years later, a **Kentucky Fried Chicken** franchise opened in Salt Lake City, the first of 25,000-plus outlets in more than 145 countries. The famous KFC bucket was introduced in 1957. Although Sanders died in 1980, his legacy and image endure.

Boone Tavern offers dishes that Kentucky's favorite frontiersman may have eaten back in the day, like spoon pudding, apple bourbon–flavored pork, and fried green tomatoes. Another throwback, the **Anchor Grill** in Covington has been serving delicious diner meals since 1946. Get your hickory-smoked mutton at **Moonlite Bar-B-Q** in Owensboro on the Ohio River.

BOTTOMS UP!

Although it's the official drink of the Kentucky Derby, the legendary **mint julep** cocktail traces its roots to ancient Persia and Moorish Spain. From there, the beloved cocktail leaped across the Atlantic to Virginia and then over the Appalachians to frontier-era Kentucky. However, **Ale-8-One soda** was born in Kentucky, invented by Winchester beverage maker George Lee Wainscott in 1902.

Moonlighting as a moonshiner, Reverend Elijah Craig is credited with creating the state's first ever **bourbon**, a blend of barley, corn, rye, and water that he conceived in the early 1790s. By the 1820s, Kentucky distillers started calling it bourbon to distinguish their liquid from the whiskey produced in other states.

The well-trodden **Kentucky Bourbon Trail** links 18 distilleries scattered across the state from **Old Pogue** (Maysville) in the east to **Casey Jones** (Hopkinsville) and **MB Roland** (Pembroke) in the west. Many of the globe's premier bourbons are made along the trail, including **Maker's Mark** (Loretto), **Wild Turkey** (Lawrenceburg), and **Jim Beam** (Clermont). Bardstown hosts the annual Kentucky Bourbon Festival (September).

With an alluring blend of Louisville cocktail bars, craft breweries, and bourbon distilleries, Louisville boasts the state's best overall drinking scene. The **NuLu (East Market) District** flaunts a dozen bars and (sunrise breakfast joints) within a short walk of one another, including **Goodwood Brewing & Spirits**, the funky **Garage Bar** in an old gas station, and **Nouvelle** wine bar with its cool backyard.

Proof on Main in the city's hip 21C Museum Hotel hosts "A Month With" program featuring craft cocktails and flights from new distilleries. **Equus & Jack's** in the St. Matthews neighborhood offers 75 bourbon varieties as well as steaks flavored with bourbon demi-glace or bourbon mustard. ∎

Bourbon blends with summery mint in the classic mint julep.

Louisiana

Louisiana cooking is legendary, a mash-up of various cultures and culinary influences that makes the southern state a global gathering place for fine dining and enchanting flavors.

THE BIG PICTURE

Founded: 1812

Population: 4.59 million

Official State Doughnut: Beignet

Also Known As: Pelican State

Culinary Influences: French (Creole/Cajun), Spanish, African

Don't Miss: New Orleans, Lafayette, Baton Rouge

Claim to Fame: Raising Cane's, gumbo, fried catfish, po'boys

Few states boast a single instantly recognizable regional cuisine, let alone two. But that's what makes Louisiana such an incredible place to eat, as Creole and Cajun foodways are both world renowned. And the Pelican State even offers awesome Italian cuisine, Jewish delis, and southern soul food.

For those who don't reside at the lower end of the Mississippi River, it's sometimes hard to differentiate between Creole and Cajun foods. There's definitely overlap, for example, with dishes like **gumbo, jambalaya**, and **crawfish pie** that appear in both cuisines (and a famous Hank Williams song). Yet, they are distinct.

Cajun cuisine was created by French-speaking Acadians who arrived in Louisiana in the late 1700s after they were banished from Canada following the British takeover. They had already developed a unique regional cuisine that blended French country cooking with ingredients available in Atlantic Canada. Over time, Cajun people living along the bayous and in rural communities blended their Acadian traditions with Spanish, West African, and Native American cooking and local ingredients they came across in Louisiana.

Among the most typical Cajun foods are **boudin** and **andouille** sausages, *cochon de lait* (suckling pig), **catfish court bouillon stew**, and **crawfish étouffée**, the latter another dish shared with Creole cooking. *Maque choux*, a popular side dish, blends corn, bell peppers, onions, garlic, and bacon in a skillet.

Also sourced from the bayou, **frog legs** and **grilled or fried gator** are other heirloom dishes. A whole **roast pig** is the star attraction at a *boucherie*, a traditional Cajun outdoor feast for friends and family. **Crawfish boils** are also popular.

Creole cuisine features many of the same gastronomic influences and evolved during the same time frame, but it was born in New Orleans rather than the Louisiana countryside. Largely pioneered by enslaved African Americans working in the kitchens of wealthy Europeans and Americans, the genre embraces a wider range of ingredients than Cajun food because of the city's status as a global entrepôt. For many years, Creole cooking was considered more refined than Cajun

A thick blanket of powdered sugar tops pillowy beignets at the perennial favorite Café du Monde in New Orleans.

A traditional crawfish boil with crustaceans, potatoes, sausage, corn on the cob, and lemon wedges

because of its urban roots. But with Cajun coming into the mainstream, that's no longer the case.

Among the typical Creole dishes are **beef grillades with grits**, **chicken creole** with a spicy tomato-based sauce on a bed of steamed rice, and ***pompano en papillote***, a delicious seafood meal traditionally served on parchment paper. Fresh Gulf shrimp are the focus of **shrimp creole, shrimp bisque**, and **shrimp rémoulade**. Access to dairy products empowered Creole cooks to develop the creamy sauces that feature in dishes like **oysters Rockefeller** and **eggs Sardou**.

New Orleans also has a knack for inventing sandwiches. The po'boy—French bread stuffed with lettuce, tomato, pickles, cheese, and either meat or seafood—was conceived in the late 1920s, allegedly by two restaurant-owning brothers who handed out free sandwiches to striking streetcar workers. The **muffuletta**—a Sicilian sesame roll filled with Italian deli meats, cheese, and marinated olive salad—was invented in 1906 by deli-owning immigrant Salvatore Lupo.

The Crescent City's contributions to the pantheon of American desserts include the **king cake** (a Mardi Gras confection baked with a tiny plastic baby figurine hidden inside and decorated with purple, gold, and green frosting), as well as **pralines, beignets**, and **bananas Foster**.

CULINARY EXPERIENCES

Louisiana boasts eight official food trails covering various regions and culinary genres. These range from the **Creole Crescent** in New Orleans, the Lower Mississippi River parishes, and the **Bayou Bounty** around Lafayette and St. Martin Parishes to the Cajun-flavored **Prairie Home Cooking** of St. Landry and Avoyelles Parishes and the southern soul food–infused **Red River Riches** of Shreveport and the state's northwest corner.

The best food festivals are also spread around the state. Louisiana's favorite freshwater shellfish is the focus of the **Breaux Bridge Crawfish Festival** near Lafayette (May) and the **World Championship**

Revelers take in the sights on Bourbon Street in New Orleans' French Quarter.

Crawfish Etouffee Cook-Off in Eunice (March). The **Natchitoches Meat Pie Festival** (September) revolves around traditional pastries stuffed with beef, pork, onions, garlic, and red peppers. In addition to roast suckling pig, the **Cochon de Lait Festival** in Mansura (May) includes a pork cracklin' cooking contest and live zydeco music.

The Baton Rouge Epicurean Society organizes several annual food and wine events, including the **Crawfete** (March) at Perkins Rowe and a **Spring Fete** (April) at historic Houmas House. Perkins Rowe also brings together a dozen mobile feasts for the **Food Truck Round Up at the Rowe** (June).

Although music is the main raison d'être of the **New Orleans Jazz & Heritage Festival** (April–May), the big bash at the Fair Grounds is also a great place to catch a wide variety of Louisiana eats. The festival includes a **Drag Queen Brunch** and a **Food Heritage Stage** where top chefs prepare local, regional, and international favorites. A single iconic New Orleans dish is the focus of the **Oak Street Po-Boy Festival** (November), where prizes are awarded for the best pork, beef, shrimp, seafood, and vegetarian/vegan sandwiches.

New Orleans is also one of the nation's best places to learn how to cook. Every Monday and Thursday, the **Southern Food & Beverage Museum** in the Central City neighborhood offers two-hour Cajun and Creole cooking classes. The long-running **New Orleans School of Cooking** in the French Quarter stages twice-daily demonstrations and hands-on sessions in Cajun and Creole cooking. Over on the north shore of Lake Pontchartrain,

PAUL PRUDHOMME: LOUISIANA'S CULINARY EMISSARY

Drawing from the food of his youth in Louisiana's Acadiana region in the 1940s, Paul Prudhomme helped raise the status of Cajun and Creole cooking from regional specialties to global renown via his restaurants, television shows, and invitations to cook at the White House and high-profile international events.

Prudhomme's early years were anything but auspicious. His first restaurant, a hamburger joint in hometown Opelousas, didn't even last a year. But he persevered, working his way up the culinary food chain to the exalted position of executive chef at the prestigious Commander's Palace in New Orleans.

He eventually opened his own New Orleans restaurant and authored 11 cookbooks. Prudhomme's fame spread with *Fork in the Road,* the first of five cooking shows that he hosted in the late 1990s and early 21st century. Among his many accolades are Culinarian of the Year in the United States (1986), Chevalier of the Ordre National du Mérite Agricole in France (1980), and Pioneer of American Cuisine from the Culinary Institute of America before his death in 2015.

creole, and frog legs Provençale.

Across the street is **GW Fins** and its modern take on seafood via innovative techniques like dry aging and whole-fish "ocean conservation cuts." The menu changes daily depending on what's available, but among their signature dishes are lobster dumplings, snapper ceviche, dry-aged bluefin tuna, and Scalibut (halibut, scallops, and shrimp risotto).

Out in the genteel Garden District, **Commander's Palace** has been serving exquisite New Orleans fare since 1893 under the direction of celebrated chefs like

Culinary Kids specializes in beginner and advanced cooking classes for children ages seven to 16.

The **Tabasco sauce** company on Avery Island offers three edible adventures: a 45-minute factory tour to see how the famous pepper sauce is made, an Acadian culinary experience, and a Cajun cooking demonstration. Depending on who you talk to, the celebrated condiment was invented by company founder Edmund McIlhenny in 1868 or several decades earlier by New Orleans entrepreneur Maunsel White.

RESTAURANTS TO DIE FOR

Founded by eccentric French wine salesman Arnaud Cazenave in 1918, **Arnaud's** is a French Quarter classic. A feast for both the eyes and taste buds, the elegant eatery features art deco murals and etched glass windows, the museum of flamboyant Mardi Gras costumes, and arguably the city's best Creole cuisine. The menu includes all-time favorites like oysters Bienville, seafood gumbo, shrimp

Bananas Foster brings the heat tableside with flambéed fruit swimming in a rum sauce.

Emeril Lagasse, Paul Prudhomme, and current kitchen maestro Meg Bickford. Nowadays the forte is New Haute Creole cuisine—dishes like Breaux Bridge crawfish strudel, prosecco-poached Louisiana blue crab, and Ponchatoula strawberry-glazed pork belly—with ingredients sourced within a 100-mile (161 km) radius of the restaurant.

Another bastion of New Orleans fine dining, **Dooky Chase** in the storied Tremé/Lafitte neighborhood started life in 1939 as a humble sandwich shop before morphing into an icon of Creole cuisine where two U.S. presidents, prominent civil rights leaders, and music stars have dined.

But it's not all white tablecloths and crystal chandeliers. Some of NOLA's best eats are found in old-time neighborhood stores like **Stein's Market & Deli**, a Jewish Italian hybrid in the Garden District that specializes in muffuletta, corned beef, hoagies, and other sandwiches.

In the heart of the French Quarter, **Central Grocery & Deli** is where the muffuletta and its beloved olive salad originated at the turn of the 20th century. Two blocks down Decatur Street, **Café du Monde** started baking its famous beignets in 1862 during the Union occupation of New Orleans.

Even though it started life as a neighborhood market, **La Petite Grocery** in Uptown New Orleans is now a classy little restaurant serving modern Louisiana cuisine. The menu is spangled with innovative eats like alligator Bolognese pasta, panéed rabbit with spaetzle, and blue crab beignets. A block west

Cajun spices add a welcome kick to shrimp and sausage jambalaya.

Catch that pig! The race is on at the Cochon de Lait Festival in Mansura.

along restaurant-packed Magazine Street, **Casamento's** has lured oyster epicures since 1919 with dishes like fried oysters, oyster salad, oysters on the half shell, oyster stew, and oyster loaf sandwich. Across the Mississippi in Westwego, family-owned **Mosca's Restaurant** started serving spaghetti and meatballs, chicken cacciatore, and other Italian standards in 1946.

The epitome of fine dining in Baton Rouge, **Mansurs on the Boulevard** has been a date-night fave for more than three decades. Signature dishes like the char-grilled oysters, cedar-roasted redfish, and creole chicken piccata complement a copious wine menu and a resident pianist. The state capital's new culinary hot spot, Mid City South also boasts **Beausoleil Coastal Cuisine** with shaded patio tables and **City Pork Jefferson** with a menu that features Mexican-Louisianan fusion foods like wild boar flautas and brisket nachos.

In keeping with Natchitoches's status as the official "meat pie

capital of Louisiana," **Merci Beaucoup Restaurant** serves the savory treats single and by the dozen. Among its other regional specialties are crawfish étouffée, Cajun potatoes, sausage gumbo, and catfish with hush puppies or dirty rice. Farther down the Red River corridor, **Lea's Lunchroom** (founded in 1928) in Lecompte is another longtime favorite for meat pies, baked ham, red beans and rice, and pies made with a family recipe.

Located in the heartland of Cajun cuisine, **Prejean's** restaurant on the north side of Lafayette sets the mood for devouring catfish Atchafalaya, smoked duck and andouille gumbo, or fried gator po'boys with live local tunes on Tuesday and Friday nights and Sunday brunch.

Established in 1937 and one of the city's oldest eateries, **Johnson's Boucanière** does Cajun-style smoked meats and barbecue, gumbo, jambalaya, beignets, and boudin balls. South Louisiana music recorded live at the restaurant is sold

Mediterranean at **Mazen's** and French with a Louisiana twist at **La Truffe Sauvage**.

BOTTOMS UP!

Loaded with both drinking establishments and bartenders who love to experiment, New Orleans may be the birthplace of more acclaimed cocktails than any other global city.

Legend holds that local apothecary Antoine Peychaud first concocted the **Sazerac** (rye whiskey, bitters, and absinthe or anise liqueur) in 1838 and that he served it in an egg cup—*coquetier* (allegedly the genesis of the word "cocktail"). Owner/barkeep Henry Ramos formulated his frothy **Ramos Gin Fizz** (gin, egg white, cream, orange flower water, lemon, and lime juice) in 1888 at the long-gone Imperial Cabinet Saloon on the outer edge of the French Quarter.

Named for the neighborhood, the **Vieux Carré** (rye whiskey, bitters, cognac, vermouth, and Bénédictine liqueur) came into this world at the Hotel Monteleone in 1938. The **Hurricane** (rum, grenadine, passion fruit juice, orange juice, and lime juice) blew into town during World War II at Pat O'Brien's bar in the French Quarter. A few years later, Napoleon House created a New Orleans version of the **Pimm's Cup** (Pimm's, lemonade, 7UP), a refreshing summer drink already popular in England.

New Orleans is also a world leader in bars: with around 1,400 at last count, or roughly one bar for every 500 residents. In other words, you'll find plenty of spots in which to sample the city's homegrown cocktails. Two of the most

Chef Meg Bickford, the first woman executive chef at the historic Commander's Palace in New Orleans

on the Valcour Records label. A block off campus, the **Olde Tyme Grocery** has been serving po'boys and flavored snowballs to University of Louisiana at Lafayette students for more than 40 years.

The po'boys at **Darrell's** and all-around menu at **Pat's of Henderson** are among the top choices for Cajun food in Lake Charles. But the southwest Louisiana city also has international eats: Greek and Eastern

renowned are the **Sazerac Bar** with its stylish art deco murals at the Roosevelt Hotel and **Carousel Bar & Lounge** with its whimsical circus decor at the Hotel Monteleone. Another oldie but goodie is the portrait-filled **Napoleon House**.

Piña coladas and mai tais top the tropical cocktails at **Beachbum Berry's Latitude 29** tiki bar near the riverfront. Opposite Louis Armstrong Park, **Bar Tonique** is a craft cocktail oasis with tasty takes on the Sazerac, Vieux Carré, Ramos Gin Fizz, and other local libations. Live jazz and cold beer are the tonics at **Kermit's Treme Mother in Law Lounge** in the Seventh Ward.

The intersection of Laurel and 3rd Streets is ground zero for the drinking scene in downtown Baton Rouge. Among the five bars within a block radius is **Blend**, a wine bar that also serves classic Louisiana cocktails. Across the street from the LSU campus, **the Chimes** is an upscale version of a student bar with local-inspired grub (think boudin egg rolls and crawfish mac and cheese) and an extensive craft beer selection. Out in the redeveloped Mid City South area, **Hayride Scandal** offers funky decor, live tunes, and an amazing array of classic, modern, and custom cocktails,

from the Navi-Daddy (tequila, coconut, lime, and nutmeg) to the cognac-and-peach-based One Twelve.

Up in Alexandria, the **Mirror Room** inside the historic Hotel Bentley does double duty as an elegant cocktail bar and tapas lounge. (Sample the hot crab claws or smoked brisket quesadilla.) Lafayette's **Blue Moon Saloon** stages roots music from around the world, including locally based Cajun, zydeco, and R & B acts. Even though it's only open on Saturdays, **Fred's Lounge** in Mamou lures Cajun music and dance fans from around the state. ■

Tabasco hot sauce matures in white oak barrels sourced from distilleries around the United States.

Maine

Lobster might be Maine's culinary magnum opus, but crustaceans aren't the only delicacy that elevates dining in the Pine Tree State.

THE BIG PICTURE

Founded: 1820

Population: 1.39 million

Official State Snack: Whoopie pie

Also Known As: Pine Tree State, Lumber State

Culinary Influences: English, French, Wabanaki

Don't Miss: Portland, Bar Harbor, Camden

Claim to Fame: Lobster roll, blueberry pie, baked beans

As hard as it is to believe today given **lobster's** popularity, the shellfish was largely a working-class food until the early 20th century, when elites of Boston, New York, and other eastern cities discovered it could be downright tasty. Realizing it could cash in on the boom, Maine soon became a leading lobster-catching state and elevated the various ways you can cook and serve lobster into the gourmet arena.

Boiled or steamed, lobsters are served whole, stuffed between bread rolls, or baked into pies. Ask a hundred locals what their favorite Maine lobster shack is, and you'll likely get as many different responses. Suffice it to say, **Young's Lobster Pound & Seafood Restaurant** in Belfast, **Harraseeket Lunch & Lobster Co.** in South Freeport, **Red's Eats** in Wiscasset, and **Rose Eden Lobster** on Mount Desert Island are among the ones that consistently make the "best lobster shack" lists. Another Maine forte, **steamers** (soft-shell clams) are served steamed, fried, in chowders, or on burger buns at many lobster joints.

Maine-style **baked beans**, made with locally grown yellow eye beans, salted pork, onions, molasses, and spices, is another local favorite.

Acadian settlers who relocated to northern Maine during the 18th century introduced two other Maine favorites: *ployes* (buckwheat pancakes) and **fiddleheads** from ostrich ferns. The state's far north is also the realm of tasty **Aroostook potatoes**.

Mainers satisfy their sweet tooth by gobbling up **blueberry pies** (the official state dessert), **whoopie pies** (the official state snack), and **Needhams candy**, a square of dark chocolate filled with coconut and potato that's been around since 1872.

CULINARY EXPERIENCES

Maine doesn't have an official state **lobster trail**, but U.S. Route 1 between Portland and the Canadian border easily fits the bill, with hundreds of spots where you can munch the scrumptious crustacean. Seagoing outfitters like **Rugosa Lobster Tours** in Kennebunkport and **Lulu Lobster Boat Ride** tours in Bar Harbor offer educational day trips during which passengers can help haul in lobster traps. Another hands-on adventure is ranger-guided steamer clam digs at **Wolfe's Neck Woods State Park**.

An easy way to explore the Maine food scene is via guided

Fluffy whoopie pies have a delicious cream filling.

Enjoy the charming coastal ambience at Eagles Nest restaurant in Bar Harbor.

foodie walking tours offered by **Maine Day Ventures** in Portland, Bar Harbor, Boothbay Harbor, and Kennebunkport. Among their many offerings are a **Portland: Savor and Saunter the East End** artisan tasting tour and a Kennebunkport **Doggy and Me Tour**, during which your canine companion also gets tasty treats.

The state celebrates its signature foods at various annual events, including the **Maine Whoopie Pie Festival** in Dover-Foxcroft (June), **Ployes Festival** in Fort Kent (August), **Maine Lobster Festival** in Rockland (August), and several blueberry jamborees throughout the seasons. Year-round, the **Portland Farmers Market** (established in 1768) offers a bounty of Pine Tree State products from land and sea.

RESTAURANTS TO DIE FOR

Announcing to the world what locals already knew, *Bon Appetit* magazine declared Portland "America's Foodiest Small Town" (2009) and the "Restaurant City of the Year" (2018). Truth be told, Maine's largest city really isn't that small (more than half a million people in the metro area alone). But the food is out of this world.

A handful of fine dining establishments lead the way. Located on one of the old finger piers along the Portland waterfront, **Scales** serves fresh-off-the-boat seafood with views of the local fishing fleet. Sure, they've got steamed lobster and lobster rolls. But some of the real treats are halibut ceviche, kingfish crudo, littleneck clams on the half shell, seafood stew, and Maine clam chowder. A few blocks off the waterfront, **Leeward** is making waves with house-made pasta dishes like *tonnarelli cacio e pepe* (cheese and pepper pasta), chicken cappelletti, and fusilli with lacinato kale pesto and pine nuts.

113

Local farmers and foragers complement the daily catch on the ever changing menu at **Fore Street** restaurant. James Beard Award winner Sam Hayward oversees an open kitchen that prepares its meat and seafood dishes on a grill, on a turnspit, and in an applewood-stoked brick oven. At **Eventide**

Oyster Co. you can have raw oysters, a unique lobster roll, and more seafood dishes paired with inventive cocktails in a casual setting. Over on the west side of Back Cove, **Woodford Food & Beverage** offers contemporary twists on American classics like smoked trout, roast chicken, Angus beef

steak, and an extraordinarily tasty brisket burger.

Portland's funky East End is a veritable foodie paradise thanks to eateries like the **Front Room** (possibly the state's best brunch), **Blue Spoon** for New American cuisine, and an **Eastern Prom Food Truck** gathering that includes 10 different culinary rigs at any given time.

From the Portland waterfront, would-be diners can hop a water taxi or ferry to dig into the oysters Rockefeller, lobster arancini, and other maritime marvels at the quaint little **Crown Jewel** café on Great Diamond Island. Farther up the coast, the "full-circle kitchen"—with nothing wasted—at **Primo** in Rockland specializes in modern, farm-to-table Italian dishes with many of the ingredients grown or raised on owner/chef Melissa Kelly's farm.

Acadia National Park harbors two unique eateries. Serving guests since 1893, **Jordan Pond House** offers incredible views from tables on the lawn behind the historic restaurant. Pond House has served its beloved tea and popovers for more than 100 years, and they should not be missed. Another Acadia favorite is the **Quiet Side & Ice Cream Shop** in Southwest Harbor, which offers a variety of artisan pizzas, specialty sandwiches, seafood baskets, and homemade pies to go with their 20 ice-cream flavors.

BOTTOMS UP!

Maine's favorite tuber is the foundation of the potato vodka and gin made by **Cold River distillery** in Freeport. Maine maple syrup flavors the **fall Old-Fashioned**, a favorite cold-weather cocktail. Even more popular with Down East drinkers are **Allen's Coffee Flavored Brandy** and its cold brew cousin.

It doesn't get much better than the brown butter lobster rolls at Portland's Eventide Oyster Co.

Portland's Fore Street restaurant utilizes hardwoods and applewood in its brick-and-soapstone-hearth oven, grill, and turnspit.

Portland owns the lion's share of Maine's best cocktail bars, including the **Portland Hunt + Alpine Club**, often named among the nation's best purveyors of mixed drinks. Down the coast in Biddeford, the mixologists at **Magnus on Water** shake and stir offbeat libations like the Van Helsing (a tequila and light beer smoothie), Tarantula (mezcal, sherry, and habanero chili), and Camo Pants (vodka, yellow chartreuse, and kiwi). Meanwhile, **Central Provisions** in Portland and **Havana** restaurant in Bar Harbor are known for their excellent and extensive wine cellars. ∎

MAINE'S FAVORITE LIBATION: MOXIE

If author Stephen King didn't occasionally mention Moxie in some of his best-selling books, the outside world probably wouldn't know about Maine's favorite soda pop. Invented by physician and Civil War veteran Dr. Augustin Thompson in 1876 and originally marketed as a medicinal drink that could cure "softening of the brain," among many other things, Moxie was proclaimed Maine's official soft drink in 2005.

Variously described as tasting bitter or like bubble gum, Moxie derives its "distinctively different" flavor from gentian root. Its popularity spread across New England, and the drink went on to be served at the inauguration of Vermont-born president Calvin Coolidge and was plugged on the radio by Boston Red Sox slugger Ted Williams.

Adoration reaches fever pitch at July's **Moxie Festival** in Lisbon Falls, Maine, which features a Moxie Recipe Contest (cakes, cookies, clam batter, etc.), Moxie Chugging Challenge, and New England Moxie Congress for those who like to discuss the drink ad infinitum. The rest of the year, duck into **Frank's Restaurant & Pub** in Lisbon Falls for Moxie swag and a sip of the legendary libation.

Maryland

Fresh seafood from the Chesapeake Bay and recipes with roots in colonial times are at the forefront of Maryland's culinary scene.

THE BIG PICTURE

Founded: 1788

Population: 6.16 million

Official State Dessert: Smith Island cake

Also Known As: Old Line State, Free State

Culinary Influences: African, English, Irish, German, Italian

Don't Miss: Ocean City, Annapolis, Baltimore

Claim to Fame: Caramel cream candies, crab cakes

The world's third largest estuary, the Chesapeake Bay is a hotbed for recreation, transportation, flora and fauna, and food—especially seafood. Almost 7,000 miles (11,265 km) of its shoreline fall within the state of Maryland. And many of the ingredients that end up on local menus—like **blue crabs, oysters,** and **rockfish**—are harvested in the bay.

It's well known that Marylanders love their **crab cakes,** especially with a dusting of **Old Bay Seasoning,** a signature blend of herbs and spices that debuted in Baltimore in 1939. But dozens of other yummy iterations of blue crab pepper the state, including **steamed crabs, Maryland crab soup, crab dip, soft-shell crab, crab imperial casserole, crab-stuffed hot dogs or pretzels or baked potatoes, crab-topped pizza,** and **Utz Crab Chips** (Old Bay–dusted potato chips that are actually made in neighboring Pennsylvania).

Away from the bay, Maryland is renowned for heirloom meaty dishes like **southern Maryland stuffed ham** (filled with cabbage, onions, and plenty of pepper), panfried **Chicken Maryland** in a cream sauce and garnished (believe it or not) with banana slices, and **Maryland-style pit beef,** a barbecue made with a saucy spread featuring garlic, onions, chili powder, and, of course, Old Bay. There's even a **Baltimore-style hot dog,** which is wrapped with a bologna slice and stuffed inside a bun with a dill pickle spear and yellow mustard.

Another oldie but goodie is **white potato pie,** a traditional holiday treat featuring cinnamon, nutmeg, vanilla, sugar, butter, and eggs (don't even ask how many calories). Among the state's other throwback desserts are the **Smearcase cheesecake** introduced by 19th-century German immigrants and many-layered **Smith Island cakes** (Maryland's official state dessert) from the eponymous isle in the Chesapeake Bay.

CULINARY EXPERIENCES

Sandy Point State Park in Annapolis hosts the **Maryland Seafood Festival** (September), where signature crab cakes and crab soup are complemented by live tunes, an arts village, kids' activities, and lots of craft beer.

Seventy miles (110 km) away on a branch of the Potomac River,

Traditionally comprising eight layers, Smith Island cakes have been made since the 1800s.

Quintessential Maryland seafood

Leonardtown is home to the **U.S. Oyster Festival** (October), which culminates in an oyster cook-off and the National Oyster Shucking Championship.

A slew of places stage early summer **strawberry festivals** that correspond with the June harvest, including Sandy Spring Museum, Cape St. Claire, Finksburg, Pittsville, and Adelphi. At the other end of the culinary spectrum, the **Maryland Chicken Wing Festival** (April) takes flight at the Anne Arundel County Fairgrounds in Crownsville.

Baltimore is one of those under-the-radar foodie destinations that doesn't get close to enough credit for its culinary savoir faire. **Bite of Baltimore** food tours are a great way to sample the city's diverse culinary offerings during a guided walking

"food crawl" of Fells Point, Mt. Vernon, or Federal Hill.

Opened in 1782, Baltimore's historic **Lexington Market** has upped its 21st-century game with the 2022 debut of a new 60,000-square-foot (5,574 m²) market hall. The 45-plus vendors range from artisan coffees and teas at **Black Acres Roastery** and Baltimore snowballs (a unique style of shaved ice) at **Sausage Master** to **Lumbini Nepali Fusion, Charro Negro** street tacos, and **Faidley's Seafood** crab cakes.

RESTAURANTS TO DIE FOR

Front and center on the Baltimore waterfront, **Charleston** delivers a divine dining experience that focuses on artistically presented oysters, soft-shell crab, and other seafood. In nearby Fells Point, the

Black Olive presents incredible Greek-style seafood in a historic brick building on a vintage cobblestone street.

Out near Druid Hill Park, James Beard Award–winning chef Spike Gjerde has transformed an old factory into a gourmet oasis called **Woodberry Kitchen** that features modern takes on American classics like fried chicken, rib eye steak, and fish and grits.

Attman's Delicatessen in the Jonestown neighborhood offers the city's best Baltimore-style, bologna-wrapped hot dogs, while **Pioneer Pit Beef** in Windsor Mill makes what many consider the state's best barbecue beef sandwiches (as well as pit ham and pit turkey).

Baltimore's hinterland hosts many great eateries, including **Tersiguel's**

French Country Restaurant and the superlative seafood at **Catonsville Gourmet** on the west side, as well as **Pairings Bistro** in Bel Air with its alluring culinary events like the five-course Whiskey Brawl dinner. **The Milton Inn** in Sparks Glencoe serves a huge dose of history with elevated American cuisine. Built in 1740, it was originally a Quaker coach stop and then a school attended by youthful John Wilkes Booth.

With its many politicos and midshipmen, it stands to reason that Annapolis boasts plenty of great grub. Crab omelets, crab cakes, and Baltimore hot dogs are among the 100-plus menu items at **Chick & Ruth's** deli, which also serves a colossal six-pound (2.7 kg) milkshake and giant sandwiches. **Cantler's Riverside Inn** serves crab a dozen different ways on a deck overlooking the Chesapeake Bay. Fresh seafood is also the strong suit at **Mike's Restaurant & Crabhouse**, with waterfront locations on either side of Annapolis.

Boaters can dock right next to **Old Salty's Restaurant** in Fishing Creek, where locals have been crabbing for more than 300 years. Another eastern shore throwback, **Smith Island Bakery** churns out traditional (chocolate) and new wave (red velvet, rainbow, coconut, etc.) versions of the island's legendary cakes.

BOTTOMS UP!

The Kentucky Derby has its signature mint julep while the Preakness Stakes at Pimlico Race Course in Baltimore is renowned for its **Black-Eyed Susan**, a customizable cocktail that combines vodka and at least one other spirit

Alma Cocina Latina in Baltimore highlights vibrant Venezuelan culture in its cuisine and decor.

Wild rockfish ceviche at Charleston restaurant in Baltimore

(bourbon, rum, schnapps, Cointreau—your choice!) with orange and pineapple juice garnished with an orange slice and maraschino cherry.

A lot of those same ingredients go into the **Orange Crush** cocktail, which blends vodka, freshly squeezed orange juice, and triple sec. The **Harborside Bar & Grill** in Ocean City claims to be the birthplace of the summer refresher, as well as its close kin, the **Grapefruit Crush**.

One of the pioneers of the Maryland craft brewing scene, **Heavy Seas Beer** offers tours and a taproom in the Baltimore suburb of Halethorpe. Among the state's other suds hubs are the **Brookeville Beer Farm** (which grows its own hops), **Burley Oak Brewing Company** in Berlin on the Delmarva Peninsula, and the **Guinness Open Gate Brewery** in Halethorpe, one of only two places in the United States where the Irish beer is made.

Maryland's oldest bar is the venerable **Middleton Tavern**, opened in 1750 on the Annapolis waterfront. Although "seafaring men" mainly frequented it, the tavern counts George Washington, Thomas Jefferson, Benjamin Franklin, and James Monroe among its bygone patrons. ■

CHARM CITY CAKES

Even though **Duff Goldman** launched his bespoke baking business in 2002, Charm City and its owner didn't become household names until the Food Network made them stars via eight seasons of the hit show *Ace of Cakes*.

Renowned for his extreme creativity and willingness to take on any confectionary challenge, Goldman has created cakes for movie premieres and television shows, baseball teams and the Super Bowl, and President Barack Obama's second inaugural ball.

Working out of a historic church building in Baltimore's Remington neighborhood, Charm City Cakes offers kids' baking camps, in-studio cake and cupcake classes, and private lessons for one to 12 people.

Massachusetts

Massachusetts fishermen and farmers have spent centuries harvesting the ingredients that anchor one of the nation's richest and most diverse culinary traditions.

THE BIG PICTURE

Founded: 1788

Population: 6.98 million

Official State Dessert: Boston cream pie

Also Known As: Bay State

Culinary Influences: English, Irish, Italian, Portuguese

Don't Miss: Boston, Cape Cod, Plymouth

Claim to Fame: Boston cream doughnut, chocolate chip cookies, Dunkin'

Native Americans were harvesting and eating **clams**—and baking them in sandy pits on the beach—for thousands of years before the Pilgrims arrived in 1620. Since then, the tasty bivalve mollusks have become a cornerstone of Massachusetts cooking.

New England clam chowder most often uses locally sourced **quahog clams** combined with clam juice, potatoes, onions, celery, bacon or salted pork, and milk or cream. Down along Buzzards Bay and neighboring Rhode Island, **Portuguese clam chowder** (tomatoes, spicy sausages, bell peppers,

garlic) is a legacy of the region's Iberian immigrants.

Quahogs and soft-shelled **littleneck clams** are also steamed and served with lemon wedges and melted butter. Both are also integral to a traditional clam bake, along with **scallops, mussels, oysters, shrimp, crab**, and **lobster**.

Given the seafaring heritage of ports like Gloucester, Chatham, and New Bedford, the state is one of the nation's best for fresh-off-the-boat fish. **Haddock, halibut, monkfish**, and **bluefin tuna** are the most common restaurant fish landed by Massachusetts fleets, although you can

also find **salmon, swordfish**, and **bluefish** on many menus. Even though the "scrod" doesn't exist, one of the state's homegrown seafood favorites is **baked stuffed scrod**: haddock or cod stuffed with breadcrumbs, butter, herbs and spices, and whatever else the cook feels like throwing in (crabmeat, clam juice, wine, etc.).

Boston lends its name to several iconic Bay State dishes. The city derives its "Beantown" nickname from **Boston baked beans**. This savory blend of molasses, salt pork or bacon, and navy beans was prepared by the city's 17th-century Puritans on Saturdays because they weren't allowed to cook on the Sabbath. Likewise for **Boston baked bread**, another Puritan favorite served alongside those Sabbath beans.

On the other hand, **Boston cream pie** is a 19th-century concoction, a decadent mix of yellow cake and vanilla custard with chocolate frosting declared the official state dessert by the commonwealth legislature.

The **Boston cream doughnut** (the official state doughnut) is basically a miniature version of the cream pie with a vanilla custard filling and

Sample classic New England fare, such as hearty clam chowder, at the historic Red Lion Inn in Stockbridge.

Dig for quahog clams—the predominant mollusk found in coves along the eastern seaboard—at low tide in Orleans Cove.

chocolate glaze. Among the state's other breakfast treasures are **apple cider doughnuts** and **grilled blueberry muffins**. The fabled **fluffernutter sandwich** involves two pieces of white bread filled with peanut butter and Marshmallow Fluff, a creamy marshmallow-like spread invented in Lynn, Massachusetts, by a couple of local lads who had recently served in World War I.

The nation's second largest **cranberry** grower, Massachusetts produces around 1.8 million barrels of the deep red fruit each year. They end up in all sorts of local foods and drinks, from jams, muffins, and Thanksgiving side dishes to pizzas, barbecue sauce, wassail mulled wine, and margaritas.

Chocolate chip cookies were famously invented in the late 1930s by Ruth Graves Wakefield at her family's Toll House Inn restaurant in Whitman, Massachusetts. Already a culinary innovator, Ruth decided to use chopped "chips" from a Nestlé semisweet chocolate bar in a cookie recipe instead of baking chocolate. Rather than melting into the dough, the chips kept their shape and enhanced the cookie's flavor.

CULINARY EXPERIENCES

Sample a range of maritime munchies at the **Boston Seafood Festival** (August), an outdoor event on Boston Fish Pier that features cooking demonstrations, an oyster-shucking contest, live

music, and people dressed up as pirates.

Year-round, local seafood and a wide range of other foods are available at two permanent locations in central Boston, one of them nearly 200 years old, the other a repurposed art deco building.

Founded in 1825 at the behest of Mayor Josiah Quincy, the historic **Quincy Market** has transitioned from a wholesale fish and produce emporium into one of the nation's original food halls, with a collection that includes the **Boston Chowda Co.** and **Ned Devine's Irish Pub**. Located in a cavernous 1920s structure that started life as a Sears and Roebuck warehouse, **Time Out Market Boston** near Fenway Park

Rich molasses and salty pork flavor batches of traditional Boston baked beans.

horse show, cider pressing, and a skillet-tossing competition.

Even though it's one of the most densely populated states, Massachusetts harbors more than 7,000 farms. The Massachusetts Department of Agricultural Resources website offers an online **Agriculture Tourism Map** with more than 400 farm attractions open to the public.

Among the family-focused farm visits are pick-your-own **Breezelands Orchards** near Sturbridge and **Davis Farmland** near Worcester, where kids can pick their own fruit, interact with farm animals, or

DUNKIN' COFFEE & DOUGHNUTS

If it seems like there's a Dunkin' on every other street corner in Massachusetts, it's because that's not far from the truth. The Bay State boasts more than 1,000 of the fast-food restaurants, which changed names from Dunkin' Donuts in 2019 to reflect its evolution from primarily coffee and baked goods into a range of all-day foods.

Dunkin' was an unexpected spin-off of World War II. During the war, shipyard worker Bill Rosenberg noticed a severe lack of breakfast and lunch choices near the factory. He decided to fill that void by starting an industrial catering service to serve workers in the Quincy area.

It soon became clear that coffee and doughnuts were far and away his best sellers. With that in mind, he founded a restaurant that became the first Dunkin' Donuts location in 1950. It's still there and still serving, at 543 Southern Artery in Quincy.

Since then, Dunkin' has exploded into more than 11,000 locations in 41 states and 36 countries around the world.

revolves around hip food and beverage outlets like chef Nina Festekjian's **Nu Burger** and the innovative Japanese cuisine (like nori sushi tacos) at **Gogo Ya**.

Bow Market in suburban Somerville boasts equally enticing eating options like the fresh, locally caught or harvested seafood of **Bluefin** and the decadent sandwiches of **Mike & Patty's**.

Out on the cape, the **Wellfleet OysterFest** (October) promises a "shucking good time" for all who attend. Wellfleet SPAT, which organizes the festival, also offers **shellfish farm tours** from July to September. Offshore, the Martha's Vineyard Agricultural Society stages an old-time **Living Local Harvest Festival** that includes local foods, a farmers market, a draft

navigate a huge seasonal corn maze with three miles (4.8 km) of corridors. **Cranberry Bog Tours** on Cape Cod offers guided tours of the state's largest organic cranberry farm, especially colorful in the fall when the ripened fruits are collected into bright red islands.

On the other hand, maple syrup boils (aka maple sugaring) are a late winter and early spring activity when the trees are tapped for their amber sap. Visitors can participate in the tapping process or watch how maple sugar is made at historic **Appleton Farms** (established in 1638) on the North Shore, **North Hadley Sugar Shack** in the Pioneer Valley, and during "Maple Days" at **Old Sturbridge Village**.

RESTAURANTS TO DIE FOR

Ask a dozen Bostonians and you'll probably get a dozen different answers on the best seafood in the Massachusetts metropolis— which means that prospective diners should probably zero in on location or specific dishes.

Tucked beneath a red-and-yellow circus tent beside the waterfront, the **Barking Crab** is hard to top for salty ambience or its heaping lobster and crab platters. At the opposite end of the Seaport District, **Legal Sea Foods—Harborside** offers one of the city's best all-around seafood menus, including an especially yummy clam chowder.

In the eatery-infused North End, two great seafood joints are found within yards of one another: **Neptune Oyster**, with its popular raw bar, and **Mare Oyster Bar**, which makes one of the city's best lobster rolls. With restaurants like **Saltie Girl** and its gourmet tinned seafood and offbeat dishes (tuna

Dusk outside Faneuil Hall Marketplace and Quincy Market in Boston

flatbread, lobster and waffles, torched salmon belly), and the stylish **Select Oyster Bar**, the Back Bay East area is another cluster of top-notch seafood. Nearby **Mooncusser** is renowned for its four-course seafood tasting menus.

Venturing beyond traditional seafood, **O Ya** restaurant serves some of the best sushi, nigiri, and sashimi on the East Coast, as well as a 20-course omakase dinner. **Chickadee** at the Boston Design Center offers Mediterranean-inspired surf and turf, while **Fox & the Knife Enoteca** features fresh fish and shellfish among its elevated Italian dishes.

Among the many laudable eating options in Boston's burbs are the hip **Tasting Counter** and modern Peruvian at **Celeste** in Somerville; **Scoop N Scootery** ice cream in Arlington; the Turkish and Middle Eastern cuisine of **Oleana** in Cambridge; **Mahaniyom** in Brookline with its Thai-style tapas; and the innovative New England food at **Town Meeting Bistro** with its alfresco Culinary Garden in Lexington.

Beyond Boston, up on the North Shore, Lynn's **Blue Ox** makes what many people consider the best burger in the Boston metro area. Meanwhile, the **Azorean Restaurant** in Gloucester presents awesome Portuguese island fare while **Mom's Kitchen** offers a chance to breakfast at 5 a.m. with the *Wicked Tuna* crowd.

Cape Cod also offers myriad dining choices that range from the classy French cuisine at **Chillingsworth** in Brewster to the vintage **Lobster Pot** in Provincetown and **Skipper Chowder House & Ice Cream Shack** in Yarmouth. For

Pickled shrimp and smoked oysters star on a serving board.

something truly special, try the Old World pastries and breads at **Provincetown Portuguese Bakery** (established in 1900) or the vodka- or tequila-infused oyster flutes at **Mac's Shack** in Wellfleet.

Local farmers and fisherfolk provide many of the ingredients that go into the New American dishes at the fashionable café **The Sweet Life** on Martha's Vineyard. Among the island's more casual eateries are **Red Cat Kitchen** and **Black Dog Dockside Café** near Oak Bluffs Harbor. Over on the mainland, the **Inn on Shipyard Park** offers a raw bar, fried seafood, and a fish or shellfish bake at historic waterfront digs in Mattapoisett.

In the Berkshires, fine dining is often served with a side dish of early American history. Among the region's oldest and most venerated culinary hot spots are the **Red Lion Inn** in Stockbridge (founded in 1773) and the **Old Inn on the Green** in New Marlborough (opened in 1760).

In central Massachusetts, **Ebenezer's Tavern** at the Publick House Historic Inn in Sturbridge (founded in 1771) offers traditional turkey dinner and baked scrod on its bill of fare. On the other hand, **Bocado** in Wooster is a thoroughly modern tapas and wine bar.

Students at Amherst and Hampshire College flock to **Atkins Farms**

Boiling sap during the Maple Days festival at Old Sturbridge Village

Country Market and its popular **Orchard Run Ice Cream** stand. Farther down the Pioneer Valley, Springfield's vintage **Student Prince & the Fort** restaurant (established in 1935) blends beer and traditional German foods like schnitzel, wurst, and sauerbraten.

BOTTOMS UP!

Brewed by the Boston Beer Company, **Samuel Adams** lager is the state's most well-known beer.

Despite the name, there is no connection to its namesake, the 18th-century politician and Founding Father. However, the original Sam Adams was in the beer business. His family owned a Boston barley malting house that Adams—a great patriot but a notoriously bad businessman—eventually inherited and drove into bankruptcy.

The flagship **Sam Adams Downtown Boston Taproom** overlooks the "Samuel Adams" statue by artist Anne Whitney outside Faneuil Hall. Tours and tastings are available at the Samuel Adams Boston Brewery in Jamaica Plain. **Harpoon Brewery** on the South Boston waterfront and **Downeast Cider House** at Jeffries Point also offer tours and tipples.

Several Boston neighborhoods are ripe for a classic pub crawl, including the sports bar–infused area around **Fenway Park**, Ivy League–certified **Harvard Yard**,

Boston's historic Fort Point Channel is home to the Barking Crab, a beloved meeting spot for locals.

and "townie" Broadway in **South Boston**, where the watering holes range from the sophisticated **Capo** and **Lincoln Tavern & Restaurant** to divey **Croke Park Whitey's**. If you don't want to drink alone, join **Boston Crawling's** "Independence Pub Crawl" of bars along the Freedom Trail.

Making your way up the food chain, Boston also boasts some cool cocktail lounges. Just off Boston Common, **Yvonne's** supper club offers several ornately decorated drinking spaces, including the underground **Gallery** bar, accessed via a hidden door behind a bookshelf in the Library dining room. A few blocks away, James Beard Award semifinalist **haley.henry** wine bar complements its fabulous vino with charcuterie boards and gourmet canned seafood.

Recently named one of the world's top 25 bars, the graffiti-laden **Backbar** anchors a casual but diverse nightlife scene in Somerville that blends Boston hipsters and the Tufts University crowd. Over in Woburn, **Baldwin & Sons Trading Co.** and its creative cocktails occupy the upper floor of the Sichuan Garden restaurant in the old Baldwin

A classic since 1984: Samuel Adams Boston Lager

Mansion. Boston's best sake bar is also in the burbs: the **Koji Club** in Brighton.

Cape Cod's nightlife scene runs a broad gamut, from traditional oceanfront hangouts like **the Beachcomber** in Wellfleet and the clubby **Thoreau's bar** in Harwich to the variety shows at the **Post Office Cafe and Cabaret** and drag queens at the **Crown & Anchor** in Provincetown.

The bar scene in western Massachusetts is equally diverse. **MoonCloud Lounge** in Great Barrington mixes some of the best cocktails in the Berkshires; try the Fuego en la Montaña with its jalapeño-infused mezcal. New England's oldest brewpub (established in 1987), **Northampton Brewery** in the Pioneer Valley flaunts a rooftop garden and wide-ranging libations from Black Cat Stout to Sap House Mead. ∎

THE REAL FIRST THANKSGIVING

Though it's nice to imagine the Pilgrims and Wampanoag people arrayed around a long wooden table gobbling roast turkey, candied yams, mashed potatoes, and pumpkin pie with copious amounts of spiked eggnog, the reality of that first Thanksgiving in 1621 is something far different.

Edward Winslow's eyewitness account says they "entertained and

feasted" for three days rather than a single supper, and that there were five deer contributed by the Wampanoag and miscellaneous birds shot by a "fowling" hunt commissioned by the Plymouth Colony's governor.

The rest of the menu wasn't recorded, but the feast probably included fish and shellfish, cornmeal porridge, squash and other

indigenous root crops, wild plums, and various types of berries.

In 1649, Connecticut was the first colony to declare Thanksgiving an official holiday, a full 20 years before the Massachusetts Bay Colony. President Washington made it a national holiday in 1789, and Abraham Lincoln fixed Thanksgiving as the last Thursday in November.

Michigan

Michigan's diverse gastronomic world varies from Detroit's sophisticated dining scene to the Fruit Belt and vintage ethnic eateries on the Upper Peninsula.

THE BIG PICTURE

Founded: 1837

Population: 10 million

Official State Fish: Brook trout

Also Known As: Great Lakes State, Wolverine State

Culinary Influences: African American, German, Dutch, Middle Eastern

Don't Miss: Mackinac Island, Detroit, Grand Rapids

Claim to Fame: Detroit-style pizza, pasty, Coney dogs, Kellogg's Corn Flakes

Cherries don't grace the Michigan state flag, but they probably should. The state grows around 75 percent of the nation's tart cherries, and cherries are the official state fruit. Three types are grown in the Fruit Belt along the western edge of the Lower Peninsula: the Montmorency tart, Balaton tart, and Michigan sweet cherries.

Cherries that aren't shipped across the country end up in locally made **cherry pies, preserves, salsa**, and other flavorsome foods, along with **cherry wine** in Traverse City.

Michigan also produces more **cucumbers** than any other state, with the lion's share slated for transformation into **pickles** by Vlasic in Imlay City, Hausbeck in Saginaw,

and a growing number of small, artisanal pickle makers.

Bordering four out of the five Great Lakes, Michigan also shines at freshwater fish. **Lake perch, pickerel**, and **whitefish** are the most common on restaurant menus. Those angling for their meals can add **trout, salmon, muskellunge**, and **splake** to the list.

Michigan's homegrown lunch specialties include the **Cudighi** sausage sandwich (aka Yooper Italian sandwich) from the Upper Peninsula and the **ground or fried bologna sandwich** of Detroit and other spots on the Lower Peninsula.

The Upper Peninsula is a hotbed for two other iconic Michigan dishes. Originally introduced by 19th-century Cornish miners, **pasties** are savory handheld pastries traditionally stuffed with beef, rutabaga, carrot, onion, and potato. Nowadays chicken and vegetarian versions are widely available. *Pannukakku* (pancakes with berry sauce or maple syrup) became a U.P. breakfast favorite via Finnish immigrants to the region.

Check out Al-Ameer Restaurant in Dearborn for authentic Mediterranean, including the falafel sandwich.

Cherry pies come fresh out of the oven bubbly and golden at the Grand Traverse Pie Company in Traverse City.

CULINARY EXPERIENCES

With nicknames like the "cherry republic" and "world's cherry capital," Traverse City wants the entire planet to know that the little red pitted fruits are its pride and joy. Founded in 1925, the city's **National Cherry Festival** (July) features cherry pit–spitting and cherry pie–eating contests and three cherry-themed parades. Year-round, the **Grand Traverse Pie Company** churns out tasty cherry pies, muffins, turnovers, and other baked goods. During the July cherry-harvesting season, visitors can pick their own at **King Orchards**.

Farther up the Fruit Belt, the **Charlevoix Apple Fest** (October) celebrates the local apple harvest, while the **National Morel Mushroom Festival** in Boyne City offers mushroom sales, seminars, tasting sessions, and an evening wine and dine. About halfway down the state's Lake Michigan coast, the Oceana County towns of Hart and Shelby host the **National Asparagus Festival** (June).

A Battle Creek tradition for more than half a century, the **World's Longest Breakfast Table** (aka National Cereal Festival) features free Frosted Flakes, Rice Krispies, Froot Loops, and other Kellogg's cereals to more than 25,000 people seated at a 2,800-foot-long (853 m) table along McCamly Street.

Detroit's historic **Eastern Market** (opened in 1891) hosts a year-round Saturday farmers market, as well as summertime Sunday and Tuesday markets. The restored redbrick building is also the cornerstone of two culinary festivals that run simultaneously in September: the **Detroit Foodie Fair** and **Detroit Vegan**. Housed in the lobby of the exquisite art deco Fisher Building, the **Pure Detroit** boutique peddles Stella Good Coffee, Better Made in Michigan potato chips, Urban Slicer pizza seasoning, and other Motor City foodstuffs.

RESTAURANTS TO DIE FOR

Set behind the huge arching gateways that once disgorged fire

Taste the original Detroit-style pizza, invented in 1946 at Buddy's.

Park offers gourmet fried bologna on a potato waffle with cream cheese jalapeño peppers, while **Green Dot Stables** near downtown makes fried bologna sliders and a wide range of other mini burgers. With its large Arab American population, Dearborn is the place for excellent Eastern Mediterranean restaurants like **Al-Ameer**.

Ann Arbor reflects its immigrant roots in restaurants like **Amadeus**, where the menu features pierogi, kielbasa, goulash, pork cutlets, and other Hungarian, Polish, and Austrian favorites. The trend continues at **Zingerman's Deli**, where diners can add sides like latkes, knishes, and kugels to a wide range of gourmet sandwiches. At the elegant **Divani** in Grand Rapids, surf or turf dinners should always be punctuated with one of their sumptuous desserts.

Mackinac Island offers numerous dining options, but none as charming as the "farm-to-ferry" dining at **Chianti**, where the five-course set menus come with panoramic views of Lake Huron. Heritage eateries—like **Lawry's Pasty Shop** in Marquette, **Suomi Home Bakery & Restaurant** with its Finnish specialties in Houghton, and **Ralph's Italian Deli** in

engines from Detroit's fire department headquarters, the **Apparatus Room** exemplifies the city's downtown renaissance with both its interior design and upscale New American cuisine. The new kid in town, **Freya** opened to raves in late 2021 and has an open-plan kitchen where the culinary team creates audacious tasting menus with dishes like Michigan whitefish bao, wild boar chops, and a range of vegan options.

With more than a dozen outlets in the metro area, including downtown Detroit, **Buddy's Pizza** is the foremost purveyor of local square-cut pies with specialty pizzas

named in honor of Motown, Henry Ford, the Detroit Zoo, and the Eastern Market.

Grey Ghost Detroit in Brush

WILLIAM DUFTY & MACROBIOTICS

Born in Grand Rapids in 1916, William Dufty had already earned a reputation as an outstanding journalist and biographer *(Lady Sings the Blues)* when he began searching for a healthier alternative to the traditional American diet.

He eventually settled on macrobiotics. Founded by Japanese educator George Ohsawa and heavily influenced by Eastern philosophical principles like yin and yang—the diet revolves around grains, fruits, vegetables, fish, and soy products rather than meat.

Along with his wife, Gloria Swanson, and influential friends like John Lennon and Yoko Ono, Dufty helped make macrobiotics one of the fad diets of the late 1960s and '70s.

Ishpeming—reflect the eclectic culinary heritage along the Lake Superior shore of the Upper Peninsula.

BOTTOMS UP!

Along with the automobile assembly line and traffic signals, Michigan gave birth to American-style **ginger ale** when Detroit pharmacist James Vernor concocted the fizzy libation in 1866. Founded by Russian immigrant brothers in 1907, Detroit's **Faygo soda pop** has expanded from an original three flavors to more than 50 different kinds.

Despite its name, the refreshing **Boston Cooler**—which combines Vernors Ginger Ale and vanilla ice cream—was actually invented in Detroit. Vanilla ice cream also goes into **the Hummer**, a milkshake-like rum and Kahlúa cocktail created at the city's Bayview Yacht Club long before the name was applied to a vehicle.

Detroit's eclectic bar scene runs an incredibly broad gamut, from the ritzy **Monarch Club** in the neo-Gothic Metropolitan Building and **Baker's Keyboard Lounge** (one of the world's oldest and most celebrated jazz clubs) to newbies like the **UFO Factory** with its record-release parties and the **Cadieux Café** in Grosse Pointe, a Belgian-themed bar serving monastery beer, steamed mussels, and pommes frites with mayonnaise alongside games of feather bowling.

Forgo the student bars in Ann Arbor and head straight for **the Ark**, the city's leading music club. In the other college town, the **Lansing Brewing Company** is the modern artisanal incarnation of a brewery originally founded in 1898.

After toiling in the copper pits of the Upper Peninsula, miners often knocked back a few cold ones at local taverns and dive bars. Some have endured into the 21st century, like **Shute's Saloon** in Calumet and **the Ambassador** in Houghton.

Those looking for quality wine don't have to hop the Atlantic. Traverse City sits on the 45th parallel, the same latitude as Bordeaux and the Rhone Valley. Vineyards here boast quality Rieslings, Chardonnay, and Merlot. ∎

Divani's bourbon-based Smokey! cocktail is infused with cinnamon-flavored smoke.

Minnesota

Already renowned for its North Woods and Nordic bounty, the Land of 10,000 Lakes now boasts a rich and diverse global food scene.

THE BIG PICTURE

Founded: 1858

Population: 5.72 million

Official State Mushroom: Morel

Also Known As: North Star State

Culinary Influences: Swedish, Norwegian, Sioux, Hmong

Don't Miss: Minneapolis, Duluth, St. Paul

Claim to Fame: Hot dish, wild rice soup, lutefisk

Scandinavian immigrants have had a profound effect on the Minnesota culinary scene. Among the state's signature dishes are **lutefisk** (pickled whitefish) and **lefse** (potato flatbread) as well as **Norwegian** *kransekake* (ring cakes). Though the northern European palate remains strong, recent years have seen an influx of immigrants from around the world who have transformed the Minneapolis–St. Paul Twin Cities region into a culinary melting pot.

The bounty of the lake-spangled North Woods contributes other iconic Minnesota dishes like the **walleye fish sandwich**, tasty **morel mushrooms**, the **wild rice** found in numerous dishes, and **strawberry delight salad**. Pineapple chunks, marshmallows, whipped cream, and mushy rice are the main ingredients of **glorified rice**, a supersweet summer dessert popular at Minnesota picnics and community gatherings. Another potluck favorite is **hot dish**, a casserole that normally features ground beef, mushroom soup, and either macaroni or Tater Tots, with melted cheese on top.

Sweet, firm, red-and-yellow **Honeycrisp apples** are the official state fruit. Literally born and bred in the Land of 10,000 Lakes, the cultivar was created at the state's horticultural research center at the University of Minnesota in the 1970s. Meanwhile, the unofficial state candy bar is the **Nut Goodie**, a peanut, milk chocolate, and maple nougat confection manufactured by Pearson's Candy Co. in Minneapolis since 1912.

Another edible with local roots is the **Juicy Lucy burger**, which entails wrapping a slice of cheese inside two thin beef patties, resulting in a molten core of melted cheese that oozes out with each bite. Two different Minneapolis bars claim invention of the Juicy Lucy during the mid-20th century. What about the burger's namesake? Lucy remains a mystery.

CULINARY EXPERIENCES

Ingebretsen's on Lake Street in the Corcoran neighborhood has been the go-to place for Scandinavian foods in the Twin Cities region since Norwegian immigrant Charles Ingebretsen opened the store in 1921. The deli counter offers lutefisk and lefse as well as a wide variety of Scandinavian-style meats and cheeses. There's also a vast array of imported gourmet foods, from Söderblandning teas and lingonberry concentrate to

Lefses (Norwegian potato flatbreads, shown with sour cream) are similar to crepes.

Ice fishermen collect their catch atop a frozen lake at sunset.

canned fish balls and Swedish pancake mix.

The nearby **Midtown Global Market** lives up to its name with edibles from Mexico and Venezuela, Morocco and the Middle East, Cambodia and Thailand, and East Africa. Wash it all down at the market's **Eastlake Craft Brewery**. And plan your visit for special events like Family Fridays with its live music, or free salsa dance lessons every other Sunday.

Staged over two weeks leading up to Labor Day, the **Minnesota State Fair** in St. Paul features wildly popular competitions to determine the best baked products and canned and preserved foods. The variety is mind-boggling: more than 100 baking and 80 canned/preserved categories ranging from berry jams to ethnic breads.

St. Paul's delectable **Uptown Food Truck Festival** (July and August) is no longer just uptown after spreading its wings to suburban Hopkins and Anoka. Meanwhile, the **Twin Cities Veg Fest** in September is the largest plant-based food gathering in the Midwest. These are relatively new events compared with old-fashioned rural food festivals like **Preston Trout Days** (May), **Henderson Sauerkraut Days** (June), the Deer River Lions Club's **Wild Rice Festival** (July), and **Potato Days** in Barnesville (August).

RESTAURANTS TO DIE FOR

Chef/owner Gavin Kaysen has crafted incredibly diverse eating adventures at **Demi** and its sister restaurant **Spoon and Stable** in the Minneapolis Warehouse District beside the Mississippi River. Out in

the burbs, **Travail Kitchen and Amusements** in Robbinsdale complements its industrial chic decor with an awesome tasting menu, gourmet dinner series, and a food-centric lakeside party each summer.

The itsy-bitsy **Nook** café in St. Paul has what many aficionados consider the best Juicy Lucy burgers in Minnesota. They offer four different kinds, including pepper Jack cheese and chorizo sausage versions, plus Cutie Lucy sliders. On the other side of the river, **Matt's Bar & Grill** and the **5-8 Club** also have their Juicy Lucy advocates. Not in the mood for a stuffed burger? Try the legendary homemade soups and corned beef sandwiches at **Cecil's Deli** in St. Paul (opened in 1949) or North Woods–inspired dishes like walleye fish-and-chips or bison

Benedict at **Hell's Kitchen** in downtown Minneapolis.

The most unexpected aspect of Twin Cities dining is the global food scene. You can eat your way around the world. **FIKA Café** at the American Swedish Institute in Minneapolis specializes in Nordic fare like gravlax, Swedish meatballs, and aquavit cocktails. The journey continues at **Red Sea Ethiopian, Victor's 1959 Café** Cuban cooking, **Pimento Jamaican Kitchen & Rum Bar, Hai Hai** Vietnamese, and the offbeat but delicious blend of Korean and Latin American dishes (like Korean pork tacos) at **Sooki & Mimi**.

Farther downstream, **Meritage** in downtown St. Paul brings a touch of Paris to the Twin Cities with its classic French cuisine and sidewalk seating. At the other end of the state capital's dining spectrum, the **HmongTown Marketplace** in Frogtown offers dozens of stalls with tasty Thai, Vietnamese, and Laotian foods, plus a daily farmers market with more Asian goodies.

BOTTOMS UP!

Between the **All Pints North** beer festival in July and outstanding lakefront breweries like **Fitger's Brewhouse** and **Canal Park Brewing**, Duluth is the undisputed champion of Minnesota craft beer. But with long, cold winters, the city on Lake Superior also produces other warm-your-body-and-soul libations, like the craft vodka, gin, whiskey, and aquavit of **Vikre Distillery** and the creative craft cocktails and "fauxtails" at **Black Water Lounge** in the landmark Greysolon Plaza building.

Two Ojibwe ricers navigate gentle waters in their canoe.

The cheese-stuffed Juicy Lucy, created at the 5-8 Club in Minneapolis

Jesse James and the Younger Brothers are long gone. But you can toast to the courageous residents who thwarted their 1876 raid on the town during the annual **Defeat of Jesse James Days** in September or any time of year at the **Contented Cow**, a modern saloon on the same street where the fabled shoot-out took place.

Minneapolis sports a diverse drinks scene that stretches from the super-chill **Prohibition Bar** on the 27th floor of the W hotel to **Gori Gori Peku**, a Japanese whisky bar in the Warehouse District. One of the city's most unique alcohol encounters is **Upstairs Circus MPLS**, which combines regularly scheduled DIY arts and crafts socials (like woodwork, leatherwork, and jewelry making) with creative sippers from the bar. For those who crave nothing more than cold beer and cool tunes, duck into **Palmer's Bar** near the University of Minnesota campus. ∎

INDIGENOUS EATS

Minnesota's Native American nations are not just reviving Indigenous cuisine for their own enjoyment. They're making traditional dishes that have been around for hundreds of years accessible to anyone who wants to sample the region's original foods.

Hand-harvested *manoomin* (wild rice, which is actually an aquatic grass), blue corn mush, elk, and Three Sisters salad are a few of the traditional Dakota, Lakota, and Ojibwe dishes on the menu at

Owamni by the Sioux Chef restaurant in Minneapolis.

Beyond his restaurant, the James Beard Award–winning Sean Sherman of the Sioux Chef has created the nonprofit **Indigenous Food Lab** to research and promote the cultivation and use of Indigenous foods and train Native American chefs in preparation methods. The lab is currently developing a test kitchen and restaurant at Midtown Global Market in Minneapolis.

Mississippi

Southern comfort and soul food dominate the gastronomic landscape of a state where good food is often paired with live tunes and music history.

THE BIG PICTURE

Founded: 1817

Population: 2.94 million

Official State Fish: Largemouth/black bass

Also Known As: Magnolia State

Culinary Influences: Mexican, African, Slovenian, Czech, French

Don't Miss: Clarksdale, Jackson, Biloxi

Claim to Fame: Biscuits, Mississippi mud pie, catfish, hush puppies

If Elvis Presley adored the **peanut butter, banana, and bacon sandwiches** his mother made while growing up in Tupelo, does that mean the dish should be considered as one of Mississippi's official foods?

Possibly, although the Magnolia State offers a lot of other dishes that could also qualify. Especially things that come from the water, like the **blue crabs** netted along the Gulf Coast or **catfish** and **largemouth bass** angled from the Mississippi River and other freshwater lakes, streams, and bayous.

And the Elvis (as the sandwich is often called) isn't even close to being the state's most bizarre sandwich. Mississippi's beloved **slugburger**, which features a patty comprising ground beef mixed with flour, cornmeal, grits, or another binder, derives its rather unappetizing name from the fact that it cost a nickel (or one "slug") when it was first devised during the Great Depression. On the other hand, the **pig ear sandwich** really does contain pig ears.

Just about any Mississippi sandwich or meat dish could come with a healthy dollop of **comeback sauce**. Originally invented by a Jackson restaurant, the topping blends just about every condiment including ketchup, mustard, and mayonnaise, with chili sauce and Worcestershire sauce to give it a little kick.

As one of the fonts of southern cooking and soul food, Mississippi's culinary catalog also embraces heirloom dishes like **collard greens, cornbread, biscuits and gravy, shrimp and grits**, and **sweet potato pie**. Another popular side is **pickles**, preferably fried or marinated in Kool-Aid.

Baked cheese straws flavored with cayenne pepper is a longtime Mississippi snack, while local dessert tables often feature **caramel cakes, Mississippi mud pies**, or **butter cookies**.

CULINARY EXPERIENCES

Filet, whole, nuggets, baked, breaded, or blackened are a few

Fried cornmeal catfish is made even better by a generous serving of tangy comeback sauce.

Borroum's Drug Store & Soda Fountain in Corinth, Mississippi

of the ways the headliner fish is served at the **World Catfish Festival** (April) in Belzoni, an event that also features the Miss Catfish Pageant and lots of local blues, gospel, and country music.

The **Pelahatchie Muscadine Jubilee** (September) revolves around a strain of wild grape (*Vitis rotundifolia*) native to Mississippi and other southeastern states. In addition to a celebrity grape stomp, the festival offers a chance to sample muscadine jams, juice, and wine.

Chefs from New Orleans and Baton Rouge join local restaurants at the **Natchez Food & Wine Festival** (July), which culminates in a Friday evening alfresco Tastings Along the River.

Discover the epicurean delights of Mississippi's most erudite city with **Oxford Food Tours**, which offers a Booze & Bites Cocktail Tour and Historic Oxford Square Walking Food Tour.

RESTAURANTS TO DIE FOR

Jackson's repute as the state's fine dining hub took a huge leap with the debut of **Elvie's** all-day café in 2020. Named for owner/chef Hunter Evans's grandmother, the house specialty is a seven-course tasting menu. The city's go-to surf and turf spot is **Char Restaurant**, which also lays on an outstanding brunch.

Down along the coast, **Mary Mahoney's Old French House** in Biloxi offers coastal classics like seafood gumbo, crab imperial, and jumbo broiled shrimp inside an elegant French colonial mansion built in 1737. Farther along the Mississippi shore, **the Chimneys** offers more elevated southern-style seafood on Gulfport Beach.

Oxford's elite eateries range from the raw bar and Creole cuisine at the stylish **Snackbar** to the **Ajax Diner** on Courthouse Square and a menu peppered with local favorites like fried catfish, fried pickles, turnip greens, and sweet tea. In the countryside near Oxford, **Taylor Grocery & Restaurant** in Taylor is renowned for catfish and other southern comfort foods served inside a clapboard building that opened in 1889 as a dry goods store.

Whether you're revisiting Highway 61 or driving the Mississippi River road for the first time, good food and great music are inseparable. Opened in 1924, **Abe's Bar-B-Q** in Clarksdale makes awesome beef, pork, and chicken sandwiches near the Delta Blues Museum and right

beside the crossroads where blues legend Robert Johnson famously sold his soul to the devil.

A couple of blocks from the B.B. King Museum & Delta Interpretive Center in Indianola, the **Crown Restaurant** offers entrées with creamy Florentine sauce or rich buttery Allison sauce, catfish salad, sandwiches, and cakes. By the time you reach Natchez, the cuisine offers a fleeting taste of New Orleans, as personified by the eggplant Orleans, pork tenderloin grillades, and beignets that accompany the live music at **Biscuits & Blues**.

Up in the state's northeast corner, **Borroum's Drug Store & Soda Fountain** in Corinth was founded by a Civil War veteran, although its classic soda fountain wasn't added until the 1930s. Complement your slugburger or cornbread salad with an old-fashioned milkshake or root beer float. There's a good chance that young Elvis Presley munched a burger or BLT at **Johnnie's Drive-In**, just a six-minute walk from the two-room Tupelo house where he was born a few years before the restaurant opened.

BOTTOMS UP!

Mississippi was the last state to repeal Prohibition, finally axing the dreaded act in 1966. Well into the 21st century, many counties remained dry. But elsewhere, beverage culture is booming.

Ole Miss college students and a thriving arts sector stoke a lively bar scene in Oxford. Among its dozens of watering holes are the rooftop **Coop** in the Graduate Hotel; **City Grocery** on Courthouse Square; the amazing array of cocktails, liqueurs,

Cozy up for a sipper under the trees at the Library Lounge in Jackson.

HOT TAMALE HOTBED

It may seem implausible, given that Mississippi is nowhere near the United States–Mexico border, but tamales are a longtime local favorite and inextricably linked to Delta blues.

Various theories abound on how the iconic Mexican dish, which originated among Mesoamerican people at least 5,000 years ago, became a Mississippi darling.

Some experts think troops returning from the 1840s Mexican War may have brought home tamales; others postulate they were introduced by early 20th-century Mexican agrarian workers. Robert Johnson's 1936 blues song "They're Red Hot" idolized a female tamale vendor.

Among the many places to sample Delta-style tamales are the **Big Apple Inn** in Jackson, **White Front Café (Joe's Hot Tamale Place)** in Rosedale, and **Solly's Hot Tamales** in Vicksburg.

A stack of tamales from the Big Apple Inn in Jackson

and wines at **Saint Leo lounge**; and the **Apothecary at Brent's Drugs**, a 21st-century addition to a vintage pharmacy that also nurtures a classic 1940s soda fountain.

Mississippi's literary heritage is on full display at the **Library Lounge** inside Jackson's historic Fairview Inn. In addition to first editions by William Faulkner, Tennessee Williams, John Grisham, and other Magnolia State scribes, the bar boasts a collection of Civil War books and "author's drinks" like the Faulkner Mint Julep, Alice Walker Celebration, and Shelby Foote Mason Dixon.

Craft beer thrives along the state's short but action-packed Gulf Coast. **Lazy Magnolia Brewing** started the trend two decades ago with a brewery and taproom in the little bayou town of Kiln near Bay St. Louis. Others followed suit, including **Chandeleur Island Brewing Co.** in Gulfport, the **Cypress Taphouse** in Ocean Springs, and **Colludium Brewing Company** in Hattiesburg, where patrons can guzzle Dungeons & Flagons bitter or Basic Rule Set ale while playing one of the taproom's 100-plus board games. ■

Missouri

From Kansas City barbecue to St. Louis–style pizza, Missouri is celebrated for unique dishes that were born and raised in the Show-Me State.

St. Louis has always had an uncanny knack for inventing new foods or modifying already existing dishes.

Legend holds that the first **ice-cream cones** were popularized at the St. Louis World's Fair of 1904, when an ice-cream vendor used rolled waffles borrowed from an adjoining food stand as a replacement for paper cups. **Gooey butter cake** was another accident, invented by a baker who added way too much butter to his coffee cake.

Toasted ravioli was also happenstance, conceived in the 1940s when a cook at Charlie Gitto's restaurant unintentionally dropped uncooked raviolis into boiling oil rather than water. However, a retired opera singer intentionally invented **St. Louis–style pizza** with its superthin crust and **Provel cheese**.

Many of the city's Chinese eateries offer the **St. Paul sandwich**, which features egg foo young, lettuce, tomatoes, and pickles between two slices of white bread. The

THE BIG PICTURE

Founded: 1821

Population: 6.18 million

Official State Dessert: Ice-cream cone

Also Known As: Show-Me State

Culinary Influences: German, African, Chinese, Italian

Don't Miss: St. Louis, Kansas City, Columbia

Claim to Fame: Ice-cream cones, hot salami sandwiches, burnt ends, gooey butter cake

Gerber sandwich (ham and Provel cheese on garlic bread) and **Amighetti's submarine sandwich** (ham, roast beef, salami, and Swiss cheese on a French roll) also hail from the Gateway City.

The St. Louis **slinger** plate

Toasted garlic-and-cheese ravioli with a sprinkling of Parmesan

Glazing smoky ribs with a Kansas City–style sauce

combines fried eggs, two hamburger patties, fried potatoes or hash browns, chili, cheese, and onions. St. Louis–style frozen custard is often called a **"concrete"** because it's so thick it won't fall out even if you turn the cup upside down.

As the onetime home of the nation's second largest stockyards (after Chicago), Kansas City has a culinary scene shaped by easy access to top-notch beef. **Kansas City–style barbecue**, with its slow-smoked meat and sweet tomato-based sauce, was largely developed by African American culinary trailblazers like Henry Perry and Arthur Bryant. **Burnt ends** are the most celebrated offshoot of the city's thriving barbecue culture.

CULINARY EXPERIENCES

The **American Royal World Series of Barbecue** takes place in Kansas City, Kansas. But there's still plenty of grilling action during the **Q Kansas City BBQ Festival** at Arrowhead Stadium (May). **Taste of Kansas City Food Tours** includes a top-notch barbecue joint in its popular Lip Smacking Foodie Tour, while booze is the focal point of their evening KC Prohibition Tour.

Delicious smoked meat and traditional Ozark music infuse the **Bluegrass & BBQ Festival** in Branson (May). Among Springfield's annual food events are **A Taste of SoMo** (June) and the **Ozark Berry Festival** (September). While Missouri Rhineland wine

and German-style sausages are the headliners at the **Hermann Wurstfest** (March), the happening also features sauerkraut-making classes and wiener dog races.

The Soulard neighborhood on the south side of St. Louis is famed for the sprawling **Soulard Farmers Market** (founded in 1779 as the first public market west of the Mississippi River) and the month-long **Soulard Mardi Gras** (January–February), which includes Taste of Soulard pub and restaurant crawl, the Bud Light Party Tent, and the Cajun Cook-Off.

RESTAURANTS TO DIE FOR

Connoisseurs continue to disagree on the best barbecue joint in Kansas City. Some prefer the burnt ends at **Arthur Bryant's Barbeque** near the Negro Leagues Baseball Museum, while others are partial to **Harp Barbecue** in suburban Raytown or **Jack Stack Barbecue** in the Crossroads Arts District.

Still, KC dining is more than smoked meat. At the classy **Corvino Supper Club & Tasting Room**, chef Michael Corvino has crafted innovative, modern versions of American classics like pork, ribs, rib eye, and fried chicken. Three other top eateries offer elevated ethnic fare: Mexican at **Jarocho**, Mediterranean at the **Antler Room**, and Franco-American at **Pot Pie**.

Many of the oldest, more traditional Italian restaurants in St. Louis—like **Charlie Gitto's** and **Mama's on the Hill**—are located on the Hill, a historic Italian American neighborhood. In nearby Maplewood, **Acero** renders modern Italian cuisine in a small, designer dining room.

Among the Gateway City's other top spots are the award-winning **Vicia** with its Farmer's Feast menus, the terrific Mediterranean cuisine at **Casa Don Alfonso**, and the innovative takes on surf and turf at the **Sidney Street Cafe**. But for good old concrete frozen custard, **Ted Drewes Frozen Custard** (founded in 1930) is still the place.

Venturing up the Missouri River, Hermann is renowned for Germanic restaurants like the **Hermann Wurst Haus** and diner-like **Swiss Meat & Sausage Co**. In Jefferson City, **Imo's Pizza** is a hot spot for St. Louis–style pies. At nearby Lake of the Ozarks,

Stewart's has been serving local faves like country biscuits and gravy, fried steak, and beer-battered onion rings since 1953. Another Ozark eating institution, **A Slice of Pie** in Rolla bakes chocolate cappuccino cheesecake, bumbleberry pie from four different berries, and dozens of other sweet things. At **Lambert's Cafe** in Ozark (and two other locations), their famous "throwed rolls" are literally flung across the dining room.

BOTTOMS UP!

German immigrants may have stoked Missouri's beer culture, but they also influenced other libations. The state's Rhineland region (or **Hermann AVA**) along the Missouri River between St. Louis and Jefferson City harbors more than half a dozen

The fresh flavors of southern Italy grace tables at Casa Don Alfonso in St. Louis.

The lush setting of Hermannhof Winery in Hermann

wineries. Founded in 1847 as the state's first winery, **Stone Hill** was the world's third largest wine producer before Prohibition and nowadays makes a range of regular, sparkling, and dessert wines.

Anheuser-Busch is the most famous name in Missouri beer, but the Show-Me State offers plenty of other amber options like **Perennial** **Artisan Ales** and **Side Project Brewing** in St. Louis, **Boulevard Brewing Co.** in Kansas City, **Mother's Brewing Company** in Springfield, and **Logboat Brewing Co.** in Columbia. For sheer novelty, **Prison Brews** replicates the jailhouse ambience of the nearby Missouri State Penitentiary (now closed) in Jefferson City.

Among the many watering holes in Kansas City's redeveloped Stockyards District are **Amigoni Urban Winery** (try its Missouri-made Cabernet Franc, Cabernet Sauvignon, Chardonnay, and Viognier made with local grapes), the creative cocktails of **the Campground**, and live music at **Lucky Boys** dive bar. In nearby Midtown, **Mesob Restaurant and Rum Bar** complements its extensive distilled menu with Ethiopian and Caribbean cuisine.

Switchgrass Spirits offers tours and tastings of its whiskey and brandy distillery in St. Louis. The **Gin Room** near Tower Grove Park stocks 300 varieties of its namesake botanical spirit, while **Planter's House** near Lafayette Square focuses on innovative craft cocktails like You Betrayed Me and No I Didn't. Perhaps the most pleasant place to quaff a cold brew in St. Louis is the **Boathouse at Forest Park**. ■

ANHEUSER-BUSCH: THE KING OF BEER

St. Louis soapmaker Eberhard Anheuser and his son-in-law Adolphus Busch, both German immigrants, started their collaboration in the 1850s after the latter's service in the Civil War.

Innovations like pasteurization, refrigerated railroad cars, advertising, and mass-bottling allowed them to ship their beer across the nation and become the first national beer brand. During a fact-finding trip to Europe to study brewing methods, Busch was especially impressed by the beer brewed in the Bohemian town of Budweis and decided to "borrow" the name for their new Budweiser beer.

The Busch family maintained control until 2008. By then, it was the world's largest brewer. The company now offers brewery tours in 12 U.S. cities, including the historic 19th-century flagship in St. Louis.

Montana

The very definition of farm-to-table, Montana's culinary world thrives on locally grown and sourced ingredients.

Montana doesn't boast an official state food, a fact that prompted the *Flathead Beacon* newspaper to ask local chefs and foodies what dish most represents the Treasure State. Opinions ranged from **bison burgers** and **pork chop sandwich** to Native American **fry bread** and the **pasty meat pies** introduced by long-ago Cornish miners.

The only thing that people seemed to agree on is that **huckleberries** should be near the top of

Montana's food pyramid, either on their own or combined with other popular dishes. Like namesake Huckleberry Finn, the tiny fruits are game for just about anything: pies, pastries, and pancakes, ice cream and milkshakes, barbecue sauce and salad dressing, coffee and tea, martinis and craft beer.

Flathead cherries are another passion. A microclimate around big Flathead Lake—warmer winters than the surrounding terrain—

enables cultivation of sweet treats. They aren't a cultivar per se, but rather a variety of different cherries (such as Lambert, Lapins, Bing, Rainier) that farmers grow around

THE BIG PICTURE

Founded: 1889

Population: 1.12 million

Official State Fish: Blackspotted cutthroat trout

Also Known As: Treasure State

Culinary Influences: English, French, multiple Native American tribes

Don't Miss: Bozeman, Whitefish, Missoula

Claim to Fame: Huckleberries, steak, hot dogs

Huckleberry bear claws fresh from the oven at Polebridge Mercantile & Bakery

Dine alongside the Blackfoot River at Cliffside Camp at the Resort at Paws Up in Greenough.

the lakeshore. Once again, Montanans employ the fruit in a range of foods, from cherry cobbler and cherry chicken salad to cherry juice and cherry vodka.

Two of Montana's major crops, **wheat** and **barley**, are among the seven grains that feature in **Cream of the West** hot cereal, produced in the state since 1914. Montana also grows around 40 percent of the nation's **lentils** each year, far more than any other state. The lens-shaped legumes feature in numerous recipes recommended by Great Falls–based **Timeless Natural Food**, which produces a line of lentils, chickpeas, and ancient grains grown in Montana.

Another local favorite, the **Pickle Barrel sandwich** is a Montana version of a sub or hero invented in the 1970s by a couple of Bozeman restaurant owners. Cold or hot, they can feature any number of meat fillings with Monterey Jack, provolone, or Swiss cheese and a sprinkling of greens.

CULINARY EXPERIENCES

Montana's favorite fruits take center stage at the **Huckleberry Festival** in Trout Creek (August) and the **Flathead Cherry Festival** in Polson (July). The former includes a hotly contested huckleberry pie–eating contest, while the latter reaches a fever pitch during a cherry pit–spitting competition.

Find a number of pick-your-own farms around Flathead Lake during cherry season (late July to early August), including **Hockaday Orchards** at Angel Point on the western shore and **Bowman Orchards** near Woods Bay on the east side.

Sprawling across four city blocks, **Yellowstone Valley Farmers Market** in Billings features more than 60 farmers and craft food vendors hawking fresh produce and gourmet foods produced within a 120-mile (193 km) radius of the southern Montana city.

Montana's ultimate foodie happening is **Master Chefs** at **Paws Up**, an upscale wilderness resort and dude ranch that stages a three-day gourmet feast each fall with meals prepared by some of the nation's leading chefs. The event includes three nights' accommodation and all meals. Paws Up also presents the **Wonder Women of Food & Wine** (April), **Montana Master Grillers** (May), and **Fish & Feast** (September).

Chico Hot Springs Resort in Paradise Valley has more great eats and offers an intimate private experience in the Tasting Room wine cellar that includes a seven- or 12-course chef's tasting menu with exceptional wine pairings.

RESTAURANTS TO DIE FOR

Montana doesn't disappoint when it comes to straight-off-the-ranch beef. **Silver Star Steak Company** in Helena complements its filet mignon and New York strip

with live country music several nights each week. For anyone with a massive appetite, **Lolo Creek Steak House** near Missoula features a 24-ounce (680 g) "Montana Steak" served with baked potato, salad, garlic bread, and optional Alaska king crab legs.

That same top-notch beef goes into burgers at places like the **Burger Dive** in Billings, where the award-winning I'm Your Huckleberry burger features huckleberry–Hatch chili barbecue sauce, goat cheese, and roasted red pepper mayo on a Grains of Montana bun. Near the North Entrance of Yellowstone National Park, the **Corral Bar, Steakhouse & Motel** in Gardiner offers elk and bison burgers.

The state's best foodie destination, Whitefish blends indigenous eats and faraway flavors. Elk tacos, bison meatloaf, and sourdough patty melts are a few of the Montana-flavored dishes at the low-key and family-friendly **Buffalo Cafe**. Crawfish cakes, cornmeal-crusted catfish, and shrimp and grits are among the southern classics at **Tupelo Grille**, while its sister restaurant, **Abruzzo,** features elevated Italian cuisine.

Montana's favorite legume takes the limelight at two upscale eateries in Missoula. **Scotty's Table** offers an outstanding warm lentil salad, while nearby **Plonk** renders an amazing *massaman* curry paired with bison flank steak and the city's best wine selection.

Sample the legendary Pickle Barrel sandwiches like the Big Sky Special, Blue Streaker, or Dragon Slayer at the original **Pickle Barrel** restaurant in Bozeman or newer outlets in Billings and Livingston.

Among the state's guilty pleasures are **Wilcoxson's Ice Cream** at the factory outlet store in Billings; saltwater taffy, Jelly Belly candy, fudge, and other nostalgic edibles at the **Sweet Palace** candy shop in Philipsburg; and huckleberry or Flathead cherry bear claws at historic **Polebridge Mercantile & Bakery** near Glacier National Park.

BOTTOMS UP!

Montana seems to have preserved more of its vintage bars than just about any other state. Among its many storied watering holes are **Bale of Hay Saloon** in Virginia City (opened in 1869), the **Old Saloon** in Emigrant (1902), the **Gold Bar** in Helena (1907), **Montana Bar** in Miles City (1908), and **Stacey's Old Faithful Bar & Steakhouse** in Gallatin (1937).

Pickle Barrel sandwiches have been a local favorite in Bozeman since 1975.

Beacon Icehouse in Great Falls is a great spot to check out summer concerts along the banks of the Sun River.

Like many states, Big Sky Country is in the midst of a spirits boom that sees local distillers making libations with locally available ingredients. "Garden-to-glass cocktails" is the motto at Whitefish's **Spotted Bear Spirits**, where they make their own huckleberry vodka, cinnamon-flavored whiskey, limoncello, and peppermint schnapps. At **Willie's Distillery** in the Madison River Valley, the output includes wild chokecherry liqueur, huckleberry cream liqueur, honey moonshine, and two different whiskeys.

Beyond distillery taprooms, many of these homegrown beverages are now found in cocktail bars ranging from the funky **Sip 'n Dip Lounge** tiki bar in Great Falls with its behind-the-bar aquarium and resident mermaids to hip, modern joints like **Bar Plata** in Missoula and **Doc Harper's** martini bar in Billings. ∎

MONTANA'S HUTTERITE CUISINE

A small, independent Christian group from eastern Europe, Hutterite migrants arrived in Montana in the first half of the 20th century, establishing 50 colonies on the remote plains north of Great Falls and Lewiston.

With skill, resolve, and community teamwork, the Hutterites eventually became successful dairy cow, chicken, and hog farmers; milk and egg producers; and grain growers. Those ingredients figure into many traditional Hutterite dishes, including their popular soups, breads, buns, and pies that are often found at Montana farmers markets.

Montana's Hutterite cuisine is similar to the fare found at former colonies in North Dakota and the Canadian prairies. But one item is uniquely Montanan: the "hoot dog," a deep-fried hot dog wrapped in fry bread invented by Hutterite cook Rita Hofer of King Colony Ranch.

Nebraska

Long before it was a hip restaurant mantra, farm-to-table was standard for home kitchens and restaurants in the Cornhusker State.

Producing more than a billion bushels a year, Nebraska is one of the nation's top three **corn** producers. Stalks of corn emblazon the Great Seal of the State of Nebraska, while the state legislature recently pondered whether or not to name corn the state's official vegetable. The plant inspired the nickname of Nebraska's favorite college football team, and its **corn on the cob** is second to none.

Nebraskans are also skilled at raising **wheat, soybeans, sugar beets, great northern beans**, and a variety of animals—crops and livestock that also head straight from the farm into local kitchens.

Omaha Steaks from corn-fed cattle has been the gold standard for American beef since the company was founded in 1917. Ground beef, cabbage, and onions are stuffed into the baked **Runza** bread pocket sandwich that was invented in Nebraska. And the **Reuben sandwich** is another local innovation, allegedly devised at Omaha's Blackstone Hotel between the two World Wars when patron Reuben Kulakofsky requested a corned beef and sauerkraut sandwich during a poker game.

The beloved **cheese Frenchee**— a deep-fried version of the grilled cheese sandwich—hails from Lincoln, Nebraska. But nobody seems to know how it got its French sobriquet. Meanwhile, little St. Paul on the Nebraska prairie is the hometown of **Dorothy Lynch Dressing**, a thick tomato-based salad cream and all-around condiment currently bottled in Duncan.

CULINARY EXPERIENCES

Enter the corn cob toss or the corn-eating contest, gobble down heaps of kettle corn or corn nuggets, and listen to lots of cool country tunes at Omaha's **Sweet Corn Festival** over Labor Day weekend.

Founded in the early 20th century, the **Omaha Farmers Market** offers food, crafts, and other goodies from more than 100 vendors at the downtown Old Market (Saturday) and Aksarben Village on the west side (Sunday) from May to October. Among its eclectic offerings are the **Deviled Egg Co., Smoking Gun Jerky, Fermented Felon** kombucha, and **Brixtix Bakery for Dogs**.

The **Nebraska State Fair** (Labor Day week) in Grand Island is a veritable smorgasbord of odd food, from the fiery "buckshot" (pulled pork, pepper Jack cheese, jalapeño crisps, and chili sauce) at **Cactus**

THE BIG PICTURE

Founded: 1867

Population: 1.97 million

Official State Fish: Channel catfish

Also Known As: Cornhusker State

Culinary Influences: Omaha, Ponca, German, Scandinavian

Don't Miss: Omaha, Lincoln, North Platte

Claim to Fame: Kool-Aid, Reuben sandwich, TV dinners

Cornfields abound in the Cornhusker State.

Whiskey-marinated steaks are a specialty at the Drover restaurant in Omaha.

Jack's Chuckwagon to the OMG Chicken Sandwich (chicken breast, cornflakes, and bacon on a glazed doughnut) at the **Hall Family Foods** stand.

RESTAURANTS TO DIE FOR

It almost goes without saying that Omaha has great steak. Among its many carnivorous choices are the elegant **Committee Chophouse** in the Kimpton Cottonwood Hotel and longtime favorite **Gorat's Steak House** (founded in 1944), where the traditional T-bone with hash browns comes with a generous helping of live music. Whiskey-marinated steaks are the specialty at **the Drover**, another Omaha old-timer.

Residents of Nebraska's largest city occasionally eat something besides beef. The hip little **Block 16** serves offbeat takes on traditional dishes like Croque Garcon Burger, Rangoon fries with crab cream cheese, and a poutine burrito. **Big Mama's Kitchen** in Prospect Hill is all about soul food.

A global menu that blends Korean barbecue meatballs or Faroe Islands salmon with locally sourced pork tenderloin or fried chicken makes **Dish** the height of fine dining in Lincoln. **Misty's Steakhouse & Lounge** offers more traditional surf and turf in the state capital. Afterward, grab a scoop or two at the popular

TV DINNERS: NEBRASKA'S CULINARY GAME CHANGER

Despite its agricultural bounty and farm-to-table roots, Nebraska is the place where the frozen TV dinner was born. Although the company that became **Swanson Foods** was founded in 1899, the Omaha-based business didn't conceive its frozen ready-made meals until the 1950s.

Initially the three-piece meals (meat and two sides) were meant for airline passengers, but Swanson quickly realized they were also ideal for the growing number of American families who ate dinner in front of their new television sets.

Declared a turning point in American cuisine in the book *Eating History* by Andrew Smith, Swanson frozen TV dinners went from sales of 5,000 the first year they were sold in supermarkets to tens of millions nowadays.

University of Nebraska–Lincoln Dairy Store.

Way out west, **Coppermill Steakhouse** in McCook serves intriguing spin-offs of Nebraska cuisine like the Farmers Bowl (mashed potatoes with corn, chicken breast, cheddar cheese, and white bacon gravy) and Nebraska Fries (potato fries cloaked in burnt ends, prime rib, cheddar cheese, scallions, and barbecue sauce).

With locations throughout Nebraska, the **Runza** restaurant chain offers variations on the iconic pocket sandwich, including Swiss mushroom, BLT, barbecued bacon, southwestern, and original. Cheese Frenchees are on the menu at **Don and Millie's** diners in Omaha, Bellevue, and Lincoln. **Crescent Moon Ale House** in Omaha offers an original Blackstone Reuben sandwich as well as salads with Dorothy Lynch Dressing.

Around 150 miles (240 km) west of Omaha, Dannebrog reflects its Scandinavian heritage in eateries like **the Danish Bakery** with its wide world of pastries and **Dannebrog Delights** old-fashioned ice-cream shop.

Anyone driving the Lincoln Highway (U.S. 30/I-80) across Nebraska can slip even more into a nostalgic mood by noshing at **Penny's Diner** in North Platte or **Grandma Jo's Café** in Sidney.

BOTTOMS UP!

Omaha boasts one of the livelier, more diverse drinking scenes in the Great Plains region. With its colorful retro decor and "killer" cocktail menu, **Mercury** is

Farm-to-table street food—like the Wagyu beef poutine burger with gravy—at Omaha's Block 16

Vibrant produce overtakes Rhizosphere Farm's booth at the Omaha Farmers Market.

a throwback to the 1970s. Beers and Bloody Marys are the thing at **Krug Park**, lodged inside a vintage 1908 brick building.

KOOL-AID: FROM HASTINGS TO THE WORLD

Hoping to transform the liquid in soda pop concentrate into a powder form that could easily be transported anywhere, Edwin Perkins created Kool-Aid in 1927 while experimenting in his mother's kitchen in Hastings, Nebraska.

Kool-Aid eventually became a worldwide phenomenon and Nebraska's official state soft drink. From the original six flavors Perkins created, the powdered "fruit" drink expanded into more than 100 variations.

Hastings continues to celebrate its famous drink with the Kool-Aid Days festival in August and Kool-Aid exhibits at the Hastings Museum.

The triple threat at the **Homy Inn** is sangria, Jell-O shots, and champagne on tap. From the psychedelic Alpine Cabin and vintage Recording Booth to the Caramel Couch Set, each of the seating areas at the **Tiny House** bar in the Little Bohemia neighborhood has a theme.

Little Bohemia is also known for its craft beer establishments, including the **Infusion Brewing Co.'s** taproom and brewery and **Beercade 2** with its 40-plus pinball machines and arcade games.

More than a dozen local winemakers strut their stuff at the **Toast Nebraska Wine Festival**, a twin event that takes place in Omaha (May) and Grand Island (November).

Although it's hard to find in Nebraska, the **Sonic Screwdriver** cocktail was invented by an Omaha fan of the classic *Dr. Who* television series and named after a powerful tool that featured in the show. ■

Nevada

Nevada's incredibly eclectic dining scene ranges from vintage Basque eateries and Rat Pack steak houses to lavish buffets and top-shelf celebrity chef restaurants.

THE BIG PICTURE

Founded: 1864

Population: 3.18 million

Official State Fish: Lahontan cutthroat trout

Also Known As: Silver State

Culinary Influences: Basque, Spanish, French

Don't Miss: Las Vegas, Lake Tahoe, Virginia City

Claim to Fame: Shrimp cocktail, steak, buffets

Nevada's most renowned meal is probably the **casino hotel buffet**. Those same eateries also popularized what are now considered the state's most iconic dishes.

The **shrimp cocktail**, possibly a spin-off of the oyster cocktails popular in gold rush–era San Francisco, has become a Las Vegas standard. In 1959, the Golden Gate Hotel & Casino was the first to introduce the maritime concoction to Sin City. Also in the 1950s, **chateaubriand** became a culinary drawing card in dining rooms along Glitter Gulch and the Strip.

Around that same time, Frank Sinatra, Dean Martin, and the rest of the Rat Pack frequented steak houses slightly off the Strip and in the process helped turn Las Vegas into a desert oasis of **steak**: filet mignon, porterhouse, rib eye, T-bone, New York strip, prime rib, you name it.

Basque cuisine is the closest the Silver State comes to a readily identifiable regional cuisine. Originally drawn to the Nevada Territory by the Comstock silver strike of 1859, many of the Basques eventually returned to sheep farming in the arid Great Basin. They also reverted to their native cuisine, succulent dishes like **baked or roast lamb** and **lamb chops, chorizo sausage**

(served on its own or in sandwiches), **Basque beans** (pinto), and **sweetbreads**.

CULINARY EXPERIENCES

With its buffets, celebrity chef restaurants, and outlets for just about every imaginable fast-food and restaurant chain, Las Vegas is basically a year-round smorgasbord. But the southern Nevada city does host epicurean events. The lineup includes the **Great American Foodie Fest** (May), **Life Is Beautiful** (September), the **Las Vegas Greek Food Festival** (September), and the **Las Vegas Food & Wine Festival** (October).

A unique way to explore the city's culinary scene is a **Hog Car Las Vegas** food tour, during which guests cruise the Strip in a convoy of little pink four-wheel scooters while visiting the huge chocolate fountain at the Bellagio and sampling goodies at top restaurants.

Nevada's biggest barbecue blowout is the annual **Best in the West Nugget Rib Cook-Off** in Sparks over Labor Day and the following week. The event draws as many as 400,000 people and several dozen of the nation's top barbecue teams

Shrimp cocktail has been a classic since it hit menus in 1959.

Tour the Las Vegas Strip's sites and tastes in pure pink fashion with Hog Car Tours.

to a four-block-long "rib village" along Victorian Avenue.

Offering various ways to try Iberian foods, the three-day **National Basque Festival** (July) takes place in downtown Elko.

RESTAURANTS TO DIE FOR

No longer a one-trick pony, Las Vegas has evolved from its all-you-can-eat buffet days into one of the globe's most diverse dining destinations.

It's become de rigueur for celebrity chefs, much like music legends, to star on the Strip. Among the higher profile are the elegant nouvelle French cuisine of **L'Atelier De Joël Robuchon** at the MGM Grand and **Restaurant Guy Savoy** at Caesars Palace, as well as the Iberian-flavored **Bazaar Meat by José Andrés** at the Sahara.

Picasso at the Bellagio celebrates its namesake with sumptuous Spanish and French regional cuisine served in a dining room decorated with original Pablo Picasso paintings and ceramics. Another artistic legend is celebrated at the Wynn resort's **Sinatra** restaurant, which serves Ol' Blue Eyes's favorite spaghetti and clams. The Wynn also excels at Asian cuisine with top-shelf eateries like **Mizumi** and the Michelin-starred **Wing Lei**. Meanwhile, the unassuming **Lotus of Siam** on East Flamingo Road boasts what many insiders consider the city's best Thai cuisine.

Time-trip back to the 1950s at old-school Vegas steak houses like the dark and delicious **Hugo's Cellar** at the downtown Four Queens, the Wild West–themed **Bob Taylor's Original Ranch House &**

Supper Club, or **Golden Steer Steakhouse**, where the likes of the Rat Pack, Elvis, Marilyn Monroe, and Muhammad Ali once dined.

Though Reno does boast high-falutin eats like **Atlantis Steakhouse**, the world's "biggest little city" isn't a pretentious food town. Tucked inside an old house, **Süp** in MidTown specializes in tasty soups, salads, and sandwiches. **Liberty Food & Wine Exchange** does triple duty as a butcher shop, wine bar, and petite restaurant with shared plates. **Peg's Glorified Ham n Eggs** is the place for a hearty breakfast, with four locations around the Reno-Sparks metro area.

The elegant **Edgewood Tahoe** restaurant in Stateline complements dishes like smoked elk loin, spring rabbit, and lobster *angelotti*

with panoramic views of Lake Tahoe. Among the top spots for grub along Interstate 80 in northern Nevada are **the Griddle** diner in Winnemucca and the Cornish pasties and fruit pies at **B.J. Bull Bakery** in Elko. The region is also renowned for the Basque cuisine served at the historic **Martin Hotel** in Winnemucca (established in 1898) and **Toki Ona** in Elko.

BOTTOMS UP!

In addition to their Iberian dishes, the Basques are responsible for some of Nevada's most distinctive drinks. **Picon Punch** (aka Basque Cocktail) blends brandy, grenadine, soda water, and Amer Picon bitter-orange liqueur into a popular northern Nevada concoction. In a rare example of reverse cultural diffusion, Picon Punch has made its way back to Europe's Basque Country.

Winnemucca coffee—the Basque version of Irish coffee—features whiskey, brandy, and anisette. On the other hand, **kalimotxo** (or calimocho) is a simple blend of red wine and cola soda served on ice in a highball glass.

Another hangover from the Rat Pack days, the signature drink in Las Vegas is the venerable **martini**. Among the many spots to sip martinis and other cocktails are the stylish **Chandelier Bar** at the Cosmopolitan, the **Caviar Bar** at Resorts World, **Bar Parasol** at the Wynn Las Vegas, and the **Underground Speakeasy & Distillery** beneath the Mob Museum.

As the neon lights of Vegas fade into your rearview mirror, so does

Seared ahi tuna at the waterfront Edgewood Restaurant at Edgewood Tahoe Resort in Stateline

The whimsical Bar Parasol at Wynn Las Vegas

the over-the-top bar scene. Located in a nondescript strip mall in Pahrump, **Stonewise Mead & Cider** offers Pineapple Express mead, Cranky Apple cider, and other unique creations. Nevada's oldest continuously operated drinking establishment, the **Genoa Bar & Saloon** near Carson City has been around since 1853. Down in Fallon, **Frey Ranch Farmers + Distillers** grows 100 percent of its whiskey grains in the surrounding fields. ■

LAS VEGAS BUFFETS

The cheap all-you-can-eat buffet was launched at El Rancho Hotel & Casino in the 1940s to lure prospective gamblers and in hopes of prolonging their dice throwing and card playing. Costing just $1 and dubbed the Buckaroo Buffet, the midnight feast was hyped as a way to "appease the howling coyote in your innards."

In the 1950s, many new casinos along the Strip adopted the idea and expanded the spread to daylight hours. Prices remained low—and the food rather ordinary—until the 1990s, when the Las Vegas eating scene went upmarket. The lavish **Carnival World Buffet** at the Rio once raised the bar with more than 300 dishes from around the globe.

Other luxury hotels rolled out their own lavish feasts, including the decadent **Bacchanal Buffet** at Caesars Palace, the often offbeat **Wicked Spoon** at the Cosmopolitan, and **the Buffet** at Wynn Las Vegas with its 15 cooking stations.

Prices have also risen. Breakfast buffets under $10 are still offered by some off-Strip casinos, but the gourmet spreads generally cost $20 to $60.

New Hampshire

Locally sourced ingredients like seafood, apples, pumpkins, and maple syrup feature in many of the drinks and dishes popular in the Granite State.

THE BIG PICTURE

Founded: 1788

Population: 1.4 million

Official State Fruit: Pumpkin

Also Known As: Granite State

Culinary Influences: French, Canadian, Abenaki

Don't Miss: Manchester, Portsmouth, Concord

Claim to Fame: Lobster, poutine, apple cider cocktails and doughnuts

New Hampshire shares a passion for **lobster, oysters, clam chowder**, and **maple syrup** with its New England neighbors. So what makes Granite State cuisine unique?

For one thing, **apples**. Many of the 200-plus apple varieties found in New England thrive in New Hampshire's rocky soil, including native strains like the sweet-tart red-and-yellow **Granite Beauty** and the crisp, sweet **New Hampshire No. 8**. The two apples have polar opposite origins: The former was discovered in the early 1800s, the latter created by horticulturalists at the University of New Hampshire. Local apples and their juices find their way into lots of foods, from apple pie, apple dumplings, and apple cornbread to apple cider, apple wine, and apple martinis.

Given its heritage, one would figure that apples would be the official state fruit. But that honor goes to a large, orange edible that most of us don't think of as a fruit—the **pumpkin**—possibly because apples were already the official state fruit in neighboring Vermont. Much like apples, pumpkins are a versatile ingredient that can be used in all sorts of things: pie, bread, fudge, pudding, ice cream, lattes, and

Hot apple cider doughnuts, fresh from the fryer, are coated in cinnamon sugar.

The Hampton Beach Seafood Festival hosts more than 50 local food vendors.

pancakes smothered in New Hampshire maple syrup.

French Canadian dishes like **poutine**, *tourtière* (meat pies), and **Montréal-style smoked meat** have drifted down from Québec. The north-of-the-border influence is especially strong in Manchester, where 40 percent of the population was Québécois in the early 20th century.

CULINARY EXPERIENCES

One of the state's biggest festivals, **Apple Harvest Day** (October) draws more than 60,000 people to downtown Dover for an apple pie–eating contest, live music, and 300-plus vendors.

Autumn is also prime time for pick-your-own visits to apple orchards. **Gould Hill Farm** in

Contoocook is also home to the **Contoocook Cider Company** and a bakery that makes apple pies and apple cider doughnuts. **Sunnycrest Farms** in Londonderry adds to the family fun with a barnyard animal petting zoo. An art gallery, nature trails, and casual café complement the 18 varieties of apples at **Windy Ridge Orchard** in North Haverhill.

The **Milford Pumpkin Festival** (October) combines adoration of the orange gourd and Halloween activities like pumpkin carving, creepy window displays, and a haunted trail.

Despite having the shortest seacoast of any coastal state (18.5 miles/30 kilometers), New Hampshire knows how to throw a seafood jamboree. The long-running

Hampton Beach Seafood Festival (September) presents dishes from dozens of top shoreline eateries, plus an almost obligatory lobster roll–eating contest. Year-round, **Portsmouth Eats** offers guided culinary tours of a city that one national newspaper ranked among the nation's 10 best small-town food scenes.

RESTAURANTS TO DIE FOR

Lobster mac and cheese in a sherry Mornay sauce, pumpkin soup with cinnamon and fried sage, and poached pear salad are some of the New Hampshire–inspired dishes that chef Julie Cutting-Kelly has crafted at her **Cure Restaurant** in Portsmouth. Another local favorite, **Black Trumpet** on the Old Harbor

Maple tree sap is collected in metal buckets before being boiled down into syrup.

specials at the same location on Lowell Street since 1922.

Dining in the White Mountains also runs a broad gamut, from the elegant **Main Dining Room** at the Omni Mount Washington Resort in Bretton Woods to little old **Polly's Pancake Parlor** in Sugar Hill, where the choices include gingerbread walnut and cornmeal coconut flapjacks.

In the nearby Lakes Region, some of the best grub is served at modest-looking establishments, like the barbecued chicken and pulled pork pizza at **Yankee Smokehouse** in West Ossipee or the paninis and deli sandwiches at **Squam Lake MarketPlace** on Golden Pond in Holderness. With roots stretching back to 1784, **Chichester Country Store** is renowned for its apple cider doughnuts.

Dropping down to southern New Hampshire, **Surf Seafood** in Nashua goes full fusion with Asian-flavored dishes like Korean barbecue scallops, miso-marinated salmon, and wakame seaweed salad. Over on the coast, the upscale **Carriage House** in Rye puts an Italian spin on many of its seafood dishes.

Tuckaway Tavern & Butchery in Raymond offers the option of eating its beef, pork, and bison steaks, top-quality burgers, marvelous meat pies, and blueberry cheesecake balls in-house or as takeout for home or hotel dining. **Parker's Maple Barn** near Mason stays true to its New Hampshire backwoods location with breakfast dishes like pumpkin pancakes, maple bacon chicken sausages, maple baked beans, and maple baby back ribs with eggs.

BOTTOMS UP!

New Hampshire seems to have a knack for making fruit-flavored beers, wines, and liqueurs. **Smuttynose Brewing Co.** in

prizes local ingredients in dishes like lamb and pine nut *börek* (pastries) with pumpkin puree, monkfish and clam bouillabaisse, and chicken, apple, and cranberry sausage.

Portsmouth may rank as New Hampshire's top foodie town, but Manchester (the state's largest city) isn't far behind.

Manchester's surprisingly diverse eating scene extends from traditional surf and turf at the **Hanover Street Chophouse** and farm-to-table New American cuisine at **the Foundry** gastropub to Indian and Nepalese dishes at **Kathmandu Spice** and French Canadian comfort foods at **Chez Vachon**. One of the city's oldest restaurants, **Red Arrow Diner** has been serving blue plate

The offerings available from Stark Brewing Co. in Manchester

Hampton makes a mighty fine pumpkin ale based on recipes dating from Colonial days, while **Stark Brewing Co.** in Manchester brews a tasty Grumpy Pumpkin Ale in the fall.

Old Hampshire Applejack, made with four varieties of New Hampshire apples; Chocorua Cider Rye; and White Mountain Lemonade are three of the signature drinks from **Tamworth Distilling** in Tamworth. The state's oldest distillery, **Flag Hill** near Newmarket, makes delicious liqueurs flavored with cranberry, blueberry, raspberry, and maple sugar, as well as Josiah Bartlett Apple Brandy. **Cathedral Ledge Distillery** in North Conway flavors its craft vodkas with figs, ginger, blueberries, and even horseradish.

Portsmouth Beer Week (March) features the official release of many new beers from New Hampshire, Maine, and Massachusetts breweries. The coastal city also boasts many of the state's best watering holes, ranging from **Earth Eagle Brewings** and its offbeat libations to classic cocktails at the erudite **Portsmouth Book & Bar** or **Cava Tapas & Wine Bar**.

Birch Beer, Maple Cream, Pale Dry Ginger Ale, and Yup (lemon) are a few of the nonalcoholic drinks **Squamscot Old Fashioned Beverages** in Newfields produces that are available at the factory store and retail outlets around the state. ∎

NEW HAMPSHIRE & PROHIBITION

Way ahead of the national curve, New Hampshire residents voted down a ballot proposition to ban the manufacture and sale of alcoholic drinks in 1889. And it wasn't even close: 54 to 45 percent against statewide Prohibition.

When national Prohibition came along in 1920, the state's motto may as well have been "Drink Free or Die" because New Hampshire became a major player in rum-running. The coastal towns of Hampton Beach and Rye were popular landing spots for boats coming down from Canada with illegal booze, while the state's border with Québec provided another avenue for liquor smuggling.

One of the epic speakeasies from that era—the Cave at Omni Mount Washington Resort in Bretton Woods—endures as a partially concealed, underground bar. Down in Nashua, CodeX B.A.R. replicates the ambience and classic cocktails of olden days.

New Jersey

The Garden State may produce a lot of fruits and vegetables, but New Jersey is better known for a wide range of novelty foods created by its classic diners and boardwalk hucksters.

THE BIG PICTURE

Founded: 1787

Population: 9.26 million

Official State Fruit: Blueberry

Also Known As: Garden State

Culinary Influences: African, Italian, Irish

Don't Miss: Jersey City, Elizabeth, Atlantic City

Claim to Fame: Jersey Mike's, pork roll sandwich, saltwater taffy

Although New Jersey is the butt of endless jokes because of its seemingly absurd nickname, it really is a garden state. The nom de plume was coined during the 19th century, when the state kept Philadelphia and New York City well stocked with fruits and vegetables. Fast-forward to the present century and agriculture remains one of New Jersey's top three industries.

With more than 9,000 farms, the state is one of the nation's top 10 producers of **apples, asparagus, bell peppers, blueberries, cranberries, cucumbers, eggplant, peaches, spinach, squash**, and **tomatoes**.

Yet when many of us think about typical New Jersey foods, our minds (and taste buds) conjure less organic things, like the **candied apples** and **saltwater taffy** popularized along the Jersey Shore. As for the taffy, local legend holds that after seawater flooded an Atlantic City Boardwalk shop in the 1880s, the owner realized the "spoiled" taffy tasted even better.

There are, of course, other local favorites, like the **Trenton tomato pie** (pizza with tomatoes covering the cheese), the **Jersey-style sloppy joe** (corned beef or pastrami, Swiss cheese, coleslaw, and Russian dressing on rye bread), and gooey **disco fries** (with gravy and melted mozzarella cheese). Other homegrown edibles include Trenton's **Taylor pork roll** (aka Taylor ham) and Newark's **Italian hot dog**, served in pizza bread and garnished with fried potatoes, onions, and bell peppers.

With a long Atlantic coast and many bays and estuaries, New Jersey also relishes great seafood. Among the maritime choices are **Barnegat Light scallops** from the mid-coast and **Cape May oysters** from the state's southern extreme.

Newark, Orange, New Brunswick, and other cities in North Jersey have evolved into hotbeds of African cuisine. Several dozen restaurants serve a variety of African foods, from Moroccan **tagine** and Ethiopian **injera** (flatbread) to Nigerian *suya* (meat skewers) and Swahili-style **tilapia**.

CULINARY EXPERIENCES

Find out why New Jersey really is a garden state at the **New Jersey Tourism** website *(visitnj.org)*, which lists greenhouses, nurseries, farms that welcome visitors, pick-your-own activities, vineyards and wineries, and farmers markets.

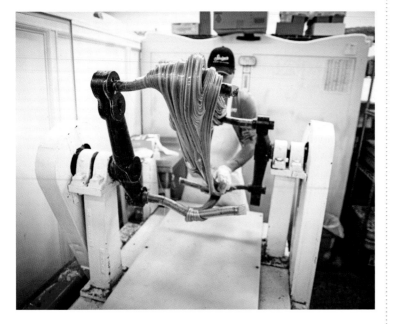

Stretching a batch of saltwater taffy at a store in Ocean City

Visit the fish market at Viking Village in Barnegat Light for responsibly harvested local seafood.

Just across the river from New York City, the **Hoboken Farmers' Market** is open every Tuesday from June to November, while the **Historic Downtown Jersey City Farmers Market** in Grove Street PATH Plaza takes place on Mondays and Thursdays from April to December.

Sample the state's homegrown and ethnic edibles at summer and fall **food truck festivals** in Elmwood Park (August) and Paramus (April), Hopatcong (June) and Neptune City (September), and South Toms River (October). Meanwhile, motorists can follow the state's **Food Truck Trail** to mobile eateries in more than half a dozen cities via a handy map online.

For those who would rather walk, **Savor and Stroll Culinary Tours** offers three ways to eat and drink your way across Morristown,

including one with a beer tasting and another that combines local history. **On the Town Food Tours** lays on guided walks of six locations in South Jersey, including Atlantic City, Hammonton, and Mount Holly.

RESTAURANTS TO DIE FOR

One of the state's top farm-to-table restaurants, **Ninety Acres at Natirar** draws many of its ingredients from the farm at the surrounding luxury estate, Natirar, which nurtures 200 kinds of sustainable produce and raises pasture-fed pigs, sheep, and fowl.

Several upscale eateries lure diners across the Hudson from the Big Apple. Perched on a finger pier in Jersey City, super-sleek **Battello** serves modern Italian seafood and Manhattan skyline views. Meanwhile,

Fascino in Montclair is renowned for its sumptuous, Italian-flavored Sunday brunch. James Beard Award winner Chris Cannon left the big city behind to create **Jockey Hollow Bar & Kitchen** in Morristown. Down the New Jersey Turnpike in New Brunswick, the **Frog and the Peach** elevates regional dishes like New Jersey scallops and Long Island duck breast.

Where to eat those Jersey-style novelty foods? **Papa's Tomato Pies** near Trenton has been serving those "upside-down" pizzas since 1912. **Jimmy Buff's** in Kenilworth claims to be the original home of the Italian hot dog, while **Town Hall Delicatessen** in South Orange is the alleged birthplace of the Jersey-style sloppy joe. **James Candy Company** on the Atlantic City Boardwalk is celebrated for its saltwater taffy and

"nostalgic confections" like Paddle Pops, peanut butter chews, and mint sticks.

With more than 500 diners, New Jersey boasts more nostalgic eateries than any other state. Among the classics are the **Summit Diner** in Summit (opened in 1928), **Bendix Diner** in Hasbrouck Heights (opened in 1947), **Tick Tock Diner** in Clifton (opened in 1948), and **Mustache Bill's Diner** in Barnegat Light (opened in 1959).

BOTTOMS UP!

The state's most celebrated bar, the **Stone Pony** in Asbury Park was just another seaside dive until local lads Bruce Springsteen and Steve Van Zandt began playing there in the mid-1970s. It's still a major music venue, and many of the shows support local charities.

The Rustic Cabin in Englewood Cliffs where Frank Sinatra got his start is long gone. But you can catch a similar view of the Hudson River and George Washington Bridge while sipping a martini at **DeNovo European Pub** in nearby Edgewater. Farther down the river, **Smorgasbar** and the **Rooftop at Exchange Place** offer panoramic riverside views of Lower Manhattan and its iconic skyscrapers.

New Jersey's first craft brewery was **Descendants Brewing Company** at the Old Ship Inn in Milford. Set beside the Delaware River, the establishment has been making British-, German-, and Flemish-style suds since 1985. Descendants is one of seven craft breweries along the **Hunterdon County Beer Trail** in west-central New Jersey.

New Jersey takes full advantage of its coastline with fresh scallops and other seafood.

Check out Jersey's food trucks at festivals and along the state's Food Truck Trail.

With nearly a million people of Irish descent, New Jersey has no shortage of Irish bars, both traditional and modern. With Guinness and Harp on tap, live Celtic music, and a Sinn Féin poster behind the bar, **Tír na nÓg** is often cited as the state's most authentic Irish pub. Among the oldest are the **Irish Pub** in Atlantic City (a popular speakeasy during Prohibition), **McGovern's Tavern** in Newark (opened in 1936), and **Tierney's Tavern** in Montclair (founded in 1934).

Atlantic City lounge lizards chill at joints like **VÜE Rooftop Bar & Lounge** on the 23rd floor of the historic Claridge Hotel. The marathon six-hour happy hour starts at noon, with entertainment three nights a week, and unobstructed ocean views over the breezy outdoor terrace. ∎

ANTHONY BOURDAIN

An erudite and widely traveled chef, author, and television personality, Anthony Bourdain was known for his eclectic palate and profound insights into the food he consumed and the places he traveled.

Although born in New York City, Bourdain grew up across the Hudson River in Leonia, New Jersey, and he always considered the Garden State his home. Neither of his parents worked in the culinary industry, but Bourdain traced his lifelong love affair with food to the dishes he sampled during a family vacation in France and summers eating seafood at the Jersey Shore.

The **Anthony Bourdain Food Trail** by Visit New Jersey includes many of his favorite eats from across the state, including the ripper hot dogs at **Hiram's Roadstand** in Fort Lee, the seafood at **Dock's Oyster House** in Atlantic City, and the cheesesteaks at **Donkey's Place** in Camden.

New Mexico

A melting pot of Indigenous, colonial, and American culinary traditions, the Land of Enchantment nurtures one of the nation's most celebrated regional food scenes.

THE BIG PICTURE

Founded: 1912

Population: 2.11 million

Official State Vegetables: Chilies and frijoles

Also Known As: Land of Enchantment

Culinary Influences: Spanish, Mexican, Navajo and other Native American tribes

Don't Miss: Santa Fe, Albuquerque, Taos

Claim to Fame: Bizcochito, chile relleno, posole, Chimayó cocktail

Along with the Creole/Cajun of Louisiana and Polynesian of Hawaii, New Mexico's extraordinarily tasty regional cuisine is the closest that American food comes to feeling (and tasting) like something from another country.

A synthesis of Native American and Hispanic influences, New Mexico's native cuisine was almost fully evolved by the time the Southwest became part of the United States in 1848. From around A.D. 700, the Pueblo people developed a flourishing urban culture in the Rio Grande Valley and northwest desert made possible by the cultivation of **corn, beans, and squash**, three cornerstones of modern New Mexican cuisine.

Although they now bear Spanish names, many of the state's iconic dishes have Pueblo origins. **Posole** is a hearty, delicious stew made with hominy, onions, chili peppers, and either pork or chicken (in pre-Columbian times it would have been game meat). Likewise with **carne adovada**, another Pueblo dish that combines meat and chili peppers, and green or red chili stew, both of which have ancient roots.

The arrival of Spanish padres, soldiers, and settlers in the 16th century added Hispanic flavors, dishes, and cooking methods to New Mexican food.

Found throughout Iberia and Latin America, **sopaipillas** are tasty little fried pastries made with nothing more than wheat flour, shortening, baking powder, salt, and water—although they taste even better with honey or jam. Wheat flour is also the main ingredient in cold **panocha** pudding and **bread** baked in traditional beehive-shaped *hornos* (ovens).

Calabacitas (little gourds), a popular sautéed summer side dish, combines squash with zucchini, corn, onion, tomato, spring onions, and, of course, chili peppers. New Mexican cooks use a variety of peppers to make **chile relleno**, a dish that involves stuffing the chilies with meat or cheese and dipping them in an egg-white batter before baking.

New Mexico's favorite sweet treat is **bizcochitos**, cookies flavored with cinnamon and anise. Often cut into stars or crescent moons, they can be munched on any time of year but are especially popular at weddings and other family occasions and during the holiday season. Bizcochitos are also the official state cookie.

Although their origins are buried deep in the state's Hispanic past,

Sopaipillas are a delicious fusion of fried pastry and quick bread often drizzled with honey.

Masa dough surrounds a chili pepper filling before being wrapped in corn husks and steamed to make tamales.

some of New Mexico's favorite dishes are 20th-century creations. Bacon, eggs, and chilies are the stuffing for **breakfast burritos**. Rather than being rolled and baked in a casserole, the **stacked enchilada** is a tower of fried corn tortillas with red chili sauce, cheese, meat between the layers, and a fried egg on top. And then there's the **Frito pie**, made with ground beef, chilies, beans, cheese, and whatever else the cook feels like tossing in served atop corn chips— and sometimes directly from the Fritos bag.

CULINARY EXPERIENCES

Located about 40 miles (63 km) north of Las Cruces in the Rio Grande Valley, the town of Hatch is the holy grail of New Mexican chilies. Not only does it have a namesake pepper (Hatch chilies); it's also home base of the renowned **Hatch Chile Festival**. The main attraction is the bounty of chili-flavored foods, but the Labor Day Weekend event also includes chili, watermelon, and ice cream–eating contests, a chilitossing competition, and lots of live music.

Chili is also the star of the **National Fiery Foods & BBQ Show** in Albuquerque (March). The state's largest city also hosts Sawmill Market, an assemblage of more than two dozen food and beverage outlets ranging from **Flora Taco** and **Hiro Sushi** to **XO Waffle** and **Neko Neko** ice cream, as well as the pop-up shops of the **New Mexico Artisan Market**.

An hour up the interstate, the **Santa Fe Wine & Chile Fiesta** offers the best of more than 60 New Mexican restaurants and 90 local wineries over five days in September. Among the many events are celebrity chef luncheons, wine dinners, auctions, tastings, and foodie seminars. Throughout the year, **Food Tour New Mexico** offers guided walks of Santa Fe and Albuquerque that combine history and restaurant visits.

New Mexico's small towns also get in on the food festival action. The vintage horse racing track at Ruidoso Downs in Lincoln National Forest presents the **Regional BBQ Competition** in October, with

The Regional BBQ Competition features a cook-off with home cooks and competitive pitmasters, a rodeo, and live entertainment at Ruidoso Downs Race Track.

awards for the best barbecued chicken, ribs, pork, and brisket, along with live entertainment.

Dozens of chocolate shops and chocolatiers from around the Southwest participate in **Chocolate Fantasia**, a February event in Silver City, a onetime Wild West boomtown. And it just seems natural that Pie Town in west-central New Mexico should host an annual **Pie Festival** (September). Year-round, **Pie-O-Neer Pies** in Pie Town offers a mouthwatering array of delicacies, from time-honored flavors like strawberry rhubarb, coconut cream, and lemon meringue to newfangled chocolate red chili pie and green chili apple pie with piñon (pine) nuts.

RESTAURANTS TO DIE FOR

The unofficial fine dining capital of the Southwest, Santa Fe is flush with amazing chefs and their incredible eateries.

The elevated Mexican cuisine at **Sazón** in the city's Historic District is overseen by Fernando Olea, named "2022 Best Chef in the Southwest" by the James Beard Awards. The elegant restaurant has also scored a recent *Wine Spectator* Award of Excellence. **The Compound** off Canyon Road offers a culinary trip around the world with dishes like Australian rack of lamb, Icelandic cod, Maine lobster, and Tuscan salad. Lodged inside the 18th-century adobe Borrego House, **Geronimo** edges closer to southwestern cuisine with Four Corners rack of lamb and honey-grilled Mexican prawns.

The common denominator among the above fine dining options is the absence of New Mexican cuisine. But not to fret: Santa Fe offers plenty of homegrown grub. **Tia Sophia's Restaurant** near the plaza often has a line to get in, especially at breakfast, and a menu that

SOME LIKE IT HOT

Though many native New Mexican foods would be delicious without chilies, it's the red and green *Capsicum annuum* that adds much of the color, flavor, and zesty oomph to the state's distinctive cuisine.

A native plant of South America that Columbus "discovered" in the Caribbean, chilies made their way to New Mexico with 16th-century Spanish conquistadors and colonists and the local Puebloan people soon adopted them.

Over 400 years, many landraces (localized varieties) evolved to the point where different pueblos produced slightly different types. By the late 1800s, pioneer horticulturist Dr. Fabián García was selective breeding chilies to create new varieties like New Mexico No. 9, the first commercial cultivar.

Many other varieties have emerged since then, including the well-known Hatch. Chilies are one of New Mexico's official state vegetables, along with frijoles (pinto beans). The official state question "Red or green?" reflects a query often asked at local restaurants regarding chili preference. New Mexican chilies have even been grown aboard the International Space Station.

stuffed sopaipillas, carne adovada, and the offbeat but tasty green chili clam chowder.

Ask locals where to grab the best local grub in Taos and they often cite **Toribios**, a nondescript roadside café near the turnoff to the Rio Grande Gorge Bridge that cooks up delicious and inexpensive Frito pies, carnitas, tamales, and chicken mole. Closer to the plaza, **Doc Martin's Restaurant** offers classic New Mexican and Mexican dishes inside an 1890s adobe house. Just around the block, **Lambert's of Taos** has been the top dog of local dining for more than three decades. If you can't snag a reservation, try the bison relleno or mole pork tostadas at the first come, first served **TreeHouse Bar**.

Albuquerque's gastronomic apogee is brunch or dinner at **Campo**

features green chili stew, posole, blue corn pancakes, and quesadillas. Or escape the tourist crush at **La** **Choza**, a local hangout beside the Santa Fe Railyard Park that serves some of the city's best chile relleno,

Chili peppers are an essential ingredient of New Mexican cuisine.

at **Los Poblanos**. Located on a historic estate on the city's north side, the restaurant sources many ingredients for its modern southwestern cuisine from its own organic farm or farmers and herdsmen in the Rio Grande Valley.

Among the city's longtime bastions of traditional New Mexican cuisine are the **Frontier Restaurant, Mary & Tito's Café**, and the petite diner inside **Duran Central Pharmacy**, while the even older **El Modelo** (founded in 1929) serves Mexican favorites.

Old-time eateries are also staples in small towns around New Mexico. **Black Bird Saloon** in Los Cerrillos complements its vintage Old West venue with dishes that have included buffalo summer sausage and the Miner's Hand Warmer Burrito. Green chili cheeseburgers are the house specialty at both the **Owl Bar & Cafe**, a 1940s diner in San Antonio, and **Sparky's** barbecue joint in Hatch.

Charred leeks at Campo at Los Poblanos in Albuquerque

BOTTOMS UP!

Tequila, apple cider, and crème de cassis make up the **Chimayó** cocktail, invented in the 1960s by Arturo Jaramillo at his Rancho de Chimayó Restaurante in the town of Chimayó. Still owned and operated by the Jaramillo family, the bar also makes a tequila **Prickly Pear Cactus Martini**.

New Mexico's other homegrown cocktail is the **Tree Martini**, a blend of gin and dry vermouth served in a small Spanish *porrón* (pitcher) and concocted at Taos Ski Valley winter resort in the late 1950s. The name derives from a tradition of placing

A portrait of John Wayne graces the dining room of Frontier Restaurant in Albuquerque.

the drinks in wooden boxes affixed to "martini trees" for skiers to imbibe on their way down the slopes.

New Mexico's terroir provides the perfect environment for the smooth, buttery flavor of **piñon nut coffee**. Nuts from the piñon pines *(Pinus edulis)* that grow high in the mountains are typically blended with imported Arabica coffee beans to make the brew. At the three Piñon Coffee House locations in greater Albuquerque, patrons can sip piñon latte or cold brew with bizcochito cookies or piñon nut bear claws.

Historic Route 66 (aka Central Avenue) through central Albuquerque is ground zero for vintage architecture and classic watering holes. **Happy Accidents** mixes an

incredible range of cocktails including "Spanish-style" gin and tonics, mezcal-based drinks, and creative exotics like whiskey flavored with coconut and pandan leaves. Among the strip's other cocktail emporiums are **Founders Speakeasy** (password required!) and the **Apothecary Lounge** rooftop bar in the Hotel Parq Central, which flavors many of its drinks with cranberry, orange, rhubarb, and other bitters.

Discover your inner cowpoke while shooting pool, guzzling longnecks, and line dancing to live country tunes at the **Cowgirl** bar in Santa Fe. Or relish a laid-back glass of wine or sangria at the stylish **Anaconda Bar** at El Monte Sagrado resort in Taos. ∎

New York

With New York City in the vanguard, the Empire State kicked off its conquest of the culinary world in the 19th century, with the industrial revolution and the rise of Wall Street fueling its ascent to the pinnacle of global dining.

THE BIG PICTURE

Founded: 1788

Population: 19.85 million

Official State Muffin: Apple muffin

Also Known As: Empire State

Culinary Influences: Jewish, Italian, Chinese

Don't Miss: New York City, Syracuse, Fire Island

Claim to Fame: Coal oven pizza, bagels and lox, cheesecake

New York State is three gastronomic worlds rolled into one. When it comes to food, western New York has more in common with the Great Lakes region than the rest of the state. The Hudson Valley, Catskills, and Adirondacks feel more like New England. Though New York City harbors everything from the upper echelon of fine dining to legendary beach boardwalk snacks.

As the main gateway of American immigration for more than 150 years, New York City owes much of its culinary innovation to people who came from abroad.

Various migrant groups have established culinary beachheads in the Big Apple, but Jewish arrivals from eastern Europe were responsible for many dishes that have become quintessentially New York,

from **bagels** and **matzo ball soup** to **kosher pickles** and **pastrami sandwiches**.

Modifying foods they knew from Sicily, Naples, and elsewhere, Italian immigrants created New York–style **thin crust pizza, pasta primavera**, and even that feed-the-family Italian standby **spaghetti with meatballs**.

Among other dishes with New York roots are **Manhattan clam chowder** (possibly spawned at the original Fulton Fish Market), the **Waldorf salad** (created in the 1890s at the Waldorf-Astoria hotel), **Tootsie Rolls** (invented at a Brooklyn candy shop in 1884), and **Oreo cookies** (conceived at the Nabisco factory in Chelsea in 1912).

Long before New York City was dubbed the Big Apple, the state of New York was big on **apples**. The climate and soils are ideal for growing 31 commercial varieties of *Malus domestica*—more than any other state. New York harbors more than 11 million apple trees spread across 600-plus orchards.

Western and central New York are far enough away from New York City to have developed their own unique dishes, like **beef on weck**, a sandwich comprising

With a crushed graham cracker crust and creamy filling, New York–style cheesecake is a true classic.

New York's oldest deli, Katz's Delicatessen, was established in 1888.

roast beef stuffed into a caraway-seeded kummelweck roll. In the 1960s, Buffalo's bars helped transform the least appreciated part of a chicken's anatomy into an international phenomenon called **Buffalo wings** by dousing them with spicy pepper sauce. **Hemstrought's Bakery** in Utica still makes the popular half-moon cookies it launched in 1920.

Forget Philadelphia. The town of Chester in the Catskills region is the original hometown of **cream cheese**, invented in the 1870s by dairy farmer William A. Lawrence. He shipped his creamy concoction to the city, where local bakeries combined it with graham crackers to create **New York–style cheesecake**.

CULINARY EXPERIENCES

It's a no-brainer that New York's second biggest city should host the **National Buffalo Wing Fest**, a Labor Day weekend event that plays out in Highmark Stadium, where the Buffalo Bills of the NFL play their home games.

Taste of Syracuse (June) takes place in and around Clinton Square, as more than 70 restaurants, beverage makers, snack vendors, and 30-plus musical acts invade the city center. Year-round, the new Salt City Market food hall on the southern edge of downtown Syracuse offers ethnic eats from around the globe, like Southeast Asian cuisine at **Firecracker Thai Kitchen** and **Big in Burma**, Jamaican dishes at **Erma's Island**, and Middle Eastern at **Baghdad Restaurant**.

Rochester eaters revel in the return of the popular **Food Truck Rodeos** at Rochester Public Market, every Wednesday between April and September. The downtown market also flaunts permanent feasts like **Juan & Maria's Empanada Stop**, the coastal cuisine of **Velvet Belly**, and country-style French at **Cure at the Market**.

The aptly named **Troy Pig Out** (July) is the state's official barbecue festival, a day of heated cooking

contests, cornhole tournaments, fireworks, and live tunes in Riverfront Park. Held every Saturday throughout the year, the **Troy Waterfront Farmers Market** takes over Monument Square and River Street during the warmer months but moves into the nearby Troy Atrium during the winter.

Farther down the Hudson Valley, the **Warwick Valley Apple Trail** connects U-pick orchards, cidermakers, apple stands, and shops selling apple pies, cider doughnuts, and other treats. Best during the autumn apple harvest, the trail is around a two-hour drive from Manhattan.

Speaking of the Big Apple, the city's culinary carnivals range from the legendary (and admittedly lowbrow) **Nathan's Famous Hot Dog Eating Contest** on Coney Island on the Fourth of July to celebrity-spangled events like the **New York Times Food Festival** (October).

Although it started life in 1926 as a religious celebration, the **Feast of San Gennaro** (September) in Little Italy has evolved into an 11-day street fair that revolves around zeppole- and cannoli-eating contests, flavorsome street stalls, and culinary landmarks like **Ferrara Bakery** (opened in 1892), **Lombardi's** pizzeria (1905), and **Di Palo's** deli (1925).

Across the East River, **Tastes of Brooklyn** has evolved into a multi-neighborhood event that includes food crawls between April and June in Bedford-Stuyvesant, Carroll Gardens-Cobble Hill, Gowanus, Park Slope, and elsewhere.

Established in 1914, Russ & Daughters is now a New York City institution famous for its bagels and lox.

Chefs garnish servings of tomato tartare at Blue Hill at Stone Barns in Tarrytown.

RESTAURANTS TO DIE FOR

New York City

Where does one even start to take a bite out of the Big Apple? There's certainly a lot of choice: More than 24,000 restaurants and other dining outlets are spread across the five boroughs. You can eat at a different spot each night for more than 65 years and not patronize the same one twice.

The metro area boasts 73 Michelin-starred restaurants, all but 10 on the island of Manhattan, including celebrated three-star establishments like **Eleven Madison Park** with its plant-based tasting menus, the innovative modern Japanese cuisine of sushi master Masayoshi Takayama at his self-titled **Masa** restaurant, the exquisite seafood and vegetarian dishes at **Le Bernardin**, and the farmers- and foragers-based tasting menus at Thomas Keller's elegant **Per Se** overlooking Central Park.

One of Manhattan's most exclusive eating adventures is **Chef's Table at Brooklyn Fare** in the rear of a gourmet grocery store in

The Upward Burger D-Lux at Upward Brewing Company in Livingston Manor

Hudson Yards, where the tasting menus feature artistically presented Japanese dishes created with French culinary techniques. Among the island's other gastronomic superstars are **Aquavit** for modern Scandinavian, **Al Coro** for contemporary Italian, **Jungsik** for avant-garde Korean, and the Moorish- and Sephardic Jewish–influenced southern Spanish cuisine at **La Vara**.

Perhaps even more so than its star-hung eateries, New York City is renowned for delicatessens. Founded in 1888, **Katz's Delicatessen** on the Lower East Side is the oldest and most celebrated of the lot. Over the years, it's been featured in numerous movies and television episodes, including a very memorable scene in *When Harry Met Sally*. With two locations in Manhattan, **2nd Ave Deli** specializes in classic kosher dishes like gefilte fish, matzo ball soup, kugel, knish, and deli sandwiches.

Another denizen of the Lower East Side, **Russ & Daughters** has been baking what many people (including the late Anthony Bourdain) consider New York's best bagels since 1914—although hipsters who religiously line up outside **Tompkins Square Bagels** in the East Village might beg to differ. On the Upper West Side, **Barney Greengrass** specializes in smoked fish platters, fish sandwiches, caviar, and breakfast eggs with various sorts of fish.

Junior's Restaurant in Brooklyn and Midtown makes traditional

AMERICA'S FIRST CULINARY SUPERSTAR

What do Mark Twain, Theodore Roosevelt, Nikola Tesla, Elvis Presley, Denzel Washington, and King Edward VII of England have in common? They've all dined at **Delmonico's** restaurant in Lower Manhattan.

The legendary eatery started as a modest café opened by Swiss immigrant brothers Giovanni and Pietro Delmonico in 1827. Within a decade, it had grown into a refined restaurant with tablecloths, printed menus, and a celebrated chef—items virtually unknown in America at the time. In 1859, it became the first ever restaurant reviewed by the *New York Times*.

Although its signature dish remains the rib eye steak, Delmonico's has been credited with numerous food firsts, including chicken à la king, lobster Newberg, eggs Benedict, the wedge salad, and the baked Alaska dessert.

The original family-owned Delmonico's closed in 1923. Subsequent owners kept the restaurant going until 2020, when it fell victim to the COVID-19 pandemic. Plans are under way to reopen the famed dining spot at its longtime 56 Beaver Street location.

New York cheesecakes, while **Eileen's Special Cheesecake** in SoHo is renowned for its modern takes on the confectionary art like chocolate cappuccino, salted caramel, dulce de leche, and sprinkles.

If you can't make it to Coney Island, the Big Apple's hot spot for hot dogs is a one-block stretch of 86th Street on the Upper East Side that harbors the **Schaller's Stube Sausage Bar** and **Papaya King**, a longtime favorite that also offers fresh tropical fruit drinks.

Brooklyn's finest dining spot—owing to the exemplary American cuisine, glittering Manhattan skyline views, and number of celebrity chefs who have left their marks on the kitchen—is the **River Café**. Literally in the shadow of the Brooklyn Bridge, the restaurant's summer outdoor seating is heavenly. The elevated Mexican cuisine of chef Cosme Aguilar at **Casa Enrique** is well worth the schlep to Long Island City in Queens.

At the opposite end of Long Island, the seasonal rich and famous buoy an upscale Hamptons eating scene that includes superior surf and turf at **1770 House** restaurant and locally sourced seafood dishes like broiled or fried flounder and fluke sautéed with a panko crust at **Bostwick's Chowder House**.

Hudson Valley/Catskills/Adirondacks

With its own vegetable fields, greenhouses, and herb garden, **Blue Hill** restaurant at the Stone Barns Center for Food & Agriculture near Tarrytown presents true farm-to-table dining in a lovely bucolic setting.

Smoked salmon flatbread and smoked maple-cheddar omelets highlight brunch alongside waterfall views at the 200-year-old **Roundhouse** in Beacon. Discover Irish haute cuisine—Guinness-braised beef short ribs, venison bangers, gin-and-juniper-cured salmon, and divine Irish coffee—at **Bia** in

Coney Island hosts Nathan's Famous International Hot Dog Eating Contest every Fourth of July.

Rhinebeck. Grab a whole-bird spinning chicken, some sides, and a bottle of Accordion wine at **Kitty's Market & Café** in Hudson and picnic at nearby Henry Hudson Riverfront Park.

If you're heading to a concert at Woodstock, grab some grub beforehand at the **Local Table & Tap** on the shore of Kauneonga Lake, a 10-minute drive from the music venue and the spot where the historic music festival played out in 1969. On your way out the next morning, **Java Love Bethel** brews pretty good coffee and organic tea to accompany their fresh bakery bites.

Elsewhere in the Catskills region, **Upward Brewing Company** kitchen and taproom in Livingston Manor offers fish tacos, Bavarian bratwurst, vegetarian wraps, and other dishes to down with its craft beers on the big rolling lawn out front. If you're antiquing in the region, pop into the **Tusten Cup** in Narrowsburg for breakfast, lunch, or sweet snacks.

Even in the dog-eat-dog political world of Albany there's romance: classic Italian cuisine in the wood-paneled dining room or vintage brick patio at **Café Capriccio**. Yet the state capital's biggest surprise is **Yono's**, a stylish Indonesian American meld with dishes like Maine lobster *nasi goreng* and beef short rib *rendang*.

In addition to hundreds of lakes and 46 high peaks, the Adirondacks region renders myriad eating and dining spots. True to its name, **Well Dressed Food** in Tupper Lake styles great-looking (and -tasting) sandwiches, flatbread pizzas, rotisserie chicken dishes, and fully decked-out bagels. **Campfire Adirondack Grill** in the historic Hotel Saranac reflects

Eileen's Special Cheesecake in New York City has been a local mainstay since 1974.

both the decor and the hearty comfort food once served at the region's millionaire Great Camps.

In keeping with the town's winter sports ambience, **Generations Tap & Grill** in Lake Placid offers Alpine-inspired dishes like German onion soup, German Dip roast beef sandwich, and bratwurst meatloaf with apple-bacon sauerkraut. Down the Northway in Chestertown, **the Bullhouse** does tapas, steaks, and seafood with a Latin twist.

Western and Central New York

Three blocks from where Teddy Roosevelt was sworn in as the 26th president, the old **Anchor Bar** on Main Street continues to specialize in spicy Buffalo wings, although you now have an option of bone-in or boneless, and a combo that includes wings and a roast beef on weck sandwich.

At the opposite end of the Buffalo eating spectrum, the stylish **Bacchus Wine Bar & Restaurant** in the city's theater district does upscale surf and turf in a candlelit setting. The Italian-Renaissance-style lobby of the Ellicott Square Building in downtown Buffalo provides an elegant setting for lunching on the signature beef and turkey dishes at **Charlie's the Butcher Carvery**.

The Buffalo area's oldest restaurants are out in the burbs. Nearly 200 years after it was founded by a German immigrant, **Schwabl's** in West Seneca is still known for its roast beef on weck, goulash, Bavarian-style pretzel sticks, and summertime Ebenezer Punch. Founded in 1827, the **Eagle House** in Williamsville offers classic comfort food like chicken pot pie, Welsh rarebit, and pork chops in apple bourbon sauce in a dining

Butter-poached lobster, one of Thomas Keller's classic dishes. No ingredients are ever repeated throughout the meal in the tasting menus at Per Se in New York City.

room reminiscent of the era when Buffalo was the western frontier.

Rochester's contribution to the western New York food compendium is the legendary Garbage Plate, a medley of hamburger patties, baked beans, home fries, chopped onion, macaroni salad, hot sauce, and

TAKE THE 7 TRAIN TO TASTE TOWN

Manhattan remains the epicenter of New York dining, but Queens is giving the island a run for its money when it comes to global cuisine. With residents who speak more than 140 languages, the borough is home to hundreds of eateries "unceremoniously serving unadulterated national cuisine to working-class compatriots," says the *New York Times*.

The selection is truly astounding, a literal A to Z of global cuisine—from Albanian, Burmese, and Cantonese to Tibetan, Uzbeki, and Zulu. Astoria is a hotbed for North African and Middle Eastern cuisine, while Flushing is the place to head for Chinese regional foods. Jackson Heights and Long Island City are bastions of Indian cuisine, and the Jamaica neighborhood is (naturally) an urban island of Caribbean flavors.

Sample a wide range of international bites at Queens Night Market, Saturday nights from June to October inside New York Hall of Science in Flushing Meadows. Or catch the 7 Train at Grand Central or Times Square to sample ethnic eateries in Woodside, Jackson Heights, Elmhurst, Corona, and Flushing.

Pair a flight with the tasty Firetower pretzel at Generations Tap & Grill in Lake Placid.

Diner with its Betty Boop memorabilia near Washington Square Park and **Dinosaur Bar-B-Que** near Clinton Square. Among Salt City's other favorites are **Alto Cinco** for modern Mexican cuisine, swanky **Saint Urban Wine Bar** on the same block, and **Darwin** gourmet sandwich shop in downtown.

BOTTOMS UP!

How did the iconic **Manhattan** cocktail (whiskey, vermouth, and bitters) get its name? It was definitely born on Manhattan Island, but the moniker actually derives from its 19th-century invention at the old Manhattan Club for gentlemen.

Though the first martini was probably created in gold rush–era California, the **dry martini** (dry gin, dry vermouth, and orange bitters) was likely invented by bartender Martini di Arma di Taggia at New York's original Knickerbocker hotel in the early 20th century. Almost a century later, an Australian bartender at Milk & Honey (now **Attaboy**) on the Lower East Side concocted the **Penicillin** cocktail (whiskey, lemon juice, ginger, and honey).

The town of Long Island, the state of Tennessee, and Oak Beach Inn in the Hamptons all have competing claims regarding who pioneered the potent brew called **Long Island Iced Tea** (gin, rum, tequila, vodka, and triple sec). The genesis of the **Cosmopolitan** (Cointreau, vodka, and cranberry juice) is also contentious, although no one disputes that **the Odeon** in Tribeca and the hit TV show *Sex and the City* made the "Cosmo" a 1990s sensation.

Manhattan offers plenty of places to knock one back.

various other condiments first concocted at **Nick Tahou Hots** on Main Street.

The city's most romantic eatery is **Pane Vino on the River**, where dishes like spicy Sicilian calamari, caprese *confrutti*, and linguine with clam sauce complement a nice Chianti, Genesee River views, and live music on the outdoor patio. On the outer edge of Rochester, **Black & Blue Steak & Crab** near Pittsford offers an array of American seafood dishes, from she-crab soup and crab cakes to Maine lobster and Alaska king crab.

Syracuse flaunts its solid working-class roots at eateries like **Stella's**

Mixologists at **Death & Co.** penned the bar's James Beard Award–winning *Cocktail Codex: Fundamentals, Formulas, Evolutions.* Continuing the literary riff, **Bemelmans Bar** in the Carlyle hotel on the Upper East Side is decorated with original murals by Ludwig Bemelmans, author of the Madeline children's books.

Katana Kitten in the West Village offers high-end sake and cocktails made with Japanese whiskey, vodka, and gin. The **Stonewall Inn** on Christopher Street and **Julius'** around the corner on Waverly Place are two of the Big Apple's legendary gay bars.

Peer down on Manhattan from **Overstory** on the 64th floor of the 70 Pine Street skyscraper or **Manhatta** on the 60th floor of the 28 Liberty Street building.

Tucked inside a vintage brick waterworks building, **C.H. Evans Brewing** in the Albany Pump Station carries on a legacy of making local craft beer that stretches back to 1786. With divey **Frizzy's Bar**, gay mainstay **Cathode Ray**, and live tunes at **Nietzsche's**, the Allen Street strip is Buffalo's nightlife hub. The upstairs attic at the **Daily Refresher** in Rochester offers a cozy spot for sampling the bar's 300-plus whiskeys, while **Middle Ages Brewing** in Syracuse concentrates on British-style stouts, porters, and IPAs.

South of Syracuse, the **Finger Lakes region** has been making wines since the early 1800s and in 1982 became one of the first regions east of the Mississippi to achieve American Viticultural Area (AVA) status. Although several dozen varieties are produced, the area is especially adept at German-style wines like Riesling. **Hermann J. Wiemer Vineyard** and **Red Newt Cellars** near Lake Seneca and **Weis Vineyards** on Keuka Lake make some of the region's top-rated wines. ∎

Pause for a tasting at Dr. Konstantin Frank Winery overlooking Keuka Lake in Hammondsport.

North Carolina

Much like their college basketball allegiances, North Carolinians have strong opinions when it comes to barbecue. But no one disputes the fine seafood served along the state's Atlantic shores.

THE BIG PICTURE

Founded: 1789

Population: 10.7 million

Official State Fruit: Scuppernong grape

Also Known As: Tar Heel State, Old North State

Culinary Influences: Spanish, French, German

Don't Miss: The Triangle, Asheville, Outer Banks

Claim to Fame: Krispy Kreme doughnuts, Moravian cookies, barbecue

North Carolina is a state divided. Not by conventional things like city versus country, but rather, by barbecue. Residents of the Tar Heel State tend to be advocates of either **Lexington-style barbecue** in the west or **eastern-style barbecue** below the fall line (the geological line that marks the division between the Piedmont and the Atlantic Coastal Plain).

Though both regions use pork as the primary meat—although eastern tends to utilize the entire pig, Lexington just the shoulder—the main distinction is in the sauce. Lexington revolves around a tomato-based concoction flavored with various spices slathered on the pork as it cooks. On the other hand, eastern adheres to a vinegar-based sauce normally added at the dinner table. Politico proponents of each style have tried at various times in the past to get their favored style declared the official state barbecue.

But cooler heads prevailed, and North Carolina remains a two-barbecue state.

With the nation's sixth longest coastline and a broad coastal plain composing nearly half of the state, North Carolina also excels at seafood. The state's been serving tasty **shrimp, blue crabs**, and a variety of **ocean and estuary fish** for centuries. Calabash village near the southern extreme of the state's Atlantic coast is renowned for **Calabash-style seafood**: fish, shrimp, oysters, and other shellfish deep-fried in a cornmeal coating.

The state's most distinctive dessert is the **Moravian cookie**. Introduced by German-speaking Moravians who settled Winston-Salem in the 1750s, the superthin cookies are flavored with ginger, sugar, and whatever else the baker feels like tossing in, from chocolate and coffee to lemon, lime, and pumpkin.

CULINARY EXPERIENCES

North Carolina is a national leader in the adaptive reuse of old factory buildings into hip, modern food and beverage centers. Once

Eastern-style pulled pork barbecue with a tangy vinegar sauce

Seafood straight from the source on the Calabash River

an intercity bus garage, **Transfer Co. Food Hall** in Raleigh now harbors Dank Burrito, Mama Crow's Burger & Salad Shop, and an amazing charcuterie shop called Alimentari at Left Bank. On the western side of the metro area, an old tobacco warehouse has morphed into **Durham Food Hall**, an ideal stop for breakfast or lunch while browsing the **Durham Farmers' Market** in the adjacent park. Half a dozen blocks away, the historic **American Tobacco Campus** now churns out gourmet coffees, craft cocktails, and soul food rather than cigarettes.

Decide for yourself which style 'cue is best by following North Carolina's **Historic Barbecue Trail** to 20 traditional barbecue restaurants scattered between Murphy in the Appalachians and Ayden on the Coastal Plain. Although it mainly features the western style, the **Lexington Barbecue Festival** in October is the state's premier showcase for smoked or grilled pork. Meanwhile, the 200-year-old **C. Winkler Bakery** in Old Salem is the place to splurge on authentic Moravian cookies.

From the **North Carolina Seafood Festival** at Morehead City to the **Outer Banks Seafood Festival** at Nags Head (both in October), there are plenty of ways to sample the state's maritime bounty. You can also visit places that are farming the sea. At **Oysters Carolina** on Harkers Island, owner Ryan Bethea offers all-you-can-eat tastings of Beau Sels and other oysters. At **Marshallberg Farm** in Smyrna, Lianne and Brian Reburn lead tours of indoor tanks holding more than 6,000 of the ornery-looking **sturgeon** followed by a tasting that includes Osetra caviar, smoked sturgeon, and North Carolina distiller Social House Vodka.

RESTAURANTS TO DIE FOR

The easternmost stop on the Historic Barbecue Trail, Ayden's **Skylight Inn BBQ** (opened in 1947) is popular with local truckers, farmers, state troopers, and anyone questing for great meat. Try the

pulled pork sandwich with slaw and a bottle of Cheerwine. Another bastion of the eastern style, **Parker's Barbecue** in Wilson is perpetually packed with local families who have been dining there for generations. Another longtime favorite, **King's BBQ** in Kinston offers daily specials (like meatloaf on Tuesdays and sliced turkey on Sundays) for those who want to venture into other local comfort foods.

Appropriately located on Smokehouse Lane, **Lexington Barbecue** in the town of the same name cooks its pork shoulders over hickory or oak coals. Often listed among the nation's top barbecue joints, the modest diner-style eatery serves its western-style pork chopped or pulled. **Willie Brooks BBQ** in Boone complements its meats with extravagant dessert cakes and a tasty craft beer and whiskey menu. Founded in 1930, **Stamey's Barbecue** cooks up amazing pork, chicken, and hot dogs at two locations in Greensboro. Way out west, **Buxton Hall BBQ** in Asheville offers modern takes on smoked meats and other southern favorites in a hip, industrial chic setting.

Down on the shore, two vintage restaurants, **Beck's** and the **Waterfront Seafood Shack**, have long vied for the title of best Calabash-style seafood. Both offer clams, crab, shrimp, and oysters. But their ambience is decidedly different: Beck's has indoor dining in downtown Calabash, while the Shack features alfresco dining on picnic tables beside fishing boats docked along the Calabash River. If you've had your fill of seafood, grab a burger and shake at **El's Drive-In** in

Goat cheese burrata at Rhubarb in Asheville

Transfer Co. Food Hall is a popular meeting spot housed in the historic Carolina Coach Garage and Shops in Raleigh.

Morehead City and dine beneath the big shade trees.

Moving up the coastal food chain, **Blue Moon Bistro** in Beaufort offers a refined French twist on surf and turf in a romantic, candlelit dining room half a block off the harbor. Among its signature dishes are

Coquille St. Jacques scallops in a cognac-mushroom cream sauce, lobster bisque, and tasso shrimp and grits. Novel takes on traditional southern cuisine are the hallmark of the uber-hip **Cypress Hall Kitchen + Bar** in New Bern, with a menu that varies from cider-braised

KRISPY KREME DOUGHNUTS

For Vernon Rudolph, it was always about doughnuts. He learned the baking business as a teenager working in his uncle's doughnut shop in Paducah, Kentucky. At the age of 22, determined to blaze his own path in the pastry world, Rudolph moved to Winston-Salem, North Carolina, and opened the Krispy Kreme doughnut shop.

Using the "secret" recipe that his uncle bought off a New Orleans chef, Rudolph began production in the summer of 1937. Initially, he sold his glazed delights to local grocery stores. But such was the demand from the doughnut-loving public, he soon opened his bakery to walk-in

customers. Despite lines down the block, there was no indication that Krispy Kreme would become a global phenomenon.

Although Rudolph died in 1973, his dream of spreading Krispy Kreme endured. During the 1990s the chain spread across the United States, and in the early 21st century a global expansion kicked off. Krispy Kreme now has stores in 30 countries.

The original shop is long gone, the spot marked by a plaque at a park at 534 South Main Street in Old Salem. One of the oldest shops still in existence graces the corner of Person and Peace Streets in Raleigh.

pork cheeks and smoked deviled eggs to collards with bacon and Mema's Famous Strawberry Cake.

Sure, you can down half a dozen different types of oysters and slurp spicy oyster shooters at **St. Roch Fine Oysters + Bar** in Raleigh, but the menu also boasts creative takes on New Orleans cuisine like crawfish hush puppies, duck rillette, and house-made andouille sausage. For many diners and food writers, the pinnacle of North Carolina cuisine is **Chef & the Farmer**, a gourmet eatery in Kinston that featured in the PBS series *A Chef's Life*. The chef in question is Vivian Howard, who, along with her husband, Ben Knight, opened the renowned New American eatery in 2006.

The epitome of fine dining in Durham is the **Counting House** on the ground floor of the 21C Museum Hotel. Once upon a time the venue was a bank. Nowadays it's a swank dining room draped in funky modern art with a petite but tasty menu that features meat and fish mains, pasta, and eclectic small dishes. If you're craving something more down-to-earth, try the Puerto Rican dishes at **Boricua Soul** in the American Tobacco Campus or the house specialty at **Dame's Chicken & Waffles** in the Liberty Warehouse complex.

Despite its unassuming gray brick facade, **Haberdish** cooks up some of the best food in Charlotte. This self-proclaimed "mill-town kitchen" reimagines southern classics like fried chicken, barbecued ribs, and panfried trout with mouthwatering sides like sweet potato dumplings and cheddar cheese grits. One of the city's oldest and most beloved eating spots, **Green's Lunch** near Bank of America Stadium (home to the Carolina Panthers) has been serving mighty fine breakfasts, burgers, ham sandwiches, and hot dogs since 1926.

Magnolia House in Greensboro is even older. It's a Victorian-era restaurant and inn that once featured in the historic *Negro Motorist Green Book* as a site where Black travelers were safe to eat and sleep. Nowadays, the upscale restaurant brings in jazz bands for Saturday and Sunday brunch. Another local favorite, **Yum Yum Better Ice Cream and Hot Dogs** started life in 1906 as a food cart in downtown Greensboro.

Raleigh Beer Garden has three floors of gathering space and more than 350 beers on tap.

Ever trendy Asheville complements its lively art and music scene with global food. **Cúrate Bar de Tapas** offers more familiar small plates like chorizo sausage and Iberian ham, as well as less common dishes like *ajo blanco* (chilled almond and garlic soup), *rossejat* (paella-style pasta), and *almejas* (clams) steamed with pork belly. Just down the block, **Rhubarb** offers an equally eclectic take on modern American cuisine crafted by chef and owner John Fleer, whom the James Beard Foundation named one of the "Rising Stars of the 21st Century."

Breakfast is often a long, drawn-out, and very social affair in North Carolina, especially at vintage restaurants like **Lovick's Cafe** in Kinston. The busy diner was launched in 1941 by the grandparents of the current owners, who borrowed $180 to open an early morning eatery that originally catered to tobacco workers. Nowadays the clientele varies from tourists and schoolkids to cops, farmers, craft brewery workers, and miscellaneous old-timers.

Another blast from the past, **Big Ed's Restaurant** in Raleigh originally opened in 1958. Four blocks from the state capitol, the City Market location often has a line out the front door of people craving its country-fresh southern breakfasts. On the other hand, **Biscuit Head** in Asheville brings a 21st-century spin to the traditional Carolina breakfast with dishes like gluten-free vegan biscuits and gravy and veggie sausage patties.

BOTTOMS UP!

Invented in Salisbury in 1917, **Cheerwine** is a cherry-flavored, burgundy-colored carbonated soft drink that complements eastern or

The iconic southern beverage, Cheerwine, has been sold since 1917.

western barbecue. Despite the name, it contains no alcohol, but just a smidge of caffeine. Available at many old-timey restaurants, Cheerwine also lends its distinctive flavor to ice cream, cakes, and other confections.

North Carolina is also the birthplace of another beloved soda: **Pepsi**. The cola traces its roots to New Bern, North Carolina, where drugstore owner Caleb Bradham invented and started selling the drink in 1893. That corner store is now a Pepsi soda fountain, museum, and swag shop.

Raleigh Beer Garden in the state capital claims to offer the world's largest selection of draft beers: more than 350 at any given time from all around the globe. Their selection ranges from old standbys like Bud Light and Corona to rarely found suds like Dragon's

Milk, Golden Monkey, and Astronaut Sauce.

With more than 370 breweries and brewpubs, North Carolina is the undisputed king of southern craft beer. Asheville and Charlotte boast dozens of outlets. But the craft beer boom has spread throughout the state to out-of-the-way spots like Kinston, where **Mother Earth Brewery & Spirits** produces great craft beers and small-batch malt whiskey and botanical gin.

Nuvole Rooftop TwentyTwo in Charlotte serves craft cocktails with a panoramic view of the state's largest city, while **Young Hearts Distilling** in downtown Raleigh offers killer cocktails like the Violet Delight and Honeysuckle Mule. Yet North Carolina's top mixologist might just be Travis Harper at tiny **Stanley's Saloon** in Kinston. ∎

North Dakota

North Dakota's culinary smorgasbord blends foods introduced by Scandinavian and German immigrants with modern takes on old-time prairie favorites.

THE BIG PICTURE

Founded: 1889

Population: 779,261

Official State Fruit: Chokecherry

Also Known As: Peace Garden State

Culinary Influences: Scandinavian, German

Don't Miss: Fargo, Bismarck, Grand Forks

Claim to Fame: Bison, Juneberry pie, chippers, krumkakes

With around one out of every three North Dakotans claiming Scandinavian ancestry—and a heritage that stretches back to the arrival of the first Norwegian immigrants in 1869—Scandinavian culinary traditions have always loomed large in the state's food culture.

Besides well-known dishes like **lutefisk** (pickled whitefish) and **lefse** (potato flatbread), North Dakota kitchens also concoct soup with *knoephla* (dumplings), *kase knoephla* (cheese buttons), and *rømmegrøt* (porridge), as well as *æbleskiver* (baked apple snacks) and *krumkakes*, a thin cookie made in a metal press and then rolled into a cone and eaten alone or à la mode.

Among the state's other sweet treats are **Juneberry pie** and **chippers**, which are potato chips covered in chocolate or peanut butter rather than that famous implement of destruction in the movie *Fargo*.

As one of the states where the buffalo still roam—on ranches and in Theodore Roosevelt National Park—North Dakota has **bison** on many restaurant menus. But sampling some of North Dakota's carnivorous favorites requires a trip to the store: the **beef jerky** and **smoked bacon** at Myers' in Parshall and Garrison and the **Wishek sausage** made using the original 1909 recipe at Stan's Supermarket in Wishek.

CULINARY EXPERIENCES

North America's largest celebration of Scandinavian culture, **Norsk Høstfest** in Minot (September) features plenty of Nordic cuisine and A-list country music acts. **Uffda Day** in Rutland (October) offers a small-town version of the large fest, including æbleskivers at the American Legion Hall and rømmegrøt at the Senior Center.

North Dakotans enliven warm-weather months with plenty of other food events, including the **Rhubarb Festival** at the Prairie Village Museum in Rugby (June) and the **Chokecherry Festival** in Williston (August). **Pitchfork Steak Fondue** is an outdoor dinner with Western flair that takes place nightly between June and September in Medora. The **World's Largest French Fry Feed** in Grand Forks coincides with a University of North Dakota home football game each fall. Come winter, cold-weather comfort food is the flavorsome forte of **Frostival** in Fargo.

Potato flatbread (lefse) is a popular staple.

Norsk Høstfest in Minot is North America's largest Scandinavian festival.

North Dakota offers various pick-your-own opportunities, including **Patrie's Raspberries on the Prairie** in Bowdon, the **Old Juneberry Patch** near Velva, and **Angelic Gardens** in Minot, which also features a Victorian walk-through garden and family-oriented holiday activities.

As well as funding research into growing pinto, navy, kidney, and other varieties, Fargo's **Bean Institute** manages a great website with bean recipes, cooking tips, and nutrition facts for both professional chefs and home cooks.

RESTAURANTS TO DIE FOR

Overlooking the Missouri River, **Huckleberry House** in Bismarck prepares Norwegian specialties like a *smørrebrød* (open-faced sandwich) with beef and Danish blue cheese and *frikadeller* (Swedish meatballs). The Sons of Norway **Kringen Lodge** in Fargo offers an occasional lutefisk and meatball dinner, as well as *kringle* (Danish pastries) with morning coffee. **Freddy's Lefse** in West Fargo has been the go-to place for takeaway lefse since 1946.

With locations in Bismarck, Fargo, and Minot, **Kroll's Diners** are a North Dakota institution. Besides traditional American diner dishes like burgers, grilled chicken, and country-fried steak, Kroll's serves German specialties like cabbage rolls, sauerkraut, sausages, and *fleischkuechle* (dumplings). **Würst Bier Hall** in Fargo complements its imported German beers with schnitzel, currywurst, and spaetzle noodles.

Kitchens at several of Bismarck's upscale eateries revolve around modern American cuisine. **Pirogue**

Outdoor cooking and dining rule at Pitchfork Steak Fondue in Medora.

Grille creates new takes on prairie favorites like sautéed bison medallions with Bordelaise, venison sausage with grilled onion relish, and Grandma Flo's ham loaf sliders. Another favorite in the state capital is **Bistró 1100**, located in a frontier-era carriage house flanked by vintage railroad cars. For lighter fare like soups, salads, and sandwiches, it's hard to beat **Bread Poets**, which also makes the city's best cookies and scones.

Located in a meticulously restored 1917 brick building with pressed-tin ceilings, **Mezzaluna** offers elegant dining in downtown Fargo, courtesy of a menu that features steak, fish, and pasta dishes as well as vegan, vegetarian, and gluten-free options. In the southside Clara Barton neighborhood, **Luna Fargo** (no relation) offers Italian-flavored prairie dishes like braised-beef lasagna and spaghetti squash carbonara.

Blending Scandinavian and Jewish flavors, **BernBaum's** bagel shop on Broadway serves brunch and lunch dishes like classic potato latkes, matzo-breaded chicken schnitzel, Nordic lamb, and Iceland gravlax. Half a block south, the modish **Rosewild** restaurant in the Jasper Hotel offers its own take on "farm-to-Fargo" cuisine with North Dakota beef in the leading role.

With a menu ranging from rack of lamb and roast duck to ahi tuna and filet mignon, **Sky's Fine Dining** is the epitome of elegant dining in Grand Forks. Way out west, **Theodore's Dining Room** in Medora channels the spirit of the 26th president and onetime North Dakota rancher with dishes like braised bison shanks, pan-seared walleye, and prime rib. **Northside Café** is a local favorite for hearty breakfast and lunch.

North Dakotans satiate their sweet tooth at the old-fashioned **Pride Dairy** ice-cream shop in Bottineau (the state's only remaining small-town creamery) and with chocolate chippers at **Widman's Candy Shop** in Grand Forks.

MOLLY ON THE RANGE

Proving that beautiful music and food aren't all that far apart, Molly Yeh has made a career of both pursuits. After studying percussion at the Juilliard School, Yeh fully expected to pursue a career in the acoustic world. But life took an unforeseen turn when she married fellow Juilliard graduate Nick Hagen and the couple moved to the Hagen family sugar beet farm along the North Dakota–Minnesota border.

While playing and teaching music in the Grand Forks area, Yeh blogged about food, a sideline that segued into her first cookbook, *Molly on the Range: Recipes and Stories From an Unlikely Life on a Farm*. Food Network later spun her unlikely life into *Girl Meets Farm,* a hit culinary show that blends upper Midwest dishes with recipes gleaned from Yeh's Chinese Jewish heritage.

Yeh is perhaps best known for her cakes and other confections. But given her culinary roots, her recipes range far and wide: lemongrass chicken rice bowls and kosher pretzel challah, classic Tater Tots and corn dogs, Asian breakfast tacos and brussels sprout latkes.

BOTTOMS UP!

Norths Dakota's cowboys and cowgirls gather to drink and dance at the **Lonesome Dove** near the rodeo grounds in Mandan. For something more upscale (and less beer-centric), hop across the Missouri River to **Peacock Alley** bar in downtown Bismarck, where the martini menu features the Monkey Tail, Espresso, Lemon Drop, and other tasty libations.

And lest you think that mead comes in just one (medieval British) flavor, **Prairie Rose Meadery** in Fargo crafts orange spice, caramel apple, honey mojito, and chokecherry meads. The latter is also the main ingredient of the chokecherry wine produced at **Maple River Winery** in Casselton, which makes several offbeat drinks, including rhubarb, dandelion, and cucumber lime wines. ∎

Luna Fargo sources from local purveyors for its seasonal Midwest-inspired menu.

Ohio

Ohioans have leveraged their talent for innovation into foods, beverages, bars, and restaurants that define the state's unique culinary culture.

THE BIG PICTURE

Founded: 1803

Population: 11.8 million

Official State Fruit: Tomato

Also Known As: Buckeye State

Culinary Influences: Serbian, Polish, German, Italian

Don't Miss: Cleveland, Cincinnati, Columbus

Claim to Fame: Cleveland-style barbecue, Hungarian hot dogs, Cincinnati-style chili

From Thomas Edison to Wilbur and Orville Wright, Ohio has always had a penchant for invention. And that includes food.

Among the state's many gastronomic innovations is **Cincinnati-style chili** (aka chili spaghetti), conceived by Macedonian brothers who relocated from the Balkans in the 1920s. The city's iconic **Goetta sausage sandwich** traces its roots to late 19th-century German émigrés.

Cleveland's beloved **Polish boy** is a kielbasa sausage in a bun stuffed with french fries, coleslaw, and barbecue sauce. The Akron area was the birthplace of **sauerkraut balls**: deep-fried, bite-size blends of ham and cabbage.

Barberton in central Ohio is where a Serbian husband and wife started serving their uniquely seasoned **Barberton fried chicken** in the 1930s. However, the hot and often messy **shredded chicken sandwich**, a fowl version of the sloppy joe, doesn't owe its allegiance to any particular city.

Ohio's dessert and snack innovations are equally impressive. A combination of peanut butter and chocolate called **Buckeye candy** gets its name from a resemblance to the nutlike seeds of the buckeye tree. Traditional **Ohio Shaker lemon pie** filling contains just three ingredients: lemons, eggs, and sugar.

And we owe the invention of **Life Savers** candy to Ohio's hot summers. In 1912, fed up that his stock kept melting, Cleveland chocolatier Clarence Crane concocted a hard, fruit-flavored "summer candy" shaped like an old-fashioned life preserver.

Buckeye candies: peanut butter bites covered in chocolate

Shredded cheddar, meat-and-bean chili, and onions smother a mound of spaghetti for Cincinnati-style chili.

CULINARY EXPERIENCES

Ohio has sketched out more than half a dozen food routes that unveil various aspects of the Buckeye dining scene. The state capital offers several choices, including the **Columbus Tikka Trail** of great Indian eateries and the **Columbus Taco Trail** of can't-miss Mexican places.

Just north of Cincinnati, the **Butler County Donut Trail** links 13 mom-and-pop bakeries and pastry shops, from **Stan the Donut Man** in West Chester to the **Donut Dude** in Liberty Township. More sweet treats await along the **Ohio Ice Cream Trail** between Cleveland and Cincinnati, and the **Ohio Buckeye Candy Trail**, which features buckeye candymakers and chocolatiers throughout the state.

The state's largest food festival, a **Taste of Cincinnati** (May) features food and beverages from more than 65 restaurants, food trucks, and market vendors along a four-block stretch of 5th Street in downtown. The **Ohio Sauerkraut Festival** in Waynesville might be the place where you finally sample sauerkraut balls.

RESTAURANTS TO DIE FOR

Michelin-starred chef Dante Boccuzzi has created three amazing restaurants right next to one another in restored buildings along Cleveland's Professor Avenue: **Next Door** for casual Italian, **Ginko** for delicious sushi, and his flagship **Dante** for elevated American cuisine.

Among Cleveland's other divine dining experiences are the small plates at **Salt+** in Lakewood; **Momocho** for Mexican inside a funky red clapboard house in the Ohio City neighborhood; the Mediterranean-flavored **Astoria Café & Market** on Detroit Avenue; and **Edwins Leadership & Restaurant Institute** in the eastside Buckeye-Shaker area, where former inmates honing their hospitality skills cook and serve upscale French cuisine.

French fare and a romantic setting are also the forte of **the Refectory**, which occupies an old church

Take a tour through the restaurants of the historic German Village neighborhood with Columbus Food Adventures.

in Columbus and flaunts the city's best wine selection. Another North Side eatery, the erudite **Asterisk Supper Club** in Uptown Westerville invites patrons to browse its extensive book collection during afternoon tea or craft cocktails, or pop in at night for gourmet meatloaf, chicken pot pie, or lamb chops. Out on the Gold Coast, **Pier W** restaurant offers freshwater and saltwater seafood with views of Lake Erie.

Cincinnati's downtown restaurant world is anchored by eateries like **Boca**, where the global menu wanders from hamachi crudo and Scottish salmon to Amish chicken and Colorado lamb. Just three blocks away, **Orchids at Palm Court** serves creative surf and turf

dishes in a spectacular art deco dining room and bar.

Over-the-Rhine, Cincinnati's historic German American neighborhood, is another hot dining spot. The menu at **Sacred Beast Diner** runs a time-traveling gamut from oldies like Goetta and schnitzel to newbies like pork rinds with shishito peppers and lobster bisque fries. Across the street, **Pepp & Dolores** specializes in homestyle Italian pasta dishes. Out on the west side, **Price Hill Chili** serves its namesake over spaghetti, on hot dogs, in cheese sandwiches, or on its own. Or make the short drive up to Dayton for the heavenly Peruvian cuisine at **Salar Restaurant & Lounge**.

Smaller cities host many of the state's oldest eateries. Founded in 1932, **Packo's Eastern European Kitchen** in Toledo is renowned for its Hungarian hot dogs, sauerkraut pierogi, and chicken paprika, while **Kewpee Hamburgers** in Lima (opened in 1928) makes ordering easy with just seven burger and sandwich choices.

BOTTOMS UP!

Established in 1827, Yellow Spring's **Ye Olde Trail Tavern** is the state's oldest bar and one of the best places for German fare, from Hofbräu Pilsner and Moselle wines to currywurst, Goetta sandwiches, and bratwurst.

More suds are on tap along the

OHIO'S "HERB CAPITAL"

From basil and lavender to rosemary and thyme, **Gahanna** is obsessed with herbs. Not long after the central Ohio city was founded in 1849, residents began to hone their skills at growing botanicals for food and drink, candles and cosmetics, and other aromatic products. A 1972 resolution by the state legislature named Gahanna the "herb capital of Ohio."

But the opening of the **Ohio Herb Center** in one of the town's oldest houses really placed it on the herbal map. The center offers herbal workshops and classes including "The Art of Tea" and "Backyard Foragers," and also helps stage **Herb Day** and the **Herb n' Arts Fair** each spring.

Gahanna also has an **Herbal Cocktail Trail** featuring restaurants, bars, and breweries with herb-infused beverages, as well as an **Herb'n Restaurant Week** (May) and the **Geroux Herb Gardens** with sections dedicated to culinary, medicinal, scented, and biblical plants.

Route 33 Brew Trail south of Columbus, an itinerary that includes the **BrewDog, Double Edge,** and **Combustion** craft breweries. If spirits are more your thing, cruise the **Celtic Cocktail Trail** in Dublin on the north side of the state capital.

With more than 60,000 students on the Ohio State University campus, Columbus is easily the king of the college bar scene, including slightly offbeat hangouts like **Alibi Bourbon & Cocktail Lounge** and **Ivan Kane's Forty Deuce Pizzeria & Speakeasy**, with a burlesque supper club and cabaret.

You're not going to find coconut palm–shaded beaches on Lake Erie. But Cleveland's **Porco Lounge & Tiki Room** does a good job of setting a tropical mood via its mai tais, daiquiris, and Singapore slings. Climax a sultry summer afternoon in Cincinnati with cocktails at the **View at Shires' Garden**, a rooftop bar overlooking downtown and the riverfront.

Manufactured in Akron since 1924, **Norka Sparkling Beverages** are such a local treasure they're sold at the Akron Art Museum, the Crawford Auto-Aviation Museum in Cleveland, and the Ohio Statehouse in Columbus. ∎

The Celtic Cocktail Trail highlights the dining and craft cocktail scene in Dublin.

Oklahoma

Old West cooking and culinary traditions inspired many of Oklahoma's signature dishes. But new chefs and concepts stoke the state's modern big-city food scenes.

Fried okra, chicken corn pudding, and **fried catfish**—dishes that the Sooners of the 1880s and later pioneers brought with them from their previous homes—still count among the state's beloved foods. Among Oklahoma's other vintage dishes are savory **sparerib pies** and **deep-fried sweet pies** stuffed with fruit or nuts. Native American foods like **sand plums** (aka Cherokee or Chickasaw plums) and fry bread **Indian tacos** are also old-time favorites. And believe it or not, the official state

"vegetable" is the **watermelon**.

There's also an **official state meal**, a feast that includes barbecued pork, chicken-fried steak, and biscuits and sausage gravy, as well as cornbread, fried okra, squash, black-eyed peas, corn on the cob, and fresh strawberries and pecan pie for dessert. Add **milk** (the official state beverage) and you're all set.

More recent times have brought the advent of offbeat Oklahoma delicacies like **smoked bologna sausage, fried onion burger**, and the **Theta burger**. Slathered with

hickory barbecue sauce, dill pickles, and shredded cheddar cheese, the Theta burger was allegedly invented at the now defunct Town Tavern in Norman and named for a University of Oklahoma sorority.

THE BIG PICTURE

Founded: 1907

Population: 4.02 million

Official State Meal: Barbecued pork, cornbread, biscuits and sausage gravy, fried okra, and more

Also Known As: Sooner State

Culinary Influences: Old West, African American, Cherokee and other Native American tribes

Don't Miss: Oklahoma City, Tulsa, Bartlesville

Claim to Fame: Fried onion burgers, Indian tacos, barbecue

Fry bread tacos with traditional fixings: ground beef, lettuce, onions, tomatoes, and cheese

Learn about Native American and cowboy food traditions at the annual Chuck Wagon Festival in Oklahoma City.

CULINARY EXPERIENCES

Part of the yearly '89er Celebration that commemorates the 1889 Oklahoma Land Rush, the **Guthrie Chuck Wagon Feed** offers a tasty time-travel trip back to pioneer days. "America's first food truck" is also the focus of the annual **Chuck Wagon Festival** over Memorial Day weekend at the National Cowboy & Western Heritage Museum in Oklahoma City.

Some of Oklahoma's iconic foods are the focus of the **Fried Onion Burger Day Festival** in El Reno (May), the **Rush Springs Watermelon Festival** (August), and the **National Indian Taco Championship** in Pawhuska (October). And even though it seems out of character, the **Bristow Tabouleh Fest** (May) was inspired by Middle Eastern immigrants who settled in Oklahoma during pioneer days.

But it's not all old-school. **Oklahoma Food Tours** organizes guided walking and tasting excursions in the state capital's foodie-centric Plaza and Paseo Arts Districts.

RESTAURANTS TO DIE FOR

Serving cowboys, ranchers, cattle haulers, and other hungry diners since 1910, **Cattlemen's Steakhouse** in the old stockyards district is Oklahoma City's most venerated restaurant. If there's a long wait for a table, grab a seat at the bar and order a thick, juicy sirloin, rib eye, or T-bone.

While restaurants in the refurbished **Bricktown** district lure hungry eaters in with outdoor canal-side dining, the food is much better in eateries along Automobile Alley (North Broadway) and the hip **Paseo, Plaza**, and **Uptown 23rd Districts** north of downtown. In addition to straight-up great steak, **Red PrimeSteak** in the 1911 Buick Building offers innovative dishes like beef tenderloin tamales and beluga lentil chile rellenos. Located in a former flower shop, **Cheever's Cafe** combines southwestern cuisine and southern comfort food.

Farther west on 23rd Street, the **Asian District** harbors enduring favorites like the menu of dim sum meets sushi at **Grand House China Bistro** or Vietnamese noodles at **Pho Lien Hoa**, followed by Taiwanese-style bubble tea at **Gong Cha**. However, OKC's hottest new Asian eatery is **Ma Der Lao Kitchen** on NW 16th Street.

Jamil's Steakhouse is the place for classic Oklahoma dishes like smoked bologna, fried okra, and

Try award-winning farm-to-table cuisine, like the spring pea and mushroom risotto, at downtown Tulsa's Juniper.

Oklahoma restaurant to get a nod from *Wine Spectator,* the upscale **Polo Grill** in Utica Square offers eclectic eats ranging from escargot and gazpacho to Colorado rack of lamb and lobster tails. Two of Tulsa's oldest and most treasured dining spots are the **White River Fish Market & Seafood Restaurant** (opened in 1932) and **Ike's Chili** (opened in 1908). But a lot of locals swear that **BurnCo Barbeque** makes the best brisket, ribs, and pulled pork.

Out in the hinterland, the **Old Plantation Restaurant** in Medicine Park offers southern comfort food in a historic cobblestone inn that was allegedly a hangout for Bonnie and Clyde, Pretty Boy Floyd, and other gangsters in the 1920s and '30s. A bastion of Native American cooking in Shawnee, **FireLake Fry Bread Taco** also serves traditional corn soup, meat pies, three different beans, and a choice of bison, beef, or chicken on your Indian taco. With seven outlets around Oklahoma, **Arbuckle Mountain Fried Pies** is the place for pastries stuffed with peaches, pecans, pineapple, and other sweet things.

BOTTOMS UP!

One of many eye-catching attractions along historic Route 66 in Oklahoma, **Pops 66** gas station and restaurant in Arcadia lies beneath a giant neon soda pop bottle and distinctive cantilevered roof. Besides fountain drinks, this homage to the humble soft drink also serves shakes, sundaes, floats, and meals throughout the day.

The **Pump Bar** in Oklahoma City's trendy Uptown 23rd District has switched octane to another liquid pick-me-up: craft cocktails like the bourbon-based Velvet Elvis, the mango and pineapple vodka–

fried catfish, while **Tim's Drive Inn** in suburban Warr Acres boasts what many consider the city's best Indian tacos. The main event at **Waffle Champion** in Midtown is obvious, although they also make avocado toast, smoothie bowls, and breakfast tacos. Meanwhile, **Vast** offers

something that no other OKC restaurant can claim: a tableside view from the 49th floor of Devon Tower, the state's tallest building.

Up the interstate in downtown Tulsa, **Juniper** is the epitome of farm-to-table fine dining and decadent weekend brunch. The only

WORLD'S GREATEST BARBECUE

Governor Jack Walton celebrated his inauguration on January 9, 1923. The event was billed at the time as the "world's greatest barbecue," with an outdoor feast at the **Oklahoma State Fairgrounds** that attracted more than 100,000 eaters.

Fifteen different meats—beef, lamb, pork, turkey, rabbit, and exotics like buffalo, bear, reindeer, antelope, and even possum—were cooked in trenches said to stretch more than a mile. The meal also featured 100,000 loaves of bread, "wagonloads" of fresh buns, and 20,000 gallons (75,710 L) of coffee.

An Associated Press report described the barbecue as "a feeding of the multitudes on a scale heretofore not recorded even in biblical history," while a *New York Times* correspondent noted that the throng included "farmers, businessmen, the idly curious, politicians, Indians, statesmen, New Yorkers and women."

The barbecue was preceded by an inaugural parade featuring multiple bands, cowboys in their finest holiday regalia, prairie schooners and stage-coaches, scores of buglers, and Native Americans from various tribes stretching an estimated 10 miles (16 km).

infused Haterade, and coconut rum Kahiki Kai. The bar at **Mary Eddy's Dining Room** in the OKC Arts District flaunts its own creative cocktails, while the **Sidecar Barley & Wine Bar** in the old Pontiac Building likes to serve things straight up, on the rocks or not.

Sidecar in Tulsa sits atop a four-story building along the city's boozy East 15th Street, with another on Riverfront Drive in Jenks. **Hodges Bend** in Tulsa's trendy East Village neighborhood morphs from a day-time gourmet coffee shop into a popular after-dark wine bar and cocktail lounge.

East Main Street in Norman is flush with bars like **Bison Witches** and **the Garage**, frequented by University of Oklahoma students. South Washington Street (aka the Strip) serves a similar function in Stillwater, where the country music of **Outlaws**, shots at **Willies Saloon**, and pool tables at the **Copper Penny** attract the Oklahoma State crowd. ∎

The iconic Pops 66 restaurant and service station on Route 66 in Arcadia

Oregon

When they're not crafting artisanal wine and beer—or new planet-friendly foods—Oregonians excel at Pacific Northwest cuisine made with fresh ingredients from farm, forest, and sea.

O ne of the bastions of sixties counterculture and its later iterations, Oregon is a longtime proponent of "animal-friendly eating" and organic farming. A blend of soybean tofu and wheat protein, **Tofurky** was invented in 1980 by Forest Grove tree house–dwelling hippie Seth Tibbot. Around the same time, vegetarian restaurant owner Paul Wenner was pioneering the **Gardenburger**.

Ironically, the state is also responsible for some of the nation's most beloved snack foods. **Tater Tots** were developed in the 1950s at the Ore-Ida potato processing plant at Ontario in eastern Oregon. Though its origin is hotly disputed between several states, the "Pronto Pup" hot dog on a stick developed by Versa and George Boyington of Rockaway Beach in the late 1930s may have been the world's first **corn dog**.

The state is also at the leading edge of a sustainable seafood effort that puts the likes of locally caught **wild salmon, pink shrimp, black cod, rockfish, Dover sole**, and **Dungeness crab** onto local menus and into fish markets.

The evergreen forests of western Oregon produce a bounty of small edible fruits—**blackberries, marionberries, blueberries, raspberries**, and others—that end up in pies, preserves, milkshakes, ice creams, and myriad other goodies. The

THE BIG PICTURE

Founded: 1859

Population: 4.24 million

Official State Mushroom: Pacific golden chanterelle

Also Known As: Beaver State

Culinary Influences: Spanish, Burns Paiute and other Native American tribes

Don't Miss: Portland, Ashland, Eugene

Claim to Fame: Tater Tots, marionberry pie, Pinot Noir, Tofurky and other animal-friendly foods

woods are also a leading source of edible **wild mushrooms**.

Oregon grows around 99 percent of U.S. **hazelnuts**, derived from farms rather than the wild. The state is also a major producer of the hand-harvested Pacific Ocean **sea salt** that many chefs prize.

CULINARY EXPERIENCES

O regon's version of a yellow brick road is a **Cheese Trail** that includes more than 15 craft cheesemakers. Stops range from the celebrated **Tillamook County Creamery Association** on the coast and **Rogue Creamery** near Grants Pass to **Briar Rose Creamery** in the Willamette Valley wine country and **TMK Creamery** south of Portland.

Oregon's other delicious journey is the **Hood River Fruit Loop**, a 35-mile (56 km) route through orchards, berry patches, farm stands, flower fields, wineries, breweries, and cider producers in the lush valley east of Portland.

Among Oregon's educational food encounters are the crabbing experience at **Kelly's Brighton Marina** near Rockaway Beach; foraging and

Wild mushrooms are foraged in the lush forests around the state.

The 35-mile (56 km) Hood River Fruit Loop explores 28 culinary sites in the Hood River Valley.

mushroom-hunting classes with naturalist **Rebecca Lexa**; and **WildCraft** workshops on clamming, intertidal foraging, and maple sugaring.

Fungi are the focus of the annual **Mushroom Festival** at Mount Pisgah Arboretum in Eugene (October or November) and the **Yachats Mushroom Festival** (October).

RESTAURANTS TO DIE FOR

Elevated Pacific Northwest cuisine is the lure of upscale eateries like **Higgins** in downtown Portland and **Canard** across the river in Burnside, as well as Quaintrelle in the Hosford-Abernethy neighborhood.

But the City of Roses also excels at global edibles: Spanish tapas and Basque at **Urdaneta**; Haitian and other Caribbean cookery at **Kann**; vegan and gluten-free Sri Lankan at **Mirisata**; Russian and eastern

European dishes at **Kachka**; ceviche, pisco, and other Peruvian standards at **Casa Zoraya**; and the irresistible "deep-fried funk" at **Eem PDX Thai BBQ**.

As the location of the most famous food fight of all time, Eugene has come a long way, gastronomically speaking, since *Animal House* was filmed there in the late 1970s. French-flavored **Bar Purlieu** is renowned for its five-course tasting menu and wine pairing, while **King Estate Restaurant** on the outskirts of town matches exceptional Oregon wines with Northwest seafood, meats, and artisanal cheeses.

The long-running Oregon Shakespeare Festival in Ashland has attracted both theatergoers and fine dining to the southern Oregon city. **MÄS** and its modern "Cascadian cuisine" recently made the *New York*

Times list of the nation's 50 best restaurants. **Larks Home Kitchen Cuisine** and **Alchemy Restaurant and Bar** inside a Victorian-era mansion also cater to the pretheater crowd.

The Oregon coast offers abundant choices in seafood ambience, from the sleek, glass-enclosed waterfront home of **Local Ocean** in Newport to the old gillnet boat that harbors takeout-only **Bowpicker Fish & Chips** along the Columbia River in Astoria.

BOTTOMS UP!

The great American (and now global) craft beer revolution kicked off in Oregon in 1980 when Chuck and Shirley Coury started Cartwright Brewing in Portland. The tiny brewery lasted just a single year, but it served as a precedent for other pioneering craft brewers like the

Widmer and McMenamin families to launch their own artisanal tipples.

With so many avid brewer-entrepreneurs and near-ideal conditions for growing hops, the Beaver State now boasts more than 300 craft breweries.

Many have come and gone, but the **Widmer Brothers Brewing Company** endures, offering tours and tastings at their flagship brewery in Portland's Eliot neighborhood. Across the Willamette River, the revitalized Pearl District is flush with drinking establishments, including the **Deschutes Brewery Portland Public House, Backwoods Brewing Company**, and **Von Ebert Brewing**.

Since opening the Hillsdale Brewery & Public House in 1985, the **McMenamins** have spread far and wide, establishing taprooms and gastropubs at more than two dozen locations around Oregon, including historic or offbeat venues. Their **Roseburg Station Pub & Brewery** in Roseburg occupies a 1916 railroad depot. An old Catholic school in Bend proved a perfect location for **Old St. Francis Pub**. And a former funeral home in Portland has morphed into the **Chapel Pub**.

Oregon's craft beer boom is exceeded only by the rise of wine. More than 750 wineries have sprouted across five distinct wine regions: the Willamette Valley, Columbia Valley, Snake River Valley, Umpqua Valley, and Rogue Valley.

Though Oregonian vintages are rarely mentioned in the same breath as French or Californian wines, consider the fact that numerous Oregon

A spread of Russian favorites with the family of chef Bonnie Frumkin Morales, owner of Kachka in Portland

Cascadian cuisine, such as this canapé of Wagyu beef and aged tuna, stars at the acclaimed MÄS in Ashland.

vintners have landed on the annual *Wine Spectator* lists of the world's best wines. Among them are **Alexana Winery** and **Maresh Red Barn** in the Dundee Hills near Portland, as well as **Cayuse Vineyards** and **Force Majeure Vineyards** way out east near Pendleton.

While the rest of the state is obsessed with suds and plonk, **Elixir craft distillery** in Eugene has been quietly building a reputation for Old World–style spirits like Fête vodka, a Florentine iris liqueur, and Calisaya made with the herbaceous bark of a South American shrub. ■

THE "DEAN OF AMERICAN COOKERY"

Born in Portland in 1903, **James Andrew Beard** grew up in a family that employed a Chinese cook and spent summers fishing and foraging along the Oregon coast. So his early culinary influences were diverse.

When he was expelled from college (presumably because he was gay), Beard moved to Paris with its progressive sexual mores and incredible cuisine, opened a small gourmet food shop, and began to pen cookbooks. Returning to the United States after World War II, Beard hosted the first TV cooking show (*I Love to Eat*) and launched the James Beard Cooking School in New York City and Seaside, Oregon.

By raising the image and standard of American food, promoting local ingredients and food producers, and influencing generations of chefs and cookbook authors, Beard had a profound influence on the way that Americans purchase, prepare, and consume food. Long after his death in 1985, he continues to impact the way we eat via the prestigious James Beard Foundation.

Pennsylvania

From Philly cheesesteaks and scrapple to Heinz 57 and Hershey's chocolate, Pennsylvania has played a pivotal role in defining American food.

THE BIG PICTURE

Founded: 1787

Population: 12.97 million

Official State Fish: Brook trout

Also Known As: Keystone State

Culinary Influences: Italian, German (Pennsylvania Dutch)

Don't Miss: Philadelphia, Gettysburg, Pittsburgh

Claim to Fame: Heinz 57, Hershey's chocolate, Philly cheesesteaks, shoofly pie

American independence wasn't the only thing born in Philadelphia. The city is also the birthplace for several seminal Pennsylvania dishes that carry its name. Most prominent of these is the beloved **Philly cheesesteak**, which features thinly sliced sautéed beef, onions, and American cheese on a hoagie roll. Culinary legend claims brothers Pat and Harry Olivieri invented the sandwich at their Philadelphia hot dog stand in the early 1930s.

The city also lends its name to the **Philadelphia pepper pot**, a hearty stew of beef tripe and various vegetables with herbs, spices, and peppercorns to give it a kick. Its roots run back to enslaved West Africans, who introduced the tasty dish to the fledgling United States in the mid-18th century, where it gradually became ubiquitous within Philadelphia.

Another Philly favorite is the **hoagie**. The city's official sandwich is a meat lover's dream, a combination of salami, capicola, Italian cured ham, and provolone cheese garnished with tomato, onion, iceberg lettuce, cherry peppers, virgin olive oil, and red wine vinegar on a hoagie roll. The City of Brotherly Love also craves the **roast pork sandwich**, named the "Best Sandwich in America" in 2012's *Adam Richman's Best Sandwich in America* television food competition.

The city's Italian American residents conceived both the cheesesteak and hoagie, as well as the **stromboli**. Variously described as a turnover or wrap—and often compared to a calzone—the dish features Italian meats and cheeses stuffed inside pizza dough rolled into a cylinder shape and then baked or deep-fried.

German-speaking immigrants—who came to be called the Pennsylvania Dutch—introduced **pretzels** during the 17th century. Pennsylvania was home to America's first pretzel factory (1861) and, until recently, produced around half of the nation's pretzels.

Two other popular Pennsylvania Dutch concoctions are **apple dumplings** and **shoofly pie**. Made with brown sugar and molasses, the pie allegedly draws its name from the fact that cooks had to shoo away flies while the sweet, sticky pie was cooling down in a window or on a counter after baking. And the same folks conceived **scrapple**, a savory breakfast loaf that combines minced pork with spices and flour or cornmeal, served on its own or with eggs.

One side of the Philly cheesesteak war: Pat's King of Steaks signature cheesesteak sandwich

An Amish food stall inside the Reading Terminal Market in Philadelphia

The **banana split** is also Pennsylvania born and raised, invented in 1904 by Latrobe pharmacy owner David Strickler, who had the idea to split a banana in half lengthwise and cover it with three types of ice cream and whipped cream. Founded in Philadelphia in 1853, the **Keebler Company** evolved from a single bakery into a cookie empire that made the first **Girl Scout cookies**.

CULINARY EXPERIENCES

Located in the heart of Pennsylvania Dutch country, Lancaster has become a huge foodie destination. The redbrick **Lancaster Central Market** is the nation's oldest continuously operating public farmers market (founded in 1730).

Though the lineup includes Amish and Pennsylvania Dutch food vendors, the market has evolved into a global smorgasbord with Cuban, Thai, Italian, and Uruguayan cuisines.

The Lancaster version of **Taste! Festival of Food, Wine & Spirits** (November) is the big annual culinary event. Among the food-related activities at the city's **Amish Farm & House** are the summertime Sunset Picnic and Christmas Cookie Tour. In addition to the Amish Experience Theater and Amish dairy tour in a classic horse-drawn buggy, **Plain & Fancy Farm** in nearby Bird-in-Hand village offers a restaurant with dishes like meatloaf, chowchow, and shoofly pie.

About an hour's drive north of Lancaster, the **Kutztown Folk Festival** (July) features regional folk art, crafts, entertainment, Pennsylvania Dutch food, and a traditional ox roast. Another long-running summer event, the **Pittston Tomato Festival** revolves around a parade with tomato-themed floats and a contest to choose the largest, smallest, ugliest, and most perfect tomatoes. **Julius Sturgis Pretzel Bakery** in Lititz offers interactive tours with pretzel-twisting lessons.

One of the nation's largest and oldest public markets, **Reading Terminal Market** in downtown Philadelphia has expanded from local foods to global eats since it opened in 1893. On the other side of the

Julius Sturgis Pretzel Bakery in Lititz was America's first commercial pretzel company.

Schuylkill River, **Franklin's Table food hall** on the University of Pennsylvania campus showcases the culinary magic of several top restaurants, including **DK Sushi, High Street Hoagies**, and **Goldie** falafel shop.

The Philly version of the **Taste! Festival of Food, Wine & Spirits** (October) and the **Philadelphia Street Food Festival** (November) are among that city's top gastronomic events, while Pittsburgh gastronomes eagerly await the eclectic edibles at **Food Truck-a-Palooza** (January).

RESTAURANTS TO DIE FOR

The Strip District may sound like an especially sordid area, but it's actually one of Pittsburgh's top dining neighborhoods. Among its delicious denizens are **Pamela's Diner** for breakfast, **Bar Marco's** modern Italian cuisine, Middle Eastern at **Salem's Market & Grill**, and out-of-this-world sushi and sashimi at **Mola**.

For sheer spectacle, nothing tops the **Grand Concourse Restaurant**, inside a flamboyant former Gilded Age train station lobby on the south bank of the Monongahela River. The city's best food with a view is the **Monterey Bay Fish Grotto** near the top of the 1877 Duquesne Incline funicular. However, the Steel City's most talked-about restaurant these days is probably **Apteka**, with a mélange of eastern European dishes like *kapuśniak* (cabbage soup), *kluski śląskie* (Silesian potato dumplings), and *kotlet selerowy* (celeriac schnitzel).

Back in Philly, **Pat's** and **Geno's**—across the intersection from one another on South 9th Street—duke it out in the ongoing clash for the best cheesesteak, along with other local favorites like **Tony Luke's** and **John's Roast Pork**. The same southside neighborhood also boasts some of the city's tastiest Mexican food: the slow-barbecued lamb, pork, and beef tacos at **South Philly Barbacoa** and just about anything on the menu at chef Jennifer Zavala's **Juana Tamale**.

Downtown continues to dominate the Philadelphia fine dining scene with offerings like the elegant **XIX Nineteen restaurant** on the 19th floor of the Bellevue Hotel, classic surf and turf at **Butcher and Singer** with its vintage chophouse decor, and the lavish eight-course tasting menu at **Friday Saturday Sunday** (which is actually open five days a week). Yet the ultimate Philly treat is probably **Morimoto**, the upscale Japanese eatery created by legendary Iron Chef Masaharu Morimoto.

The food is pretty good in the hinterland, too, especially at **Andiario** in West Chester, where Italian meets local farm-to-table in dishes like Poconos trout with forest foragings, tagliatelle with Pennsylvania porcini, and pawpaw cake with crème anglaise.

Harrisburg diners can splash out on French cuisine at **Rubicon** opposite the state capital or feast on craft beer, artisanal pizza, and local art at **the Millworks**. Up in the Poconos, **Moya** restaurant in Jim Thorpe elevates local dining with seasonal meat, fish, and pasta dishes and an astounding wine cellar.

Take a trip down memory lane at the classic **Village Diner** in Milford (built in 1956), **White Horse Luncheonette** in Lancaster County (opened in 1968), or lakeside **Sally's Diner** in Erie (built in 1957).

BOTTOMS UP!

Pennsylvania's two huge metro areas boast the lion's share of bars, breweries, and cocktail lounges. But there's plenty of

---

HEINZ 57

Contrary to popular belief, Henry J. Heinz didn't launch the slogan "Heinz 57" because that's how many products his Pittsburgh factory produced. Instead, it was a mash-up of his favorite number (five) and his wife's (seven).

The son of German immigrants, Heinz started making horseradish (according to his mother's recipe) in his parents' basement in 1869. That first venture went belly-up. But his second stab at condiments was a roaring success: **Heinz Tomato Ketchup**, which debuted in 1876.

Heinz never looked back, building the company into one of the world's largest and most familiar food brands before his death in 1919.

Still based in Pittsburgh, the company now makes more than 5,000 products sold in 200-plus countries, including a "Heinz 57 Collection" of gourmet condiments like Infused Honey With Black Truffle, Culinary Crunch Roasted Garlic Crunch Sauce, and Mandarin Orange Miso Crunch Sauce.

---

booze—and places to quaff it—in the hinterland, too.

The lakefront **Sloppy Duck Saloon** in Erie has a tiki bar and oddball sculpture garden. **Ale Mary's at the Bittenbender** in Scranton pairs its 100 rotating craft beers with modern pub grub in a restored 1870s redbrick building. **Zeno's Pub** in State College has

Soft-shell crab sushi at Iron Chef Masaharu Morimoto's flagship restaurant, Morimoto, in Philadelphia

IN FIDE VIVO FILII DEI QUI DILEXIT ME ET TRADIDIT SEMETIPSUM PRO ME

been serving drinks, food, and live tunes to townies and Nittany Lions for more than 50 years. The **North Country Corn Crib** craft beer tap-room near Butler shares space with the **Freedom Farms Farmers Market & Kitchen**.

The Euro-themed **Lorelei Beer Hall** in Pittsburgh's East Liberty neighborhood specializes in German and Belgian beers, hard ciders, and Alpine wines. The former old-time Moose Lodge in Upper Lawrenceville has morphed into a hip drinking and entertainment space called **Spirit**, which also boasts a pizzeria.

Another miraculous transformation, **Church Brew Works** occupies the former St. John the Baptist Church (built in 1902) with its gorgeous stained glass windows. A laid-back lounge called the **Allegheny Wine Mixer** complements Pittsburgh's best wine selection with live opera music.

Philadelphia also boasts an amazing array of drinking establishments. The speakeasy-style **Hop Sing Laundromat** bar in China-town is renowned for creative craft cocktails, while the wacky **Tattooed Mom** on bar-spangled South Street stages comedy shows, poetry readings, and even a (very loud) Metal Diva Brunch. Another South Street denizen, divey **Bob and Barbara's Lounge** draws crowds for its live jazz, drag shows, and "the Special": a shot of Jim Beam bourbon with a Pabst Blue Ribbon chaser.

Open from April to October, the rooftop **Bok Bar** pairs its libations with live music and a guest chef residency program that offers grub from many of Philly's top female and

Pittsburgh's Church Brew Works is located in a former Catholic church built in 1902.

Visit the craft cocktail bar and lounge at Philadelphia Distilling to sample seasonal cocktails and classics.

minority-owned restaurants. Down by the river, **Cuba Libre Restaurant & Rum Bar** blends mojitos with island food and flamboyant floor shows. Farther up the waterfront, **Philadelphia Distilling** serves craft vodka, gin, absinthe, and cocktails in a restored factory setting. ∎

HERSHEY'S CHOCOLATE

Born in 1857 into a Pennsylvania Dutch family in Derry Township, **Milton Hershey** grew up to start America's best known chocolate company and founded the city and theme park that now bear his name.

After dropping out of school at 14, Hershey apprenticed to a Lancaster confectioner, and by the age of 19 was running his own candy-making business. He eventually found success making caramel candies.

Chocolate didn't come into the picture until 1893, when Hershey found himself intrigued by a German chocolate-making machine at the World's Columbian Exposition in Chicago. Taking a huge gamble, he sold his caramel business to fund a chocolate factory in his hometown.

After launching Hershey's milk chocolate bars in 1900, the company introduced the Hershey's Kiss in 1907, Mr. Goodbar in 1925, and M&M's in 1941.

Rhode Island

Between its oceanfront setting and Italian American heritage, little Rhode Island has forged a huge culinary reputation and many unique local foods.

Rhode Islanders would like the rest of the nation to know that Boston and Manhattan are not the only versions of the scrumptious shellfish soup. Dairy-free, clear-broth **Rhode Island clam chowder** with bacon and diced celery, potatoes, and onion offers a unique take on one of America's all-time favorite dishes.

The Ocean State creates plenty of other seafood munchies, including savory **clam cakes**; zesty **Rhode Island–style calamari** with onions, garlic, and hot peppers; and beloved **stuffies**: quahog clams on the half shell loaded with chorizo or linguiça sausage, breadcrumbs or stuffing

mix, and various herbs and spices.

Unlike their maritime equivalent, **Rhode Island johnnycakes** are a tasty cornmeal concoction that originated in North America long before Roger Williams established his breakaway colony. Different versions prevail in various parts of the state, with fierce debate between their respective advocates. The rivalry reached fever pitch in the 1940s when a fistfight broke out during a state legislature session to determine the official version.

The state's Italian American cooks popularized two other baked treats: the **zeppole** (deep-fried, powdered

sugar–covered pastry), and the cheeseless, meatless, tomato paste–heavy **pizza strip**. A Greek immigrant is responsible for launching Rhode Island's cherished **hot wiener**, a frankfurter smothered in meat sauce, mustard, and chopped onion in a steamed bun.

THE BIG PICTURE

Founded: 1790

Population: 1.09 million

Official State Appetizer: Calamari

Also Known As: Ocean State

Culinary Influences: Italian, French, Portuguese, Irish, African American

Don't Miss: Newport, Providence, Block Island

Claim to Fame: Coffee milk, doughboys, Del's Frozen Lemonade

CULINARY EXPERIENCES

Between the **Newport Burger Bender** (February), **Newport Restaurant Week** (April and November), **Newport Oyster & Chowder Festival** (May), **Newport Mansions Wine + Food** (September), and **Bowen's Wharf Seafood Festival** (October), the seaside city is never wanting for big-time food events.

The **Wharf Southern Kitchen & Whiskey Bar** in Newport is one of a half dozen stops on the **Rhode Island Oyster Trail** that stretches between the Bristol Oyster Bar in Bristol to Matunuck Oyster Bar in Wakefield.

India Point Park in Providence provides a waterfront venue for the **Rhode Island Seafood Festival** (September). The edibles of 85 plant-based restaurants offer Earth-friendly

Broth, instead of cream, makes up the base of Rhode Island clam chowder.

Many of the state's best restaurants serve up tasty bites at the Rhode Island Seafood Festival in Providence.

sustenance at the **RI VegFest** (February) in the state capital.

The culinary nonprofit **Fresh Farm RI** organizes six seasonal farmers markets in the greater Providence area as well as a year-round Saturday market, and permanent residents like Tallulah's Taqueria, Anchor Toffee, and New Harvest Coffee Roasters at 10 Sims Avenue in Providence.

Plant City offers a whole new concept in dining—not just in Providence, but the entire nation—with its entirely plant-based food hall and marketplace. The vegan and vegetarian food hall harbors eight restaurants ranging from New Burgers bistro and Besina Mexican cuisine to Double Zero pizza bar and Make Out sandwiches and smoothies.

Dive deep into Ocean State cuisine via the Downtown Providence and Newport neighborhood guided gourmet walks offered by **Rhode Island Red Food Tours**.

RESTAURANTS TO DIE FOR

Newport has been an upscale foodie destination since the Gilded Age, a fine dining tradition that continues in esteemed eateries like the **Dining Room at Castle Hill Inn** and the **Dining Room at the Vanderbilt**, a luxury hotel that also hosts Gilded Age dinners, "Tower of Bubbles" champagne parties, and martini sessions.

The high society hangouts share Aquidneck Island with blue-collar favorites like **Flo's Clam Shack** in Middletown and Portsmouth.

Established in 1936, Flo's is known for Rhode Island fortes like clam chowder, stuffed quahogs, and calamari. A historic lifesaving station in Narragansett provides a venue for the **Coast Guard House**, serving super-fresh seafood since the 1940s.

Date night in Providence probably means a candlelit table at **Gracie's** with its popular chef's tasting menus, rosé and oysters at **Nicks on Broadway**, or perhaps sake paired with the incredible raw fish platter at **Oberlin**.

Further down the metro area food chain are oldies but goodies like **Stanley's Famous Hamburgers** in Central Falls (opened in 1932), hot wieners and coffee milk at **Olneyville New York System** cafés in Providence and Cranston

Adirondack chairs dot The Lawn at Castle Hill Inn in Newport.

(founded in the 1930s), and the **Modern Diner** in Pawtucket, one of the classic Sterling Streamliners built during the 1930s and '40s and the very first diner listed on the National Register of Historic Places.

Federal Hill in Providence began to evolve into the city's "Little Italy" in the 1870s, when the first Italian migrants arrived. Nowadays the neighborhood is revered for the classic Italian cuisine served at **Il Massimo, Andino's Italian Restaurant, Costantino's Venda Bar & Ristorante**, and more than a dozen other Italian eateries.

Locals get their sugar rush from the creative ice-cream tacos or sandwiches at **Tricycle Ice Cream** in Federal Hill, or the heavenly baklava and other Middle Eastern delights at **Aleppo Sweets** near the Brown University campus.

With the entire state a short drive from Providence or the coast, it's easy to explore the culinary landscape of the rest of Rhode Island. Try places like **Ella's Food & Drink** in Westerly and its innovative fusion dishes like duck udon and miso salmon, and the bucolic **Tree House Tavern**, which occupies a converted 1860s farmhouse and barn in Warwick.

BOTTOMS UP!

Rhode Island's official state drink is **coffee milk**, a blend of coffee syrup and chilled milk traditionally served in a short, glass coffee cup. Add vanilla ice cream and it becomes a **Coffee Cabinet milkshake**.

Those who crave even more caffeine can quaff **Espresso Martini** (on draft) at **the Eddy** cocktail lounge or **Dean Hotel Bar** in Providence. Among the city's other watering holes are the speakeasy-style **Justine's**, hidden behind a lingerie shop in Olneyville, and **the Avery**, with its blend of craft cocktails and uncommon beers, tucked down a residential street on Federal Hill.

Two other Rhode Island born and bred beverages are **Del's Frozen Lemonade** (unveiled in Cranston in 1948) and **Narragansett Beer** (brewed in Cranston since 1890). Del's Lemonade stands are found at locations around the state, while Narragansett offers live tunes, tastings, and food trucks at its flagship brewery in Providence.

True to its upper-crust image, Newport offers a refined drinking scene. Swig gin and tonics while watching sailboats race on Narragansett Bay from the comfort of an Adirondack chair on **The Lawn at**

THE FOOD NETWORK

Celebrity chefs Emeril Lagasse, Bobby Flay, and Rachael Ray might not have become household names if an idea that was hatched in Providence, Rhode Island, in 1990 had never come to fruition.

Hoping to expand his company's footprint, *Providence Journal* newspaper company president Trygve Myhren decided to break into the burgeoning cable television world by launching a channel all about food.

Myhren and co-founder Reese Schonfeld initially dubbed it the Cooking Channel before a last-minute switch to the Television Food Network just before it launched in 1993. With those celebrity chefs as the main drawing card, the channel now reaches more than 90 million American households and has expanded to more than half a dozen overseas versions.

Castle Hill Inn. Knock back a Whaler's Drift or Seaside Spritz at the **Top of Newport Bar + Lounge**, which crowns the Hotel Viking. Or turn back the clock with a locally brewed Rhode Trip IPA at the **White Horse Tavern**, the nation's oldest bar (founded in 1673). ■

Local favorites make up a classic Rhode Island food truck meal.

South Carolina

Three of the nation's most storied cuisines—Low Country, southern, and Gullah Geechee—come together in a state that's evolved into a major American foodie destination.

THE BIG PICTURE

Founded: 1788

Population: 5.28 million

Official State Vegetable: Collard greens

Also Known As: Palmetto State

Culinary Influences: West African, Catawba and other Native American tribes

Don't Miss: Charleston, Myrtle Beach, Hilton Head Island

Claim to Fame: Barbecue, she-crab soup, sweet tea, boiled peanuts

South Carolina's iconic Low Country cuisine includes many elements of classic southern cooking and soul food but with a lot more fresh-from-the-dock seafood.

Local favorites like **collard greens, fried okra, shrimp and grits, chowchow** relish, **Brunswick stew,** and **hoppin' John** (aka Carolina beans and rice) are crossover dishes found throughout the American South.

But the Palmetto State has created its own distinctive seafood dishes. **Oyster roasts** are festive gatherings that often involve family members, friends, and neighbors. The oysters are half-steamed, half-grilled over hot coals on a make-shift grill grate draped with a wet burlap bag.

A South Carolina shrimp boil—also called a **Low Country boil** or **Frogmore stew,** after the town on St. Helena Island—complements the tasty crustaceans with sausage, red potatoes, corn on the cob, and copious amounts of seasoning in a large pot.

Another distinctive coastal dish, **she-crab soup** is a delicious bisque-like concoction that adds sautéed celery and onions, fresh scallions and chives, a dash of hot sauce, and a splash of sherry—plus heavy cream or milk and a thickening agent like flour—to crab roe and crabmeat.

The state also boasts its own meat-grilling traditions. Said to have originated in the Pee Dee region north of Charleston during colonial times, **South Carolina barbecue** entails cooking pork ribs, shoulders, or even the whole hog *very* slowly over oak or hickory coals in an open pit.

Barbecue sauce varies across the state, with vinegar or light tomato popular in the east and coastal areas, sweet, heavy tomato in the mountainous west, and mustard-based sauces as the tangy darling of the Midlands or Piedmont regions.

The Pee Dee region is also the cradle of **chicken bog**. Variously described as pilaf, stew, or even casserole, the dish combines chicken and rice with sausage, onion, and seasoning in a savory broth. The grain of choice is **Carolina Gold rice**, originally from West Africa and cultivated in South Carolina since the American Revolution.

Creamy grits are the base for Low Country favorite shrimp and grits.

Hefting oysters onto a table at the Lowcountry Oyster Festival at Boone Hall Plantation & Gardens in Mount Pleasant

Benne wafers, a crunchy cookie made with sesame seeds, brown sugar, and vanilla extract, are an abiding passion. However, the official state snack is actually **boiled peanuts**. Although Georgia and South Carolina may debate which state has more claim to the **peach**, the latter produces more than twice as many peaches as Georgia each year—which is the main reason (rather than to troll Georgians) that peaches are the official state fruit.

Despite its mid-Atlantic moniker, **Lady Baltimore cake** originated in South Carolina. The layer cake, which features white frosting and dried fruit, is said to have originated in the early 20th century when a Charleston housewife baked a special dessert for Owen Wister, author of the recently published *Lady Baltimore* novel.

CULINARY EXPERIENCES

South Carolina's quintessential foods are on full display at various festivals around the state. Seafood takes center stage at the **Lowcountry Oyster Festival** at Boone Hall Plantation & Gardens in Mount Pleasant (January) and the music-filled **Beaufort Shrimp Festival** (October).

Among the highlights of the **World Grits Festival** in St. George (April) are a corn toss and grits-eating contest, as well as a Rolling in the Grits competition in which contestants dive into a huge tub of grits and try to get as much as possible to stick to their bodies.

The **Loris Bog-Off Festival** (September) revolves around the yummy chicken and rice dish, while the **South Carolina Pelion Peanut Party** (November) features a giant

community peanut boil. One of the state's oldest food festivals, the **Irmo Okra Strut** (September) offers fried, pickled, and other ways to eat the green pods. A giant peach-shaped water tower is the centerpiece of the **South Carolina Peach Festival** in Gaffney (July).

One of the nation's rare statewide gastronomic events, **Restaurant Week South Carolina** is an 11-day feast featuring more than 100 restaurants in Charleston, Columbia, Greenville, Spartanburg, Myrtle Beach, and elsewhere. **Charleston Wine + Food** (March) spotlights the coastal region's top chefs and sommeliers, fishermen and farmers, mixologists, distillers, winemakers, and craft beer maestros.

"Chucktown" is also flush with guided food and beverage adventures. **Charleston Culinary Tours**

offers 2.5-hour downtown and historic Upper King Street outings, as well as a three-hour farm-to-table experience. In addition to its popular cocktail walks, **Bulldog Tours** offers foodie walks in appetizing areas like South of Broad and Shem Creek.

Carnivores can follow three different **barbecue trails** through South Carolina, covering eateries along the coast, in the Midlands, and up in the western mountains.

RESTAURANTS TO DIE FOR

One of the nation's top dining destinations, Charleston is world renowned for elevated Low Country cuisine and innovative southern cooking, especially at restaurants that combine incredible food and intriguing locations.

Circa 1886 is set within the original carriage house of the historic Wentworth Mansion, while the elegant **Husk** is inside a Queen Anne Victorian home and backyard garden on Queen Street. **Delaney Oyster House** fills a 19th-century clapboard "single house" with an elongated porch on the side rather than the front of the building, while **Church & Union** inhabits an early 20th-century redbrick chapel overlooking Charleston City Market. Given the fact that it occupies a 1920s bank building—with the kitchen inside the old vault—**the Ordinary** is anything but.

At the opposite end of the city's culinary spectrum are stylish modern eateries like **FIG** and its creative transatlantic dishes and **Wild Common** with its offbeat "living wallpaper" decor, chef's

You'll find everything from smoked turkey and pulled pork to sausage and from-scratch sides at Bobby's Wood-Smoked BBQ in Fountain Inn.

All smiles at the Charleston Wine + Food festival

GULLAH GEECHEE CUISINE

Descendants of West Africans who were enslaved to work rice, cotton, and indigo plantations in the antebellum Sea Islands, the Gullah Geechee people of the Carolinas and Georgia coast have evolved their own arts and crafts, language, music, and cuisine.

The Gullah Geechee from Africa introduced many ingredients and dishes that are now integral to southern and Low Country cooking, including okra, yams, peanuts, black-eyed peas, watermelon, peppers, sorghum, and golden rice.

Combining African and Native American ingredients with local seafood and African cooking methods, the Gullah Geechee developed novel dishes like okra soup, oyster stew, shrimp and grits, she-crab soup, rice purloo, deviled crab, red rice, Frogmore stew, and reezy peezy (rice and peas).

Among the seminal places to sample Gullah Geechee food along the South Carolina shore are **Hannibal's Soul Kitchen** in Charleston, **Bertha's Kitchen** in North Charleston, **Workmen's Café** on James Island, and **Gullah Grub Restaurant** on St. Helena Island.

table experience, and culinary mash-ups like oysters with chorizo, shrimp *har gow* (dumpling), and grits *pain de mie*. Tucked away in the off-the-beaten-path Cannonborough Elliotborough neighborhood, **Chubby Fish** also goes full fusion via smoked conger eel curry, black sea bass tempura, and Wagyu beef tartare with trout roe and Alabama white barbecue sauce.

Adventurous eaters venture beyond the city limits for unique eats like the modern Asian American food at **Jackrabbit Filly** in North Charleston, Low Country versions of pizza and pasta at the **Obstinate Daughter** on Sullivan's Island, or she-crab soup, mustard-based barbecue, and sweet potato casserole (topped with apples, raisins, and

pecans) at **Stono Market & Tomato Shed Café** on Johns Island.

Hilton Head's well-heeled residents frequent longtime island hangouts like **Michael Anthony's Cucina Italiana** and the **Market Cafe**, the romantic **Charlie's Coastal Bistro (L'etoile Verte)** with its classic French cuisine, and **Ruby Lee's** with its soul food, live tunes, and updated juke joint vibe. Hop a ferry to nearby Daufuskie Island for a double espresso or frozen lemonade at **School Grounds Coffee**, in the one-room schoolhouse where young Pat Conroy taught in the 1960s before his rise to literary fame and fortune.

Bay Street in Beaufort is a veritable restaurant row, with more than a dozen different eateries along a

five-block stretch, many of which overlook the Beaufort River. Anchoring the street are the **Ribaut Social Club** restaurant inside a historic antebellum mansion with Civil War tales, and the esteemed **Saltus River Grill**, where daily fresh catch is served with a Low Country or Carolina set featuring local bites like shrimp purloo, pickled okra, sweet corn chowchow, and smoked pimento cheese grits.

"Farm to fork" is the creed at the **Motor Supply Company Bistro** in Columbia, a state capital mainstay dedicated to locally sourced produce, fish, and meats. French flavors, and dishes from around the former French empire, dominate the menu at **Black Rooster**.

Some of the best Midlands-style

The watermelon salad at Motor Supply Company Bistro in Columbia

barbecue is served in nearby Lexington at joints like **Hudson's Smokehouse** and **Willie Jewell's Old School Bar-B-Q**. Established in the early 1940s, **Midway BBQ** in Buffalo is the last of 50 slow-cooked meat "hash houses" that once fed Union County. On the outskirts of Greenville, **Bobby's Wood-Smoked BBQ** offers sandwiches, meat by the pound, and barbecued tacos.

BOTTOMS UP!

The common Asian **tea** plant (*Camellia sinensis*) was first cultivated in North America along South Carolina's Ashley River in the late 18th century. Almost a century later, Dr. Charles Shepard established a highly regarded tea plantation in Summerville. His American Classic tea bushes were transferred to a new plantation on Wadmalaw Island in 1963. Now called the **Charleston Tea Garden**, it's the nation's only large-scale tea producer. Trolley and factory tours end at a gift shop, where bagged and loose tea, as well as American Classic shower gels, hand creams, soaps, and lip balms are sold.

Thus, it should come as no surprise that sweet tea—*Camellia sinensis* with ice, sugar, and perhaps a lemon wedge—is South Carolina's official state "hospitality beverage." Summerville's **Sweet Tea Trail** highlights a sweet tea mural, the world's largest mason jar of sweet tea (2,524 gallons/9,554 liters), and bars like the **Day Drink Brunch Lounge** and **Frothy Beard Off World** that feature sweet tea–infused cocktails or beers. The drink even gets infused into vodka at Charleston's Firefly Distillery.

First created in the 1890s as a cure for upset stomach, **Blenheim Ginger Ale** is the state's homegrown

The showstopping grilled pompano with ginger-scallion sauce at Charleston's Chubby Fish

soda. Another old-time favorite, **sweet potato beer** has evolved into a popular craft brew made by the likes of **Palmetto Brewing** in Charleston.

With its balmy coastal climate, Charleston is the perfect place to frequent high-rise bars like the **Citrus Club** atop the Dewberry hotel, the **Rooftop Bar** at the Vendue hotel, **Fiat Lux** above the Hotel Bennett, or the **Élevé** rooftop lounge crowning the Grand Bohemian Hotel.

Columbia's best bars cluster around the state capitol building and University of South Carolina campus. **Bourbon** whiskey bar stocks more than 500 different whiskeys and a food menu with bourbon-flavored steaks, pork chops, burgers, and gumbo. **The Aristocrat** gastropub offers live tunes and craft cocktails. Rare vintages from around the world and locally produced craft beers lure drinkers with a sophisticated palate to **Lula Drake Wine Parlour**. ∎

South Dakota

A confluence of prairie ingredients, Indigenous cooking, and pioneer-era comfort foods, South Dakota's eating scene reaches far beyond beefsteaks and corn on the cob.

THE BIG PICTURE

Founded: 1889

Population: 909,824

Official State Dessert: Kuchen

Also Known As: Mount Rushmore State

Culinary Influences: German, Czech, Lakota and other Native American tribes

Don't Miss: Rapid City, Sioux Falls, Deadwood

Claim to Fame: Kolaches, bison steak and burgers, corn

The four presidential figures on Mount Rushmore gaze across a state of infinite variety when it comes to food. Ingredients that existed long before the first rustlers and wagon trains rumbled across its endless prairies still form the base of many South Dakota dishes.

Native wildlife makes up traditional favorites like **bison steaks and burgers, fried or grilled walleye**, or **roast pheasant** and **pheasant salad sandwiches**.

Indigenous peoples were the first to cultivate **corn** in a state that ranks among the nation's top 10 producers. Among their other contributions are sweet ***wojapi* sauce** (made with chokecherries or other berries) and ***wasna*** (a patty made with ground bison, deer, or elk meat mixed with chokecherries and cooked in the animal's fat).

And Native Americans introduced newer dishes like **Indian tacos** and **fry bread** (the official state bread). **Tanka Bars**—a high-protein snack made by Oglala Lakota on the Pine Ridge Reservation—are a modern version of wasna that combines bison meat and cranberries.

The next culinary wave came from 19th-century European immigrants who packed recipes for **kolache** pastries, *fleischkuekle* (meat pies), and **kuchen**, the official state dessert, in the meager belongings they brought to the prairies. It's also thought that early European pioneers devised the **chislic stick**—cubed meat on a stick and the official state nosh.

CULINARY EXPERIENCES

Demonstrations by celebrated Native American chefs, sampling decolonized foods, and talks on food sovereignty, as well as Indigenous entertainment and games, are among the ongoing attractions of the **Lakota Food Summit** in Rapid City (February).

Kolache and other traditional Czech foods take center stage at **Tabor Czech Days** near Yankton (June), started in 1872 and one of the nation's oldest food festivals. The **South Dakota Chislic Festival** at the Prairie Arboretum in Freeman (July) shines a spotlight on succulent skewered meats.

Housed inside a historic pioneer-era stone bar, the free **Sioux Falls Stockyards Ag Experience** illuminates the role of farming and ranching on South Dakota life

A hefty scoop of caramelized onions tops an equally hefty bison burger.

Visitors are greeted with a smile at the Corn Palace in Mitchell.

through family-friendly hands-on exhibits. **Sioux Falls Food Tours** offers year-round guided walks of four or five restaurants and craft breweries in the downtown area. The **Hartford Area Burger Battle** takes place in January as five eateries near Sioux Falls vie for the coveted title of best burger.

RESTAURANTS TO DIE FOR

Far and away the state's largest urban area, Sioux Falls also boasts the lion's share of fine dining establishments. **Minervas** is renowned for surf and turf, as well as shareable chislic skewers and locally sourced dishes like the potato-crusted walleye, buffalo burger, and Tatanka bison fillet in a Buffalo Trace Bourbon demi.

Housed inside a vintage 1908 hydroelectric powerhouse, **Falls Overlook Café** offers casual dining in Falls Park on the banks of the Big Sioux River. A combination Airstream trailer and brick-and-mortar structure, **Phillips Avenue Diner** offers all-American classics like meatloaf, chicken-fried steak, Cobb salad, and corned beef hash.

Between the **Carnaval Brazilian Grill** ("a festival of meat!"), **Lalibela** Ethiopian cuisine, and **Sanaa's 8th Street Gourmet** for Eastern Mediterranean cooking, Sioux Falls flaunts a surprising array of global cuisines.

Way out west (both in location and spirit), Rapid City is another culinary hub. An enclave for slow

food, great steaks, and elegant dining, **Delmonico Grill** might be the state's single best restaurant. Just around the corner, **Tally's Silver Spoon** raises South Dakota standards to new heights with dishes like autumn oak pheasant in apple cider, root beer bison with glazed prunes, and marinated rib eye chislic with pickled bananas and peanuts.

Out in the Badlands, **Wall Drug** is nearly as iconic as South Dakota's Corn Palace. Opened in 1931, the sprawling emporium features a restaurant (famous for its homemade doughnuts) that doubles as a gallery of Western art, as well as a soda fountain and ice-cream shop, apothecary shop, and pharmacy museum. **Cattleman's**

Club Steakhouse in Pierre is another old-timer.

The Black Hills have plenty of good grub. Located inside the Indian Museum of North America at the Crazy Horse Memorial, **Laughing Water Restaurant** offers Native American specialties like Indian tacos, bison stew, and fry bread with wojapi sauce. Fry bread tacos, bison burgers, and fry bread dessert with powdered sugar and wojabi sauce highlight the menu at the **Stage Stop Cafe** (opened in 1878) at Cheyenne Crossing in the town of Lead.

MITCHELL CORN PALACE

South Dakota's most distinctive building, the whimsical Corn Palace rises above the town of Mitchell, about an hour's drive west of Sioux Falls.

Originally established as a multi-purpose community center and a means to promote the region's paramount crop, the palace opened in 1892 but was completely reworked in the 1920s and '30s, when it assumed its much photographed Moorish Revival facade.

Fashioned from corn and other grains and native grasses, the building's beloved murals are created by design and digital media students from Dakota Wesleyan University. The old murals are dismantled each August and new ones are unveiled the following October.

Free guided tours are offered throughout the summer, but the Corn Palace is busy year-round with basketball games, rodeos, concerts, an autumn polka festival, a farmers market, and a popular **Corn Palace Festival** (August) that features carnival rides, live music, and food vendors.

Traditional southern Brazilian roasting and serving techniques are on display at Carnaval Brazilian Grill in Sioux Falls.

In-season food and wine pairings at Hill City's Prairie Berry Winery

Along the state's eastern edge in Brookings, **Pheasant Restaurant & Lounge** (opened in 1949) offers innovative twists on northern prairie dishes, including peasant salad lettuce wraps, sweet corn and sunflower hummus, lamb chislic, and rhubarb jerk chicken. Down on Main, **Nick's Hamburger Shop** (established in 1929) offers burgers "by the bag," as the slogan goes, and homemade pies.

Fleischkuekle is one of the specialties at **Meridian Corner** in Freeman, which also serves corn nuggets, mutton or lamb chislic, various potato-focused dishes, and amazing steaks. Forty-five minutes to the west, **Dimock Dairy** churns out delicious artisanal cheeses, cheese curds, cheese spreads, and 13-pound (6 kg) South Dakota cheese horns.

BOTTOMS UP!

It may not seem that tempting at first glance, but the **South Dakota Martini** (aka Beertini) is an invigorating blend of draft beer, tomato juice, green olives, and perhaps a few pickle slices that's especially refreshing on a hot summer day on the prairie.

Just about any bar can create a SoDak Martini on request. However, only a few specialize in the art of mixology, including the **Carpenter Bar** in downtown Sioux Falls or the Vertex Sky Bar on the roof of the historic **Hotel Alex Johnson** in Rapid City.

Deadwood doesn't boast nearly as many saloons as in its Wild West days, but you can still undertake a pretty good pub crawl along Main Street, hopping between the **Nugget Saloon, Mustang Sally's** sports bar, **Mavericks Steaks & Cocktails, Sick-N-Twisted Brewery**, and **Saloon No. 10,** where Wild Bill Hickok was shot dead during an 1876 poker game.

For something totally different, try the cranberry, black currant, pear, pumpkin, edelweiss, rhubarb, or other fruity flavors at **Prairie Berry Winery** in the Black Hills. ■

Tennessee

Wedged between the Mississippi River and the Appalachian Mountains, the Volunteer State melds southern foods, flavors, and cooking methods with its unique culinary ways and means.

THE BIG PICTURE

Founded: 1796

Population: 7.05 million

Official State Fruit: Tomato

Also Known As: Volunteer State

Culinary Influences: West African, southeastern Indian, western European

Don't Miss: Gatlinburg, Memphis, Nashville

Claim to Fame: Goo Goo Clusters, Jack Daniel's, Memphis-style barbecue, doodle soup

One of the four cornerstones of American smoked meats, **Memphis-style barbecue** is almost always pork ribs or shoulders, brushed with a wet or dry rub with as many as 40 different spices before being slow-cooked over a pit.

Nashville may not have a unique barbecue style, but it does have **hot chicken sandwiches**, tangy concoctions that should include hot sauce and paprika or cayenne pepper, plus mayonnaise, bread-and-butter pickles, and thinly sliced cabbage. Tennesseans are also partial to **country ham**, **catfish**, and a restaurant dish called **meat and three** in which three sides (like **hush puppies,** **macaroni and cheese, baked beans**, or **fried pickles**) accompany the carnivorous main.

Another Tennessee standby is **doodle soup**, a vinegar-based broth with some kind of meat (chicken, pork, rabbit, you name it) and a bit of cayenne pepper to give it a kick. The origin of the name is lost in time—perhaps from the general merchandise doodle wagons that roamed Tennessee in the 19th century.

Among the state's much loved desserts are **banana pudding, stack cake, Ambrosia icebox cake**, and **moon pies**. With a flavored marshmallow filling between two graham crackers, all covered in chocolate, MoonPies are really more like supersize cookies. Invented in 1917 by the same Chattanooga bakery that makes them today, they are traditionally consumed with **RC Cola**, although nobody seems to know why. The official candy of Nashville, **Goo Goo Clusters**, featuring chocolate, peanut, and marshmallow, were first sold in 1912 and became a popular snack at the Grand Ole Opry.

CULINARY EXPERIENCES

Doodle Soup Days in September draws hungry and curious eaters to Bradford in western Tennessee (the self-proclaimed "doodle soup capital of the world" since 1957). South Pittsburg on the Tennessee River offers the **National Cornbread Festival** in April, a shindig that includes a cornbread cookoff, eating competition, and Cornbread Alley recipe exchange. Bell Buckle is home to the **RC Cola–MoonPie Festival** (June).

Nashville's supper club shows combine dinner, drinks, and live entertainment. If the popular **Nashville Nightlife Dinner Theater** or the **General Jackson Showboat** seem a little too touristy, try more locally

Cut the heat of a Nashville hot chicken sandwich with toppings like creamy coleslaw and tangy pickles.

Pitmaster Robert Cox grills ribs over charcoal for the award-winning Rendezvous in Memphis.

focused shows like the **Twelve Thirty Club** on Lower Broadway or **Cabana Taps** near Vanderbilt University.

The Twelve Thirty Club is part of the **Assembly Food Hall** complex, which boasts 30 bars and restaurants, plus live music on Nashville's largest entertainment rooftop. Among its many eating options are **Hōru Sushi Kitchen, Chilangos Tacos, Istanbul Shawarma**, and **Thai Esane**.

RESTAURANTS TO DIE FOR

Memphis barbecue reaches a delectable peak at vintage joints like **Cozy Corner BBQ** in Uptown and **Charles Vergos' Rendezvous** near the AutoZone Park baseball diamond. Fried green tomatoes, chitterlings, catfish, and pork

chops are some of the southern delights at **Four Way** soul food in Washington Heights.

Audacious new eateries have expanded the Memphis food scene in recent years. **Erling Jensen** restaurant and its namesake Danish chef offer a wonderful tasting menu that can include lamb barbacoa or bluefin tuna poke paired with international wines. **Flight** restaurant in downtown Memphis puts an upscale twist on southern favorites like shrimp and grits, chicken and waffles, and Louisiana redfish. **Magnolia & May** also blends old and new in dishes like Tacos con Mempho with pulled pork or their collard green, Swiss cheese, and fried chicken melt sandwich.

Nashville boasts southern feasts at places like **Arnold's Country Kitchen** with its fried chicken, fried catfish, and cherrywood-smoked ribs, or the upscale **Husk**, tucked into a historic mansion on Rutledge Hill.

But given an influx of new residents (and tourists) from around the globe, the Music City eating scene has become increasingly international. Under James Beard Award winner Tony Mantuano, **Yolan** has evolved into the city's top Italian eatery. At **City House** restaurant, soul food meets Italian in dishes like turnip greens ravioli and peaches and mozzarella pizza. A similar transatlantic blend colors the modern Mediterranean menu at **Butcher & Bee**. Nashville's Asian eating scene is

out of this world, with choices like **Tánsuǒ** and its contemporary Chinese cuisine, the Asian fusion menu at **Locust**, and **Suzy Wong's Drag'n Brunch**.

A restored early 20th-century hotel and brothel provides an elegant setting for **St. John's Restaurant** in Chattanooga and its upscale surf and turf offerings. Modern takes on southern stalwarts like fried chicken, pot roast, and voodoo shrimp are the forte at **Public House Chattanooga**. Doing double duty as a butcher shop and café, **Main Street Meats** offers a range of meat sandwich and steak options.

BOTTOMS UP!

Nashville's Lower Broadway is lined by honky-tonk bars like **Legends Corner, the Stage**, and the fabled **Tootsies Orchid Lounge**, where Willie Nelson, Keith Urban, and many other country music legends have appeared over the years.

The **Black Rabbit** on 3rd Avenue in the Arts District also stages live tunes, but earlier in the evening it's a hip choice for creative cocktails like the Goat Rodeo, Hot Lips Houlihan, or Quarter Tank of Gasoline. On the south side, the **Big Bar at Bastion** presents an equally enticing cocktail menu in a restored warehouse setting, while the historic Marathon Motor Works offers the triple threat of **Grinder's Switch Winery, Corsair Distillery**, and **Tennessee Legend** whiskey distillery.

Legendary Beale Street in Memphis is the epicenter of blues, soul, and classic rock-and-roll in the riverside city. **Alfred's on Beale** flaunts a vast collection of gold records and diverse live music that ranges all the

Yolan offers seasonal Italian fine dining at the luxurious Joseph hotel in Nashville.

way from Elvis tribute shows to the Memphis Jazz Orchestra. **Silky O'Sullivan's** is renowned for its dueling pianos, patio band, and (believe it or not) live goats. All-time greats lend their names and musical cred to **B.B. King's Blues Club** and **Jerry Lee Lewis' Cafe & Honky Tonk**.

Chattanooga may not have the musical heritage, but the city in southeast Tennessee has some mighty fine spots to drink. With its brick and wood decor, **the Social** on Market Street offers a casual space for conversation and cocktails. A few blocks away, the **Flying Squirrel** bar flaunts a great craft beer selection in an eye-catching structure with a massive canopy roof. The **Proof Bar & Incubator** derives its unusual name from the pairing of a traditional cocktail bar with an experimental kitchen where local chefs can test new concepts. ■

Catch a show and taste some classic southern fare at B.B. King's Blues Club on Beale Street in Memphis.

JACK DANIEL'S

One of the world's most popular whiskey brands—with more than 15 million cases sold each year—got its start in Lynchburg, Tennessee, shortly after the Civil War. Its namesake was **Jasper "Jack" Daniel**, who learned the fine art of whiskeymaking from a local preacher and former enslaved man named "Nearest" Green, who would become his first head distiller.

By the end of the 19th century, Daniel's **Old No. 7 Tennessee** sour mash whiskey was a nationwide sensation. More often called "Black Label" owing to the color of its original packaging, the whiskey is said to draw its distinctive flavor from the mineral-rich water of Cave Spring Hollow and charcoal "mellowing," or filtering, after distillation.

Though **Black Label** remains the company's flagship drink, Jack Daniel's now produces a variety of libations, including rye and flavored whiskey liqueurs. Located on the original site Jack Daniel chose, the distillery in Lynchburg offers daily tours.

Texas

Texas is a big state with a huge appetite that runs all the way from Tex-Mex and Gulf of Mexico seafood to classic barbecue joints and vintage roadside diners.

One of the nation's most iconic regional cuisines, **Tex-Mex** is a fusion of Mexican foods and cooking methods that began melding in the 1680s, when the first Spanish colonial settlers crossed the Rio Grande and the ingredients that typify the dishes became readily available in what later became the state of Texas.

Many of the dishes—**tamales, tacos, enchiladas, fajitas**—are

THE BIG PICTURE

Founded: 1845

Population: 30.03 million

Official State Food: Chili con carne

Also Known As: Lone Star State

Culinary Influences: Mexican, Spanish, German

Don't Miss: San Antonio, Austin, Houston

Claim to Fame: Brisket, queso, Whataburger, Blue Bell ice cream, Fritos

standard Mexican fare. But over the years, others have taken on a unique Tejano/Texas character, including a chili-flavored beef and kidney bean stew called **chili con carne** (the Texas state food), which was pioneered during frontier days by chuck wagon cooks, and the "Chili Queens" of 1930s San Antonio with their popular roadside stalls. On the other hand, **Texas red chili** nixes the beans in favor of more tomatoes and chili pepper. Another blast from the past, *pan de campo* (the Texas state bread) was a cowboy campfire staple that originated among the Tejano vaqueros of South Texas.

Thanks to politicians partial to local grub, Texas has a lot of official state foods. There are both overall (**jalapeño**) and native (**chiltepin**) state peppers and also two state pastries: the **strudel**, introduced by German-speaking immigrants, and **sopaipilla** from south of the border. **Tortilla chips and salsa** are the state snack, **sweet onions** the state vegetable, **red grapefruit** the state fruit, and so on. There's even an official state cooking implement: the **Dutch oven**.

The state crustacean is the **Gulf shrimp**, which competes for

Big, bold Texas staple chili con carne

Texas longhorn cattle roam a field near Bee.

popularity with other aquatic edibles like **Gulf oysters, blue crab, flounder, red drum, grouper, sheepshead**, and **tuna**. With so many rivers and reservoirs, Texas also boasts a bounty of freshwater denizens: **catfish, crappie, bass**, and **crawfish**.

Seeing as the fabled Texas longhorn is the official large mammal—and as much a part of local lore as the Alamo and Texas Rangers—it comes as no surprise that **beef** is also a big deal. Menus feature steaks, sausages, ribs, brisket, and **chicken-fried steak** smothered in zesty white gravy.

At the end of a meal, Texans like to dig into official state desserts like **pecan pie** or **peach cobbler**, which are best eaten à la mode with Texas-made **Blue Bell ice cream**. Despite its name, **Texas pecan fruitcake** does not have official status despite its popularity far beyond the Lone Star State.

CULINARY EXPERIENCES

Texas is such a huge state—and barbecue such a huge deal—that there's more than one route for carnivorous gastronomes to follow. The **Texas Barbecue Trail** loops through the Hill Country between Austin and San Antonio with stops in smoked meat–loving towns like Taylor, Elgin, Lockhart, and Luling. The **Great Coastal Texas Barbecue Trail** features eight options in and around Victoria.

Delicious brisket, ribs, pulled pork, and chicken are the focus of several fall events: the **Southern Smoke Festival** in Houston (October), the **Q BBQ Fest** at AT&T Stadium in the Dallas–Fort Worth (DFW) metro area (November), and the long-running *Texas Monthly* **BBQ Festival** in Lockhart (November).

The Lone Star love for chili reaches fever pitch at the **Terlingua International Chili Cookoff** near Big Bend National Park (November). Founded in 1967, the desert ghost town extravaganza also includes the World Championship Margarita Mix-Off and the Jimmy Doherty Memorial Salsa Contest.

Up in the Big D, the **Dallas Kosher Chili Cookoff** (March) features meat and vegetarian categories. Dallas also hosts the **State Fair of Texas** (September–October), which kicked off in 1886 and boasts its own barbecue and chili contests, as

Crown your steak with Carpet Topping (a fried oyster, Buffalo sauce, blue cheese, and bacon) for the ultimate indulgence at B&B Butchers & Restaurant in Houston.

well as a celebrity chef kitchen, wine garden, and Big Tex Choice Awards for offbeat midway foods like deep-fried Blue Bell rocky road ice cream or a fried charcuterie board.

Those who want a deeper dive into the state's favorite ice cream can visit the **Blue Bell Creamery** in Brenham (near Houston), which includes an old-fashioned ice-cream parlor, country store, Blue Bell Museum, and observation deck above the factory floor.

With a long shore along the Gulf of Mexico, Texas also stages seafood events like the **Fulton Oysterfest** near Corpus Christi (March) with its oyster-eating and -decorating contests; a crab gumbo cook-off and crab nachos at the **Texas Crab Festival** in Crystal Beach (May), and **Shrimporee** in Aransas Pass (May).

RESTAURANTS TO DIE FOR

No one would dispute that Dallas knows how to eat well.

The **Mansion Restaurant** raised the bar on local dining when it debuted in 1980, and the Turtle Creek sanctum continues to excel at nouvelle American cuisine, including an exquisite tasting menu with wine pairings. The only restaurant in the Big D that's more formal is the elegant **French Room** in the downtown Adolphus Hotel, known for both its lavish afternoon tea and over-the-top Louis XVI decor.

North Dallas has transformed into something of a culinary oasis via eateries like **Matt's Rancho Martinez** and its awesome Tex-Mex offerings, and **Sister**'s menu of Texas meets Mediterranean has fusion dishes like Calabrian chili ravioli and pork *secreto* with apricot honey and grilled fennel. Down in Deep Ellum, the **AllGood Cafe** serves Texas-flavored favorites like tenderloin beef stew with green chilies, jalapeño cheddar cornbread, and pecan chocolate sheet cake.

Fort Worth is also bullish on Lone Star grub. **Lonesome Dove Western Bistro** in the Stockyards district goes full frontier with dishes like rattlesnake and rabbit sausage, buffalo rib eye steak, elk sliders, and red chili. **Bonnell's Fine Texas Cuisine** is celebrated for its elevated southwestern, Mexican, and creole cuisine.

Cowtown is also home to **Goldee's Barbecue**, a southside shack that *Texas Monthly* magazine named the best barbecue in Texas. For something totally different, try the Texas Ethiopian barbecue at **Smoke'N Ash** in Arlington.

Houston is an energy powerhouse that lures plenty of petrodollars for meals at posh restaurants like **March** with its Mediterranean tasting menus, or caviar and steak at **B&B Butchers & Restaurant**. Modern

---

THE BIRTH OF FRITOS

Fritos were born of the Great Depression and an unlikely encounter between two San Antonio men striving to survive the economic downturn.

In 1932, restaurateur Gustavo Olguin placed a classified ad in a local newspaper offering to sell the recipe for a small fried corn chip snack made with masa dough. Olguin dubbed them "fritos" after the Spanish word for "fried."

Looking to expand his own

fortunes, young San Antonio candy store owner Charles Doolin purchased the recipes and began making "Fritos" (with a capital *F*) in his mother's basement.

By 1945, Doolin inked a deal with snack entrepreneur Herman Lay—already famous for automating potato chip manufacturing—to distribute Fritos nationwide. By 1961 they had merged to form **Frito-Lay**, the world's largest snack maker.

Euro-American cuisine is the attraction at hip hangouts like **Nancy's Hustle** in East Downtown and **Squable** in the Heights.

Houston can also do comfort food. With four locations around the metro area, **House of Pies** offers an astounding array of chicken dinners, chicken burgers, chicken salads, and even chicken breakfasts with country gravy. **Turkey Leg Hut** in Museum Park focuses on dishes from that other bird, with offerings like Alfredo turkey balls, turkey-stuffed baked potatoes, and its signature stuffed turkey legs.

But what really makes Houston special is abundant global cuisine.

Take a gastronomic trip across Mexico with coastal cuisine at **Caracol**, Oaxacan fare at **Xochi**, the Mexico City bistro vibe at **Cuchara**, and **Hugo's** with bites from all around Mexico. Or travel to Africa with Ethiopian dishes at **Blue Nile**, Ghanaian specialties like goat meat soup and jollof rice at **Afrikiko**, or the authentic Nigerian cooking at **Safari**. Finish the culinary journey with modern Vietnamese at **Xin Chào** or Malaysian street food at **Phat Eatery** in Katy.

Dig into culinary history and delicious Tex-Mex dishes in San Antonio at **La Fonda on Main**, one of the spots where the cuisine was

conceived in the 1930s. Overlooking the River Walk, **Acenar** offers a contemporary take on Tex-Mex with dishes like chicken-fried oyster tacos or roasted mushrooms and squash served fajita style.

San Antonio is also one of the top spots in Texas to sample Mexican regional cuisines, especially at innovative eateries of chef Johnny Hernandez. **La Gloria** serves street foods from as far apart as Mexico City and Oaxaca, while **La Frutería** on the south side does Mexican-style tapas and primo tequilas.

Leave it to an Englishman (Bruce Auden) to create one of San Antonio's bastions of nouvelle Texas

A selection of vibrant favorites at San Antonio's La Gloria: *tlayuda* with *cochinita pibil* (Yucatán-style pork), pickled red onions, Mexican street corn, and stone-ground corn tortillas

cuisine, a River Walk bistro called **Biga** with quirky dishes like habanero jerk scallops with cheesy grits and 11 spiced South Texas antelope and Lockhart quail. Down in Southtown, book the chef's table at **Bliss** and order the seven-course contemporary American tasting menu.

Austin's eclectic eating scene ranges between relative old-timers like **Güero's Taco Bar** or **Joe's Bakery & Coffee Shop** and newfangled places made to look old. Among the latter are downtown's **24 Diner**, which specializes in burgers and all-day breakfast, and **Distant Relatives**, a trendy soul food and barbecue joint in southeast Austin.

They say don't eat seafood far from the ocean, but **Uchi** is that rare exception with American sushi master Tyson Cole's mouthwatering morsels like bluefin akami crudo and oak-grilled walu walu (mackerel). Just up South Lamar Boulevard, **Odd Duck** complements its industrial chic home with innovative American food. Some of Austin's most intriguing eats are served at **Canje** with its Guyana Caribbean cooking.

To paraphrase Marty Robbins, you'll fall in love with the Mexican food out in the West Texas town of El Paso at places like the **L&J Cafe** (opened in 1927) across the street from Concordia Cemetery and eco-friendly **Café Mayapán** in the Eucalyptus district. For upscale dining in the border city, nothing beats the elegant **Cafe Central**, originally founded in Juarez in 1918 before it moved across the Rio Grande.

Great eats are few and far apart in most of West Texas. But you'll

Grab breakfast all day at Austin's 24 Diner, where the crispy fried chicken pairs perfectly with Belgian-style yeast waffles.

Famous Big Tex overseeing the State Fair of Texas in Dallas

find great grub at the **Starlight Theatre** restaurant in Terlingua ghost town; awesome burgers, sandwiches, and a vintage soda fountain at the **Drug Store** in Fort Davis (founded in 1913); and amazing breakfast at the **Water Stop** in artsy Marfa.

Goodson's Cafe in Tomball (north of Houston) and **Mary's Café** in Strawn (west of Fort Worth) are both famed for their chicken-fried steak and other comfort foods. Opened in 1896, **Collin Street Bakery & Café** in Corsicana (south of Dallas) serves Texas-style fruitcake, Frito pie, Texas chili (without beans!), and other Lone Star favorites. The **Beehive Restaurant & Saloon**— founded by Iranian brothers Ali and Nariman Esfandiary—serves amazing steaks on the outskirts of Abilene.

Enjoy a scoop while touring Blue Bell Creamery in Brenham.

Antonio Museum of Art (SAMA). **Pearl Brewery**, the city's other big beermaking factory, has morphed into a fashionable residential and entertainment complex with multiple bars and restaurants.

San Antonio is also flush with historic bars. Opposite the Alamo, the **Menger Bar** (opened in 1887) is where Teddy Roosevelt recruited local cowboys into his Rough Riders troupe for the Spanish-American War. A few blocks away, the **Buckhorn Saloon & Museum** is famed for its Old West ambience and vast collection of Texas memorabilia displayed in two museums off the main bar. Albert Friedrich started collecting in the 1880s and eventually

THE FATHER OF SOUTHWESTERN CUISINE

A Food Network celebrity chef and best-selling cookbook author, **Dean Fearing** has been a major player on the Texas food scene since the 1980s, when he was appointed executive chef at the Mansion on Turtle Creek.

An early advocate of American southwestern cuisine, Fearing rose to national fame via his Texas-inspired culinary creations on the PBS series *Great Chefs,* as well as highly acclaimed books like *The Texas Food Bible: From Legendary Dishes to New Classics* and *Dean Fearing's Southwest Cuisine: Blending Asia and the Americas.*

Departing the Mansion on Turtle Creek in 2007, Fearing founded his self-titled restaurant at the Ritz-Carlton in Dallas. Among the enticing items at **Fearing's Restaurant** are mesquite fire-grilled Wagyu steaks, Lone Star surf and turf carpaccio, and barbecued short rib enchiladas with chorizo *queso fundido* (melted cheese).

BOTTOMS UP!

Like so many fabled sodas, **Dr Pepper** was discovered by a pharmacist tinkering with carbonated flavors. In this case, it was Charles Alderton who invented the drink in 1885 while working at Morrison's Old Corner Drug Store in Waco, although no one is exactly sure why he gave it that name. Located in a former bottling plant, Waco's **Dr Pepper Museum** includes an "Extreme Pepper Experience" with a private guide. Popular in much of the American South, **Big Red** soda is another Waco contrivance (1937) and is still bottled in the Texas city.

Inspired by a Slurpee machine he saw in a 7-Eleven store, Dallas restaurant owner Mariano Martinez purchased a blender and instructed his bartenders on how to make the first **frozen margaritas** in 1971. Nowadays, **Mariano's Hacienda** in North Dallas serves 15 different flavors of the frosty cocktail by the glass or gallon. An import from south of the border, the michelada (beer, lime juice, chili peppers, salt, and hot sauce) is another popular Lone Star libation.

Dubbed the "National Beer of Texas," **Lone Star** opened its famous San Antonio brewery in 1884. The brewery tour eventually became one of the city's leading tourist attractions, but the sprawling facility now houses the San

transferred everything to the Buckhorn's first iteration.

One of the nation's renowned hipster hangouts and a college party town, Austin is famed for its nightlife. **Upstairs at Caroline** offers a vast, enclosed roof space with billiards, table games, southwestern eats, and craft cocktails (like its signature rum coconut Hipster-Jito) on draft. Craft beer buffs gather at the **Brass Tap** in Round Rock for the extensive selection of local and exotic suds and live music in the back garden.

Austin also boasts some pretty cool dives. Country music and a big dance floor are the lures at the **White Horse Honky Tonk**, while billiards and the Baton Creole food truck attract a crowd to the **Shangri-La** tiki bar, both of them

along Comal Street in the East Cesar Chavez neighborhood.

The Hill Country around Austin and San Antonio remains a hotbed for old-fashioned, Texas-style country music bars, including exalted spots like **Luckenbach Dance Hall** in Fredericksburg and **Mercer Dancehall** in Dripping Springs.

The DFW metro area is also flush with country music bars. Billed as the world's largest honky-tonk, **Billy Bob's Texas** in Fort Worth's historic Stockyards area offers dancing, dining, and mechanical bulls. Up in Plano, **Love & War in Texas** flavors its country tunes with southwestern and south-of-the-border cuisine. The funky Deep Ellum neighborhood is the place to catch country music in Dallas, with

Adair's Saloon and **Double Wide** leading the charge.

Houston may have its honky-tonks—like the **Goode Company Armadillo Palace**—but the Magnolia City is more of a cocktail town. Two areas lend themselves to a spirited cocktail crawl. Yale Street in the Heights is home to **Better Luck Tomorrow** with its creative riffs on classic cocktails, and **Eight Row Flint**, where patrons can choose between expensive rare bourbons or "Cheap Thrills" like Wild Turkey or Jim Beam. South of Buffalo Bayou Park, **Anvil** bar mixes 100 different cocktails, while the **93' Til** record bar spins classic discs, offbeat mixed drinks, and Lone Star Beer with a shot of mezcal or rye. ■

Innovative drinks get pride of place at Mariano's Hacienda in Dallas.

Utah

Utah's unique food culture traces its roots to early Mormon kitchens and campfires. But the state's modern chefs, brewers, and distillers have expanded the culinary scene with a wide variety of new tastes, textures, and singular eating spots.

THE BIG PICTURE

Founded: 1896

Population: 3.38 million

Official State Snack: Jell-O

Also Known As: Beehive State

Culinary Influences: Mormon, Ute and other Native American tribes

Don't Miss: Park City, Provo, Salt Lake City

Claim to Fame: Fry sauce, funeral potatoes, dirty sodas

As with many aspects of Utahan culture, the Church of Jesus Christ of Latter-day Saints has had a profound impact on the state's food culture. Though it's tempting to assume that many iconic Mormon dishes were first created in pioneer days, some of them are 20th-century creations.

After years of lobbying by local advocates, **Jell-O** was declared the official state snack food in 2001. Although invented in upstate New York, the wiggly, jiggly gelatin is the cornerstone of the popular Mormon dish **green Jell-O salad**. Another favorite is **frog eye salad**, which blends *acini de pepe* pasta, pineapple, mandarin oranges, and whipped cream. Pineapple also features in the **Hawaiian haystack**, a mound of steamed rice cloaked in chicken, chow mein noodles, shredded coconut, assorted vegetables, and canned pineapple. **Funeral potatoes** have evolved from a post-burial casserole into a popular anytime dish that combines potatoes, cream of chicken soup, cornflakes, and sour cream. And **fry sauce** (mayonnaise mixed with ketchup and spices) is a 1940s invention that's still a mainstay.

Mormon dishes are rare on restaurant menus. However, the Chuck-A-Rama Buffet chain carries three of these dishes, as well as other Utah favorites like **bread pudding** and deep-fried **scones** served with honey and powdered sugar.

Living up to its nickname, the Beehive State produces some mighty fine **honey**. And it should come as no surprise that **salt**—including ordinary Morton table salt and gourmet Redmond Real Salt—is produced in a state that boasts the Great Salt Lake. Among other local delicacies are **Morgan Valley Lamb**, soft and flaky **Mile High biscuits**, and the succulent **Bear Lake raspberries** found in shakes, jams, pies, and other sweet things.

CULINARY EXPERIENCES

Besides the midway food stalls at the **Utah State Fair** (September), look for traditional Mormon dishes at the **Salt Lake City Downtown Farmers Market** (November–April) and its equivalents around the state.

Foodie Field Trips organizes guided culinary walking tours that include popular restaurants and local foods in St. George, Kanab, and Springdale near Zion National Park in southern Utah.

Among Utah's flavorsome food festivals are **Savor the Summit** outdoor dining party in Park City

Sprinkle deep-fried Utah scones with sugar before drizzling with honey.

Park City locals hit the streets for Savor the Summit, an outdoor dinner party down the center of Main Street.

(June), **Bear Lake Raspberry Days** in Garden City (August), **Melon Days** in Green River (September), and **Brigham City Peach Days** (September).

RESTAURANTS TO DIE FOR

The brasserie-style **Copper Onion** in Salt Lake City takes full advantage of the intermontane setting with dishes like duck confit cassoulet, rainbow trout, and Wagyu beef stroganoff. **Table X** on the city's south side presents two nightly tasting menus (five and seven courses) paired with wines or nonalcoholic beverages, with the option of making the entire menu vegetarian. Though the gourmet mushrooms and braised lamb pasta may catch your eye, don't overlook the restaurant's extraordinary sourdough bread.

Yet the superstar of Utah fine dining is Park City, the mountain town less than an hour's drive from SLC famous for snow sports, a legendary film festival, and frequent celebrity sightings. With its airy dining room and exemplary service—and dishes like seared trout salad, shiitake fritters, and double-wide pork chops—**Twisted Fern** leads the pack. Often listed among the nation's top restaurants, **Riverhorse on Main** complements its artfully presented New American cuisine with an extensive wine cellar and live music.

Closer to the slopes, **the Farm** at Park City Mountain resort creates French dishes with locally sourced ingredients in a cozy bistro atmosphere. **Glitretind** restaurant at Stein Eriksen Lodge serves incredible views with its sustainable seafood and free-range lamb, beef, and bison dishes. And on Main Street, **No Name Saloon** offers dive bar–style digs and delicious bison burgers.

One of the great things about Utah is the fact that you don't have to spend a small fortune for awesome food. An old auto repair shop in Salt Lake City has morphed into **Garage on Beck** with its modern takes on comfort foods like chicken and waffles, meatloaf,

FRUITA FRUIT PICKING

One of Utah's more unusual food experiences is fruit picking in **Capitol Reef National Park**. Founded by Mormon pioneers in 1880, historic Fruita village inside the park harbors around 1,900 heirloom fruit trees—including apples, apricots, peaches, pears, and cherries—in 19 vintage orchards along the Fremont River.

Visitors are free to harvest ripe fruit at orchards marked with U-pick signs. Wooden fruit-picking sticks, ladders, and bags are available to aid with the roundup. Once finished, visitors are asked to weigh their haul and slip the recommended amount per pound into the self-pay station box. Funds are used to help maintain the orchards. More information is available on the Capitol Reef website.

Try a fusion of Native American and southwestern cuisines at Provo's Black Sheep Cafe.

chicken pot pie, and funeral potatoes. **Red Iguana** near Temple Square serves some of the capital's best Mexican food, while **Ruth's Diner** is renowned for its Mile High biscuits and rustic setting in Emigration Canyon in the Wasatch Range.

Black Sheep Cafe in Provo offers contemporary Native American dishes like Navajo tacos, green chili stew, and honey-lavender fry bread. Another Provo taste treat is the **BYU Creamery on Ninth**, an ice-cream parlor on the Brigham Young University campus with offbeat flavors like Blue Goggles, Fluffernutter, and Bishop's Bash.

A longtime favorite in south-central Utah, **Hell's Backbone Grill** in Boulder harvests many of the ingredients for its dishes, jams, and pet treats from its own organic farm. Farther east, Moab's favorite lunch joint is **Milt's Stop & Eat**, serving burgers, shakes, patty melts, and more since 1954. The zenith of dining in St. George is the southwestern cuisine at the art-filled **Painted Pony** in Ancestor Square.

BOTTOMS UP!

Like so many other states, Utah boasts an ever expanding craft

Everything is sourced locally or made in-house at James Beard Award semifinalist Table X in Salt Lake City.

beer scene with local twists. Founded in 1986, **Wasatch Brewery** in Park City is the state's oldest purveyor of fine suds like Snow Bank Amber Lager, Ghost Rider IPA, and Polygamy Porter. Another Park City pioneer is **High West Saloon**, a craft whiskey distillery with a bar and restaurant that patrons can reach by road, foot, skis, or snowboard. Rounding out the city's beverage choices, **Old Town Cellars** makes private-label wines with grapes imported from the Napa Valley, Russian River Valley, and other West Coast AVAs.

One of the state's most popular nonalcoholic drinks is **apple beer**, a naturally flavored soda manufactured in Holladay. Another uniquely Utahan drink is **honey wine**, a traditional mead that can be sampled at the **Hive Winery & Spirits Company** in Layton. **Dirty soda** is a new favorite on the drinks scene: a mix of a soft drink of your choice, cream, and flavored syrup or fruit.

Utah's oldest bar—and allegedly the oldest continuously operating drinking establishment west of the Mississippi—the tiny **Shooting Star Saloon** in Huntsville served its first drink in 1879. Salt Lake City's hippest cocktail lounge, **Under Current** offers show biz–themed libations like the Veronica Corningstone and Montepython. Four blocks down Broadway, the irreverent **Tavernacle Social Club** hosts dueling pianos and a weekly drag queen brunch. ∎

Vermont

From oldies but goodies like maple syrup and heirloom apples to newfangled ice-cream flavors and artisanal pizzas, Vermont offers a surprising array of food flavors, aromas, and textures.

True to the cliché, Vermont collects more **maple syrup** than any other state. And it's not even close. Its annual production of around 2.5 million gallons (9.4 million L) is more than the next six states combined. Though a good deal of that syrup goes onto pancakes, it also features in **maple cream pie** and other dishes.

Vermonters are also bullish on dairy, especially when it comes to **ice cream** and organic **artisanal cheese**. There are scores of different cheeses,

many with newfangled names like Gore-Dawn-Zola, Les Pyramids, Cosmos, and Orb Weaver.

Creamy **Gilfeather turnips** are the official state vegetable. Meanwhile, **parsnips** and **ramps** (wild leeks) are key ingredients in many recipes. Local **heirloom apples** find their way into cider, apple pies, and other treats. **Fiddleheads**—the curled fronds of young ferns—are avidly foraged in the forests of Vermont and prepared in a variety of ways, from beer-battered and

THE BIG PICTURE

Founded: 1791

Population: 647,064

Official State Dessert: Apple pie

Also Known As: Green Mountain State

Culinary Influences: British, French

Don't Miss: Burlington, Stowe, Champlain Islands

Claim to Fame: Ben & Jerry's, chicken pot pie, aged cheddar

pickled to sautéed and in salads.

The state's baking tradition and local favorites like **chicken pot pie, apple cider doughnuts**, and **apple slab pie** take the spotlight on the long-running Food Network show *Baked in Vermont,* hosted by Gesine Bullock-Prado (actor Sandra Bullock's younger sister).

Follow the Vermont Cheese Trail to sample an endless variety of the state's specialty.

From amber to very dark: The varying grades of Vermont maple syrup line a windowsill.

CULINARY EXPERIENCES

Follow the pungent **Vermont Cheese Trail** to dairy farms, creameries, and artisanal cheesemakers scattered up and down the Green Mountains and the eastern shore of Lake Champlain. The 60 cheesy stops include three goat dairies and the **Billings Farm & Museum**, an ode to Vermont rural life that revolves around a restored 1890 farmhouse.

Among the other agricultural entities that welcome visitors are **Shelburne Farms** near Burlington with its educational programs, craft farm products, and farm-to-table restaurant; the maple syrup–producing **Bragg Farm** near Montpelier; and **Sugarbush Farm** near Woodstock, which churns out 15 different cheeses and four grades of maple syrup.

If you still don't have your fill of the sweet, sticky stuff, consider attending the **Vermont Maple Festival** in St. Albans (April), which features a maple cooking contest, maple syrup and products contest, and a maple-themed Sappy Art Show.

Creativity is also the focus of **ArtsRiot** in Burlington, a combination art gallery, live music space, food truck hangout, and craft spirits distillery. Vermont's largest city is also home to the **City Market/ Onion River Co-op**, a hip farmers market and craft food emporium with a hot food bar, foodie events, and children's programs.

Over in the Connecticut River Valley, **King Arthur Baking Company** in Norwich revolves around a shop, a café, and the highly regarded Baking School with classes for professionals, children, and home bakers.

RESTAURANTS TO DIE FOR

Although ice cream may be at the top of your Burlington bucket list, the city also offers some delicious appetizers and entrées. **Hen of the Wood** relies on the bounty of the Vermont waterways and countryside to create innovative dishes like duck pastrami with smoked apple, mushroom toast with house bacon, and kale cannelloni.

On the north side of town, **Misery Loves Co.** and sister eatery, **Onion City Chicken & Oyster**, offer an amazing array of flavors on Main Street in downtown Winooski. One of Burlington's favorite

King Arthur Baking Company in Norwich offers hands-on and virtual classes for bakers of every skill level.

casual lunch spots, **Kountry Kart Deli** opposite the city hall offers subs, shiners, wraps, and specialty sandwiches like the Cajun chicken Philly and Montréal smoked meat.

As a college town and cultural enclave, Burlington is loaded with global eats. Sample diverse Asian flavors at **Sherpa Kitchen** with its savory Nepalese dishes, while **A Single Pebble** serves classic Cantonese cuisine. There are two great spots for

French food: **Leunig's Bistro & Café** and **Bistro de Margot**, just a block apart on College Street in the heart of downtown. From Turkish mezes to *güveç* casseroles, **Istanbul Kebab House** is the go-to place for Eastern Mediterranean cuisine.

Lake Champlain provides a rustic, romantic setting for **Blue Paddle Bistro** on South Hero Island. Chef Phoebe Bright's global travels have inspired new takes on traditional comfort dishes, including coffee-crusted pork tenderloin with goat cheese mashed potatoes and soy-glazed salmon with cranberry-ginger Asiago risotto.

Tucked inside a restored 18th-century farmhouse in South Londonderry, **SoLo Farm & Table** specializes in five-course chef's tasting menus served communally around the bar and a large, shared table. Farm-to-table tasting menus, including a "Platinum" dinner with a choice of Maine lobster or pasture-raised beef tenderloin, are also the forte at **Michael's on the Hill**, in an early 19th-century farmhouse between Waterbury and Stowe.

How far are you willing to venture for heavenly pizza? The **Parker Pie Co.** in Vermont's Northeast Kingdom makes the drive worthwhile with gourmet pizzas like the Malibu Barbie, Bangkok Disco, and Green Mountain Special with spinach, onion, bacon, apple, garlic, and cheddar cheese drizzled with maple syrup. At the opposite end of the state, the super-casual **Mojo Cafe** in Ludlow brings Mexican and New Orleans cooking to the south Vermont mountains.

BOTTOMS UP!

Saxtons River Distillery in Brattleboro and **Bent Hill Brewery** in West Braintree are among the

---

BEN & JERRY'S

Growing up on Long Island, **Ben Cohen** and **Jerry Greenfield** attended middle and high school together, then reunited after college for a 1977 Penn State correspondence course on making ice cream. A year later, their youthful confidence compelled them to open their own ice-cream parlor in an old gas station in Burlington, Vermont.

At first, they used a tiny Volkswagen station wagon to deliver to local grocery stores and restaurants. Hoping to spread their frozen treats nationwide, they transformed an old bus into the "Cowmobile" for a 1986

cross-country promotional road trip. By the end of the '80s, business was thriving, and the dynamic ice-cream-making duo had been named "U.S. Small Business Persons of the Year."

Way beyond iconic flavors like Cherry Garcia and Chunky Monkey, Ben & Jerry's is a staunch advocate of organic farming, fair trade, and a wide variety of social and environmental causes. Their flagship store on Cherry Street in Burlington and their factory tour and Flavor Graveyard in Waterbury are among Vermont's leading tourist attractions.

Vermont brewers making maple sap beer, which combines typical beer ingredients like grain, hops, and yeast with maple syrup. Founded by fifth-generation Vermont maple farmers, **Sap! Beverages** in Burlington makes nonalcoholic maple seltzers and sodas.

Another traditional Vermont beverage, **switchel** is a blend of water, apple cider vinegar, and ginger that can be sweetened with honey or maple syrup. Also called haymaker's punch because of its popularity with farmers, the drink may have originated in the 17th- or 18th-century Caribbean during the era when the islanders keenly traded with New England.

Vermont churns out a variety of **apple beverages**, including sweet cider, hard cider, and ice cider (aka ice apple wine). **Eden Ciders** offers even more choice: Imperial 11° heirloom apple rosé, sparkling Brut Nature, and Golden Russet single-variety cider. Sample the lot at the **Eden Ciders Tasting Bar** in Newport.

The hills come alive with the aroma of craft beer in Stowe, where the **Von Trapp Brewing Bierhall Restaurant** pours Schwarz Dark Lager, Vienna Style Lager, Bohemian Pilsner, and other craft beers made by the family that inspired *The Sound of Music*. ∎

Farm-to-table cuisine—like this roasted chicken nestled atop a plate of fresh seafood in a delicate sauce—thrives in Vermont.

Virginia

When it comes to food, Virginia has southern roots with mid-Atlantic leanings, and a legacy in both food and drink pioneered by George Washington, Thomas Jefferson, and other early Virginians.

With myriad estuaries and a deeply indented shoreline along the Atlantic Ocean and the Chesapeake Bay, Virginia takes its seafood seriously. **Blue crab cakes, Rappahannock oysters** on the half shell, **cornmeal-crusted croaker,** **Chesapeake Bay ray**, and Virginia-style **chowders and gumbo** are a few of the state's maritime choices.

Despite claims from a town of the same name in Georgia, Virginia was most likely the birthplace of **Brunswick stew**. The original recipe

THE BIG PICTURE

Founded: 1788

Population: 8.68 million

Official State First Food: Virginia oyster

Also Known As: Old Dominion State, Mother of Presidents State

Culinary Influences: West African, English

Don't Miss: Williamsburg, Charlottesville, Virginia Beach

Claim to Fame: Fried pies, cured country ham, Virginia oysters

called for squirrel, but nowadays chicken is the meat of choice, complemented by tomato, potato, onion, corn, and lima beans.

The commonwealth's beloved **country ham** traces its roots to colonial days, when locals began feeding peanuts and peaches to their pigs before smoking the meat over an oak, hickory, or applewood fire. The quirky diet infuses the ham with a compelling sweetness. Another heirloom dish is **peanut soup**, a creamy concoction introduced by enslaved people from West Africa.

With ideal conditions for cultivating temperate-climate fruits, Virginia is one of the nation's leading **apple** growers. More than 16 varieties are found across the state, many of them turned into **apple pies, muffins, ciders**, and **butter.**

CULINARY EXPERIENCES

Take a bite of history during **apple tasting at Monticello**, where Thomas Jefferson grew more than a dozen different varieties. The experience includes a chance to compare his heirloom apples with

Step back in time with old-fashioned peanut soup.

Pippin Hill Farm & Vineyards in North Garden

modern examples, quiz a Jefferson impersonator (who's also an apple expert), and sample local artisanal cheeses.

Virginia spotlights its favorite fruit in annual events including the **Shenandoah Apple Blossom Festival** in Winchester (April–May), the **Boones Mill Apple Festival** in southern Virginia (September–October), and the **Graves Mountain Apple Harvest Festival** in Syria (October).

Down in the Hampton Roads region, the **Suffolk Peanut Fest** (October) features an old-fashioned clogging jamboree, demolition derby, and a peanut butter sculpting contest. The Chesapeake Bay watershed also hosts the **Urbanna Oyster Festival** (November) and **West Point Crab Carnival** (October).

Richmond's top chefs face off in cook-offs for the best overall, dessert, and healthy dishes during Richmond's **Broad Appetit** festival (June). Year-round, **Discover Richmond Food Tours** offers tours of delectable neighborhoods like Carytown, Church Hill, Scott's Addition, and the Arts District. An hour's drive south of the state capital, Brunswick County pays homage to its legendary stew during the annual **Taste of Brunswick Festival** in Alberta (October).

RESTAURANTS TO DIE FOR

Diners drive for hours to feast at the **Inn at Little Washington**, the only three-Michelin-starred restaurant in the mid-Atlantic region. Skippered by chef Patrick O'Connell, the rural eatery is renowned for its surf and turf Gastronaut and vegetarian Good Earth tasting menus, as well as a wine cellar that runs 14,000 bottles strong.

Rural Virginia is spangled with similar culinary treasures like the "earth-to-table" cuisine at the **Restaurant at Patowmack Farm** in riverside Lovettsville, **Harrimans Virginia Piedmont Grill** at the posh Salamander Resort in Middleburg, and the elevated southern cuisine at **Taste of Smithfield** near Newport News.

Not everything is highfalutin. Just as yummy are humble spots like **Virginia Diner** in Wakefield, which has been making country ham, Brunswick stew, and other local favorites since 1929. Way out west, the **Log House 1776 Restaurant** in Wytheville serves locally caught trout and catfish with sides like fried grits or corn pudding in a historic 18th-century residence. Up in the Shenandoah Valley, **Mrs. Rowe's Restaurant & Bakery** in Staunton does southern classics like chicken with dumplings, fried green apples, and stewed tomatoes with black-eyed peas.

Across the Potomac from the nation's capital, the Alexandria-Arlington area is loaded with great eating options. Opened in 1770, **Gadsby's Tavern** retains its colonial-era ambience and heirloom dishes like crab cakes and peanut soup, as well as the roast duck that George Washington favored when he ate there. By way of contrast, **Ada's on the River** serves up minimalist modern decor and sunny riverside tables for brunch. **Ruthie's All-Day** in Arlington offers gourmet soups, salads, and sandwiches inside a historic mid-century modern building that was once a chocolate factory.

The ultimate date night in Richmond is French cuisine at **L'Opossum** in Richmond, where the whimsically named dishes include Viva Las Vegan Avec Za'atar, Orgy on Texas Beach, and A Brisk Fall Cookout in the Boneyard.

For everyday grub in the state capital, bite into a mammoth burger at **Cobra Cabana**, munch one of the signature frittata "messes" at **Millie's Diner**, or scoff a Tuna Schmelt, Goy Vey, Jewbano, or other specialty sandwiches at **Perly's** restaurant and delicatessen. For ethnic eats in Richmond, try the Alpine-inspired cuisine at **Brenner Pass** or modern Afghan dishes at **the Mantu**. In nearby Petersburg, **Croaker's Spot** presents seafood with a soul food twist and live blues, jazz, and other tunes.

BOTTOMS UP!

Given the state's long love affair with apples, it was inevitable that Virginia should transform into one of the nation's top cider producers. Among the 20-plus cideries spread across the commonwealth are urban **Lost Boy Cider** in Alexandria, rustic **Old Hill Hard Cider** at Showalter's Orchard in Timberville, and the **Bryant's Dry Cider** "tasting meadow" in rural Roseland.

As one of the oldest and largest grape producers along the eastern seaboard, Virginia has cultivated seven American Viticultural Areas, including the **Monticello AVA** around Charlottesville and the **Northern Neck George Washington Birthplace AVA** between the Potomac and Rappahannock Rivers. A bona fide oenophile, Thomas Jefferson introduced European wines to America and tried making wine from native grapes. Washington

Understated luxury meets refined American cuisine—like this butter pecan pie ice-cream sandwich with hot caramel sauce—at the Inn at Little Washington.

carried out similar unsuccessful experiments at Mount Vernon.

Where the two presidents failed, Virginia's modern vintners have succeeded. More than 40 winemakers, including the award-winning **Wisdom Oak Winery** and **Horton Vineyards**, are scattered along the **Monticello Wine Trail**. A 10-minute drive from George Washington's birthplace, **Ingleside Vineyards** is one of the key stops along the **Chesapeake Bay Wine Trail**.

Based in Charlottesville, **Virginia Hop on Tours** offers packages for

FARMER PRESIDENT: GEORGE WASHINGTON

George Washington may have chopped down a cherry tree, but he was far more interested in other crops. Though tobacco cultivated by enslaved people supported the Mount Vernon estate and its five farms, the future general and president believed that wealthy landowners should engage in agricultural experimentation to diversify the economy and ensure future prosperity.

A decade before the Revolution, Washington began to phase out tobacco in favor of food crops, especially wheat. He also adopted what were then considered radical ideas like crop rotation, various fertilizers, intensive plowing, and newfangled farm tools.

His experiments continued after the war and his presidency, when Washington retired to Mount Vernon and concentrated on farming once again. By his death in 1799, he had tried growing around 60 different food and fodder plants, from ordinary potatoes, carrots, and cabbage to uncommon crops like fenugreek, spelt, and Jerusalem artichokes.

The handcrafted smoked whiskey cocktail at Harrimans Virginia Piedmont Grill in Middleburg

craft breweries, distilleries, cideries, and wineries in the college town as well as nearby Blue Ridge burgs like Afton, Crozet, and Barboursville. Farther south, the **Blue Ridge Cheers Trail** roams past more than two dozen beer, wine, and spirits makers in Roanoke and its hinterland.

If you're in the mood for nothing more than a cool cocktail, try **the Jasper** in Richmond for drinks like Bark at the Moon and Hoodoo U Think U R?, the offerings at the lofty **Sky Bar** overlooking the Virginia Beach Boardwalk, or the signature sangria at the riverside **Hi-Tide Lounge** in Alexandria. ■

Washington

Microclimates, geographical diversity, and entrepreneurial spirit have boosted the Evergreen State from comfort foods and culinary obscurity into one of the nation's most exciting foodie destinations.

THE BIG PICTURE

Founded: 1889

Population: 7.79 million

Official State Vegetable: Walla Walla sweet onion

Also Known As: Evergreen State

Culinary Influences: Japanese, Mexican, French, Russian, Yakama and other Native American tribes

Don't Miss: Seattle, Spokane, Bellevue

Claim to Fame: Starbucks, sockeye salmon, steamed mussels and clams

Blame it on the world's fair. The Century 21 Exposition of 1962 created the iconic Space Needle and brought global food to Seattle. Rather than treat it as a passing fancy, locals decided that dietary innovation should be a permanent thing. And thus began the evolution of Washington State into a culinary powerhouse. The local food scene took another giant leap in the 1990s with the rise of companies like Microsoft, Amazon, T-Mobile, and Expedia and their legions of young techies and office workers with disposable income and eclectic appetites.

The raw ingredients were already there. As the region's Native Americans knew well, the Pacific coast and Puget Sound produced an incredible seafood bounty—**crabs, oysters, mussels**, and other shellfish. Rivers running into the sea were flush with **salmon**. The temperate rainforest that gives the state its nickname was ripe with **berries, nuts**, and **edible mushrooms**.

Arriving in the 19th century, the first Euro-American settlers soon discovered the state's rich soil was ideal for growing vegetables, fruits, grains, and you name it—more than 300 different food crops.

Nowadays Washington State grows around 60 percent of the nation's **apples**. Though Golden Delicious and Granny Smith are the most recognizable varieties, the state also produces Braeburn, Cameo, Fuji, Gala, Honeycrisp, Jonagold, Pink Lady, and Red Delicious apples. Washington also harvests more **pears, blueberries**, and **sweet cherries** than any other state and is among the leading producers of **apricots, raspberries, potatoes**, and **asparagus**.

Locally grown produce and Pacific crabmeat are among the main ingredients in a pioneering Washington State dish: the **crab Louis salad**. Ironically, it wasn't invented anywhere near the coast, but in Spokane by Lewellyn "Louis" Davenport, who opened a hotel in the eastern Washington city in 1914. More than a century later,

Ellenos Peppermint Bark Latte, Cranberry Orange, and Biscoff Cookie Butter yogurts

Seattle's famed Pike Place Market at Christmastime

crab Louis is a signature dish at the **Palm Court Grill** in the Davenport Hotel.

CULINARY EXPERIENCES

Opened in 1907, **Pike Place Market** along the Seattle waterfront is a multistory maze of food stalls, snack bars, restaurants, specialty food shops, bars, restaurants, flower stalls, and a farmers market. With more than 10 million visitors each year, it can get more than a little crowded, especially on sunny summer weekends. But no maiden visit to Seattle is complete without a walk-through.

Pike Place Market is especially known for its longtime seafood vendors—like Sol "Cod Father" Amon—and their artful displays. Among the many specialty food shops are **Tenzing Momo** Tibetan herb store, **Ellenos Yogurt**, **Truffle Queen**, and **Totem Smokehouse** for smoked salmon.

The state's premier food fest is the annual **Bite of Seattle** (July), which brings together more than 200 food and beverage vendors in Seattle Center beneath the Space Needle. The event also includes food cook-offs, competitions, and demonstrations, as well as 70 live bands.

Year-round, **Savor Seattle Food Tours** offers guided culinary adventures ranging from a VIP early-access Pike Place Market walk to a gourmet kayak paddle through the San Juan Islands.

Guided foraging is another possibility. **Earthwalk Northwest** organizes one-day and single overnight courses like Seaweeds & Coastal Foraging in the San Juan Islands, Wild Edible Plants of the Cascades, and Primitive Cooking.

With more than 30 types of edible mushrooms, Washington is also a hotbed for mycological foraging and cookery. Learn everything you always wanted to know about fungi at the Puget Sound Mycological Society's annual **Wild Mushroom Show** in Shoreline (October). Other quintessential Evergreen State edibles are the focus of Ocean Shores's **Razor Clam and Seafood Festival** (March), **Cider Swig** in Gig Harbor (September), **Wenatchee River Salmon Festival** (September), and **OysterFest** in Shelton (October).

RESTAURANTS TO DIE FOR

Diners can find similar seafood fare at scores of waterfront eateries in Seattle. What sets some apart from the rest are the quality, presentation, service, and especially atmosphere. **Ray's Boathouse** in Ballard scores on all four points, from the excellent Washington State wines and signature dishes like Pacific Northwest sablefish, to a view of the snowcapped peaks of the Olympic Peninsula across Puget Sound. Oyster aficionados swear by the **Walrus & the Carpenter**, which serves half a dozen kinds of Washington-raised oysters in an intimate dining room in Ballard.

Ray's Boathouse is a Seattle must for fresh seafood with views of Puget Sound.

SEATTLE COFFEE CULTURE

Even though coffee plants don't grow anywhere near Seattle, the city has emerged as a global force in coffee culture.

Founded in 1971 with a single small store on Western Avenue, **Starbucks** has mushroomed into more than 30,000 outlets in 80-plus countries around the world. Love it or shun it, there's no disputing the Seattle chain has revolutionized coffee drinking via the introduction of the Frappuccino, barrel-aged coffee, and other innovations. There's often a line out the door at the landmark **Pike Place Starbucks**, but the industrial chic **Starbucks Reserve Roastery** on Capitol Hill is large enough to accommodate the crowds.

Starbucks may rule the roost, but Seattle boasts plenty of other java hot spots. Often on the list of the nation's best coffee makers, **Caffé Vita Coffee Roasting Company** has expanded from its original location on East Pike Street to four other outlets in the metro area. **Seattle Coffee Works, Victrola**, and **Herkimer Coffee** are among the city's other top independent roasters.

Another of Seattle's oldest eateries, **AQUA by El Gaucho** on Pier 70 serves seafood classics in an elegant dining room and breezy outside terrace.

For casual lunch or brunch on the water, nothing beats **Westward** in Northlake with its panoramic views of Lake Union and creative seafood twists like the fried oyster po'boy sandwich, halibut rillette, Dungeness crab tostada, and marinated mussels. Occupying a stunning mid-century modern structure overlooking Lake

Union, **Canlis** and its revolving four-course menu have been a touchstone of Pacific Northwest cuisine since the 1950s.

Away from the water, Seattle's Capitol Hill area does double duty as the city's LGBTQIA+ nexus and inland dining oasis. Among its scores of cafés and restaurants are **Single Shot Kitchen & Saloon** for artful New American food, **Kedai Makan** for exotic Malaysian, **Plum Bistro** for gourmet vegan, **Plenty of Clouds** for regional Chinese dishes, and **Spinasse** for modern Italian. In the nearby University District, **Off the Rez** café offers contemporary takes on Native American favorites like Indian tacos and fry bread. Moving out into the burbs, **the Herbfarm** in Woodinville was one of the state's first genuine farm-to-table restaurants, with many dishes prepared with ingredients grown on the property.

Heading down the Puget Sound, Tacoma also boasts a lively food scene that varies from old-timers like the waterfront **Duke's Seafood** on Ruston Way to the savory Asian cuisine of the Lakewood area at restaurants like **Cham Garden Korean BBQ, Tacoma Szechuan**, and **i5 Pho & Boba**.

As it wraps around the Olympic Peninsula, Highway 101 leads to several intriguing eateries. Owned and operated by the Jamestown S'Klallam Tribe, the **House of Seven Brothers** restaurant in Sequim complements its surf and turf dishes with a forest of totem poles and other Native American art. **Blackberry Cafe** in Joyce and **Forks Outfitters Deli & Store** are great spots to grab breakfast or lunch on the drive from Port Angeles to the Pacific coast. Renamed for FDR after the president lunched there in 1937, the

Out on the lake? Tie up at Westward's dock on Lake Union before popping in for oysters and more.

historic **Roosevelt Dining Room** on Lake Quinault delivers woodsy, rustic ambience on the outskirts of Olympic National Park.

The San Juan Islands offer another eclectic eating experience. **Friday's Crabhouse** in Friday Harbor presents classic pub grub like fish-and-chips and fresh local seafood served steamed, grilled, or raw, while the upscale **Duck Soup** elevates island dining with dishes like lamb meatballs, king salmon tartare, and duck breast with a soy glaze. At **Westcott Bay Shellfish Co.**, visitors can learn how they raise Olympia oysters and Manila clams and then lunch on those very items. Over on Orcas Island, the elegant **Mansion Restaurant** at historic Rosario Resort serves breakfast and dinner on the veranda of an early 20th-century Victorian villa overlooking Cascade Bay.

Pacific Northwest seafood and pan-Asian cuisine manage to make their way more than 200 miles (320 km) inland to Spokane. Salmon with pea risotto and charred radicchio, and oysters with frozen champagne granita and a citrus mignonette sauce are a few of the signature dishes at **Inland Pacific Kitchen**. Ginger-jalapeño crab cakes and shiitake mushroom lettuce wraps highlight an innovative menu at **Mizuna**.

BOTTOMS UP!

Olympia may have been relegated to the scrap heap of beer history—the beloved Tumwater brewery closed in 2003—but craft breweries are more than compensating for the loss of Washington's longtime local favorite. **Old Stove Brewing Co.** in Pike Place Market serves a range of stouts, IPAs, and lagers, plus barley wine and hard cider, with awesome views of Puget Sound. In addition to numerous after-dark **Seattle ghost tours and haunted pub crawls** on offer, the state's largest city also hosts **Seattle Beer Week** (May) and **Oktoberfest Northwest** (October).

Given its ample hipsters, the Emerald City also boasts some cool cocktail spots. Many of them have specific themes, like the vintage carnival ambience of the **Unicorn** on Capitol Hill, the **Founders Club** speakeasy in the Fairmont Olympic Hotel, and **Stampede Cocktail Club** with its neo-Western theme. For killer cocktails without the frills, nothing tops

An abundance of riches: Maine lobster tails, seasonal fish, scallops, prawns, and sides doused in a beurre blanc at AQUA by El Gaucho in Seattle

Testing Cabernet from the barrel at Owen Roe Winery in Wapato

Ben Paris on the ground floor of the State Hotel.

With its stained glass ceiling and over-the-top decor, the **Peacock Room Lounge** rules the cocktail roost in Spokane. Meanwhile, out in the Salish Sea, tiny **Westcott Bay Cider and San Juan Island Distillery** offers an incredibly tasty array of artisanal gin, brandy, and liqueurs. ∎

VINTAGE WASHINGTON

It's a no-brainer that California produces more wine than any other state. But not a lot of people know that Washington State is number two. More than 1,000 wineries spread across 20 American Viticultural Areas, unique growing areas with microclimates and soil variations that produce more than 80 wine varieties.

The heart of Washington's wine country is the semiarid rain shadow area on the eastern side of the Cascade Range. This includes the Columbia, Yakima, and Walla Walla Valleys in the Columbia River watershed. However, the state's first vines were planted much closer to the coast, an 1825 effort by the Hudson's Bay Company to grow grapes at Fort Vancouver near the mouth of the Columbia River.

Washington wines didn't gain much traction with oenophiles outside the state until the 1990s, when they began winning national and international awards. In 2021, four of them made *Wine Spectator* magazine's list of the top 100 most exciting wines, including the 2018 Cailloux Vineyard Syrah from **Cayuse Vineyards** (No. 19), the 2018 Holler Cabernet Sauvignon from **Sparkman Cellars** (No. 29), the 2019 Eroica Riesling from **Chateau Ste. Michelle-Dr. Loosen** (No. 42), and the 2018 Syrah from **Force Majeure** (No. 60).

West Virginia

Fully embracing its Appalachian roots, West Virginia is cultivating a culinary renaissance that brings heirloom fare like ramps, pawpaws, and mountain moonshine back into the limelight.

THE BIG PICTURE

Founded: 1863

Population: 1.78 million

Official State Food: Pepperoni roll

Also Known As: Mountain State

Culinary Influences: Italian, Shawnee and other Native American tribes

Don't Miss: Fairmont, Huntington, Martinsburg

Claim to Fame: Ramps, pawpaw, molly moochers

In the 1920s, Giuseppe Argiro moved from southern Italy to West Virginia to work the coal mines. He eventually opened a bakery and invented the **pepperoni roll**. A combination of Italian sausage and freshly baked bread, the quintessential Mountain State food remains wildly popular and now boasts many variations.

West Virginia's Italian eateries have also developed local **pizza** styles, including a square variety that isn't sprinkled with cold shredded provolone cheese until *after* it comes out of the oven.

Sometimes called wild leeks, **ramps** are another favorite. When pulled from the soil, the smallish bulbs, a type of wild onion, resemble scallions. Though often served with potatoes, eggs, or ham, ramps appear in all sorts of West Virginia recipes, including casseroles, pasta, and pizza.

Another versatile West Virginia food is the **pawpaw**, a type of custard apple that was already a staple of local Native American people before Euro-American settlers adopted it. Although it resembles a tropical papaya in color and shape, *Asimina triloba* is the only member of the family that can survive in a northern temperate climate. West Virginians use them in cakes, pies, jams, ice creams, and puddings.

Come spring, many locals wander the woods in search of **molly moochers**: wild morel mushrooms. Local cooks sauté the 'shrooms with butter or bacon fat before eating them straight from the pan or adding them to meat dishes, pasta sauces, soups, or salads.

CULINARY EXPERIENCES

West Virginia runs rampant with ramps come spring, when the wild things are harvested (though care needs to be taken to avoid overharvesting). Connoisseurs can buy them at roadside stands or indulge at community ramp dinners in various towns. Meanwhile, the pungent bulb is the star attraction at April events like the **Ramp & Rails Festival** in Elkins, Camp Creek State Park's **Ramp Dinner and Lumberjack Competition**, and **Stinkfest** in Huntington.

Harvest wild ramps sustainably by cutting off one leaf and leaving the bulb and second leaf in the soil for continued growth.

A window at the historic Hatfield & McCoy Moonshine distillery in Gilbert

Its namesake may not be available year-round, but the **Wild Ramp** indoor market in Huntington has plenty of other locally grown or foraged foodstuffs from more than 100 local farmers. Morel mushrooms, kombucha, microgreens, and maple syrup are a few of the local products available at the summer-to-winter **Morgantown Farmers Market**.

Livestock shows, a Farmer's Day Parade, and buckwheat pancakes and sausage dinners lure crowds to the **Preston County Buckwheat Festival** in Kingwood (September–October). West Virginia's official state fruit is the centerpiece of the **Clay County Golden Delicious Festival** (September). But the state's oddest culinary event has to be the **West Virginia Roadkill Cook-Off & Autumn Harvest Festival** in Marlinton (September), which features dishes like biscuits with squirrel gravy, deer with sun-dried maggots, elk bratwurst, and rabbit sausage.

RESTAURANTS TO DIE FOR

West Virginia's most sublime dining experience is the **Farm & Forage Supper Club** at Lost Creek Farm. Staged in Harrison County about an hour's drive south of Morgantown, the six-course feast features heritage-inspired "mountain cuisine" grown at Lost Creek and other farms or foraged in nearby forests.

The Greenbrier resort down in the state's southeast corner boasts several of West Virginia's most elegant eating options, including three restaurants dedicated to larger-than-life personalities: **Draper's** with its flamboyant Dorothy Draper–inspired decor; **Sam Snead's** at the resort golf club; and **Prime 44 West**, a top-shelf steak house named for West Virginia basketball superstar Jerry West (his jersey number was 44).

Politicos in Charleston gather at upscale eateries like **1010 Bridge** with its fusion of New American and

Try a half-and-half pie at Pies & Pints in Fayetteville.

The Italian coal miners who flocked to Fairmont stoked the evolution of West Virginia's best Italian foods, including the **Country Club Bakery**, where Giuseppe Argiro invented the pepperoni roll, and **Muriale's Italian Kitchen** with its classic dishes. **Original DiCarlo's** in Wheeling was a pioneer of West Virginia–style pizza. But **Pie & Pints** in Fayetteville (and two other cities) is the cutting edge these days, with pies that feature red grapes, street corn, chipotle, and capicola pork shoulder sausage.

West Virginia's country roads also lead to vintage **King Tut Drive-In** in Beckley (opened by the Tutweiler family in the early 1940s) and **Hillbilly Hotdogs** in Lesage and its wide world of weenies, including its infamous six-pound (2.7 kg), 30-inch (76 cm) Original Widow-Maker dog.

BOTTOMS UP!

An almost perfect blend of liquor and local history, the **Hatfield & McCoy Moonshine distillery** in Gilbert makes small-batch 90-proof firewater with heirloom recipes on land that once belonged to the Hatfield family of

Mediterranean cuisines, or **Noah's Restaurant & Lounge**, where the menu runs a broad gamut from pork belly lettuce wraps to lamb sliders and shrimp bruschetta.

Yet the state capital also flaunts incredible comfort food: out-of-this-world soul food at **Dem 2 Brothers and a Grill BBQ**, the enormous Wagyu burgers and pimento cheese fries at **Hale House** bistro, and gelato, sherbet, and sorbet at **Ellen's Homemade Ice Cream**.

Up in the state's skinny northern panhandle, **Vagabond Kitchen** gastropub offers great grub downtown, a farm-to-table menu that includes beef-and-pork meatloaf, salt mine steak with Appalachian killed greens (a regional specialty where the greens are lightly wilted in bacon drippings or a vinaigrette), and an Elvis tribute burger with peanut butter and banana slices. The city's best meal with a view is the **Ihlenfeld Dining**

Room at the Oglebay resort in the hills above Wheeling.

Farther down the Ohio River, Huntington excels at bars and cafés frequented by students from Marshall University. Standing far apart from that crowd is **Le Bistro** with its funky French country decor and dishes that range from chateaubriand to shrimp and grits.

MOUNTAIN MUSIC MUNCHIES

Stretching 175 miles (280 km) between Thomas and Greenville, West Virginia's Mountain Music Trail along U.S. 219 features legendary music venues like Pocahontas County Opera House in Marlinton and Carnegie Hall in Lewisburg. Along the way are plenty of spots that serve food and beverage with live tunes.

The **Purple Fiddle** in Thomas stages more than 300 live music

events each year alongside its sandwiches, wraps, and vegetarian fare. Around the corner from the opera house, **Alfredo's** in downtown Marlinton is the place for pepperoni rolls and square pizza.

Farther down the pike, the **Wild Bean** in Lewisburg showcases local music talent in addition to gourmet coffees, baked goods, vegetarian fare, and tacos from the neighboring Mexican restaurant.

Hatfield and McCoy feud fame. After the behind-the-scenes tour, which recounts details of a bloody rivalry that spanned three decades of the 19th century, sample the product indoors or on the porch overlooking Gilbert Creek.

Since the turn of the 21st century, moonshine distilleries have sprouted throughout the Mountain State. Most don't have a compelling backstory like the Hatfields and McCoys, so they try to distinguish themselves in other ways.

In addition to moonshine, vodka, and whiskey tasting, **Black Draft Farm & Distillery** in Martinsburg offers live music and food trucks. **Appalachian Distillery** in Ripley makes moonshine in offbeat flavors like pawpaw, peach, apple pie, and strawberry lemonade. The combined might of **Kirkwood Winery & Isaiah Morgan Distillery** near Summersville produces some of the state's most distinctive drinks, including wild elderberry, dandelion, and Appalachian ramp wine, as well as moonshine, corn whiskey, and grappa. ■

Add some pep to your step with spirits, including coffee vodka, from Black Draft Farm & Distillery in Martinsburg.

Wisconsin

While Wisconsin continues to excel at cheese, beer, and supper club fish fries, the state's dining scene has progressed into a wide variety of tasty victuals and gastronomic adventures.

Wisconsinites call themselves "Cheeseheads" for good reason: Their state produces more **cheese** than any other state, roughly a quarter of the nation's annual production. Around 1,200 cheesemakers create more than 600 varieties from mega-popular **mozzarella** and **cheddar** to specialty cheeses like **Canaria, Chandoka, fenugreek Gouda, mascarpone**, and **Oaxaca**.

The raw ingredient for all that cheese derives from the state's 1.2 million dairy cows, which means that "America's Dairyland" also excels at **milk, butter, ice cream**, and other cow-based dairy products. Milk is also a main ingredient of **cheddar beer soup**, a Wisconsin favorite that involves sharp cheddar, dark beer, and the cook's choice of sliced or diced vegetables.

THE BIG PICTURE

Founded: 1848

Population: 5.89 million

Official State Pastry: Kringle

Also Known As: Badger State

Culinary Influences: German, English, Scandinavian, Polish

Don't Miss: Bayfield, Milwaukee, Madison

Claim to Fame: Bratwurst, cream puffs, Colby cheese

In addition to bringing dairy farming to Wisconsin in the early 19th century, immigrants from north and central Europe also introduced the oval-shaped, fruit- and nut-suffused **kringle** (the official state pastry), fruit-filled **kolache** turnovers, and the flavorsome **beer brats** (bratwurst sausages boiled in beer) popular at Milwaukee Brewers baseball games and other sporting events.

Although five different American cities claim invention of the **ice-cream sundae**, the earliest origin story (1881) comes from Two Rivers, when a patron walked into Berners' Soda Fountain and abruptly asked for chocolate sauce poured over his ice cream. Among the state's other dessert darlings are the **cream puffs** sold at the Wisconsin State Fair in West Allis (August) and **Kopp's Frozen Custard** in Milwaukee.

CULINARY EXPERIENCES

Learn how cheeses like quark, chèvre, and cheddar are made during a tour of **Clock Shadow Creamery** in Milwaukee's trendy Walker's Point neighborhood. Or take one of the many online classes—like "Building a Cheese

Sweet icing drizzled atop a kringle pastry

Try a cheese sample at the counter of Fromagination cheese shop in Madison.

Board" or "The Science of Cheese"—offered by **Fromagination** from its retail store opposite the state capitol in Madison.

Cheese is also the focus of the **Dairy State Cheese & Beer Festival** in Kenosha (April), the **Wisconsin Grilled Cheese Championship** in Dodgeville (April), and the **Cheese Curd Festival** in Ellsworth (June), which features more than 20 dishes made with cheese curds. Meanwhile, sausages take center stage at Madison's **Brat Fest** (May), during which four million bratwursts are consumed.

American Family Field in Milwaukee offers a variety of Wisconsin dishes during Brewers games, from beer brats and cheesy fries to the cheese-slathered Wisconsin on My Mind hot dog and the Yeli Melt grilled cheese sandwich (named after cheese-loving all-star Christian Yelich).

Milwaukee's new **3rd St. Market Hall** offers an airy, glass-enclosed downtown space for vendors like **Dairyland** (burgers, cheese curds, sundaes, frozen custard), **Kawa** (sushi and ramen), and the **3rd St. Market Bar** (local craft brews).

Wisconsin's fresh food emporiums range from urban spreads like the **Dane County Farmers' Market** in Madison and the **West Allis Farmers Market** to bucolic country bazaars like **Koepsel's Farm Market** on the Door Peninsula and **Beloit Farmers Market**.

RESTAURANTS TO DIE FOR

With its 12-course tasting menus and impeccable wine selection, **Ardent** has been the gold standard of Milwaukee fine dining since it opened in 2013. Another paragon of fine dining, **Sanford** creates seasonal four-course tasting menus featuring copious local ingredients inside a vintage redbrick building on the city's East Side. Overlooking Lake Michigan, **Bartolotta's Lake Park Bistro** and its French cuisine offers the best blend of fine dining and fantastic view.

Milwaukee's global food scene covers a lot of geography, from traditional German fare at **Mader's** (opened in 1902) and **Wioletta's Polish Market** to empanadas and pisco cocktails at

Triciclo Perú, the eclectic Asian eats at **Momo Mee**, and the modern Mexican cuisine of **Café Corazón**. For good old American comfort food, nothing beats the **Nite Owl Drive In Ice Cream Parlour & Sandwich Shoppe** near the airport (open March to November).

Eno Vino Downtown lures Madison diners with its jaw-dropping views of the state capitol copula and a tapas menu that includes many Wisconsin-made artisanal cheeses. On nearby Capitol Square, the **Old Fashioned Tavern & Restaurant** serves iconic Wisconsin dishes like beer cheese soup, beer-battered cheese curds, bratwurst, fish fry, and Door County cherry salad. "We put the grease in greasy spoon," says **Mickie's Dairy Bar**, a longtime breakfast and lunch

WISCONSIN'S BELOVED SUPPER CLUBS

Wisconsin's supper clubs started life as roadhouses, dance halls, and lakeside resorts during Prohibition, before evolving into formal restaurants with familiar dishes and frequent entertainment.

They're most renowned for Friday fish fry dinners featuring fried or beer-battered walleye, perch, cod, or other fish. Other supper club traditions include prime rib on Saturday and chicken or ribs on Sunday, as well as Wisconsin plates, local beers, and Old-Fashioneds.

The state boasts more than 260 supper clubs, including stalwarts like the log cabin–style **Ishnala Supper Club** in Wisconsin Dells, the lakeside **Buckhorn Supper Club** in Milton, and **Schwarz's Supper Club** in New Holstein, as well as the new **Harvey House** supper club in Madison, which debuted in 2021.

hangout for Badger football fans and University of Wisconsin students. An hour up Interstate 90, **Field's at the Wilderness** offers refined steak house dining among all the fast-food joints in Wisconsin Dells.

Though it's tempting to order surf and turf at Green Bay's **Chefusion** gastropub, the more intriguing dishes are offbeat small plates like the Philly steak egg rolls, harvest pumpkin bisque, or pork belly

A collection of appetizers and desserts at the Harvey House in Madison

The beer hall at Milwaukee's Lakefront Brewery fills up for Friday fish fries.

ramen. At the northern end of the Door Peninsula, **Al Johnson's Swedish Restaurant & Butik** in Sister Bay offers Scandinavian fare and great Lake Michigan fish dishes. Farther south along the lakeshore, **Larsen Bakery** in Racine is a bastion of Danish delights like kringle, Seven Sisters coffee cake, and thumbprint cookies.

BOTTOMS UP!

Schlitz may have been the "beer that made Milwaukee famous" (along with other oldies like **Blatz** and **Pabst Blue Ribbon**), but nowadays Wisconsin suds lovers flock to the growing number of craft breweries.

King of the hill is **Lakefront Brewery**, which, contrary to its name, is actually on the Milwaukee River rather than Lake Michigan. In addition to its regular lagers and ales, Lakefront produced the nation's first organic beer and was a pioneer of gluten-free beer. Other top breweries include **Eagle Park Brewing & Distilling Company** on the Lower East Side and **Good City Brewing** in the Deer District.

Milwaukee's cocktail circuit ranges from the **Foundation** tiki bar and frontier-themed **Boone & Crockett** (think Daniel Boone and Davy Crockett) to historic **Bryant's Cocktail Lounge**, which opened its doors in 1938 and serves more than 450 different libations.

Home to numerous politicos and 50,000 students at the University of Wisconsin–Madison, the state capital offers scores of places to toss back a drink. One of the most esteemed is the **Kollege Klub**, founded in 1953 with the motto "Never Let School Interfere With Your Education." Popular with western Wisconsin college students, the **Library Bar** in La Crosse blends books and booze.

You really can see storied Lambeau Field (home of the Packers) from the outdoor tables in front of the **Stadium View Bar** in Green Bay. An 1882 saloon in Egg Harbor has evolved into the modern **Shipwrecked Brew Pub** on the Door Peninsula, while **Little Bohemia Lodge** and its bar in Manitowish Waters is where the FBI ambushed John Dillinger in 1934. ■

Wyoming

Wyoming's modern frontier food draws inspiration from the cowboy cooking of yore and the culinary heritage of the region's Indigenous peoples.

THE BIG PICTURE

Founded: 1890

Population: 581,381

Official State Fish: Cutthroat trout

Also Known As: Equality State

Culinary Influences: English, French, Cheyenne and other Native American tribes

Don't Miss: Jackson Hole, Cody, Cheyenne

Claim to Fame: Bison burgers, prime rib, soda bread

Where the Great Plains meet the Rockies, Wyoming still feels a lot like the untamed frontier. Wide-open spaces are par for the course for a place that has fewer people than any other state and features foods the state's cowboys and Native Americans once prepared.

Wyoming cuisine played a key role in saving the American bison from extinction—thanks to the Yellowstone herd—as the large, sometimes ornery bovine took center stage as **bison steaks, bison burgers, bison jerky, bison sausage**, and other dishes.

Elk, venison, and **pronghorn antelope** are the main game—and **trout** the most popular freshwater fish—found on restaurant menus.

Given the fact that Wyoming is home to more than 1.3 million cattle and fewer than 600,000 humans, it should come as no surprise that the **beef** is also fabulous. It's not for everyone, but Wyoming could be the place where you finally sample **Rocky Mountain oysters** (breaded deep-fried bull testicles).

Strange as it may seem given that situation, chicken rather than beef is the main ingredient of **Wyoming white chili**, along with flavorsome white beans.

Native Americans have also contributed to the state's gastronomic repertoire via dishes like **fry bread** and **three sisters stew**, a delicious blend of corn, beans, and squash, three crops that were widespread among the Indigenous people of the Great Plains long before the first Europeans arrived.

CULINARY EXPERIENCES

Crank back the clock at **Cheyenne Frontier Days** (July), a 10-day celebration of cowboy culture with bull riding, barrel racing, a wild horse race, country dancing at the Buckin' A Saloon, a popular pancake breakfast, and dozens of carnival midway food choices, including fresh-from-the-ranch steaks and burgers. **Laramie Jubilee Days** (July) complements its rodeo events and country music with the Flaming Gorge Jalapeño Eating Contest and Betty Kiser Memorial CASI Chili Cookoff.

Wyoming's leading culinary event is the two-part **Jackson Hole Food & Wine** festival, which includes a winter edition in March and a summer version in June. The events feature a variety of local and guest chefs, winemakers, cocktail mixologists, and craft brewers.

Way up north, Grinnell Plaza is the center of the gastronomic universe in Sheridan with events like the **Wine Fest** (September),

Three sisters stew marries corn, beans, and squash into a one-pot wonder.

Cheyenne Frontier Days highlights Western culture with a parade, carnival fare, a giant pancake breakfast, and more.

3rd Thursday Street Festival (once a month between June and September), and **Sheridan Farmers Market**, which takes place every Thursday between early June and mid-September.

Get up close (but not too personal) with roaming buffalo at **Terry Bison Ranch** on the outskirts of Cheyenne. Among the activities are chugging across the open range in a miniature train or munching the award-winning short ribs and burgers at **Senator's Steakhouse**.

RESTAURANTS TO DIE FOR

A culinary oasis in the wilderness, Jackson Hole offers some of the finest dining in the Rocky Mountains region, thanks to restaurants like **Wild Sage** at Rusty Parrot Lodge, where the reimagined frontier cuisine includes dry-aged duck

with smoked mushrooms and wild-caught salmon with artichokes. Another top choice, **Gather in Jackson Hole** flavors its menu with Korean marinated strip loin, bone marrow fried rice, pork belly bao buns, and other Asian-influenced edibles. For a quick bite, pop into **Liberty Burger** on Cache Street.

Well worth the gondola ride from Teton Village, **Piste Mountain Bistro** pairs its surf and turf selections with incredible views across the Jackson Hole Valley. Up the road in Grand Teton National Park, the **Jenny Lake Lodge Dining Room** elevates frontier dining to new heights with its log cabin ambience and dishes like pan-seared pheasant, salmon crudo, venison tartare, and rabbit roulade as well as the region's best wine selection.

Topping the Cheyenne dining

charts, the **Metropolitan Downtown** offers a brunch with dishes as varied as crab Benedict, chorizo potato hash, bison pasta, and street tacos. At the other end of the state capital food spectrum, the little old **Luxury Diner** (opened in 1964) is renowned for its daily breakfast and lunch specials.

Cavalryman Steakhouse on the southern outskirts of Laramie overlooks the former parade ground at historic Fort Sanders, a U.S. Cavalry outpost established after the Civil War. In downtown Laramie, **Sweet Melissa Café** offers an eclectic selection of American, Mediterranean, Mexican, and Asian favorites.

Tucked inside a 1906 Victorian home and adjoining sunroom, Casper's **Cottage Café** offers soups, salads, wraps, and artisanal sandwiches like the tandoori chicken,

herb-crusted salmon, and California veggie.

The epitome of frontier dining, **Irma Hotel Restaurant & Saloon** in Cody was established by Buffalo Bill in 1902 and named for his youngest daughter. The menu is spangled with iconic Wild West dishes like bison rib eye, Rocky Mountain oysters, Wyoming legacy steak, and rainbow trout. After lunch or dinner, step across the street to **Annie's Soda Saloon** for a sundae, milkshake, or ice-cream soda.

BOTTOMS UP!

If Wyoming had a state cocktail it would probably be the **Sloshie**, an alcohol-infused version of the good old slushy that comes in a variety of flavors and colors. Since it first appeared in Jackson Hole liquor stores and grocery markets in 2012, the frozen drink has spread across much of the state and is now available in many restaurants. If you're really thirsty, some outlets will let you fill a plastic milk jug with Sloshie.

Founded by a couple of cattle ranchers and a river guide in 2012, **Wyoming Whiskey** in Kirby was the state's first distillery. Among its appellations is a National Parks Limited Edition straight bourbon whiskey with a first run that celebrates Grand Teton National Park.

Wyoming Whiskey, honey syrup, and lemon juice make up the Gold Rush cocktail at the **Million Dollar Cowboy Bar** in Jackson, a local hotbed for live country-and-western tunes (Glen Campbell, Willie Nelson, Tanya Tucker) since its grand opening in 1937.

The **Bear Pit Lounge** in the Old Faithful Inn is the best spot to grab a

Saddle-covered bar stools at Million Dollar Cowboy Bar in Jackson

The bison burger at Senator's Steakhouse in Cheyenne

locally flavored drink—like the Huckleberry Martini or Wild Huckleberry Wheat Lager—in Yellowstone National Park. Along the southern edge of Grand Teton National Park, the historic **Stagecoach Bar** has been serving cowpokes, rangers, and visiting city slickers since 1942. Weekly highlights include Disco Night on Thursday and live music at the Sunday Church sessions.

Among the state's other vintage watering holes are the **Buckhorn Bar & Parlor** in Laramie (opened in 1900) and the **Occidental Saloon** in Buffalo (founded in 1880), where the likes of Buffalo Bill, Calamity Jane, and Butch Cassidy once drank. Tracing its roots to a saloon that opened in 1883, the **Woods Landing Dancehall** in south-central Wyoming is on the National Register of Historic Places and features a dance floor cushioned by railroad boxcar springs. ■

FOOD ON THE RANGE: COWBOY GRUB

Whether roasted on a spit over an open fire or cooked in a Dutch oven, the food consumed by the men and women who worked with cattle had to be hearty, protein packed, and durable enough for days, weeks, or even months on the range.

Though hunting and foraging certainly contributed to the cowboy diet, several distinctive dishes emerged during the 19th century. Among the most common ingredients were **smoked beef jerky**, **salted pork**, and **bacon**. And as the satirical movie *Blazing Saddles* (1974) humorously pointed out,

beans were another common dish.

Masters of mobile baking, "cookies" made **corn dodgers, sourdough, camp bread**, and **biscuits** that were eaten hard, tossed into soups, or dipped in **Arbuckles' coffee**. Another popular meal was **Son of a Gun (aka Rascal or SOB) stew** using leftover animal parts and innards.

Potatoes, eggs, hard cheese, and **dried or fresh fruit** rounded out the chuck wagon pantry. One thing they rarely ever ate were their literal cash cows—the little dogies they were driving to market.

U.S. Territories
(Puerto Rico, USVI, Guam)

With their diverse history and cultural heritage, Puerto Rico, the U.S. Virgin Islands, and Guam present very different takes on the American food experience.

THE BIG PICTURE

Founded: 1917 (Puerto Rico and USVI); 1898 (Guam)

Population: 3.22 million (Puerto Rico); 87,146 (USVI); 153,836 (Guam)

Official Dish: Arroz con gandules (Puerto Rico); fish and fungi (USVI); kelaguen (Guam)

Culinary Influences: Spanish, Taíno, West African (Puerto Rico); West African, British, Indian, Taíno (USVI); Spanish, Mexican, American, Japanese, Filipino (Guam)

Don't Miss: San Juan (Puerto Rico); St. Thomas (USVI); Tamuning (Guam)

Claim to Fame: Mofongo, lechón asado, asopao de pollo (Puerto Rico); johnnycake, cow heel soup (USVI); Latiya cake, guyuria cookies (Guam)

PUERTO RICO

A mouthwatering mash-up of tropical island fixings and 400 years of Spanish colonial cuisine, Puerto Rico's native foods are among the most distinctive in the entire Caribbean.

Mashed **plantains** are the main ingredient in **mofongo**, the island's signature dish. Traditionally made with pork rinds and garlic, the dish lends itself to lots of other add-ons, including chicken, beef, seafood, and vegetarian versions.

When you fry mashed plantain and pound it into thin slices, it becomes **tostones**, consumed as a snack, appetizer, or side dish and often served with a tangy garlic sauce. Another popular appetizer is *alcapurrias*, turnovers made with plantain flour and stuffed with meat, cheese, seafood, or vegetables.

Though fresh seafood is available throughout Puerto Rico, many of the island's other signature dishes revolve around meat. As the name suggests, the *tripleta* sandwich features three types of meat—boiled ham, grilled steak, and *lechón* (roasted) pork—accompanied by lettuce, tomato, cheese, and perhaps french fries or plantain. **Lechón asado** is succulent roast pork.

Saborea Puerto Rico stages several high-profile food and beverage events each year, many of them at the Caribe Hilton hotel in San Juan. They range from a **Winter Party** that showcases more than 40 local chefs and restaurants, to a **Rums of Puerto Rico** event that highlights the island's homegrown

An assortment of dishes at Puerto Rico's Mario Pagán, including an adobo pork chop, lobster thermidor, and arroz con pollo

Grab an artisan Puerto Rican coffee at Hacienda San Pedro.

spirit. Other local favorites are the focus of the **Fiesta Nacional del Mango** in Mayaguez (June) and the **Maricao Coffee Festival** (February).

The cutting-edge side of San Juan's eclectic dining scene is spearheaded by Condado eateries like superchic **Mario Pagán** with its fusion dishes, the globally inspired tasting menus at **Cocina Abierta**, and the intimate **Sage Italian Steak Loft** in the Olive Boutique Hotel. For traditional Puerto Rican cuisine, locals frequent vintage eateries like the colorful, upstairs **Casita Miramar** and the tiny **Deaverdura** café in Old San Juan.

Venturing into the island's mountainous interior, the Cayey area is renowned for casual barbecue joints like **Lechonera Los Pinos**. On the main plaza in Ponce, **King's Cream** scoops an amazing array of tropical ice-cream flavors, including mango, coconut, tamarind, guayaba, and guanabana (soursop). Out on the east coast, **La Estación** in Fajardo barbecues out-of-this-world meat and seafood dishes in an abandoned Esso gas station.

Both the **Caribar** at the Caribe Hilton and **Barrachina** restaurant in Old San Juan claim their bartenders invented the **piña colada** in the 1950s. Across the harbor, **Casa Bacardí** offers tours and tastings of its sprawling rum factory. It may be called **La Factoría**, but the legendary bar in Old San Juan now manufactures craft cocktails and music videos like "Despacito."

U.S. VIRGIN ISLANDS

Anyone familiar with Jamaican cuisine and the foods of other English-speaking Caribbean islands will quickly recognize many of the USVI's signature dishes—salt fish and conch fritters, rice and peas, johnnycakes and meat patties, callaloo soup and oxtail stew, dasheen, and fried plantains.

However, there are some unique eats. Like **fish and fungi**, which isn't nearly as strange as it sounds. Originally a staple prepared by enslaved people of the Danish colonial era, it features salted herring and cornmeal dumplings (fungi) and is now

18°64° the Restaurant on St. John, U.S. Virgin Islands

proudly considered the archipelago's national dish.

Cow heel soup (made with real cow feet) and **pot fish** (so called because they were traditionally caught in a pot) also trace their roots to early Afro-Caribbean residents. Despite the fact that it sounds like a catch of the day, **red grout** is a dessert that blends tapioca, guava nectar, vanilla, cinnamon, and nutmeg.

Local dishes are readily available at the **Carnival Village Food Fair** that appears in Charlotte Amalie on St. Thomas, Cruz Bay on St. John, and Christiansted on St. Croix during the territory's pre-Lent carnival in February or March.

Billed as the Caribbean's largest food event, **Taste of St. Croix**

(April) spotlights more than 60 of the island's top chefs, restaurants, bartenders, and beverage makers. Over on St. Thomas, the **King of the Wing** competition at Magens Bay Beach (June) pits local pros and amateurs in a battle to decide the island's best chicken barbecue.

Wealthy Americans began flocking to the islands after the United States purchased them from Denmark in 1917. Part of the legacy is an abundance of fine dining. Considered one of the best restaurants in the Caribbean, **Savant** offers locally flavored surf and turf, as well as its signature curries and noodle bowls, near the historic Danish fort in Christiansted. With a name that refers to its latitude and longitude

rather than a date, **18°64° the Restaurant** in Mongoose Junction draws St. John's most discerning diners for its sushi, raw bar, and super-fresh fish.

From the **Cruzan Rum** that's been distilled since 1760 to the craft beers made by **Leatherback Brewing** since 2018, the USVI boasts more than its fair share of local libations. Among the best cocktail spots are **Lime Out**, which literally floats in the middle of Coral Bay on St. John, and the whimsical **Breakers Roar Tiki Bar** at the King Christian Hotel on St. Croix.

GUAM

Floating in the western Pacific around 2,000 miles (3,220 km) from the Asian mainland, Guam blends aspects of Spanish, American, and Asian in its Indigenous Chamorro cuisine.

One of the most popular is **chicken *kelaguen*** marinated in a tangy lemon sauce and cooked with fresh coconut. Ceviche-like versions feature raw, marinated seafood. Either way, kelaguen is often served with coconut flour *titiyas* similar to naan. Chicken is also the main ingredient of *kadon pika*, a spicy stew with peppers, onions, and coconut milk.

The Spanish influence on Chamorro cuisine is seen in dishes like **escabeche**, fish marinated in vinegar and fried with various vegetables. Guam's ubiquitous *eneksa agaga* (red rice) gets its color and kick from achiote seeds. Locals who like it even spicier add a tad of

finadene, a condiment that blends vinegar, soy sauce, and chili peppers. Barbecued chicken or beef is also popular, but special occasions call for *hotnon babui*, a whole roast pig.

Guam's Indigenous snacks and desserts include *guyuria* "jaw-breaker" cookies, *kalamai* (coconut pudding), and a delicious vanilla custard cake called *latiya*.

The **Wednesday Night Market** at Chamorro Village in Hagåtña is a great place to sample local cuisine at outdoor stalls or sit-down restaurants like **Chamorro Island BBQ**. A block east of the market, **Meskla Chamoru Fusion Bistro** goes pan-Pacific with dishes like barbecued chicken quesadillas, seafood lumpia, ahi poke, and its popular Chamoru Platter.

Tumon harbors two other culinary bastions. Hawaii meets Korea at **Pika's Cafe**, where the lineup includes

loco moco, Spam musubi, and kimchi and bulgogi fried rice. Barbecue is the big thing at **Proa Restaurant**, including a Big Feller Trio of short ribs, spareribs, and chicken.

One of the island's biggest food events is the **Hagåt Mango Festival** (May) on the island's south side. Visitors can combine Chamorro cuisine and Pacific islands culture at the **TaoTao Tasi** outdoor dinner show in Tumon.

The glass-fronted **Lobby Lounge** at the Dusit Thani resort is one of the best places to sip a sundowner. Mojitos and margaritas are the signature drinks at the open-air **Beach Restaurant & Bar**, perched right on the sand at Gun Beach. On the non-alcoholic side, **Bubbly Tea Cafe** near Dungcas Beach does bubbly shakes, snow cream, shave ice, and other cool treats. ∎

The view at sunset from Guam's Beach Restaurant & Bar

Canada

Wild blueberries can be found in every province in Canada.
They add a tart burst of flavor to freshly baked muffins.

Alberta

Alberta's food scene has evolved from its old-time reliance on beef into a multifaceted culinary world with ethnic eats, creative young chefs, and skilled craft beverage makers.

It didn't take Canada's westward-bound pioneers long to figure out that Alberta's golden prairies are ideal for raising cattle. It started in 1877 with just 22 head on the outskirts of Fort Macleod. With the arrival of the railroad a few years later, Alberta's cattle industry kicked into high gear.

Nowadays Alberta is the king of Canadian **beef**. The province accounts for around 40 percent of the nation's cattle population (4.5 million animals), and **steak** is far and away the most iconic dish. Alberta is also big when it comes to **bison**, who cherish the same lush grasslands.

Those same plains are ideal for growing **red fife wheat** and **canola (rapeseed)** with its golden flowers and seeds that are crushed into an edible oil with low saturated fat. By the way, the name "canola" is an acronym of "Canada oil."

Alberta's other golden treasure is **honey**. In fact, Alberta is the world's fifth largest honey producer. The province's 25 billion bees produced more than half of Canada's honey and by-products like **mead** (fermented honey, water, and yeast) and **honey ice cream**.

Ethnic foods also flourish. Frontier-era Ukrainian immigrants

THE BIG PICTURE

Founded: 1905

Population: 4.65 million

Official Provincial Fish: Bull trout

Also Known As: Princess Province, Energy Province

Culinary Influences: Ukrainian, Chinese, Lebanese

Don't Miss: Calgary, Edmonton, Canmore

Claim to Fame: Grilled steak, bison, saskatoon berries

introduced **pierogi** to the province while the descendants of Chinese workers who helped build the Canadian Pacific Railway created unique Chinese Canadian dishes like **ginger beef**. In the 1980s, Lebanese Canadians opened the first donair (or *döner*, aka gyro sandwich) shops in Alberta and evolved a unique style called the **Edmonton donair** garnished with onions, tomatoes, lettuce, and a sweet sauce.

Alberta's favorite sweet thing is the **saskatoon berry** with its reddish purple hue and a taste similar to blueberries. Wild saskatoon berries were gathered by the Indigenous and eagerly adopted by European pioneers. Nowadays, they're found in everything from pies, preserves, and ice cream to cheesecake, cookies, and barbecue sauce.

CULINARY EXPERIENCES

The annual **Calgary Stampede** in July is Alberta's biggest bash, and one of its signature components is the **pancake breakfast**: You'll find dozens of versions around the city, from the food truck Tikka N Tequila's Stampede Breakfast and OMO Teppanyaki Green Tea Pancake Breakfast to the Calgary Dream

The main attraction at Hy's Steakhouse & Cocktail Bar in Calgary

Taste for Adventure in Banff hosts top chefs from the region for two weeks of exclusive events.

Centre Homecoming Hoedown and Pacific Hut's Pinoy-style pancake breakfast.

Calgary's newest foodie haven, the recently resurrected **Simmons Building** transformed a derelict brick factory into a culinary outpost in the city's East Village neighborhood. Among its tenants are **Phil & Sebastian Coffee Roasters** and **charbar** restaurant with its Argentinian-style wood-fired grill.

Another vintage redbrick building hosts the **Old Strathcona Farmers' Market** in Edmonton's historic Strathcona district. Staged every Saturday, the eclectic spread specializes in fresh fruit and vegetables, but vendors also sell wine and spirits,

quilts, and candy, as well as Asian, Ukrainian, and Jamaican foods.

A great way to discover Edmonton's burgeoning Latin food scene are Vanessa Ojeda's **Food Bike Tours**, which utilize e-bikes on a circuit that includes three or four ethnic eateries and a ride along trails in the leafy North Saskatchewan River Valley. Ojeda recently launched similar tours in Calgary, Canmore, and Banff.

Just west of downtown, Edmonton's **124th Street** is an easily walkable "snack crawl" that includes unique eateries like **Chocorrant Pâtisserie + Café, Destination Doughnuts, Zwick's Pretzels, Duchess Bake Shop**, and **Tiramisu Bistro**.

Despite its name, the annual

Rocky Mountain Wine & Food Festival takes place on the Alberta prairies, with food- and beverage-filled indoor events in Calgary (October) and Edmonton (November). The festival also features Alberta vintners and distillers. However, the Rockies are actually home to **Eat the Castle**, a one-of-a-kind food and drink experience hosted by **Alberta Food Tours** at the legendary Fairmont Banff Springs Hotel that includes samples at four different upscale outlets. Banff also hosts **Taste for Adventure** (October–November), a two-week culinary fest that highlights foods from two dozen local restaurants.

Rural Alberta is flush with culinary adventures. **Chinook Honey**

271

A fresh comb of Alberta honey

Company in Okotoks offers honey and mead tastings, homemade honey ice cream, and a "backstage" program that includes working with the buzzing insects while clad in a full bee suit. A combined dairy, beef, and potato spread, **Lakeside Farmstead** in Sturgeon County features a year-round shop with charcuterie platters, chaga cheddar and other specialty cheeses, butter, honey, mead, and maybe the freshest glass of milk you've ever gulped.

RESTAURANTS TO DIE FOR

Calgary's riverside **Rouge** is one of those rare eateries that combines history, personality, and

Free pancake breakfasts are served throughout the city during the Calgary Stampede.

exceptional cuisine. Housed inside the 1891 Cross House, the restaurant comes with its own vegetable and herb garden. Owners Paul Rogalski and Olivier Reynaud have crafted an extraordinary French-influenced menu with dishes like sous vide beef tenderloin mignonette, wild boar belly with stuffed morels, and brioche pain perdu with stone fruit compote.

Serving only the best Alberta beef, **Hy's Steakhouse & Cocktail Bar** has been a Calgary eating institution since 1955. But the dining scene now reaches far beyond the province's boundaries to places like **Orchard** with its edgy Asian fusion food, the rustic Mediterranean of **Kama**, and the creative Latin American–inspired dishes at the hip, new **Fortuna's Row**.

The city's bustling 17th Street SW is flush with Asian and Italian offerings like the Wagyu carpaccio, walnut-stuffed Medjool dates, and decadent truffle honey–infused 4-Maggi pie at **Una Pizza + Wine**. Farther up the street, **Ollia Macarons & Tea** offers more than 20 colorful macaron flavors created by French chef extraordinaire David Rousseau.

Calgary's other restaurant row is 9th Avenue SE in Inglewood, a stretch that includes **Monki Breakfast Club & Bistro** with its heavenly French toast and the classic comfort food of **Blackfoot Truckstop Diner** (opened in 1956).

Sublime service and incredible beef are the hallmarks of the elegant **1888 Chop House** at the

Banff Springs Hotel. Their A5-rated Wagyu steak might be the best in the entire province. Breakfast at **Juniper Bistro** comes with a picture-window panorama of sunrise over the Rockies, while **Sky Bistro** at the top of the Banff Gondola offers equally stunning views with locally sourced dishes like the pulled bison burger with saskatoon berry aioli and chickpea stew. **Bluebird** focuses on prime rib served in a cozy ski chalet atmosphere.

Syrahs of Jasper exemplifies its Rocky Mountain location with dishes like smoked bison ragout, wild mushroom loaf, and elk

Wellington. But the national park town's most stunning eating and drinking location belongs to **Maligne Canyon Wilderness Kitchen** beside the dramatic gorge and its multiple waterfalls. Out on the plains, the **Boulevard Restaurant + Lounge** offers a menu that combines Asian fusion and Alberta-bred beef.

The Marc French bistro and **LaRonde** high-rise restaurant still count among Edmonton's longtime favorites. But some of the town's best chow is being served at upstarts like **RGE RD** (Range Road), a tiny dining room beside a butchery renowned for its

free-range bison steaks, heritage pork, and butcher's cut beef.

The provincial capital has spread its culinary wings to foods from around the globe. Hipsters flock to **Fu's Repair Shop** for the 1940s film noir ambience and innovative takes on Chinese classics, while chef Adelino "Lino" Oliveira has fashioned **Sabor** into a bastion of upscale Portuguese and Spanish gastronomy. Though not nearly as chic, **Swiss Donair** in north Edmonton serves top-notch gyro sandwiches. With downtown and southside locations, **Padmanadi** is the place for vegan fare.

In spite (or perhaps because) of

Get your savory with your sweet with a bacon doughnut burger, like this one at Soda Jerks in Edmonton.

the chilly winter clime, Edmonton is a tried-and-true ice-cream town, with some of the best served at **Kind Ice Cream** shops in Ritchie and Highlands.

BOTTOMS UP!

It's no surprise that craft breweries and distilleries have sprouted throughout Alberta, with so much grain grown in the province.

Using water gleaned from six Rocky Mountains glaciers, **Park Distillery** makes gin, vodka, and rye available at their flagship outlet in Banff and liquor outlets around the province. Down the hill in Calgary, **Burwood Distillery** recently moved into new digs in restored stables at the historic Currie Barracks, a space it shares with **Vaycay Brew Co.** and a communal cocktail lounge serving Burwood's gin, whisky, rum, and nonalcoholic kombucha.

Canada's beloved **Old Style Pilsner** beer was originally brewed in Lethbridge starting in 1926. The suds scene legacy lives on in Edmonton, where more than seven breweries anchor **"Happy Beer Street"**—a stretch of 99th Street on the south side. The cluster includes **Blind Enthusiasm Brewing**, which serves its unique wine barrel–aged and wine barrel–fermented beers at two outlets in the area: **the Market** brewery and **the Monolith** taproom.

In southern Alberta, the **Highway 3 Ale Trail** along the Crowsnest Highway links eight craft breweries in Fort Macleod, Lethbridge, and Medicine Hat.

Located in an 1880s log cabin, **Jolene's Tea House** in downtown Banff sells more than 60 handblended organic teas, including exotics like Wild Blueberry Rooibos from South Africa and yerba maté from South America.

A tasting flight at Park Distillery in Banff

Calgary's thriving coffeehouse scene includes several roasters dedicated to special causes. Founded by wildland firefighters, **Calgary Heritage Roasting Company** on the east side is dedicated to planting a million trees in Canada by 2030. In downtown Calgary, **Lil E Coffee Cafe**—whose name is inspired by the owner's daughter, who has Down syndrome—is staffed by individuals with intellectual and developmental disabilities. ∎

RESTAURANT NOT REQUIRED

How does a chef get nominated for Canadian "Restaurant of the Year" without having an actual restaurant? Ask Edmonton's **Scott Iserhoff,** who's quickly rising to prominence as one of the nation's top Indigenous chefs without a permanent fixed abode to serve his hungry followers.

Born and raised in Ontario's remote Attawapiskat First Nation community, Iserhoff rose through the ranks of Toronto's highly competitive restaurant world before moving out west. Along with his wife, Svitlana Kravchuk, he started **Pei Pei Chei Ow,** an offbeat food company based at Whiskeyjack Art House,

an Indigenous cultural center.

Cooking out of the center's tiny kitchen, Iserhoff prepares take-out dishes, conducts online culinary classes, and organizes sought-after pop-up events like Bannock & Drag, which features Indigenous dishes and performances by drag queens.

Among his signature dishes are bison stew, various wild plum and wild mushroom concoctions, and three-berry barbecued brisket sandwiches. But don't ask him to publish his recipes. "Indigenous people have an oral tradition," says Iserhoff. "I don't write anything down. So you better write fast if you ask me for a recipe."

British Columbia

At the geographical intersection of the Pacific coast and the Rocky Mountains, and the cultural crossroads of Canada's European, Asian, and First Nations peoples, British Columbia boasts an incredibly diverse and delicious food scene.

THE BIG PICTURE

Founded: 1871

Population: 5.37 million

Official Provincial Fish: Pacific salmon

Also Known As: Pacific Province

Culinary Influences: Japanese, First Nations, Russian, Indian

Don't Miss: Vancouver, Victoria, Whistler

Claim to Fame: California rolls, Nanaimo bars, sockeye salmon

With more than 40,000 islands and a coastline stretching for nearly 16,000 miles (25,750 km) between Alaska and Washington State, British Columbia offers rich pickings for seafood aficionados.

If the province had a national dish, it would probably star **wild Pacific salmon**. British Columbians have found dozens of ways to prepare the savory fish, whether smoked or candied or cooked up in a casse-role, burger, taco, or eggs Benedict.

But locals harvest so much more from the sea: **geoduck clams, West Coast oysters**, and **bay scallops**. **Dungeness crab** and **white sturgeon caviar**. Or **B.C.-style bouillabaisse**, West Coast salmon and shellfish cooked with onion, tomato, peppers, and the chef's choice of herbs and spices. Seafood also features in local Asian food, not just the ubiquitous **B.C. sushi rolls** with cucumber and barbecued salmon, but **salmon poke bowls** and **salmon satay sticks**, as well as **seafood noodle** and **stir-fry dishes**.

One B.C.-Asian fusion dish that definitely doesn't include seafood is the **Japadog**, a wiener made from Kurobuta or Kobe beef and stuffed inside a bun with Japanese toppings like seaweed, grated radish, red pickled ginger, and teriyaki sauce. Noriki Tamura and his wife, Miki, started Japadog as Vancouver street vendors before expanding citywide to 10 food trailers, trucks, walk-up counters, and a sit-down restaurant.

The province's legendary **Salt Spring Island lamb** comes from free-range animals raised on one of the Gulf Islands between Vancouver and Victoria. The distinctive flavor is attributed to a diet that includes wild blueberries, salal shrubs, and grasses. B.C.'s 70,000-plus dairy cows provide the raw ingredients for artisanal cheeses like **Kabritt, Castle Blue, Lady Jane**, and **Comox Brie**.

In addition to the grapes that flourish in the Okanagan Valley, the province is also renowned for apples. Among the 15 major varieties is the bright red **Spartan apple**, which was "invented" in the 1930s at a

Japadog in Vancouver pairs savory hot dogs with Japanese flavor profiles.

Wild Pacific salmon with a whipped cream sauce

Canadian government research station in Summerland and allegedly the first ever apple cultivar created via a scientific research program.

The hearty **lumberjack breakfast** was also born in B.C., an origin story that revolves around an 1870s hotel restaurant frequented by hungry loggers who eagerly scarfed down a heap of bacon, potatoes, pancakes, and six eggs.

Named after the city on Vancouver Island where they may (or may not) have originated in the 1950s, **Nanaimo bars** are a three-layer chocolate, custard, and cookie treat. Bakeries, coffee shops, and cafés along the **Nanaimo Bar Trail** create myriad variations on the original theme.

CULINARY EXPERIENCES

Launched in 2023, the **Feast! Vancouver** festival (April) features collaborative dinners prepared by teams comprising top local and visiting chefs, as well as culinary classes, a salon with alcoholic beverages distilled in B.C., and a RTD (ready-to-drink) cocktail bar.

The city's other big culinary bash—billed as Canada's largest food and drinks festival—**Dine Out Vancouver Festival** (January/February) revolves around hundreds of restaurants offering three-course (or more) menus, plus cooking and cocktail classes, B.C. wine and beer tastings, and foraging excursions.

B.C.'s global food scene is the focus of Richmond's **Dumpling Trail** and Surrey's **Spice Trail** in cities on either side of the Fraser River just south of Vancouver. Though the former concentrates on Chinese menus, the latter offers a smorgasbord of various cuisines, from Jamaican, Nepalese, and Salvadoran to Afghan, African, and Arab restaurants.

Chew on This Tasty Tours leads forays along Surrey's Spice Trail, as well as guided culinary tours of Langley, Maple Ridge, White Rock, and Fort Langley in Vancouver's hinterland. **Dine Around & Stay in Town Victoria** (January–February) gives eaters in the provincial capital a chance to beat the winter blues with special (reasonably priced) three-course menus from 40-plus of the area's best restaurants.

On the Sunshine Coast north of Vancouver, **Shaggy Jack's Wild Mushrooms** offers foraging adventures, tincture-making workshops, and mushroom therapy forest bathing hikes.

Not a one-trick pony, the Okanagan Valley pairs its exalted wine with a bounty of fresh fruit available year-round at **Kelowna Farmers' & Crafters' Market, Penticton Farmers' Market** (April through October), or **Vernon Farmers' Market** (also April through October). With contributions from more than 400 local farmers, the **BC Tree Fruits Cooperative** stocks its own market and cider tasting bar in Kelowna.

RESTAURANTS TO DIE FOR

British Columbia scored more eateries on the latest compilation of Canada's top 100 restaurants—accounting for nearly a quarter of the entire list—than any other province. And the majority of those were in the Vancouver metro area.

The city's elite scene ranges from cutting-edge contemporary Canadian and Pacific Northwest cuisine at **Hawksworth Restaurant** and timeless French dishes at **St. Lawrence** to sustainable seafood and organic produce at **Botanist** in the Fairmont Pacific Rim hotel. B.C. fusion reaches sublime heights with dishes like hamachi crudo, nori-wrapped steelhead salmon, and albacore tuna tataki at the chic **Boulevard Kitchen & Oyster Bar** in the Sutton Place Hotel Vancouver.

Rising from the rust of Vancouver's industrial past, **Granville Island Public Market** offers more than 50 independent food and beverage purveyors, from bakers and butchers to salmon pizza and Dungeness crab cakes at **the Sandbar**. Across the harbor in North Vancouver, **Fishworks** specializes in creative Pacific Northwest seafood dishes like sockeye salmon Wellington and wild halibut poutine.

Blueberry pancakes, eggs Benedict, burgers, and Canadian beer anchor the menu at the **Ovaltine Cafe**, a neon-fronted diner established in 1942 in the city's gritty Eastside neighborhood. And, yep, they have Ovaltine.

Among the city's many Asian eating adventures are the novel Japanese dishes made with Pacific Northwest seafood at **Tojo's**, where owner/chef Hidekazu Tojo invented the avocado-and-crab-stuffed California roll in the 1970s. (The roll's creation is also claimed by Los Angeles chef Ichiro Mashita.)

Hailed by a *New York Times* reviewer as one of the world's best Indian dining experiences, **Vij's Restaurant** is found along an Asian-infused stretch of Cambie Street that also includes Chinese, Japanese, Turkish, and Thai eateries. Half a dozen blocks to the east, South Main Street is another hub for Asian dining, with selections ranging from the succulent Malaysian cuisine at **Hawkers Delight Deli** to Vietnamese at **Anh and Chi**.

The Okanagan Valley pairs its divine wine with fine dining like the Mediterranean-inspired menu at **Miradoro at Tinhorn Creek** in Oliver and the modern Canadian cuisine at **Block One Restaurant** at the 50th Parallel Estate Winery just north of Lake Country. Away from the vineyards, **Little Hobo Soup & Sandwich Shop** in downtown Kelowna offers some of the wine region's yummiest comfort food.

Explore the Nanaimo Bar Trail for spots around the city and beyond where you can sample the tasty bar and other treats it has inspired.

Ask locals about the best reasonably priced seafood in Victoria, and they'll likely point you to **Red Fish Blue Fish**, a modest waterfront shack that specializes in seafood "tacones" (hand-rolled tacos), and fish-and-chips made with salmon, cod, or halibut. Just off the Inner Harbour, **Ferris' Upstairs Seafood & Oyster Bar** serves a splendid B.C.-style bouillabaisse, grilled Humboldt squid, and oysters with horseradish-infused vodka.

INEZ COOK'S CULTURAL & CULINARY JOURNEY

With around 200,000 Indigenous people from more than 200 different groups, British Columbia is at the forefront of nurturing and promoting First Nations culinary traditions.

One of the best known First Nations chefs and restaurateurs is Inez Cook. Born into the Nuxalk Nation, she was forcibly removed as a young child and "resettled" with a non-Indigenous family where she could "assimilate" into Euro-Canadian society.

Food helped Cook rediscover her Indigenous roots, a passage that culminated with the creation of **Salmon n' Bannock** in Vancouver's Fairview neighborhood. The restaurant offers modern interpretations of traditional First Nations dishes from around Canada, like mushrooms on toasted bannock, pemmican mousse, bison pot roast, and wild sockeye salmon with Ojibwe wild rice.

The staff at Salmon n' Bannock represents 20 different First Nations groups. And Cook defiantly declares that her restaurant sits on the "unceded traditional territories of the xʷməθkʷəyʼəm (Musqueam), Sḵwx̱wú7mesh (Squamish), and səlilwətałʼ (Tsleil-Waututh) Nations."

Treat yourself to modern Japanese fare at Tojo's in Vancouver.

Have breakfast or lunch with local movers and shakers in the **Parliamentary Dining Room** inside the imposing provincial legislative assembly building. Or go really old school by ordering the traditional English roast that the **Q at the Empress** restaurant serves each Sunday. A block away, **10 Acres Bistro** puts a modern twist on Vancouver Island seafood via fresh dock-to-table dishes.

With an array of après-adventure eats no matter what the season, Whistler Village in the Coast Range has transformed into a mountaintop culinary aerie. An ever changing chef's tasting menu with wine pairings is the peak of perfection at the upscale **Bearfoot Bistro** in the same building as the Listel Hotel Whistler. Since its opening in 2022, *Iron Chef* winner Alex Chen has elevated his **Wild Blue Restaurant + Bar** into Whistler's top seafood choice. Duck from the Fraser River Valley, Cascadian mountain trout, and Haida Gwaii halibut highlight the B.C.-inspired menu at **Araxi**. For a quick bite, **Zog's Dogs Whistler** on Skiers Plaza is the spot for hot dogs or poutine.

Fresh takes on flavor meld with Old World technique at small-batch distillery Odd Society Spirits in Vancouver.

BOTTOMS UP!

Running 155 miles (250 km) from north to south, the **Okanagan Valley** may be second to Ontario's Niagara Peninsula when it comes to overall production, but it's far and away the country's most revered wine region. More than 180 wineries grow 60-plus grape varieties in 11 subregions with diverse soils and microclimates that allow the valley to produce everything from hearty reds and mellow rosé to sweet whites and the region's signature ice wines.

Sacred altar wine produced starting in 1859 at **Father Pandosy Mission** (now a museum) was the

High tea at the Fairmont Empress hotel in Victoria

genesis of Okanagan wine, but the region didn't burst onto the global wine scene until the 1980s. **Mission Hill Family Estate** was one of the first to earn international kudos and to establish Napa Valley–style wine tourism with a variety of tasting and culinary experiences as well as a musical headliner concert series. Among the other big names are **Burrowing Owl Estate Winery** and **Black Hills Estate Winery** in Oliver and **Painted Rock Estate Winery** in Penticton.

Two novel ways to explore the Okanagan wine country are the summertime **Grand Sommelier Express** food-and-wine train or renting electric bikes from **E-Kruise** in Kelowna or Penticton and pedaling one of the region's five designated wine trails.

Much like the city's diverse food scene, Vancouver offers a range of drinking establishments, from the ocean-view cocktail lounge at the **Sylvia Hotel** overlooking English Bay Beach to the happily tacky **Shameful Tiki Room** along South Main. Tucked between the Eastside warehouses and container yards, **Odd Society Spirits** serves creative cocktails made with its own smallbatch whiskies, gins, and vodkas.

Often called Canada's most English city, Victoria reminisces about Dominion days with relics like **Garrick's Head Pub** (opened in 1867), the historic **Fairmont Empress** hotel with its afternoon high tea, and **Bard & Banker** bar inside a historic 1880s bank building. ∎

Manitoba

A bounty of freshwater fish highlights a Manitoba menu that also embraces eastern European immigrant foods and traditional Indigenous dishes.

Canada's land of 100,000 lakes, Manitoba is a freshwater fishing wonderland, with waterways that boast more than 100 edible species. The prize catch is **pickerel** (called "walleye" south of the border), a predatory member of the pike family that makes for awfully good eating. The fish is cooked various ways, but **pickerel cheeks** are especially prized (and a lot more expensive than fried, baked, etc.), while **pickerel jerky** rivals terrestrial varieties.

Smoked goldeye and **whitefish caviar** are other freshwater delicacies. **Northern pike, smallmouth bass, brown trout, whitefish**, and **channel catfish** are among the province's other angling prizes, but unlike pickerel are rarely found on restaurant menus.

Manitoba's First Nations people have contributed foods like **bannock, bison**, and **wild rice** to the culinary repertoire, while European immigrants brought along **borscht,**

THE BIG PICTURE

Founded: 1870

Population: 1.41 million

Official Provincial Fish: Pickerel (walleye)

Also Known As: Keystone Province

Culinary Influences: First Nations, eastern European, English, Icelandic

Don't Miss: Winnipeg, Clear Lake Country, Churchill

Claim to Fame: Bannock, pickerel cheeks, Winnipeg-style rye bread

pierogi, *kubasa* sausage, and **cabbage rolls** from their motherlands.

Winnipeg-style rye bread—made with cracked rye and white flour rather than just rye flour—is a tasty fusion of eastern European tradition and Canadian prairie ingredients. On the other hand, the popular **Fat Boy burger**, garnished with chili sauce, was pioneered in the 1950s by Winnipeg's Greek eateries.

Locals satisfy their sweet tooth via various snacks and desserts. One of the most traditional is the **Manitoba dainty tray**, a dessert platter featuring a variety of local goodies like imperial cookies, Nanaimo bars, lemon squares, butter tarts, and more. Icelandic immigrants introduced the multilayer *vínarterta* (Vienna cake), while a Russian Jewish resident invented the **schmoo torte** more than a century ago.

CULINARY EXPERIENCES

Poised at the confluence of the Red and Assiniboine Rivers, Winnipeg's **Forks Market** features a food hall with more than 30 food

Pair the Lake Manitoba pickerel (walleye) from Feast Café Bistro in Winnipeg with a pint from Torque Brewing.

A fresh loaf of sourdough made with rye and Manitoba flour

and beverage vendors ranging from **the Common** beer and wine bar to **Grass Roots Prairie Kitchen, Taste of Sri Lanka**, and **Bindy's Caribbean Delights**.

Highlighting Winnipeg's many ethnocultural communities, the long-running **Folklorama** festival (August) harmonizes live music and dance performances at 40 locations around the city with food and drink from many of those same groups. Ethnic diversity is also the focus of **Around the World in a Few Blocks**, a guided restaurant tour of the West End neighborhood.

Another foodie walk called **Bon Appétit Saint-Boniface** explores the culinary heritage of Winnipeg's historic French Quarter.

A two-hour drive southwest from Winnipeg, Clearwater village in the Pembina Valley brings local farmers and eaters from out of town together for the **Harvest Moon Festival** (September) with special emphasis on organic agriculture. Nearby Morden celebrates its cornerstone crops with the **Corn & Apple Festival** (August), which includes a beer garden and farmers market, plus free corn and apple juice.

Manitoba's First Nations art, culture, and cuisine are the focus of the **Manito Ahbee** festival in Whiteshell Provincial Park (May), with Winnipeg's **Feast Café Bistro** headlining the culinary lineup.

RESTAURANTS TO DIE FOR

With the daily mean temperature below freezing for much of the winter, Winnipeg is the perfect place for a cozy indoor meal at spots like **Máquè**, where the menu is peppered with Asian fusion small plates, or its sister eatery, **Enoteca**, with its avant-garde Italian cuisine.

Sample French cuisine in Winnipeg's Resto Gare, housed inside a 1913 train station and car.

True to its name, **Deer + Almond** reflects Manitoba's natural bounty in dishes like bison tostadas, beer-battered northern pike, and deer carpaccio. Housed inside a former Canadian National depot in St. Boniface, **Resto Gare** bistro and train car bar presents classic French dishes from escargot and chateau-briand to crepes. One of the city's most acclaimed restaurants, **Feast Café Bistro** offers innovative Indigenous dishes like fire-roasted buffalo lasagna, lemon pepper pickerel, and bannock with poached eggs and lemon chive hollandaise.

At the casual end of Winnipeg's dining range, **King + Bannatyne** in the Exchange District creates a range of artisanal slow-cooked, smoked meat sandwiches; the **Falafel Place** in Crescentwood serves both meaty pitas and numerous vegan and vegetarian choices;

and **VJ's Drive Inn** near the Forks offers a time trip back to the 1950s and some of the province's best burgers.

Manitoba's best hot dogs are found a half-hour drive north of the big city at **Skinner's Highway 44** in

Lockport. Opened in 1929, Skinner's also boasts a fishing shop where anglers headed for the Red River or Lake Winnipeg can purchase bait, tackle, and fishing licenses.

The beach towns along the western shore of Lake Winnipeg are

MANITOBA'S MENNONITE CUISINE

Mennonites from eastern Europe who arrived in Manitoba in the late 1800s brought heirloom recipes from home that have endured into modern times.

Half-moon-shaped *vareniki* (dumplings) are normally filled with mushrooms and potatoes and covered in a creamy *schmauntfatt* (gravy). Enlivened with peppercorns, *komst borscht* is a hearty soup with cabbage and assorted other vegetables.

The menu also includes *foarma*

worscht (farmer sausage), *kielke* (egg noodles), and stone-ground whole wheat *brot* (bread). And for dessert? Cake-like rhubarb *platz* and cold *pluma moos* (dried plum soup).

Among the best places to sample "Menno" dishes are the **Livery Barn Restaurant** at the Mennonite Heritage Village in Steinbach and the **Don Restaurant** in downtown Winnipeg. **Pizza Haven** in Altona does a Funky Menno pizza with farmer sausage and schmauntfatt.

flush with waterfront eateries serving freshwater fish. Pickerel cheeks, pan-seared pickerel, and pickerel tacos highlight the menu at **Seagulls Restaurant & Lounge** in Gimli. Across the road, **Kris' Fish & Chips** offers a range of deep-fried seafood with french fries, as well as poutine, pierogi, and pickerel burgers.

It's all about bears in Churchill, Manitoba's northernmost city, renowned for its polar bear migration in the fall and two bruin-inspired restaurants. Housed inside a large log cabin with a stone fireplace, **Lazy Bear Cafe** goes full frontier with lunch and dinner dishes like braised peppered elk, slow-roasted bison, and panfried arctic char. Earlier in the day, catch breakfast at the **Dancing Bear Restaurant** in the Churchill Hotel.

BOTTOMS UP!

Manitoba offers some of Canada's more colorful drinkeries. At **Joe Beeverz Canadian Pub** in Brandon, patrons can quaff Prairie Berry (Vodka) Lemonade or Maple BBQ Caesar cocktails while watching the Wheat Kings minor league ice hockey team on TV. Meanwhile, visitors to the **Tundra Pub** in Churchill can down their Borealis Burger with a 1919 Belgian Pale Ale from Winnipeg's **Little Brown Jug** brewing while polar bears (literally) roam outside.

Little Brown Jug is part of a thriving Winnipeg craft beer scene that includes **Nonsuch Brewing Co.** in the Exchange District, **Sookram's Brewing Co.** in Osborne Village, and sprawling **Trans Canada Brewing Company** on the south side.

Housed in a historic livery stable, **Patent 5** is on the leading edge of the city's craft distillery wave. The inventory output includes a variety of gin flavors (including Manitoba Berry), bottle cocktails like the Elettaria Old Fashioned and Pornstar Martini, and offbeat blends like Super Princess Peach (vodka, schnapps, and sake) and Rosalina (gin, tequila, and blue curaçao).

The provincial capital renders plenty of cocktail options, too. The **Amsterdam Tea Room & Bar** pairs its Dutch cuisine with "tea cocktails" that blend alcohol with Earl Grey, Lapsang Souchong, and other teas served cold and hot. Tabbed as one of Canada's 50 best bars, **Langside Grocery** serves cocktails inside a century-old neighborhood store. Renowned for its live music, the **Times Change(d) High & Lonesome Club** occupies an even older structure: the 1882 Fortune Block. ∎

Stop by the taproom at Little Brown Jug in Winnipeg for sips and treats to share.

New Brunswick

Acadian cooking traditions are still strong in a Maritime province that also has a soft spot for seafood and a sweet tooth for chocolate.

THE BIG PICTURE

Founded: 1867

Population: 812,061

Official Provincial Tree: Balsam fir

Also Known As: Picture Province

Culinary Influences: French

Don't Miss: Moncton, St. Andrews, Edmundston

Claim to Fame: Poutine râpée, chicken fricot, fried clams

Fresh-from-the-fryer clams

It's been more than 260 years since the French relinquished control of continental Acadia to the British after the Seven Years' War. Despite a name change (to New Brunswick) and the rise of English as the dominant language, French influence lingers, especially in the province's cuisine.

Almost everything that's considered quintessential New Brunswick food has deep roots in the French past, like **poutine râpée,** which isn't the gravy-and-cheese-curd-covered french fries you find elsewhere in Canada, but rather pork-filled potato dumplings. Potatoes are also a main ingredient of a casserole-like dish called **chiard** or **râpure** and hearty **chicken fricot** (stew).

Among the province's other Acadian holdovers are **cipâte** (savory meat or fish pies) and a superthin flatbread called **ployes** that can be served with any meal or eaten as a snack.

With a long and deeply indented coast along both the Gulf of St. Lawrence and Bay of Fundy, New Brunswick also excels at seafood. Although its name derives from the fact that the scallops were served to French pilgrims on their way to Santiago de Compostela, **Coquilles**

Covered Bridge Potato Chips is a fourth-generation family-run business in the heart of New Brunswick.

Saint-Jacques, cooked with Gruyère cheese and wine, became wildly popular on the other side of the Atlantic.

Among other Maritime favorites are **fried clam strips** and **dulce**, a reddish seaweed that's harvested by hand between June and September and then sun-dried. New Brunswickers use dulce in soups and salads or as a snack either plain or toasted.

New Brunswick desserts also bear a distinctive Gallic touch. *Pets de sœur* has risen from humble French Canadian boarding school fodder (hence the name "nun's farts") to a special holiday treat that entails pie dough stuffed with butter and brown sugar. *Poutines à trou* are tasty turnovers filled with apple, raisins, and cranberries.

Anglo residents pioneered several other iconic foods, including **Lady Ashburnham pickles**, a tangy relish flavored with mustard, onion, and peppers and named after the wife of a British peer who retired to Fredericton. **Covered Bridge Potato Chips** are produced by the fourth generation of a potato-farming family in the St. John River Valley, where most of the province's **potatoes** are grown.

CULINARY EXPERIENCES

The original Acadians may have been expelled long ago, but their culture and cuisine endure at places like the **Village Historique Acadien** in Bertrand. The open-air museum harbors two restaurants—the **Table des Ancêtres** and **Café-Bistro du Village**—serving

Acadian classics like chicken fricot.

Set on a tiny island with its own red-and-white lighthouse, **Le Pays de la Sagouine** is an Acadian living history attraction with summertime and holiday season brunch and dinner shows and a reputation for making divine pets de sœur. On the other side of the harbor, the **Société Culturelle Kent-Sud** in Bouctouche offers French Canadian–flavored concerts, art exhibits, and cuisine in a petite café.

Seafood is the raison d'être of the long-running **Salmon Festival** in Campbellton (June–July) and the **Lobster Festival** in Shediac (July). Meanwhile, the humble spud takes steps into the limelight at **Potato World** in Florenceville-Bristol, a small, bucolic theme park in the St. John River Valley that includes

Local lobster and all the fixings

hands-on exhibits, educational videos, guided tours, a New Brunswick potato hall of fame, and a restaurant serving poutine and gourmet fries, potato soup, potato smoothies, and chocolate potato cake.

For more than 70 years, the **Fredericton Boyce Farmers Market** has been the place to browse and buy fresh produce, baked goods, dairy products, gourmet foods, and arts and crafts. Among its 200 vendors are the **Cheese Market, Floko Kombucha, Black Forest Bakery**, and **Elke's BBQ**.

RESTAURANTS TO DIE FOR

Overlooking the Gulf of St. Lawrence, **Origines Cuisine Maritime** in Caraquet village blends New Brunswick ingredients and French cooking methods on sublime tasting menus that feature dishes like duck *magret,* Acadian sturgeon caviar, scallop carpaccio, and maple salmon.

Farther south along the coast, **Lafiouk Diner** in Kouchibouguac creates tasty clam strips, poutine râpée, and over-the-top holiday displays. **Restaurant la Sagouine** in Bouctouche offers an even wider array of Acadian dishes, including chicken fricot, clam pie, and seafood crepes. Clams and scallops are the forte at **Chez Léo** at Shediac Bridge on the coast road. Away from the shore, **Little Louis' Oyster Bar** in Moncton offers an elegant white-tablecloth setting for a fresh seafood pot-au-feu that includes sea bass, salmon, lobster, mussels, and scallops.

Among the gastronomic highlights of St. John's Uptown area are gourmet antipasto, pizza, and pasta at **Italian by Night** and inventive eats like chorizo and fennel boiled salmon, gnocchi à la Parisienne, and chocolate bête noire at **East Coast Bistro**. The three-course tasting menu at nearby **Port City Royal** features mouthwatering dishes like smoked mackerel fish cakes with lobster bisque and fried panko-crusted pork schnitzel.

CANADA'S "CHOCOLATE TOWN"

Located on the St. Croix River opposite Calais in northern Maine, St. Stephen is Canada's official "Chocolate Town." The local love affair with chocolate began in 1873, when brothers James and Gilbert Ganong opened a candy factory that accrued many Canadian firsts, including the first wrapped chocolate bar and first heart-shaped chocolate box.

The original Ganong factory is now the town's Chocolate Museum, while a new factory on Chocolate Drive makes sweets for the Chocolatier boutique in downtown St. Stephen. And, naturally, the town's biggest bash is the annual Chocolate Fest (July–August) with its chocolate pudding–eating contest, chocolate bar bingo, treasure hunt at Chocolate Park, and adult Choctail Hour.

Lodged inside the historic York County Court House (built in 1855), **Isaac's Way** in Fredericton complements offbeat dishes like squash Wellington, vegan smoked tofu carbonara, and curried lamb burgers with copious artworks and a riverside location.

BOTTOMS UP!

New Brunswick may seem like an unlikely candidate for Canada's best pub crawls, but two of the Maritime province's cities are made for a night of revelry.

Queen Street in Fredericton is renowned for its lively music scene, with live tunes at hangouts like the **Broken Record Bar & Music Room, Dolan's Pub**, and **the Cap**. Down on the coast, St. John's Uptown neighborhood offers a

diverse range of watering holes, from the **Hopscotch Whisky Bar** and **Happinez Wine Bar** to the **Cask & Kettle Irish Gastropub** and **Picaroons General Store**.

Perched along the river in Fredericton, **Picaroons Roundhouse Brewtique** offers a huge selection of craft beers, ciders, wines, and spirits made in New Brunswick, as well as a taproom with indoor/outdoor seating. On the other side of town, **Red Rover Cider House** produces some of the best craft

cider in the Maritimes, with the Four Seasons series and Le Brut sparkling dry cider among their best sellers.

About an hour's drive from St. John, the **1810 Carter House Tea Room & Heritage Site** in Kingston village serves traditional afternoon tea with squares, biscuits, and other dainty treats within the confines of a historic home built by a Loyalist who fled the 13 colonies during the American Revolution. ∎

Sampling at Distillerie Fils du Roy in Petit-Paquetville

Newfoundland & Labrador

Separated from the rest of Canada by distance and geopolitics, Newfoundland and Labrador evolved a distinctive food culture that blends European customs and local ingredients.

THE BIG PICTURE

Founded: 1949

Population: 525,972

Official Provincial Game Bird: Partridge

Also Known As: The Rock

Culinary Influences: British, Inuit and other First Nations

Don't Miss: St. John's, Bonavista, Battle Harbour

Claim to Fame: Figgy duff, cold plate, moose

A drizzle of molasses and pancake-like *toutons* are ready to be served.

The last part of Canada to join the confederation, the island of Newfoundland and mainland Labrador remained a British dominion until 1949. As a result, the province's culinary legacy—and local accents—often seems more Old World than those of the rest of the maple leaf nation.

Newfoundland's signature dish is the **Jiggs dinner**—corned beef served with cabbage, potatoes, peas, turnips, carrots, and **figgy duff** (blueberry) pudding—which traces its roots to Ireland and Cornwall.

Another local favorite, especially on Sundays and holidays, is a **Newfoundland cold plate** featuring turkey, ham, and other leftover meats with sliced tomatoes and beets, lettuce, pasta salad, coleslaw, and three different kinds of potato salad.

Codfish is served any number of ways, including as **codfish cakes** and a traditional local dish called **fish and brewis** that combines salted cod, potatoes, onions, and hardtack bread (brewis) soaked in cold water overnight before boiling. The dish is often served with **scrunchions**, small pieces of fried pork fat. One of the province's traditional breakfast treats are **toutons,**

Ferryland Lighthouse (built in 1870) is home to Lighthouse Picnics, complete with freshly squeezed lemonade.

panfried bread dough covered in molasses.

There's also plenty of living off the land. Local cooks forage along the coast for **oyster leaves** (which have a slight shellfish taste) and tiny **periwinkle** sea snails (aka "wrinkles"). **Caribou moss** from the tundra and boreal forest makes its way into numerous dishes, including scrambled eggs. Game meats like **moose** and **caribou** are popular as steaks, burgers, sausages, and even carpaccio.

The province also makes unique desserts like **partridgeberry pie, lassy mog** and **jam jam** cookies,

and quirky confections like the **Peppermint Nobs, Bulls Eyes**, and **Climax Mixture** made by the Purity Factories candymaker in St. John's.

CULINARY EXPERIENCES

Historic coastal beacons provide romantic venues for alfresco summer feasts like the four-course **Lighthouse Dinners** at Point Amour Lighthouse (built in the 1850s) and **Lighthouse Picnics** at Ferryland Lighthouse (built in 1870).

Culinary workshops, traditional folk music, and the Newfoundland Fishcake Championship are all part

of the fun at the five-day **Songs, Stages, and Seafood Festival** in Bay Roberts (May). On the other side of summer, the **Roots, Rants and Roars** food festival in Elliston (September) features a seven-course wilderness feast, a culinary hike with wine, beer, and music along the way, and a "Cod War" that pits local chefs in a battle to create the best fish dish.

One of the top food experiences in St. John's, the provincial capital, is the **McCarthy's Party "Rally in the Alley"** food and drink tour, a guided pub crawl through the city's legendary nightlife district.

Moose tongue pastrami is piled high atop a slice of pommes Anna with pickles and sour cream at Mallard Cottage in St. John's.

and feathers" fish and chicken dinner. Along busy George Street in the city center, **O'Reilly's Irish Newfoundland Pub** offers Jiggs dinner, toutons with molasses, codfish cakes, seafood chowder, and a variety of moose dishes including burgers, nachos, quesadillas, stew, and spaghetti.

Out in seaside Quidi Vidi village, **Mallard Cottage** offers romantic ambience inside an early 19th-century home built by Irish immigrants. The innovative menu includes dishes like panfried cod cheeks, smoked brisket with braised king oyster, and flatbread with braised moose and partridgeberry aioli.

Among the capital's other upscale eateries, the **Merchant Tavern** nestles inside an old bank building converted into an industrial chic bar and dining room. Besides a seven-course chef's tasting menu, the tavern cooks up interesting à la carte dishes like scallop ceviche, broccoli *lumache* pasta with anchovies, and a white spice cake with blueberries and honey. Charcuterie boards with local smoked meats and cheeses are the forte at **Chinched**, in an old blue house on Bates Hill.

RESTAURANTS TO DIE FOR

A home-cooked meal is the best way to dig into most traditional Newfoundland foods. But here and there in St. John's are restaurants serving throwback dishes, such as **Caines Grocery & Deli**, one block up from the waterfront on Duckworth Street, which serves Jiggs dinner with turkey, fish and brewis, panfried codfish, and Newfoundland cold plates.

Founded in 1954, the **Big R Restaurant** near Mundy Pond also does Jiggs, as well as Newfie steak (fried bologna sausage), and a "fins

PIONEERING BASQUE FISHERMEN

Basque fishermen and whalers from northern Spain were among the first Europeans to probe the North American coast. As early as 1525 — just three decades after Christopher Columbus's first voyage — they were angling for cod and harpooning whales on the Newfoundland Banks.

For more than a century, they maintained seasonal settlements like Balea Baya (modern Red Bay) on the Labrador mainland and Port aux Basques on Newfoundland island, where they spent summers

drying codfish and boiling whale oil for shipment back to Europe.

Red Bay National Historic Site offers artifacts and living history programs about the seagoing Basque along Canada's eastern shore, including stories spun by Parks Canada interpreters clad in reproduction 16th-century clothing.

The park recently launched "Bites of Basque History," a new interpretive program that includes 16th-century music, ranger talks, and tasty Basque *pintxos* (little bites).

On the other side of the island, Gros Morne National Park anchors another cluster of excellent eating places. Freshly caught seafood from the Gulf of St. Lawrence is the specialty at **Black Spruce Restaurant** in Neddies Harbour Inn, while the menu at **Java Jack's** runs a global gamut from pad Thai and Cajun chicken to lobster linguine *tutto mare* and a Mediterranean bowl. About 90 minutes south of Gros Morne, **Newfound Sushi Izakaya** in Corner Brook goes full Asian with dishes like *hiyashi wakame* (seaweed salad), pork and cod bao buns, ramen noodles, and classic sushi rolls.

Newfoundland's chicest eats are found at the **Fogo Island Inn** on the north shore, where the menus revolve around local ingredients available with the region's seven seasons—including the pack ice season at the end of winter, the trap birth season in June, and the berry season in early fall. Open from May to October, the **Twine Loft** restaurant at the Artisan Inn on the Bonavista Peninsula provides another extraordinary seaside dining experience.

BOTTOMS UP!

It's said that St. John's boasts more pubs per capita than any other Canadian city. And many of them are located along legendary **George Street**, which started life as a 19th-century sailors' haunt before evolving into a modern iteration more like spring break in Florida.

Pick your poison: **Christian's Pub** is renowned for its Screech-In ceremony, during which patrons kiss a codfish on the mouth and down a shot of 80-proof Screech Rum. **Rob Roy** probably has the best dance scene. The **Duke of Duckworth** is said to be haunted and serves what is arguably the city's best pub grub. And **O'Reilly's Irish Newfoundland Pub** stages Celtic-flavored live music nearly every night.

Quidi Vidi Brewery in St. John's invites beer buffs to sample locally made suds like Arts & IPAs No. 9, Raspberry Creamsicle, and Iceberg Lager, made with meltwater from icebergs floating off Newfoundland.

A short drive north of St. John's, **Mrs. Liddy's** pub in Torbay claims to be Newfoundland's oldest bar. Established in 1853, the mustard-colored clapboard establishment is located in a fishing village founded by 17th-century settlers from Devon. ∎

Celebrating a Screech-In ceremony at Christian's Pub in St. John's

Nova Scotia

Surrounded by rich ocean waters and infused with the culinary traditions of France and Scotland, Nova Scotia's food scene offers dishes both mysterious and familiar.

THE BIG PICTURE

Founded: 1867

Population: 1 million

Official Provincial Fruit: Wild blueberry

Also Known As: Sea Bound Coast

Culinary Influences: Scottish, French

Don't Miss: Halifax, Dartmouth, Lunenburg

Claim to Fame: Digby scallops, donair, oatcakes

Nova Scotians have this endearing habit of disguising some of their most beloved foods with names that don't describe what they actually are. **Solomon Gundy** isn't an old nursery rhyme or DC Comics character, but pickled herring. **Digby chicken** has scales rather than feathers and lives beneath the sea rather than in a barnyard—because it's smoked herring.

Hodgepodge accurately describes its sundry ingredients: potatoes, green beans, carrots, peas, turnips, and whatever other garden crops the cook feels like tossing in … but couldn't they have just called it vegetable chowder? Rather than a dessert, **Lunenburg pudding** is beef or pork pâté often prepared with onions and various herbs and sold in a sausage-like casing.

Despite its similarity to the Spanish word for sweet *(dulce)*, Nova Scotian **dulce** is an edible red seaweed harvested in the Bay of Fundy. Even locals are apt to admit that it's anything but sweet. And **Irish moss** isn't something that grows on the roofs of old homes, but another edible seaweed (with a high concentration of gelatinous carrageenan) used in many local foods.

Almost surrounded by salt water—the Bay of Fundy, the Gulf of St. Lawrence, and the open Atlantic—much of what ends up on Nova Scotian dinner tables derives from the sea. **Haddock, quahog, lobster, scallops,** and **clam chowder** are among the province's maritime darlings.

Many of Nova Scotia's iconic dishes trace their roots to the 17th and early 18th centuries, when French Acadians settled the peninsula before their forced migration. **Rappie pie,** or *rapûre,* is probably the best known, a savory potato and meat casserole. A hearty stew called **fricot** blends potatoes, onions, and chicken, although other meats are also welcome.

The province also has its Middle Eastern specialty: the **Halifax donair**. Declared the city's official food in 2015, it's similar to a gyro or kebab but covered in a thick milk and garlic sauce and wrapped inside a pita.

CULINARY EXPERIENCES

Meandering 1,000 miles (1,600 km) across the entire province, the **Nova Scotia Chowder Trail** highlights two dozen resorts, restaurants, markets, and pubs that serve out-of-this-world clam chowder and other seafood.

Nova Scotia is also keen on special events featuring food from the sea: **Shelburne County Lobster Festival**

Acadian rappie pie with grated potatoes and chicken

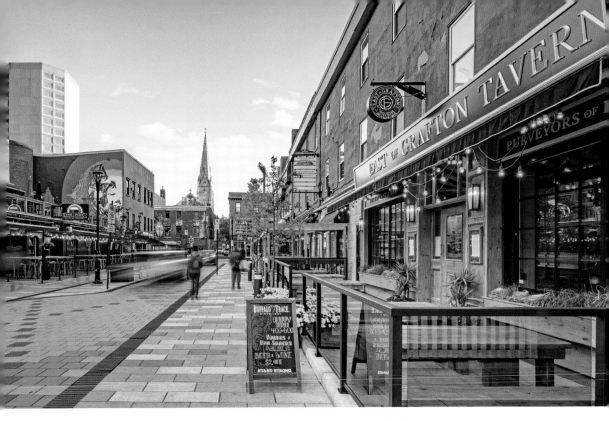

Don't miss East of Grafton Tavern in downtown Halifax for fresh takes on classic comfort foods.

(June) on the south coast; **Eastern Shore Cold Waters Seafood Festival** (June) at Memory Lane Heritage Village near Halifax; and **Digby Scallop Days** (August) on the Bay of Fundy.

Dive into Acadian culture and cuisine at **Les Beaux Vendredis Seafood Suppers** in Church Point. Staged every Friday night in July and August, the **alfresco feast in Dugas Park** features lobster, snow crab, and clams with all the fixings, plus live Acadian folk tunes. **Sugar Moon Farm** near Tatamagouche does tours and tastings at its maple sugar camp and maple-inspired chef's night meals.

Oxford village in the Northumberland region presents a two-week **Wild Blueberry Harvest Festival** each summer (August and September) that offers a chance to sample blueberry ice cream, milkshakes, mousse, pancakes, baked goods,

beer, cocktails, and just about everything else that could conceivably contain the berries. First staged in 1933, the **Apple Blossom Festival** (May) in Kentville features old-timey fun like tractor pulls, drive-in movies, and a cider bash.

RESTAURANTS TO DIE FOR

Named for a legendary postwar Italian movie, the **Bicycle**

Thief on the Halifax waterfront serves marvelous Mediterranean seafood in a city more known for North Atlantic fare. Whether sampling the cioppino, the fresh crab raviolis with Argentine shrimp, or the linguine fra diavolo with jumbo shrimp, it's hard to go wrong.

Among the innovative seafood dishes at **Bar Kismet** are crab and carrots in béarnaise, the fresh smelt

---

OUT OF OLD NOVA SCOTIA KITCHENS

More than 50 years after it was first published, *Out of Old Nova Scotia Kitchens* by Marie Nightingale remains one of the province's most cherished cookbooks.

In addition to recipes, the book includes stories about the people who brought these foods to Canada's east coast, from the early Acadian settlers to later Scottish colonization.

Dishes range from well-known carrot bread, fricasseed potatoes, and apple dumplings to rarer finds like Hogmanay shortbread and Scotch barley broth.

A veteran newspaper food writer and the founding food editor of *Saltscapes* magazine, Nightingale was inducted into the Taste Canada Hall of Fame in 2011.

sandwich, and cod with jalapeño salsa verde. Farther down the road, **Agricola Street Brasserie** puts a French twist on dishes like mussels and frites or scallops and vichyssoise, as well as tasting menus served at the kitchen-front bar or inside a rooftop igloo. The **Brooklyn Warehouse** elevates its seafood selection via pistachio butter–roasted halibut and olive oil–poached arctic char.

For seafood without the fuss, try the fish-and-chips or seafood chowder at **Freddie's Fantastic Fishhouse** on the city's west side or the oysters, lobster, and crab legs at **Shuck Seafood + Raw Bar** near the waterfront. For something totally different, **King of Donair** is where the Halifax-style gyro was invented in 1973.

Founders House in Annapolis Royal offers some of the best eats on the west coast, including a marvelous weekend brunch on the patio, while super-casual **Ed's Take Out** in Digby offers scallop rolls, clam poutine, haddock burgers, and other bites that diners can eat on the front porch with a bay view. Farther up the Fundy, the **Flying Apron Inn & Cookery** in Summerville offers lunch made with locally sourced sustainable seafood and organic produce, plus a mouthwatering array of desserts.

Over on the Atlantic coast, **Beach Pea Kitchen & Bar** in Lunenburg renders fresh seafood and pasta— and an incredible scallop and rabbit risotto—in a colorful clapboard house overlooking the harbor. Transitioning to northern Nova Scotia, **L'abri Café, Restaurant et Bar** in Chéticamp offers a delicious detour on the scenic Cabot Trail.

Get your chowder on with 38 possible stops along the Nova Scotia Chowder Trail.

Try North American cuisine with a dash of Italian influence at Halifax's Bicycle Thief.

BOTTOMS UP!

Circumnavigating the province in much the same way as the chowder route, Nova Scotia's **Good Cheer Trail** rambles to more than 60 wineries, distilleries, cideries, and craft breweries.

The largest libation concentrations are in Halifax and the Annapolis Valley. But the trail also leads to off-the-beaten-path encounters like sipping Glen Breton Rare whisky at little **Glenora Distillery** on Cape Breton Island, sampling L'Acadie Pinot Grigio at **Jost Vineyards** in Malagash, or quaffing Beth's Black Oyster Stout at **Sober Island Brewing Co.** in Sheet Harbour.

Nova Scotia's wine regions include the aforementioned Annapolis Valley on the west coast, as well as the South Shore, Northumberland Shore, and Cape Breton Island. Most are small mom-and-pop operations, but a few have evolved into bona fide oenophile destinations, including **Luckett Vineyards** and **Domaine de Grand Pré** with its upscale **Le Caveau** restaurant near Wolfville (known as the "wine capital of Nova Scotia").

The old neighborhood directly below the Halifax Citadel offers fertile ground for an old-fashioned pub crawl. Start with a Penicillin craft cocktail at **Lot Six Bar & Restaurant** before moving on to a frothy Guinness at **Durty Nelly's Irish Pub** and a shot of Nova Scotia Spirit vodka, rum, or gin at **Pacifico**. ∎

Ontario

With fertile soil in which to grow a variety of crops, myriad waterways brimming with fish, and abundant immigrants from Europe and Asia, Canada's most populous province also boasts one of the nation's richest food scenes.

THE BIG PICTURE

Founded: 1867

Population: 14.2 million

Official Provincial Tree: Eastern white pine

Also Known As: Heartland Province

Culinary Influences: English, Mohawk and other First Nations

Don't Miss: Toronto, Ottawa, Hamilton

Claim to Fame: Beavertail pastries, Hawaiian pizza, butter tart

Bordering four of the five Great Lakes and the vast Hudson Bay, and with the St. Lawrence River on its doorstep, Ontario has never been short on fish. Among the province's favorite dinner table denizens are **trout, perch**, and especially **pickerel**, a member of the pike family that's often panfried with just a pinch of salt and pepper and a smudge of butter.

Unlike so much of eastern Canada, where rocky soils stymie farming, southern Ontario's rich, loamy Guelph soil is ideal for growing scores of crops and grazing different livestock. The Niagara Peninsula between Lake Ontario and Lake Erie is renowned for succulent **peaches, pears, plums, cherries**, various **berries**, and **grapes** that stoke the region's fine wines.

By the early 19th century, dairy was one of Canada's biggest exports, and Ontario was the epicenter of an industry that was especially adept at churning out **cheddar cheese**. Around that same time, Toronto

For the beavertail dessert, fried dough is shaped into a flat beaver-esque tail and topped with various ingredients.

Canoe's eight-course tasting menu lets you sample Canadian cuisine with a breathtaking view of Toronto.

earned the sobriquet "Hogtown" because its pork business was so huge. One of the relics of that era is the **peameal bacon sandwich**: a rasher breaded with cornmeal or ground peas, fried, and stuffed into a bun.

Immigrants have introduced many of the province's best known foods, including **roti** from South Asia, **shawarma** from the Eastern Mediterranean, **jerk meats** from Jamaica, **sausages** from Germany, a plethora of **pasta** from Italy, and—perhaps the biggest surprise of all—**Hawaiian pizza**, invented by Greek Canadian chef Sam Panopoulos in 1962.

However, the region's **Persian rolls** have nothing to do with the Middle East. Concocted during the 1940s at a bakery in Thunder Bay,

the deep-fried cinnamon buns covered in a sweet berry spread are allegedly named for American general John Pershing (the baker mistakenly spelled it "Persian"), who was touring the area at the time. Among Ontario's other sweet treats are **butter tarts, Moose Tracks ice cream**, and the beloved **beavertail**, an elongated pastry (topped with bacon, butter, jam, or various other items) that resembles the tail of the dam-building rodent.

CULINARY EXPERIENCES

Pack your taste buds for journeys along Ontario's various culinary routes, including the **Oxford County Cheese Trail, Wellington County Butter Tart Trail, Apple**

Pie Trail along the south shore of Georgian Bay, and **Muskoka Cranberry Route** on the east side of Georgian Bay. Ontario's oldest cranberry growers, **Muskoka Lakes Farm & Winery** offers a guided "Bog to Bottle Discovery" walking tour that culminates with a taste of their cranberry wine.

Among Toronto's top tourist attractions are a couple of historic food bazaars. **Kensington Market** near the University of Toronto campus started life as a military parade ground and Jewish neighborhood before morphing into a multicultural cornucopia with eateries and food shops from dozens of cultures. **St. Lawrence Market** in Old Town Toronto is a cluster of vintage and

SOUTHERN ONTARIO'S MENNONITE CUISINE

Following the American Revolution, Mennonites who supported the British crown migrated from Pennsylvania to southern Ontario to continue living under the Union Jack. Joined later by migrants from Russia, they combined Old World recipes and Canadian ingredients into a unique regional cuisine.

In communities concentrated in and around the countryside near Waterloo and Kitchener, the modern Mennonite spread includes roasted chicken, smoked pork hocks, schnitzel, sauerkraut, Limburger cheese, and many different fruit pies.

Mennonite dishes are the specialty at the **Olde Heidelberg Restaurant & Tavern** in Heidelberg, **Anna Mae's Bakery & Restaurant** in Millbank northwest of Waterloo, and the buffet-style **Pebbles Family Buffet** in Durham.

modern food halls with more than 100 vendors.

Historian **Bruce Bell** guides tours of St. Lawrence Market that are equal parts eats and architecture. Sample notable and rare cheeses from around the globe during a tour with Afrim Pristine or his niece, Ardiana Pristine, of the **Cheese Boutique** in the Swansea neighborhood. Toronto's **Culinary Adventure Co.** offers guided culinary journeys through Kensington and St. Lawrence Markets, Chinatown and Little India, hip new food hubs like Riverside and Leslieville, and an Escape the City Canoe Paddle + Dining Adventure.

Founded almost 200 years ago, Ottawa's **ByWard Market** has expanded from its historic brick-and-mortar market hall to an entire neighborhood that goes by that name. The streets are packed with restaurants serving dozens of global cuisines, and there's a Saturday night market once a month between May and September. **C'est Bon Ottawa** offers two-and-a-half-hour ByWard Market tours that include sweet and savory stops.

Ottawa's Greenbelt provides a leafy location for **Mādahòkì Farm**, which offers Indigenous food events and a marketplace where First Nations farmers and artisans sell their wares. The farm hosts four seasonal festivals that celebrate Sìgwan (spring), Tagwàgi (autumn), Pibòn (winter), and the summer solstice.

RESTAURANTS TO DIE FOR

Haute cuisine meets comfort food at some of Toronto's top restaurants. A modern interpretation of the classic diner, **Aloette** lives up to its Fashion District location with spiffy decor and a hip menu that ranges from hamachi crudo and egg yolk raviolo to chicken wings and cheeseburgers. The elegant **Scaramouche** in the Summerhill area balances its caviar and lobster dishes with simpler fare like ricotta ravioli and old-fashioned Québec-style chicken. (And no, they won't do the fandango.)

Canoe complements its sky-high views on the 54th floor of the TD Bank Tower with a Canadian-slanted, eight-course tasting menu

The striking Forest Landscape dessert with juniper berries and a cashew-chocolate moon at Ottawa's Alice restaurant

Johnston's Cranberry Marsh hosts the annual Cranberry Plunge in the fall.

that might include cured bison, Atlantic oysters, or venison tartare. Down at street level, the innovative New Canadian cuisine at **Richmond Station** in Old Toronto includes some of the city's most appetizing vegetarian choices.

Toronto's culinary melting pot is reflected at Asian restaurant **DaiLo** with fusion dishes like pastrami spring rolls, lobster longevity noodles, and dumpling *pissaladière*; or **Golden Patty** for Jamaican dishes like jerk pork, oxtail, and patties with beef, goat, shrimp, or ackee. And at **Dreyfus**, the "French-ish" menu features many dishes from former French colonial possessions in North Africa and the Middle East.

Among the city's other ethnic eating stars are **Mimi Chinese** for upscale regional Chinese in the Annex, **Quetzal** in Kensington Market for sophisticated Mexican cuisine, and **Giulietta** in Little Italy, which raises the bar on local Italian fare with dishes like *brodetto di pesce* (seafood stew), black truffle–stuffed ravioli, and *bistecca alla fiorentina* (porterhouse steak).

Ottawa's status as the national capital is echoed in restaurants that raise the flag on modern Canadian cuisine. An odd little shotgun house on Rochester Street hides the uber-sophisticated **Atelier** with its 12-course tasting menus and winemaker dinners. Just around the block is **Alice**, where chef Briana Kim's fermentation-focused dishes include pumpkin seed tempura, maitake and kelp, and a forest-and-mountain landscape dessert made with juniper berries, dark chocolate, and ice cream.

Tucked into an old bank building between Parliament Hill and the Rideau Canal, **Riviera Ottawa** serves refined seafood dishes like whitefish caviar with crème fraîche, Fogo Island cod with lobster sauce, and seafood chowder with mussels, pink shrimp, and scallops.

Vintage houses in the Centretown area provide homey settings for **North & Navy** with its northern Italian–inspired menu, and **Union Local 613**, where the south-of-the-border menu features American standards like pork belly, brisket, and shrimp and grits.

Among Ottawa's best global eats are shawarma at **Three Brothers** and bygone Chinese stir-fry dishes like chop suey and chow mein at **Golden Palace**. Satisfy your sweet tooth with one of the namesake pastries at the **BeaverTails** stall in ByWard Market or the seductive croissants, cinnamon buns, and O-Towners (a cross between a doughnut and a croissant) at **Art Is In Boulangerie** in the City Centre mall.

At the eastern end of Lake Ontario, Kingston and Prince Edward County have emerged in recent years as new culinary hot spots. **Pan Chancho Bakery** and **Northside Espresso + Kitchen** in Kingston are local favorites for breakfast and lunch.

Portuguese classics like *caldo verde* soup, salt cod fritters, and *chouriço* sausage highlight the Iberian menu at **Luso Bites** inside the restored Armoury building in Picton. Or reserve a table in the elegant dining room at the historic **Royal Hotel** (opened in 1879) on the other side of Main Street.

In the nearby 1,000 Islands region, **Riva** restaurant in Gananoque serves gourmet pizzas, pastas, and heartier Italian fare inside an old stone home and outside on its garden patios. Anyone making the drive from Kingston to Ottawa should plan on lunch at **Hyde Smokehouse & Bar** in Kemptville with its awesome barbecue and vegetarian fare.

BOTTOMS UP!

With more than six million souls in the metro area, it stands to reason that Toronto boasts a wide range of nightlife and cool places to knock one back.

With decor inspired by Gaudí's whimsical design, **Bar Raval** focuses on Spanish wine, sherry, beer, and vermouth served with tapas. The Mediterranean vibe continues farther down College Street at **Birreria Volo**, where La Strada, La Luna, and Fellini Fizz are among the Italian-flavored cocktails.

Dundas Street West is awash in nouvelle Asian watering holes. The speakeasy-style **Mahjong Bar** complements its Asahi beer and Suntory

Toronto's food scene is a rich and varied landscape of cuisines from around the world.

Stop by Gaudí-inspired Bar Raval in Toronto for cocktails and Basque Country small-bite fare (known as *pintxos*).

cocktails with kimchi fries, Shanghai chicken sliders, and miso mushrooms. Half a dozen blocks to the east, **Black Dice Cafe** looks and acts like a classic Tokyo Shinjuku bar.

Tiki cocktails are the thing at the divey **Bovine Sex Club**, renowned for both its live music and bizarre Bali Hai meets industrial wasteland decor. On the lakefront, **Don Alfonso 1890 Toronto** in the Westin Harbour Castle renders one of city's best high-rise views.

Opened in 1849 when Ottawa was still a backwoods logging town rather than the national capital, **Château Lafayette** in the ByWard Market district recommends poutine, maple bacon sausage, or even a deep-fried Nanaimo bar with its

Canadian craft beers. Near Parliament Hill, **Stolen Goods Cocktail Bar** creates luscious libations from seemingly odd blends of ingredients, like the Three Brothers, which combines gin, garlic fat, turnip juice, pickled beet juice, and lime.

Toronto is bookended by a pair of wine regions that continue to earn international kudos. At the eastern end of Lake Ontario, **Prince Edward County** nurtures close to 40 wineries with a growing reputation for Pinot Noir and Chardonnay.

One of the pioneers of local winemaking, **Rosehall Run Vineyards** opened in 2001 and continues to offer one of the best wine tourism experiences. A certified

vegan winery, **Karlo Estates** pairs its wines with dairy-free cheeses and plant-based charcuterie. **Lighthall Vineyards** is known for its sparkling whites and rosé and the sheep's milk cheese made on-site. Or forsake all that vino for craft brews, ciders, and cocktails at **Kingston Brewing Company**.

On the west side of Lake Ontario, the **Niagara Peninsula**'s north side fosters around 100 wineries, with Chardonnay, Sauvignon Blanc, Riesling, Merlot, and Cabernet Franc as the most common varietals. **Cave Spring Vineyard** in Jordan, **Inniskillin** in Niagara-on-the-Lake, and **Hidden Bench Estate Winery** in Beamsville should be on everyone's Niagara wine tour list. ∎

Prince Edward Island

Seafood, beef, and potatoes are the triple crown of dining on a Canadian island where super-fresh ingredients are always right offshore or just down the road.

THE BIG PICTURE

Founded: 1873

Population: 173,954

Official Provincial Tree: Red oak

Also Known As: Garden of the Gulf, Million-Acre Farm

Culinary Influences: British, French

Don't Miss: Charlottetown, New Glasgow, O'Leary

Claim to Fame: Prince Edward Island (PEI) potatoes, PEI beef, fries with the works

Surrounded by the Gulf of St. Lawrence, Prince Edward Island lands around 15 percent of Canada's annual **lobster** catch. Harvested in the spring and fall, *Homarus americanus* features in numerous dishes, including rolls and wraps, burgers and tacos, chowders and bisques, pot pies and pastas, cakes and casseroles, curries and steamed lobster tails.

The haul from PEI's 40-plus fishing ports also features **oysters, mussels, scallops**, and **crab**, as well as a wide variety of fresh fish, including **cod** and **mackerel**.

Yet the isle is also rich in land-based edibles. The climate and iron-rich soil are ideal for growing much sought-after **Prince Edward Island potatoes**. Eighteenth-century European settlers introduced spuds to an island that now grows more than 100 varieties. And they keep getting better, thanks to research undertaken at Fox Island Elite Seed Farm. The island's restaurant chefs and home cooks create numerous potato dishes, much like with lobster, but PEI's specialty is **fries with the works**: french fries smothered in ground beef, gravy, and canned peas.

Another specialty is **Prince Edward Island beef**. Renowned for its flavor and tenderness, the beef derives from cattle raised in natural grass pastures rather than feedlots and that thrive in the salty air that wafts across the island. Local dairy cows provide the main raw material for the cheese, butter, and ice cream produced by **Cows Creamery** and sold across Canada. Another island sweet treat is **raspberry cream cheese pie**.

CULINARY EXPERIENCES

Though it's not a food event per se, **Setting Day**, the date in late April when PEI's lobster fishermen embark to much fanfare from seaports around the island to set their traps at the start of the spring season, is one of the island's biggest spectacles. A week or so later, the first catch takes center stage at the **PEI Setting Day Culinary Festival** in Charlottetown.

The provincial capital also hosts the **PEI International Shellfish Festival** in September, the cornerstone of a month-long **PEI Fall Flavours Festival** that highlights island

A selection of Prince Edward Island oysters

A fisherman shows off a giant lobster in North Rustico.

seafood, potatoes, beef, and other foods. Between June and October, **New Glasgow Lobster Suppers** serves a daily feast of lobster, blue mussels, seafood chowder, PEI potato salad, and homemade desserts in a dining room redolent of a rural community hall.

Find out everything you always wanted to know about spuds at the **Canadian Potato Museum** in O'Leary village, which also boasts the world's largest potato sculpture (selfie time!). Afterward, dig in to baked potatoes, poutine, potato skins, potato soup, and fries with the works at the museum's **PEI Potato Country Kitchen**.

PEI Burger Love (May) is a beloved month-long food competition during which local chefs produce new burger creations made with island beef. Among past winners are the Gatsby, the Mad Hatter, and the Lone Ranger. For those who want to dive deeper into island cooking, Holland College's **Culinary Bootcamps** features a variety of half- and full-day cooking courses.

RESTAURANTS TO DIE FOR

Nearly every Charlottetown eatery offers seafood, and choosing a spot for dinner or lunch can often twist your brain into knots. Among the best is the upscale **Claddagh Oyster House**, which specializes in locally harvested shellfish and island beef aged for at least 50 days. Much more casual but just as tasty, **Water Prince Corner Shop & Lobster Pound** offers a vast array of seafood dishes from chowder and

lobster rolls to fresh halibut and haddock as well as offbeat eats like the scallop burger.

On the other side of the Hillsborough River Bridge, **Phinley's Restaurant** is a two-time winner of the PEI Burger Love competition. Both champs—the Bourbon Street and Smokin' Fox burgers—highlight a menu that also includes chicken, seafood, and Mexican dishes.

One of the best things about Canada's "Food Island" is the prevalence of great meals in awesome surroundings across its entire length. Some are open year-round; others only during the summer and early fall high season.

Point Prim Chowder House on the south coast (open June–September) serves clam, seafood, and vegan chowders in a romantic oceanfront

setting, as well as a colossal steamer pot that includes shrimp, fish, mussels, clams, and snow crab legs. Over on the north shore, **Blue Mussel Café** in North Rustico (open May–October) offers a salty seafront location near the town's historic 1899 harbor lighthouse. Among the menu's more imaginative dishes are smoked seafood charcuterie board, chowder poutine, vegan mushroom Wellington, and a tangy Canadian Caesar plate that blends PEI mussels and Clamato juice.

Combine hiking, beachcombing, Canadian literary history, and good eats at Cabot Beach Provincial Park, where the **Malpeque Oyster Barn** (open June–September) serves oysters on the half shell, steamed mussels, and a delicious scallop skillet at a casual harborside location.

Away from the sea, the **Prince Edward Island Preserve Company** in New Glasgow (open May–October) serves one of the island's best breakfasts, as well as locally flavored lunch specials like a potato pie crafted with PEI spuds and cheese, potato and broccoli curry, and sandwiches garnished with the restaurant's homemade cherry and peach salsa.

Tour the farm and gardens before sitting down for a fireside multicourse meal during the Inn at Bay Fortune's FireWorks Feast.

BOTTOMS UP!

With its bucolic landscapes and British colonial heritage (the island was named for Queen Victoria's father), PEI is a most fitting place for high tea. **Blue Winds Tea Room** in New London complements its regular, herbal, and Japanese teas with scones, clotted cream, shortbread, fruitcake, and other afternoon delights. Farther west,

Golden delicious: the local favorite PEI potato-bacon pie

Tyne Valley Teas Café offers teas from around the globe, as well as tarot card and tea leaf readings.

With more than half a dozen watering holes, a two-block stretch of Kent Street in Charlottetown offers the island's best pub crawl. **Craft Beer Corner** taps locally produced Upstreet beers like White Noize IPA and Do Gooder APA, while the adjacent **Hopyard** offers beers by other island breweries like

Moth Lane and Copper Bottom. Ducking down Great George Street, **Baba's Lounge** is a hot spot for live music while **the Old Triangle Irish Alehouse** is a classic Irish pub.

For romantic waterfront drinks with seafood snacks, try the **Cork & Cast** on a floating dock at Charlottetown's SeaPort Marina, or the bar at **Peake's Quay** and a drinks menu awash with margaritas, piña coladas, and daiquiris. ∎

PEI'S FABULOUS FIREWORKS FEAST

Prince Edward Island's foremost culinary adventure is the four-hour FireWorks Feast that takes place at the **Inn at Bay Fortune** and includes a guided tour of the inn's sustainable farm, an oyster hour complemented by a multicourse dinner cooked over a large live-hearth fire, and finally, marshmallows roasted over an open fire.

FireWorks is the brainchild of Food Network celebrity chef Michael Smith and his wife,

Chastity, who in 2015 purchased the east-end lodge—which was founded in 1913 as the summer home of Broadway playwright Elmer Harris—with the aim of transforming the historic property into a feast for all the senses.

The 75-acre (30 ha) property also offers woodland paths, an herb garden, a mushroom patch, an oyster bar, and a Pots & Pans Trail that honors all the cooks and chefs who have worked at the inn.

Québec

Between Montréal's global dining scene, the European-style cafés of Québec City, and traditional French Canadian foods in the countryside, Québec Province flaunts a rich array of culinary choices.

THE BIG PICTURE

Founded: 1867

Population: 8.7 million

Official Provincial Tree: Yellow birch

Also Known As: La Belle Province

Culinary Influences: French, English

Don't Miss: Montréal, Québec City, Tremblant Village

Claim to Fame: Poutine, Montréal smoked meat sandwiches, Montréal-style bagels

Poutine is far and away the best-known Québec dish. But Canada's largest province has developed an enticing repertoire of other traditional dishes inspired by its French heritage, diverse immigrant population, and natural bounty.

Québecers are especially fond of meat or fish pies. One of the province's favorite dishes, *pâté au saumon* (salmon pie) is prepared with fresh or canned salmon, boiled or mashed potatoes, onions, and whatever herbs and spices the cook prefers.

Hailing from the Gaspé Peninsula and the south side of the St. Lawrence River, *cipaille* pie features alternating layers of dough and meat (beef, pork, fowl, wild game). On the other hand, **tourtière** meat pies are not layered, and there are regional variations within Québec. Perhaps best described as a Canadian version of shepherd's pie, *pâté chinois* blends ground beef, mashed potatoes, corn, and onion for its filling.

Another popular home-cooked meal is *bouilli*, a hearty stew in which the pot roast is enhanced by beef bouillon and complemented with potatoes, carrots, cabbage, green beans, and other vegetables.

Beef is also the main event in the **Montréal smoked meat sandwich**, thinly cut slices of beef with mustard on rye bread pioneered by the city's Jewish delis. Eaten as a side dish or snack and similar to the *chicharron* of Latin America, *oreilles de crisse* are deep-fried pork skins.

Many of those same delis are renowned for their **Montréal-style bagels**. What makes them different from any other bagel? Whether poppy seed or sesame seed, Montréal bagels are usually handmade and always poached in honey-sweetened water before baking in a wood-fired oven.

Delis are also a good place to sample some of Québec's trademark soups. *Soupe aux gourganes* revolves around a Canadian strain of fava bean called the gourgane. It's especially popular in the Charlevoix and Saguenay regions north of Québec City. Another favorite is *soupe aux pois cassés* (split pea soup).

As the largest producer of maple syrup (70 percent of global output), Québec features many desserts made with or draped in *sirop d'érable*. An easy-to-make cake featuring maple syrup and heavy cream, *pouding chômeur* ("pudding of the

Fresh snow provides a pillowy surface upon which to roll out maple taffy.

Enjoy the fresh summer brunch options at Caribou Gourmand in Montréal.

unemployed" or "poor man's pudding") was born during the Great Depression. *Sucre à la crème* is fudge made with sugar, cream, and maple syrup, while the delightful-sounding **maple taffy on snow** is maple sap or syrup boiled to 240°F (115°C) and then poured over fresh snow (or crushed ice), a process that cools it to a chewy, sticky consistency.

CULINARY EXPERIENCES

One of North America's largest open-air markets, Montréal's **Marché Jean-Talon** offers a mind-blowing array of fresh fruit and vegetables, butchers and fishmongers, kitchenware stores, snack stalls, and specialty shops like **Librairie Gourmande** culinary

bookstore and **Épices de Cru** global spice merchants. Among the city's other historic food markets are **Marché Maisonneuve** on the north side and **Marché Atwater** in the southwest.

Time Out Market Montréal is a 21st-century culinary concept. It's a collection of 19 petite eateries—many of them satellites of the city's top restaurants—at downtown's Eaton Center. Fare ranges from Asian and Caribbean to gourmet pizza, burgers, and barbecue.

Montréal's best food bash is **Le Festival Yul Eat**, a delicious mash-up of food trucks, celebrity chefs, and restaurant pop-ups. The weeklong feast takes place every September, but the venues have varied in past years from the Olympic

Stadium and Old Port to the Society for Arts and Technology campus and the Quartier des Spectacles. Meanwhile, the city's **Taste of the Caribbean** festival at the Old Port (July) focuses on the culinary offerings of the English- and French-speaking islands as well as the region's rum.

Another way to explore Montréal's food scene is Spade & Palacio's popular **Beyond the Market** walking tour, which calls on six typical restaurants and bars in the ethnically diverse Little Italy and Villeray neighborhoods, as well as Jean-Talon Market.

Québec City's biggest epicurean event is **Québec Exquis!** (April–May); past years have included special menus at more than 30

Campo's poutine with chicken, cheese curds, chorizo chips, and gravy at Time Out Market Montréal

restaurants, several outdoor dining sites, and "Aliments du Québec" take-home food boxes prepared by chefs at the Château Frontenac. Many of the city's top eateries also participate in **Québec Gourmet Table** (November) and a range of tasty table d'hôte menus. Spanning the last six weeks of the year, the city's **Grand Christmas Market** features traditional Québécois comfort foods and holiday season edibles.

Catch your own feast during the **Tomcod Ice Fishing Festival** (February) in Sainte-Anne-de-la-Pérade.

Anglers can try their luck at 400 fishing cabins on the frozen-over Rivière Sainte-Anne.

RESTAURANTS TO DIE FOR

North America's most European-feeling city, Old Québec is a warren of cobblestone streets, ancient buildings, and old-time eateries that make it feel as if you've suddenly been transported to France. Chief among the latter are **L'Entrecôte Saint-Jean** with its Parisian bistro-style menu and the classic French cuisine (and extensive

wine list) at **Chez Jules**. Going against the Franco flow, the old town's legendary **Champlain Restaurant** in the Fairmont le Château Frontenac hotel highlights regionally inspired dishes like Gaspesian wild halibut in clam sauce and Québec wild mushroom risotto.

In recent years, the St. Lawrence waterfront below the walled city has become a hotbed for edgy new restaurants like **Chez Muffy** in the Auberge Saint-Antoine, set in a restored 200-year-old warehouse, and the cellar-dwelling **Tanière[3]**, its tables set beneath ancient stone arches.

A one-block stretch of the elegant **Grande Allée** near the provincial parliament building boasts 15 gastronomic choices, including three Lebanese restaurants, a Spanish tapas café, Belgian resto-bar, chicken rotisserie, and craft brewery. Among the city's top ethnic eats are the innovative Chinese cuisine at **Restaurant Wong** in the old town and modern Italian at **Battuto** in Saint-Roch quarter.

One of the world's great melting pots, Montréal harbors more than 250 different ethnic groups. It's a good bet that somewhere in the city is a restaurant, café, snack bar, or food truck that specializes in any of those national and regional cuisines. The selection ranges from Salvadoran dishes at **Resto Los Planes** and Japanese fusion at **Restaurant Kazu** to southern U.S. comfort foods at **Dinette Triple Crown** and the marvelous smoked meats and sandwiches at **Schwartz's Deli**, founded by a Jewish Romanian immigrant in 1928.

Montréal is also loaded with Parisian-style bistros. **L'Express** on the busy Rue St. Denis has been pairing classic French dishes with wines from its 11,000-bottle-strong cellar for more than 40 years. In

Old Montréal, **Verses Bistro** offers contemporary takes on escargot, filet mignon, and *magret de canard,* while **Le Cartet Resto Boutique** is renowned for breakfast and brunch in a hip, modern bistro setting.

With so many international choices—and seemingly endless poutine purveyors—top-notch Québécois cuisine isn't always easy to find in Montréal. With dishes like Gaspesian lobster and Côte-Nord halibut, **Hoogan et Beaufort** in Rosemont is one of the better choices for high-end local seafood. You won't find caribou on the menu at **Caribou Gourmand**, but this dedicated "terroir Québécois" bistro

does have sage-roasted trout, red deer ribs, and an excellent vegetarian tart. But the ultimate in traditional cuisine is probably **La Binerie Mont-Royal**, where the menu includes pâté chinois, beef and pork tourtière, a smoked meat sandwich, and half a dozen poutines.

Another great source of traditional dishes is *cabanes à sucre* (sugar shacks) in the Québec countryside, many within a short drive of Montréal or Québec City. Taffy over snow, *oreilles de crisse* (deep-fried pork skins), and *soupe aux pois* (split pea soup) are on the menu at **Val Des Rosacées** near Mirabel, while **Sugar Shake Chez Dany**

near Trois-Rivières complements its meat pies and maple ham with folk music and dancing.

BOTTOMS UP!

Given the prevalence of maple syrup in Québécois cooking, it should come as no surprise that the province also produces *eau de vie d'érable* (maple syrup whisky). One of the better-known brands, Rosemont Laurentia is made at **Distillerie de Montréal** in the city's Rosemont quarter. Two-hour tours and tastings are available on Sundays (reservation only).

Among Québec's other spirit makers with tours and tasting rooms

Shop the (produce) rainbow at Marché Jean-Talon in Montréal.

are **Menaud Brewery & Distillery** in Clermont (vodka, gin, and berry-flavored liqueurs), **Cirka Distilleries** in Montréal (gin, vodka, whiskey, and liqueurs), and **Les Spiritueux Ungava** in Cowansville (vermouth, rum, gin, and vodka).

Montréal's repute as one of North America's top nightlife cities is buoyed by establishments like the enigmatic **Atwater Cocktail Club** with its black leather lounge and imaginative craft cocktails at **Renard** along lively St. Catherine Street in the colorful, inclusive Village district. For a more laid-back evening, grab a table at **Bar Le Record** in Villeray with its vintage vinyl collection and music-themed cocktails like the Charlie Watts, Bloody Holly, Donna Summer, and The Boss.

Booze and bird's-eye views are the forte of lofty watering holes like **Nacarat** in the Queen Elizabeth hotel with its summer outdoor terrace among the downtown Montréal skyscrapers and the airy **Terrasse Place D'Armes** rooftop bar on the eighth floor of its namesake hotel. The city's highest perch is **Les Enfants Terribles** on the 44th floor of Place Ville Marie.

Named for Scottish Canadian banker and railway tycoon Sir George Stephen—and the lodge inside his stately 1880 mansion— **Bar George** is a throwback to Dominion days with its sumptuous wood paneling and a menu featuring beef Wellington, Cornish game hen, and other British bites.

Named after the year the city was founded, **1608 Bar** in the Château Frontenac hotel affords one of the best views in Québec City, especially

Organic fall strawberries, white balsamic vinegar, and olive oil ice cream at Chez Muffy in Québec City

Distillerie de Montréal's small-batch Rosemont Pastis de Montréal uses four different types of anise seeds.

when paired with house cocktails like the Opération Neptune or Fanta-Barbara. Below the city walls in the bustling Saint-Roch quarter, **MacFly Bar Arcade** (named for the *Back to the Future* character) offers vintage pinball machines and killer grilled cheese with its beer selection, while **La Revanche** specializes in

cocktails and classic board games.

Québec City has a very active craft beer scene. Explore on your own or join a private or group pub crawl with **Broue-Tours**. The itinerary includes three cool microbreweries with beer-and-bite pairings in Saint-Roch: **Noctem, La Barberie**, and **La Korrigane**. ∎

QUÉBEC'S DELICIOUS "MESS"

Québec culinary legend holds that in 1957, when a customer asked for cheese curds on his french fries at a restaurant in Warwick village, owner Fernand Lachance quipped, *"Ça va te faire une maudite poutine!*—That will make a damned mess!" Lachance later added gravy to the concoction to keep it warm.

Since its emergence from rural Québec, that delicious mess has become an obsession with many fans around the globe. From its early days of food trucks and snack bars, poutine now appears on the menu at fine dining establishments. And nowadays it's thought of as an iconic Canadian food rather than exclusively Québecer.

From truffle and foie gras to lobster, maple bacon, and curry tikka masala poutine, many variations have evolved over the years. Montréal boasts two of Canada's top-rated poutine kitchens: the upscale **Au Pied de Cochon** restaurant and **La Banquise** with more than two dozen poutine variants.

Saskatchewan

From prime beef and plentiful berries to mashed potato doughnuts and lentil wine, the Prairie Province offers a wide and sometimes wacky variety of food and drinks.

Lentils and **mustard seeds** may not take prime billing on many restaurant menus, but Saskatchewan leads the world in the production of the two widely used ingredients. The Prairie Province produces around two-thirds of the global lentil crop and is also the world's largest exporter of mustard seeds.

What you *will* find on menus is plenty of **beef** raised on the vast plains and **freshwater fish** harvested from Saskatchewan's many lakes and rivers. **Fried pickerel cheeks** are a local delicacy. The province also produces a diverse range of **sausages**, from deer and bison to bratwurst, smokies, brown sugar

and maple, and Mennonite varieties.

Thick, chewy **Regina-style pizza**—sometimes described as a "lunch meat lasagna"—is layered with mozzarella, various deli meats, diced green peppers, and Greek seasoning, then sliced into squares rather than triangles. Another doughy favorite is **spudnuts**: deep-fried mashed potato doughnuts.

The city of Saskatoon was actually named for the **saskatoon berries** that flourished in the region rather than vice versa. The sweet, purple fruits—similar in shape, size, and taste to blueberries—feature in many local dishes, including pies, pierogi, jams, syrups, ice creams, milkshakes,

Saskatoon berry pie, a local favorite

THE BIG PICTURE

Founded: 1905

Population: 1.19 million

Official Provincial Fruit: Saskatoon berry

Also Known As: Prairie Province

Culinary Influences: Ukrainian, Russian

Don't Miss: Saskatoon, Regina, Mortlach

Claim to Fame: Regina-style pizza, spudnuts, mustard seeds

martinis, and wine, as well as the **pemmican** made by the province's First Nations people. **Prairie cherries** and **chokecherries**, which also thrive in Saskatchewan's northern clime, fill a similar culinary niche.

CULINARY EXPERIENCES

A Canadian equivalent of an American state fair, **Saskatoon EX** (August) offers a great chance to sample iconic local foods—like spudnuts and Doukhobors bread—rare in restaurants. The city also hosts **A Taste of Saskatchewan** in riverside Kiwanis Park (July) and the year-round **Saskatoon Farmers' Market** (Saturdays and Sundays) near the airport.

On the other hand, the **Saskatoon Berry Festival** takes place in Mortlach (June) and the **Great Saskatchewan Mustard Festival** in Regina (August). The latter features mustard-infused creations from two dozen local restaurants. The **Regina Farmers' Market**, which unfolds outdoors on Wednesdays and Saturdays between May and October and indoors on Saturdays between February and April, features vendors like Riverview Sausage, the Very Berry Bun Company, and Coteau Hills Creamery.

Around a 30-minute drive from downtown Saskatoon, Farm One

Saskatoon EX offers six days of music, fun, and quintessential fair food at Prairieland Park.

Forty offers a four-course **Dinner on the Farm** with canapés, cocktails, and a guided tour of its sustainable cattle, sheep, and hog farm on summer Sundays.

RESTAURANTS TO DIE FOR

With both indoor dining and a sunny terrace overlooking Wascana Lake, **Bar Willow Eatery** in Regina offers a robust array of local dishes, from Saskatchewan freshwater fish tacos and panfried pickerel to lentil meatballs, steelhead trout, bison steaks, and prairie paella.

The **Diplomat Steakhouse** in downtown Regina, the provincial capital, renders top-shelf beef and the city's best wine cellar in a vintage steak house setting where many a Canadian celebrity has dined. Inno-

vative fusion dishes like Korean-spiced bison short ribs, mushroom strudel, and a tandoori chicken "nanwich" flavor the menu at **20 Ten City Eatery** near Victoria Park.

With five locations in Regina and others in Moose Jaw, Swift Current, and Fort Qu'appelle, **Houston Pizza** is where the Regina-style pizza was born in the 1970s. One of their later inventions, the chicken Kyiv pizza, reflects the province's Ukrainian Canadian population.

Between **Primal** with its elevated Italian cuisine and **Hearth Restaurant** with its modern prairie cooking, Saskatoon placed two restaurants on the most recent list of the 100 best places to eat in Canada. *Top Chef Canada* champ Dale Mackay is the culinary mastermind behind **Little**

Grouse on the Prairie, another bastion of modern Italian cuisine.

With dishes like salmon eggs benny with asparagus and Brie, or roasted cauliflower and kale salad, Saskatoon's **Hometown Diner** puts a 21st-century spin on a classic eating establishment. Set aside a Saturday or Sunday for brunch at **Calories Bakery & Restaurant**, where the menu is spangled with tantalizing bites like savory duck hash, kimchi fried rice with pork belly, and gourmet grilled cheese.

Along the South Saskatchewan River south of town, the bright red **Berry Barn** lives up to its name via chicken wings with saskatoon berry barbecue sauce, saskatoon berry scones, saskatoon berry lemonade or iced tea, and saskatoon berry pierogi.

"Grandma's cooking with a twist" is the vibe at the **Happy Nun Cafe** in Forget, a two-hour drive from Regina in what is basically the middle of nowhere. But it's worth the trip for the comfort food and live Canadian country music. Forty-five minutes west of Regina along the Trans-Canada Highway, the elegant **Grant Hall Steakhouse & Lounge** is the essence of fine dining in Moose Jaw and perhaps the entire province.

BOTTOMS UP!

Saskatchewan's fondness for fruity flavors comes into full bloom at **Cypress Hills Winery** near Maple Creek, where the selection includes chokecherry, rhubarb, black currant, and saskatoon berry wines. On the prairie south of Saskatoon, the **Crossmount Cider Company** offers factory tours and gluten-free, organic hard apple ciders in several flavors, including black currant and rosé.

Given their proximity to fine grains and high-quality water, both Saskatoon and Regina boast flourishing craft brewery scenes.

Founded by former farm boys who grew up just nine miles (14 km) apart, **9 Mile Legacy Brewing Co.** is one of Saskatoon's premier breweries, along with **High Key Brewing Co.** and **Paddock Wood Brewing Co.** Among the top suds spots in the provincial capital are **District Brewing Co., Bushwakker Brewpub**, and **Pile O' Bones Brewing Co**.

Spadina Crescent East in downtown Saskatoon offers the province's ultimate cocktail crawl, with **Carver's Steakhouse & Lounge** in the Sheraton Cavalier Saskatoon Hotel, **Stovin's Lounge** in the historic Marriott Bessborough, **Cathedral Social Hall**

Cheers to good food and drinks from Saskatoon's 9 Mile Legacy Brewing Co.

Don't miss the fried smoked trout cake, beer-battered pike, and fried pickerel wing with tartar sauce at Hearth Restaurant in Saskatoon.

across the street, and **Hudsons Canada's Pub** just a block up 21st Street.

Regina's equivalent is a four-block stretch of Victoria Avenue that harbors **Circa 27** cocktail lounge, **Crave Kitchen + Wine Bar**, and the **Rooftop Bar & Grill**.

At Saskatoon's **Stumbletown Distilling**, patrons can sample lentil or quinoa whiskies or a Saskatoon

Sloe Gin cocktail with saskatoon berry, chokecherry, black currant, and rhubarb. The city's other premium spirits maker, **Black Fox Farm & Distillery** makes award-winning whiskies from grain grown on the estate, as well as flavored gins, liqueurs, and refreshing "mingles" produced in collaboration with **Living Sky Winery** in Perdue. ■

EASTERN EUROPEAN EATS

During 1890 and World War I, small waves of Ukrainians and Russian Doukhobors arrived in Saskatchewan. Besides their respective faiths—Ukrainian Orthodox, Ukrainian Catholic, and the Doukhobors' maverick evangelical Christianity—they also brought their respective cuisines to the Canadian prairie.

Both groups originally settled in isolated "block settlements," or rural colonies, far away from established towns and cities. However, the Ukrainians slowly became urbanized, with Saskatoon and Regina

boasting the largest numbers today.

Ukrainian delicacies like borscht beet soup, potato pierogi, cabbage rolls, and *nalysnyky* (crepes) are easy to find in both big cities and are prominent at restaurants like **Touch of Ukraine** in Saskatoon and **Peg's Kitchen** in Regina's east side.

On the other hand, the Doukhobor dishes—like *blintsi, vareniki, pyrahi* (pastries), and their own version of borscht—are mostly found at special events like Heritage Day at the **National Doukhobor Heritage Village** in Veregin (July) and the **Saskatoon EX** summer fair (August).

Yukon

Spanning a huge expanse of wilderness between British Columbia and the Arctic Ocean, the remote Yukon features an unexpectedly eclectic food scene.

Some of the earliest migrants to cross the Bering Land Bridge between Asia and the Americas, the Yukon's Indigenous peoples have lived off the land for at least 14,000 years. The Klondike gold rush of the 1890s introduced European food to the territory, while 21st-century immigrants have added culinary feasts from around the globe.

The territory's 14 First Nations tribes still access much of their food from the forest, tundra, lakes, and rivers. The harvest runs a broad gamut from **spruce tips** in spring and **salmon** and **soapberries** in summer to **moose, grouse**, and **cranberries** in fall, and **whitefish** and **caribou** in winter. It's rare to find many of these foods, other than salmon, on Yukon restaurant menus. However, many menus feature **elk** and **bison**.

Except for a few remote roadhouses along the Alaska and Klondike Highways, Whitehorse and Dawson City are the territory's epicurean epicenters. For those headed into the wilderness, both cities also offer farmers markets and well-stocked provision shops.

THE BIG PICTURE

Founded: 1898

Population: 44,160

Official Provincial Tree: Subalpine fir

Also Known As: Land of the Midnight Sun

Culinary Influences: Tr'ondëk Hwëch'in and other First Nations

Don't Miss: Whitehorse, Dawson City, Watson Lake

Claim to Fame: Elk and bison dishes, spruce tips, caribou

CULINARY EXPERIENCES

Fireweed Community Market takes over riverside Shipyards Park in Whitehorse every Thursday between early May and late September. With live music, kids' amusements, and more than 40 vendors, it's more like a weekly festival attended by hundreds of locals.

Explore local flavors as you stroll by the colorful historic buildings in Dawson City.

Lean caribou is perfect for family-style roasts served with hearty sides.

Food choices range from the **Gravy Train** poutine and **Circle D Ranch** elk sausages and haskap berry jam to **Daat Indian Cuisine, Food Ninja** Japanese cuisine, and **Klonbite** Latin American dishes.

On the northern outskirts of Whitehorse, **Tum Tum's Black Gilt Meats** sells individual cuts of grass-fed beef, pork, elk, bison, veal, goat, and lamb for cooking in the kitchen or over a campfire. They've also got ready-to-eat road foods like pepperoni and salami sticks, garlic and blueberry smokies, and biltong (jerky).

Well Bread Cooking School in Whitehorse offers private classes in how to prepare Yukon fish and meats, as well as bread baked from heirloom 1898 sourdough starter.

RESTAURANTS TO DIE FOR

Fine dining in the Yukon is a rarity. But two establishments in Whitehorse rise to the occasion. **Wayfarer Oyster House** offers a variety of Canada oysters on the half shell, as well as offbeat treats like miso brussels sprouts, burrata with nectarines and burnt honey, and sablefish collars in a miso maple glaze. Reservations are recommended on weekend evenings. **Belly of the Bison** at the foot of Main Street takes traditional Yukon ingredients to new heights with dishes like elk roulade, wild mushroom garganelli, and bison Bolognese pasta.

Variety is definitely the spice of life in modern Whitehorse, where the global dining scene includes authentic Caribbean dishes at **Antoinette's** and the arctic char tacos and other tasty Yukon takes on Mexican food at **Gather Cafe & Taphouse**.

Looking as ramshackle today as it did a century ago when it first opened as a tent-framed bakery, **Klondike Rib & Salmon** specializes in traditional surf and turf. Another oldie but goodie, **Gold Pan Saloon** (established in 1898) serves bison burgers, pulled pork poutine, and elk meatball sandwiches in a dining

Escape the city and cast a line on the beautiful Kathleen River.

room decked out with Canadian hockey paraphernalia.

With a wide selection of bakery goods and gourmet coffee, **Baked Cafe & Bakery** is an uber-popular spot for breakfast. The historic Horwoods building (built in 1905) also harbors **Cultured Fine Cheese** and **Bullet Hole Bagels**. For New Age breakfast and lunch offerings like açai bowls, chia pudding, and chai lattes, try the **Kind Café**.

Run by three generations of the same family, **Riverside Grocery** is the go-to place for locally made gluten-free, plant-based, and fair-trade foods. Among its many intriguing choices are Forager Project yogurt, Loon Kombucha, GinISH nonalcoholic botanical

spirits, and Nora's ice cream. For a quick bite, try **Azhong Noodles, Smashed YXY** burgers, or other food trucks that park across from the MacBride Museum on Front Street.

Aurora Inn Restaurant is the closest thing to fine dining in Dawson City. Its wide-ranging menu runs from traditional Yukon dishes like bison, elk, and arctic char to wood-fired barbecue brisket and pulled pork. Using meats and other products harvested locally, **BonTon & Company** butchery creates the territory's best charcuterie boards as well as innovative dishes like the zucchini, goat cheese, and leek tart and a hominy cake stuffed with pulled pork and pepper Jack cheese.

Those with a hankering for

dolmas, spanakopita, baklava, feta cheese salads, and other iconic Greek dishes can find a table at the **Drunken Goat Taverna**, which shares a historic gold rush–era house with **Back Alley Pizza**. Down along the river, **Dawson City General Store** offers a wide variety of grocery items as well as hot coffee, baked goods, and deli sandwiches.

Among the few-and-far-between eateries on the long Klondike Highway between Whitehorse and Dawson City are **Braeburn Lodge**—renowned for its giant cinnamon buns and other bakery goods—and **Coal Mine Campground & Canteen**, where you can relish a burger and shake on picnic tables beside the Yukon River. Along the Alaska

MOOSEHIDE GATHERING

Held every two years in a First Nations village downstream from Dawson City, the Moosehide Gathering has grown from a means for the local Tr'ondëk Hwëch'in people to revive their traditional songs, dances, language, and foods into a four-day celebration of Yukon Indigenous culture that attracts thousands of people each July.

All visitors are invited to join in a daily evening feast that features traditional foods, wild game, locally sourced salads, and desserts. Elders are always served first, followed by gathering performers and volunteers, then finally the visitors. Among the many workshops are sessions on the Yukon's edible plants and wild tea.

The only way to reach Moosehide village is by taking the free ferry service from Dawson City or hiking the Top of the Dome Trail (2.8 miles/4.5 kilometers) between the two Yukon River settlements.

Highway, the **Village Bakery & Deli** in Haines Junction is the "in" spot for breakfast or lunch.

BOTTOMS UP!

With five craft breweries, Whitehorse is a bona fide beer drinker's mecca. **Polarity Brewing** offers ales, stouts, and IPAs on an outdoor terrace beside the Yukon River, while **Winterlong** boasts a more rustic setting just off the Alaska Highway on the city's southern outskirts (try the Sinister Rouge). **Dirty Northern** pub on Main Street mixes locally inspired cocktails like the Buffalo Sour, Dirty Diplomat, and Skinny Girl Grows a Garden.

Whitehorse-based **Free Pour Jenny's** makes bitters and tonics made with local, organic ingredients like spruce tips, fireweed, and haskap berries that go into cocktails at **Woodcutter's Blanket**. It's generally agreed that **Bean North Coffee Roasting Co.** near the Yukon Wildlife Preserve brews the territorial capital's best coffee.

The territory's most celebrated cocktail is the Sourtoe, served at the legendary **Sourdough Saloon** in Dawson City. The libation features a dehydrated, salt-preserved human toe (for real), which drinkers are supposed to touch to their lips (but not swallow) to complete the ritual. For a less eccentric drink in the old gold rush town, try **Bombay Peggy's** pub or the bar at **Diamond Tooth Gertie's Gambling Hall**. ∎

The Yukon has a range of breweries on offer, including Deep Dark Wood Brewing Company, Woodcutter's Blanket, Yukon Brewing, and Winterlong Brewing Co.

ACKNOWLEDGMENTS

As with every book in the 50 States series, exploring the culinary world of Canada and the United States in *50 States, 1,000 Eats* was very much a team effort.

National Geographic senior editor Allyson Johnson has been there from the start and once again helped with planning and executing this ambitious book. I also worked closely with project editor Ashley Leath, designer Kay Hankins, and photo editor Susan Blair. The rest of the squad includes senior photo editors Jill Foley and Meredith Wilcox, creative director Elisa Gibson, senior production editor Michael O'Connor, marketing strategy associate Rachel Ashen, and National Geographic editorial director Lisa Thomas.

Although their talents don't come into play until the book finally drops, I'd also like to thank publicity director Ann Day, publicity manager Alexandra Serrano, and senior marketing manager Daneen Goodwin at Disney Publishing Worldwide; Anna Gartaganis at Core Four Media; Marisa Papa and Kaylie Easton at Litzky Public Relations; and publicist Martha Kiley for spreading word about the book far and wide.

Family also played a huge part in making *50 States, 1,000 Eats* a reality. Julia Clerk went way beyond the scope of marriage by proofreading this book as she has the six in the series that came before our deep dive into food. My daughters Chelsea, in San Francisco, and Shannon, in the East Village, shared their considerable foodie expertise on the Bay Area and Big Apple. Meanwhile, our feline companions, Sonic and Otis, were adept at helping me banish the occasional writer's block.

And a heartfelt thanks to the scores of others—public relations executives; state and local tourism representatives; chefs, restaurateurs, and bartenders—who helped me learn and write about their local culinary scenes.

ILLUSTRATIONS CREDITS

Cover (MAIN), Remy P/Shutterstock; (UP), Stockbusters/Shutterstock; (LO LE), forestpath/Adobe Stock; (LO CTR), Richard Salamander/Shutterstock; (LO RT), nblxer/Adobe Stock; spine, Vladislav Noseek/Shutterstock; back cover, Paul Giamou/Cavan Images; 2–3, Christopher S. Miller; 4, Scott Suchman/The Washington Post via Getty Images; 6, Jenny Marie/RdV Vineyards; 8–9, Scott Suchman/The Washington Post via Getty Images; 10, Alabama Peanut Co; 11, Alabama Tourism Department/Art Meripol; 12, Cary Norton; 13, Tad Denson/Airwind; 14, Riley Stefano; 15, Jim Kahnweiler Photography/eStock Photo; 16, Emily Mesner/Anchorage Daily News; 17, Ralph Kristopher; 18, grandriver/Getty Images; 19, StockFood/Springlane; 20, Stéphane Lemaire/hemis/Alamy Stock Photo; 21, Different Pointe of View at Hilton Phoenix Tapatio Cliffs Resort; 22, Plum Street Collective/Shannon Lyon; 23, Arizona Cocktail Weekend; 24, bhofack2/Getty Images; 25, Julie Estes Johnson; 26, hipokrat/Getty Images; 27, Marie-matata/Shutterstock; 28, Real Deal Photo/Shutterstock; 29, courtesy Gilroy Garlic Festival Association; 30, Pack-Shot/Shutterstock; 31, photo by Albert Law, courtesy Ghirardelli® Ice Cream & Chocolate Shop at Ghirardelli Square; 32, Robert Holmes/Alamy Stock Photo; 33, Gary He; 34, MishMash; 35, Melina Mara/The Washington Post via Getty Images; 36, Napa Valley Wine Train; 37, AP Photo/Eric Risberg; 38, Jeremy Papasso/Digital First Media/Boulder Daily Camera via Getty Images; 39, Telluride Ski Resort; 40, Micaela O'Mara; 41, Jerilee Bennett, The Colorado Springs Gazette; 42, Jimena Peck; 43, Horse & Dragon Brewing Company, Fort Collins, CO; 44, Jeenah Moon/The New York Times/Redux; 45, Jason R. Dubé/Silver Linings Photography; 46, Stan Tess/Alamy Stock Photo; 47, Dockside Brewery; 48, Lily Ernst/Little Sweet Baker; 49, Jessop's Tavern; 50, Kimberly Kong/NOM Digital; 51, Taya Dianna for New Castle County Department of Community Services; 52, Amanda Voisard/The Washington Post via Getty Images; 53, Mark Summerfield/Alamy Stock Photo; 54, Scott Suchman/The Washington Post via Getty Images; 55, Melina Mara/The Washington Post via Getty Images; 56, StockFood/Great Stock!; 57, Joe Raedle/Getty Images; 58, Filda Konec; 59, Matthew Pace/The Washington Post via Getty Images; 60, StockFood/Hendrik Holler; 61, Leonard Zhukovsky/Shutterstock; 62, John Angelillo/UPI/Shutterstock; 63, Gigglewaters Social Club & Screening Room in Safety Harbor, Florida; 64, bonchan/Shutterstock; 65, Sean Pavone/Shutterstock; 66, Taylor Alexandria/The Whistle Stop Cafe; 67, Mary Ann Anderson/Tribune News Service via Getty Images; 68, Peter Frank Edwards/Redux; 69, Caitlin Crawford; 70, Eldon Christenson; 71, J. Anthony Martinez Photography/Old Lahaina Lu'au; 72, Kevin Klima Photo/Shutterstock; 73, Kent Nishimura/The New York Times/Redux; 74, Bryan Chun/Getty Images; 75, Waiahole Poi Factory; 76, Lou Aaron; 77, Carol Waller; 78, The Basque Market; 79, Chandlers Prime Steaks & Fine Seafood; 80, Nichimar/Shutterstock; 81, Supitcha McAdam/Shutterstock; 82, sydneyelin/Shutterstock; 83, Jaclyn Rivas, @cosmic_ghost/Time Out Market Chicago; 84, Kevin J. Miyazaki/Redux; 85, Colin Mohr/Honey Butter Fried Chicken; 86, UnPosed Photography/Galena Cellars Vineyard & Winery; 87, Gage Hospitality Group; 88, photo by Diana Muresan, Craft and Muse Studio, recipe by Lily Ernst, Little Sweet Baker; 89, Katie Abel, Valparaiso Events; 90, Oasis Diner; 91, Dave Pluimer; 92, Scott Olson/Getty Images; 93, Maksymowicz/Getty Images; 94, Aemelia Tripp/Jaarsma Bakery; 95, Ashley McLaughlin; 96, Brent Hofacker/Shutterstock; 97, Pilsen Photo Co-op; 98, CHOTE BKK/Shutterstock; 99, David Mayes Photography; 100, bhofack2/Getty Images; 101, Tim Webb; 102, Steve Geis; 103, Brent Hofacker/Shutterstock; 104, Tim Mueller Photography; 105, Brent Hofacker/Shutterstock; 106, Pgiam/Getty Images; 107, StockFood/Brenda Spaude; 108, StockFood/Katharine Pollak; 109, Mansura Chamber of Commerce; 110, Commander's Palace; 111, McIlhenny Company Archives; 112, Hihitetlin/Shutterstock; 113, aimintang/Getty Images; 114, Eventide Oyster Co.; 115, Jen Dean Photography; 116, Edwin Remsberg/Alamy Stock Photo; 117, Jennifer Chase Photography; 118, Scott Suchman/The Washington Post via Getty Images; 119, Cheriss May/The New York Times/Redux; 120, Red Lion Inn; 121, Robert Nickelsberg/Getty Images; 122, StockFood/Keller & Keller Photography; 123, Travelpix Ltd/Getty Images; 124, John Ferrarone, courtesy Old Sturbridge Village; 125, Keith Bedford/The Boston Globe via Getty Images; 126, The Barking Crab; 127, Alexandra Schuler/picture alliance via Getty Images; 128, Al Ameer Restaurant; 129, Cat Muncey/Novum Productions/Grand Traverse Pie Company; 130, Buddy's Pizza; 131, Robert Sackyta/Divani; 132, Zoonar/Marina Saprunova/Alamy Stock Photo; 133, jimkruger/Getty Images; 134, John Noltner; 135, 5-8 Club; 136, America's Test Kitchen; 137, Carmen K. Sisson/Cloudybright/Alamy Stock Photo; 138, Drew Dempsey; 139, Visit Mississippi; 140, Stepanek Photography/Adobe Stock; 141, Mark Youngblood/Alamy Stock Photo; 142, photography by RJ Hartbeck, courtesy The Ritz-Carlton, St. Louis; 143, Jumping Rocks/Universal Images Group via Getty Images; 144, MelissaMN/Adobe Stock; 145, courtesy The Resort at Paws Up; 146, Melissa Carter/Pickle Barrel; 147, courtesy Beacon Icehouse; 148, Cavan Images/Marc Morrison/Getty Images; 149, Katie Anderson; 150, Dana Damewood Photography; 151, Ryan Soderlin/Omaha World-Herald via AP; 152, Africa Studio/Shutterstock; 153, Roy "Big Country" Nelson; 154, Brian Walker Photography; 155, David Strick/Redux; 156, Suzanne Tucker/Getty Images; 157, Hampton Area Chamber of Commerce/Matt

Parker; 158, Justin Cash/Getty Images; 159, Stark Brewing Company; 160, Al Drago/Bloomberg via Getty Images; 161, Cwieders/Getty Images; 162, Tetra Images/Getty Images; 163, Bill Denver, Equiphoto; 164, StockFood/John K Shipes; 165, Douglas Merriam; 166, Jake Rogers; 167, Brian/Adobe Stock; 168, Douglas Merriam; 169, Los Poblanos; 170, Elena Veselova/Shutterstock; 171, Wirestock Creators/Shutterstock; 172, Russ & Daughters; 173, courtesy Blue Hill at Stone Barns; 174, Dana Ball/Upward Brewing Company; 175, Tayfun Coskun/Anadolu Agency via Getty Images; 176, Jeffrey Isaac Greenberg 8+/Alamy Stock Photo; 177, Karsten Moran/The New York Times/Redux; 178, Christina Lau/Generations Tap & Grill; 179, Dr. Konstantin Frank Winery; 180, angelsimon/Getty Images; 181, Jeffrey Greenberg/Universal Images Group via Getty Images; 182, Chelsea Herre of Rhubarb; 183, Chair 8; 184, Raleigh Beer Garden; 185, Joni Hanebutt/Shutterstock; 186, SMarina/Getty Images; 187, Kara O'Byrne; 188, courtesy the Theodore Roosevelt Medora Foundation; 189, Nikki Berglund; 190, Cavan Images/Getty Images; 191, Brent Hofacker/Shutterstock; 192, Kate Djupe/Columbus Food Adventures; 193, Visit Dublin Ohio; 194, Brent Hofacker/Shutterstock; 195, Jerry Hymer; 196, Valerie Wei-Haas/Juniper; 197, Heeb Photos/eStock Photo; 198, alexkoral/Adobe Stock; 199, Larry Geddis/Alamy Stock Photo; 200, Leah Nash/The New York Times/Redux; 201, Joshua Dorcak/MÄS; 202, Paul Taggart/Bloomberg via Getty Images; 203, Ashley Gilbertson/VII/Redux; 204, Julius Sturgis Pretzel Bakery, Lititz, PA; 205, Gab Bonghi, The Infatuation; 206, courtesy The Church Brew Works/Priscilla Briggs; 207, Philadelphia Distilling; 208, Anastasia Kopa/Shutterstock; 209, Eric Voigt; 210, Erin McGinn Photography; 211, Eric Voigt; 212, bonchan/Shutterstock; 213, Robbin Knight Photography/Lowcountry Oyster Festival; 214, photo by ElectricSoul @electrcsoul courtesy Bobby's BBQ @eatbobbys; 215, Charleston Wine + Food; 216, Forrest Clonts;

217, Ruta Smith; 218, Straw Photography and Media; 219, AP Photo/Amber Hunt, File; 220, Carnaval Brazilian Grill; 221, Prairie Berry Winery; 222, Joshua Resnick/Shutterstock; 223, The Rendezvous; 224, Paul McKinnon/Alamy Stock Photo; 225, Yolan at The Joseph Nashville; 226, Eva Baughman/The New York Times/Redux; 227, Teresa Kopec/Getty Images; 228, Kirsten Gilliam for B&B Butchers Houston; 229, Jonathan Alonzo for La Gloria; 230, State Fair of Texas; 231, Consumable Content for 24 Diner; 232, courtesy Blue Bell Creameries; 233, Brooke Kasper 2015; 234, Brent Hofacker/Shutterstock; 235, Park City Area Restaurant Association; 236, Black Sheep Cafe; 237, Jean Mendieta Photography/Table X; 238, Brian Snyder/Reuters/Redux; 239, Eric Dale/Shutterstock; 240, King Arthur Baking Company, photo by Danielle Sykes, food styling by Liz Neily; 241, Don Landwehrle/Adobe Stock; 242, Blair Lonergan, author and recipe developer at The Seasoned Mom; 243, Emanuel Tanjala/Alamy Stock Photo; 244, Joseph Victor Stefanchik/The Washington Post via Getty Images; 245, Scott Suchman; 246, Ellenos; 247, Cavan-Images/Shutterstock; 248, Ray's Boathouse; 249, Jim Henkens/Westward Restaurant; 250, Alabastro Photography for AQUA by El Gaucho; 251, Tegra Stone Nuess/Getty Images; 252, StockFood/StockFood Studios/Oliver Brachat; 253, Scott James/Dreamstime; 254, U!Creative/Pies & Pints; 255, Black Draft Distillery; 256, StockFood/Keller & Keller Photography; 257, Fromagination; 258, Nicole Franzen/The Harvey House; 259, Ian Johnson; 260, Rikki Snyder/The New York Times/Redux; 261, Steve Girt, Cheyenne Frontier Days; 262, Million Dollar Cowboy Bar; 263, Autumn Parry/The Washington Post via Getty Images; 264, Rafael N. Ruiz Mederos @ruizrafi; 265, Michael Dwyer/Alamy Stock Photo; 266, Sarah B Swan Photography; 267, Annie Joo/The Beach Restaurant & Bar Guam; 268–9, Archbould Photography; 270, Clinton Hussey/Hy's Steakhouse & Cocktail Bar; 271, Drew Butler/drewbutlerphoto; 272, AP Photo/Larry Mac-

Dougal; 273, Aksana Yasiucheia/Getty Images; 274, Felix Choo/Alamy Stock Photo; 275, PARK Distillery/Banff Hospitality Collective; 276, Chris Helgren/Reuters/Redux; 277, Karsten Moran/The New York Times/Redux; 278, photo by Diana Muresan, Craft and Muse Studio, recipe by Lily Ernst, Little Sweet Baker; 279, Leila Kwok/Tojo's Restaurant; 280, Fairmont Empress; 281, R.D. Cane; 282, Feast Café Bistro; 283, StockFood/StockFood Studios/Uta Gleiser Photography; 284, courtesy Resto Gare Bistro; 285, Jensen Maxwell, Little Brown Jug Brewing Co.; 286, Ezume Images/Shutterstock; 287, Covered Bridge Potato Chip Company; 288, Stuart Forster/Alamy Stock Photo; 289, Tourism New Brunswick; 290, Carolyn Parsons-Janes/Shutterstock; 291, S. Vincent/Shutterstock; 292, Mallard Cottage; 293, The Canadian Press/Paul Daly; 294, Fudio/Getty Images; 295, Acorn Art & Photography; 296, MayaV Images/Offset; 297, Holly Davy; 298, beaulaz/Shutterstock; 299, courtesy Oliver & Bonacini Hospitality; 300, Miv Photography/Briana Kim; 301, Muskoka Lakes Farm & Winery; 302, Andrew Francis Wallace/Toronto Star via Getty Images; 303, Alexa Fernando/Bar Raval; 304, Barry Vincent/Alamy Stock Photo; 305, JFGagnonPhoto/Shutterstock; 306, PEI Potato Board; 307, Alex Bruce Photography; 308, Marc Bruxelle/Shutterstock; 309, Audrey Leynaert—Caribou Gourmand; 310, JF Galipeau for Time Out Market Montreal; 311, BalkansCat/Getty Images; 312, Auberge Saint-Antoine; 313, Ophélie Boisvert, photographer, and Méghane Boisvert, artistic director, courtesy Distillerie de Montréal; 314, Carey Jaman/Shutterstock; 315, Discover Saskatoon, Nick Biblow; 316, Nathan Jones; 317, Bob Deutscher/Hearth Restaurant; 318, EB Adventure Photography/Shutterstock; 319, Archbould Photography; 320, Scalia Media/Shutterstock; 321, Archbould Photography.

INDEX

ABOUT THE AUTHOR

During three decades as an editor, writer, and photographer, Joe Yogerst has lived and worked in Asia, Africa, Europe, and North America. His writing has appeared in *Condé Nast Traveler,* CNN Travel, *Islands* magazine, the *International New York Times* (Paris), *Washington Post, Los Angeles Times,* and *National Geographic Traveler*. He has written for more than 35 National Geographic books, including authoring the best-selling *50 States, 5,000 Ideas* and *100 Parks, 5,000 Ideas*. He is also the author of a murder mystery titled *Nemesis,* as well as the host of the National Geographic/Great Courses video series on America's state parks.

50 STATES 1000 EATS

Since 1888, the National Geographic Society has funded more than 14,000 research, conservation, education, and storytelling projects around the world. National Geographic Partners distributes a portion of the funds it receives from your purchase to National Geographic Society to support programs including the conservation of animals and their habitats.

National Geographic Partners, LLC
1145 17th Street NW
Washington, DC 20036-4688 USA

Get closer to National Geographic Explorers and photographers, and connect with our global community. Join us today at nationalgeographic.org/joinus

For rights or permissions inquiries, please contact National Geographic Books Subsidiary Rights: bookrights@natgeo.com

The information in this book has been carefully checked and to the best of our knowledge is accurate. However, details are subject to change, and the publisher cannot be responsible for such changes, or for errors or omissions. Assessments of sites, hotels, and restaurants are based on the author's subjective opinions, which do not necessarily reflect the publisher's opinion.

Copyright © 2024 National Geographic Partners, LLC. All rights reserved. Reproduction of the whole or any part of the contents without written permission from the publisher is prohibited.

The Walt Disney Company is majority owner of National Geographic Partners.

NATIONAL GEOGRAPHIC and Yellow Border Design are trademarks of the National Geographic Society, used under license.

Library of Congress Cataloging-in-Publication Data
Names: Yogerst, Joseph R. author.
Title: 50 states, 1,000 eats : where to go, when to go, what to eat, what to drink / Joe Yogerst.
Other titles: Fifty states, one thousand eats
Description: Washington, DC : National Geographic Partners, LLC, [2024] | Includes index. | Summary: "This culinary guide reveals the best food experiences across all 50 states and Canada"-- Provided by publisher.
Identifiers: LCCN 2023017343 | ISBN 9781426222825 (paperback)
Subjects: LCSH: United States--Guidebooks. | Canada--Guidebooks. | Food--Miscellanea. | Restaurants--Guidebooks.
Classification: LCC E158 .Y636 2024 | DDC 917.304--dc23/eng/20230621
LC record available at https://lccn.loc.gov/2023017343

ISBN: 978-1-4262-2282-5

Printed in South Korea
23/QPSK/1